PENGUIN  CLASSICS

CHRONICLES OF THE FIRST CRUSADE

CHRISTOPHER TYERMAN is a Fellow and Tutor in History at Hertford College, Oxford, and Lecturer in Medieval History at New College, Oxford. He has written extensively on the crusades, most recently *God's War: A New History of the Crusades* (2006) and *The Debate on the Crusades* (2011).

D1475682

Chronicles of the First Crusade
1096–1099

Edited and with an Introduction by
CHRISTOPHER TYERMAN

PENGUIN BOOKS

PENGUIN CLASSICS

Published by the Penguin Group
Penguin Books Ltd, 80 Strand, London WC2R ORL, England
Penguin Group (USA) Inc., 375 Hudson Street, New York, New York 10014, USA
Penguin Group (Canada), 90 Eglinton Avenue East, Suite 700, Toronto, Ontario, Canada M4P 2Y3
(a division of Pearson Penguin Canada Inc.)
Penguin Ireland, 25 St Stephen's Green, Dublin 2, Ireland (a division of Penguin Books Ltd)
Penguin Group (Australia), 250 Camberwell Road, Camberwell, Victoria 3124, Australia
(a division of Pearson Australia Group Pty Ltd)
Penguin Books India Pvt Ltd, 11 Community Centre, Panchsheel Park, New Delhi – 110 017, India
Penguin Group (NZ), 67 Apollo Drive, Rosedale, Auckland 0632, New Zealand
(a division of Pearson New Zealand Ltd)
Penguin Books (South Africa) (Pty) Ltd, 24 Sturdee Avenue, Rosebank, Johannesburg 2196, South Africa

Penguin Books Ltd, Registered Offices: 80 Strand, London WC2R ORL, England

www.penguin.com

This edition first published by The Folio Society Ltd 2004
First published in Penguin Classics 2012

014

Selection, foreword, introduction and editorial matter copyright © The Folio Society Ltd, 2004
Maps by Reginald Piggot
All rights reserved

The moral right of the author of editorial matter has been asserted

Printed and bound in Great Britain by Clays Ltd, Elcograf S.p.A.

ISBN: 978-0-241-95522-2

www.greenpenguin.co.uk

Contents

Foreword   vii
Introduction
   The First Crusade, 1096–1099   xv
   The Sources   xxii
Editorial Note   xxxiii
Chronology   xxxv
Maps   xli

   I   The Call to Arms   1
   II   The First Victims   30
   III   The Journey to the East   71
   IV   The First Victories   108
   V   The Siege of Antioch   143
   VI   The Holy Lance   197
   VII   Divided Leadership   246
   VIII   Miracles on the Road   274
   IX   Jerusalem   309
   X   Rejoicing and Lamentation   349

Appendix
   The Commanders   375
Further Reading   379
Acknowledgements   381
Index   385

Foreword

The eighteenth-century Scottish philosopher and historian David Hume regarded the crusades as 'the most signal and most durable monument of human folly that has yet appeared in any age or nation'. He also conceded that they 'engrossed the attention of Europe and have ever since engaged the curiosity of mankind'. These two themes of judgement and fascination have supplied the strands for the cultural rope that binds these medieval holy wars to modern interest. Hume was right. Since 1095, when Pope Urban II answered the call for help from the Byzantine emperor Alexius I Comnenus by summoning a vast army to fight in the name of God to recover the Holy City of Jerusalem and liberate eastern Christianity, there has never been a time when the consequences of this act have not gripped minds and imaginations, primarily in western society but increasingly, since the nineteenth century, among communities that have seen themselves as heirs of the victims of this form of religious violence. Throughout, the crusades have been configured to reflect later concerns and circumstances in a process that matches the protean quality of the phenomenon itself. Of all aspects of the European world in the so-called medieval period, the crusades enjoy the clearest recognition in modern times.

Of the drama and dislocation involved in crusading, there is no doubt. For more than four centuries from the end of the eleventh century, although with slackening intensity from the fourteenth, western Europeans, more used to lives circumscribed by the narrow geography of localities and regions, found themselves fighting under the banner of the Cross on battlefields as far apart as Lake Chud in western Russia and the Nile Delta, from Portugal to the Arabian deserts, in wars justified as holy against, among others, Syrians, Palestinians, Egyptians, Greeks, Slavs, Balts, Livs, Russians, Bosnians, Turks and Spaniards, Muslims both Sunni and Shiah, pagans and Christian enemies of the pope.

The personalities and actions of figures such as Godfrey of Bouillon, Richard Cœur de Lion, Saladin, Frederick Barbarossa or St Louis have haunted literature, myth and popular imagination ever since. The word 'crusade', although a non-medieval Franco-Spanish hybrid, has entered the Anglo-American language as a synonym for a good cause vigorously pursued, religious or secular. However floridly and misleadingly romantic, the image of mailed knights bearing crosses on their surcoats or banners, fighting for their faith under an alien sun, occupies a familiar niche in the façade of modern western perceptions of the past. Their story still moves.

In this lies a strong irony, for crusading has always lacked objective precision in definition, practice, perception or approval. Such startling intrusions into the customary procedures of western life inevitably elicited complex responses even when the activity became integrated into the devotional practices and assumptions of the western Church. By turns and at the same time, crusading has been understood by participants, contemporaries or later observers as warfare to defend a beleaguered faith; the ultimate expression of secular piety; a decisive ecclesiastical compromise with base secular habits; a defining commitment of the Church to accommodate the spiritual aspirations of the laity; the pinnacle of admired ambition for a ruling military élite; an agent as well as symbol of religious, cultural and ethnic identity, even superiority; a vehicle for personal self-aggrandisement, commercial expansion and political conquest; an expression of the authority of the papacy, and a means of imposing uniformity and order within Christendom as well as securing and extending its external frontiers; a manifestation of Christian love for fellow believers and of divine care for God's people; an experiment in European colonialism; an example of recrudescent western racism; an excuse and incentive for religious persecution, ethnic cleansing and acts of barbarism; a noble cause; or, as Steven Runciman, the best-known crusade historian of the twentieth century, imperishably intoned: 'one long act of intolerance in the name of God, which is the sin against the Holy Ghost'. While not all these views can necessarily be accommodated simultaneously, if at all, they indicate why their subject continues to intrigue.

Throughout its history, crusading, always a minority, if strikingly disruptive, activity among the Christian faithful of western Europe, had attracted criticism as well as enthusiasm, from those appalled at such overt embracing of physical, violent war as an act of spiritual penance, those who regarded the conduct of crusaders as beneath contempt, and those who distinguished between campaigns fought under the Cross for selfless or selfish political ends. Crusading was born in controversy, the struggle between supporters of the pope or the German emperor over the appropriate independence of the Church from lay influence. The direction of the special privileges associated with the initial expedition to Jerusalem of 1096–9 (remission of the penalties of sin, Church protection of property and family, immunity from litigation and debt reclamation, etc.) to other conflicts, against the Muslim rulers in Spain, the pagans of the Baltic, religious heretics or Christian enemies of popes, widened the scope for both commitment and criticism. The cries of many victims went largely unheard in the west: the Jews massacred by the First and Second Crusaders in the Rhineland in 1096 and 1146–7 or butchered by the triumphant Christian army in the streets of Jerusalem in July 1099; or the Muslims who shared that fate not just in Jerusalem in 1099 but in countless cities, towns, villages and forts across the Near East. Warfare, however dressed up in moral or religious terms, brutalises, kills and maims victors and vanquished. Christian, Muslim or Jewish polemic, alike in articulate passion, rarely impinged on each other. In Christendom the blunt certainty of the *Song of Roland* determined reactions: 'Christians are right and pagans are wrong.' The crusades provide a good example of how contact can breed hardening of intercultural attitudes even while channels of material transmission flow more freely. This was most catastrophically confirmed when an army of crusaders in 1204 sacked the Orthodox Christian city of Constantinople, with most showing only a few qualms. The sense of embattlement upon which the ideology of crusading rested ensured that the wars of the Cross persisted as long as the religious assumptions that had given rise to and sustained them remained intact: the authority of the pope and Church to mediate penance and redemption.

However, those critics within the pale of western culture who felt victimised or disappointed by some or all of the wars of the Cross were less easy to ignore, although easy to exaggerate. The papacy's sponsorship of the brutal conquest of Languedoc by crusader armies from northern France (1209–29) was justified by the need to extirpate the threat of Cathar heresy, a dualist creed that had caught hold in the region and undermined the established Church. Many troubadours from the area castigated the crusaders for preferring war in southern France to fighting the infidel. This smacked of *parti pris*. Elsewhere, the premise of the military action to eradicate a cancer that endangered the spiritual health of all Christendom and the salvation of Christians was more readily accepted. Crusading, on all fronts, attracted interest not because it was thought eccentric, evil or corrupt. Few would have subscribed as a practical option to Francis of Assisi's preference for conversion over combat with Islam, any more than did Sultan al-Kamil of Egypt when Francis visited him during the Fifth Crusade in 1219.* While many disapproved of the papacy's increasing obsession from the thirteenth century with using wars of the Cross to eradicate enemies within Christendom, others were happy to join these campaigns and take advantage of the spiritual and material benefits on offer. Few doubted the almost apocalyptic efficacy of Christian rule in the Holy Land, even long after its political realisation had become more of a distant memory than even a pipe-dream. Crusading continued to hold the gaze at least of prominent politicians and members of both lay and clerical élites, and, judging by wills, lesser propertied people, both men and women, because it appeared to embrace some of the constant and dangerous issues

* See *An Eyewitness History of the Crusades: The Fourth Crusade* (Folio Society, London, 2004), p. 190.

facing western European Christians: how to earn salvation in a sinful world; how to lead a strenuously active, not just passive, good and faithful life; how to measure God's approbation of individuals and society on the gauge of physical victory and defeat; even how to ensure the political survival of their entire religion.

Perhaps the strangest aspects of crusading to the Holy Land lay in its lack of connection with the territories to which the armies were directed. This is where comparisons with modern imperialism collapse. There existed no strategic interest for the knights of the west to occupy parts of Syria and Palestine. The alleged commercial imperatives driving Italian trading cities could have been achieved, if more gradually and possibly on a smaller scale, at smaller cost and with far less risk through peaceful means, as they demonstrated in their dealings with Muslim Egypt after the loss of the Holy Land. Trade piggybacked the crusades, not vice versa. The presence of western warriors and settlers in Muslim Iberia or the pagan Baltic made some economic and political sense; these were immediate frontiers. This was not true for the Holy Land, whose occupation depended on its status as a relic of Christ on earth. Whatever else, the justification if not explanation for the Palestinian wars from 1096 to 1291 lay in aspirations of faith. *Mutatis mutandis*, this applied to all Holy Wars of the Cross. Hence one central paradox of crusading history: the grip of crusade ideology and practice was decisively loosened not by Muslim victories, although they were frequent enough, but by the Reformation, which challenged the belief system that underlay the crusade – papal authority, a penitential system based on the granting of indulgences and dependent on a view of the centrality of priests and the Church in mediating the grace of God to believers. Protestants did not cavil at Holy War; but they rejected the form of the crusade as theologically spurious and ecclesiastically corrupt. In a further irony, this coincided with the greatest external Muslim threat to Christendom's survival, the advance of the Ottomans, who reached the gates of Vienna in 1529, the very year the German evangelical princes signed the 'Protest' from which the term 'Protestant' derives.

As a demonstration of the protean and forceful effect of faith, the crusades inevitably attracted the attention of historians of all denominations (and none) as well as of Enlightenment philosophers analysing the imperfections of mankind and human society. Each generation has managed to reinvent the crusades in its own image. As the pattern of nation states achieved dominance in European affairs from the seventeenth century, so the crusades were appropriated to national myths, especially in France, where the equation of the medieval term 'Frank' with the modern French proved irresistible if unsound. To many eighteenth-century savants, crusading appeared a classic example of barbaric enthusiasm: irrational, pointless and destructive, even if energetic and heroic. Yet with the removal of the Ottoman political threat, the growing fashion for eastern travel and artefacts, and the beginning of systematic commercial and political exploitation of the Near East by western powers combined with the escapist, often politically reactionary medieval revival to create a new nineteenth-century set of images. The crusades increasingly featured in academic and popular literature as stirring tales, part of the ascent of the west, tribute, in Ernest Barker's purple prose, to 'the majesty of man's incessant struggle towards an ideal good'. Although some still maintained that the whole enterprise was misguided, the picture of the crusaders as chivalric heroes or gilded thugs became firmly established, their actions part of what Edward Gibbon so misleadingly called 'the World's debate'. This last interpretation, that the crusades operated as the medieval act in an immemorial contest between east and west, Christianity and Islam, apart from being historically meaningless, was adopted in the late nineteenth century both by western colonisers and, as witness to that exploitation, by elements in the Muslim Near East seeking a future beyond the senescent Ottoman empire. When General Allenby entered Jerusalem in December 1917 some in the British army and press corps saw this as the fulfilment of some crusading destiny; so, drawing rather different conclusions, did some of their opponents. The French even claimed a Syrian mandate in 1919 on the spurious grounds of their historic interests in the area. As Amir Faisal, soon to be palmed off with the newly made throne of Iraq, sardonically enquired: 'Could I be reminded just who won the crusades?' With the rise of Zionism and the creation of the state of Israel, primarily by Jews from the European diaspora, with borders not so very different from the twelfth-century kingdom of Jerusalem, an equation with or rejection of the crusading past became in some quarters more plausible. At a banal level, when we read of the negotiations between Saladin and Richard I over the partition of Palestine in 1191–2 coming unstuck on the question of jurisdiction within the city of Jerusalem, we can experience a tremor of recognition, however false. It is one of the most savage of many bitter ironies that a nineteenth-century depiction of the crusades as a prototype for modern imperial exploitation and western cultural aggression or, alternatively, as a just war in defence of core but culturally specific western moral values, has so destructively entered twenty-first-century international politics.

Modern society is no less captivated by belief systems than any other, even if the western liberal European tradition harbours suspicion of organised religion. The crusades' combination of religion and politics, faith and materialism, has proved, if anything, increasingly captivating. This cannot surprise. The history of the crusades has left its litter. Shopping would not be pursued in Knightsbridge, nor cricket in St John's Wood, nor the law in the Temple if it had not been for the Military Orders of the Temple and the Hospital of St John, whose estates these London medieval suburbs once were, religious Orders founded to protect and succour pilgrims to Jerusalem in the aftermath of its conquest by an army from western Europe in 1099; Orders that later found themselves leading the defence of the land these westerners conquered and the political settlement they carved out from the indigenous peoples and their own no less violent rulers. Even more perhaps than in these historic survivals, the history of the crusades throws up concerns central to all societies, about the forging of identity, the communal force of shared faith, the use and abuse of legitimate violence, the nature of political authority and organised religion, the exploitation or fear of what sociologists call 'the other', alien people or concepts ranged against which social groups can find cohesion: communism and capitalism; democracy and fascism; Christians and non-Christians; east and west; them and us. The first great anti-Semitic pogrom in western Europe came as the result of recruiting for a new form of Holy War in 1096, the war of the Cross, the First Crusade.

There can be no indifference to such issues. However, there can equally be no summoning of the past to take sides in the present. The plundering of history to pronounce modern indictments serves no rational purpose and merely clouds understanding of a distant actuality whose interest lies as much if not more in its uniqueness and difference from other times, and especially from today. To observe the past through the lens of the present invites delusion. Only by trying to treat the evidence of the past as far as is possible on its own terms can any semblance of clear insight be achieved. That must be the justification for what follows, where eyewitnesses with their own distinct voices, preoccupations and experience can speak for themselves. Given the scope of the wars of the Cross, selection is inevitable. This one concerns only the witnesses to the Holy Land enterprise between 1095 and 1099. Yet throughout, the burden of understanding lies on us to appreciate their world, not on them to provide ours with facile precedents or good stories.

CHRISTOPHER TYERMAN

Introduction

Contemporaries and subsequent generations alike have been astonished, moved and intrigued by the exploits of the armies and fleets from western Europe successfully forcing their way into the Muslim Near East between 1096 and 1099 to seize and sack Jerusalem – which had been under Muslim rule for three and a half centuries, since its capture in AD 638 – in distant Palestine in July 1099. Searching for explanations for such unprecedented and dramatic events, excited western Christian intellectuals employed the language of theology: 'the greatest miracle since the Resurrection', a new 'way of salvation', almost a renewal of God's covenant with his Chosen People. Others appeared no less impressed, even if their analyses were grounded in more temporal interpretations: for the Christians of the ancient empire of Byzantium a new barbarian infusion; for Armenian Christians in Syria a fraternal act of liberation; for the Jews of the Rhineland a sudden eruption of impious and bestial persecution; for Muslims, appalled at the massacres perpetrated by the victorious westerners, an outrage and a desecration as well as a defeat. Few involved remained neutral or untouched. For Europeans and western Asians, what is now known as the First Crusade seemed to mark a caesura in world affairs, easily the equal of 1492, 1789 or 1914.

The political context of these military and naval operations revolved around the invitation sent to Pope Urban II (1088–99) by the Byzantine emperor Alexius Comnenus (1081–1118) in the early spring of 1095. Half a century later, in her extensive biographical panegyric the *Alexiad*, his daughter, Anna Comnena, recalled her father's motives in sponsoring the westerners, so that 'they, being organised by us [i.e. Alexius], might destroy the cities of the Ishmaelites [i.e. Muslims] or force them to make terms with the Roman [i.e. Byzantine] sovereigns and thus extend the bounds of Roman territory'.* For decades previously, either through direct imperial inducement or through recruiting agents whose activities have been traced as far west as Winchester, Byzantine emperors had recruited western troops into their armies, in particular the Varangian Guard from northern Europeans, including Englishmen; Normans who had settled in southern Italy; and Frenchmen, most recently a contingent of five hundred knights sent by Count Robert I of Flanders c.1090. In addition to fighting men, cosmopolitan Byzantium attracted a constant stream of western travellers, merchants, pilgrims and clerics, many of whom settled temporarily or permanently, providing a context in which western aid appeared both natural and traditional.

Behind Alexius' invitation of 1095 lay a particular strategic opportunity. In 1071, the Byzantine army had been defeated at the battle of Manzikert in north-eastern Anatolia by the Seljuk Turks who, having already overrun the Muslim heartlands of Iran and Iraq, now proceeded to impose their rule on most of Syria and Asia Minor. Within twenty years, the Turks had established a sultanate of Rum (i.e. most of western and central Asia Minor) with a capital at Nicaea, within striking distance of the Greek capital of Constantinople; and had excluded Byzantine power from northern Syria, with Antioch falling in 1084. Yet, in 1092, with the death of Malik Shah, the Seljuk sultan of Baghdad, Turkish control over the city states of Armenia, Syria and Palestine fragmented, making any support for the Seljuks of Rum improbable. In Asia Minor itself, the Seljuks faced opposition from the nomadic tribal alliance of Danishmends in the north-east as well as economically resurgent Greek cities in the west. More widely, Alexius could hope for support from the recently subjugated Armenian Christian princes of northern Syria and Cilicia and to exploit the fault lines in Near Eastern Muslim politics between the orthodox Sunnis, reinvigorated by the Seljuks, and the Shiites, whose large communities through-

* *The Alexiad of Anna Comnena*, trans. E. R. A. Sewter (Penguin, 1969), p. 439.

out the region lacked political power except in Egypt, where the Fatimid Shiite caliphs had ruled since 969. More specifically, successive eleventh-century Greek emperors had associated themselves with the Holy Places in Jerusalem, not least as patrons of the rebuilding of the church of the Holy Sepulchre after its destruction by Caliph al-Hakim of Egypt in 1009; Alexius' diplomatic and ecclesiastical embrace included Symeon, the current Greek patriarch of Jerusalem with whom the crusaders were to co-operate closely on their arrival in Syria in 1097–8. In the Balkans, Alexius had repulsed the concerted attempts by the Normans of southern Italy under their leader Robert Guiscard to annex the Adriatic and Ionian provinces in 1085, and more recently had defeated the threatening Cumans and faced down a dangerous conspiracy against him within the aristocratic officer corps. A usurper himself, Alexius needed continuing military success and effective security to maintain his position. Success in the Balkans and disunity among the Muslim powers to the east offered a chance to achieve both, provided Alexius could recruit enough élite western troops. This task would have appeared easier with the completion in 1091–2 of the conquest of Sicily by the Normans of southern Italy. Since his victory over Robert Guiscard, Alexius had recruited steadily from his former enemies; now, with the conquest of Sicily and the disposal of landed spoils complete, Alexius could expect a further peace dividend in the form of experienced Norman soldiers and commanders for hire.

In western Europe, circumstances seemed propitious for a request for military aid. The eleventh-century Investiture Wars between the papacy and Holy Roman empire, apart from accustoming western arms-bearers to fighting ideological wars soaked in theological propaganda and rhetoric, had neutralised any threat to Byzantine interests in central Europe or the Adriatic from the German western emperor, Henry IV (1056–1106), while forging an alliance of convenience between the Normans of southern Italy and the papacy (which, despite the tricky theological and legal conflicts that separated the eastern and western

Christian Churches, sought Constantinople as an ally against the Germans). By 1094–5, Pope Urban II (1088–99) had restored papal authority to the extent of being confident enough to summon a council at Piacenza in March 1095 to consider international issues such as the excommunications imposed on Henry IV and the adulterous Philip I 'the Fat' of France (1060–1108). To Piacenza Alexius sent ambassadors who appealed for western aid, recognising both Urban's use as an ally and his establishment of a wide, independent network of diplomatic contacts throughout western Europe. The appeal, which, given his knowledge of the Italian Normans and the Byzantine court, may not have caught the pope by surprise, fitted Urban's tactical, strategic and even theological sense. For years, Urban had promoted Christian expansion in Spain, as his predecessors had in Sicily. The Greek invitation, which may have included a reference to Jerusalem, matched a view that the time was ripe to reverse the historical retreat of Christianity before Islam, a belief bolstered by the papal agenda of Church reform that emphasised the need to return to the purity of the early Church in Jerusalem. In 1074, Urban II's forceful predecessor Gregory VII (1073–85), in the wake of Manzikert and dynastic instability in Byzantium, had proposed a papally led expedition to the east to help Christendom and recover the Holy Sepulchre.

Nothing came of Gregory's scheme. By contrast, Urban II, while not the initiator, eagerly seized on Alexius' request to promote the new campaign as a means of secular spiritual reform and a novel demonstration of papal authority in the temporal world. At Piacenza, Urban encouraged 'many to promise, by taking an oath, to aid the emperor most faithfully as far as they were able against the pagans'. He then embarked on an extended tour of France between August 1095 and September 1096 preaching the new war; establishing the ceremonies of taking the Cross as a sign of commitment and penitential renewal; broadcasting, by letter, legate and sermon, the necessity of the expedition and the spiritual privileges on offer to those who joined up; and recruiting personally some of the leaders of the campaign, including his representative, the papal legate Adhemar, bishop of Le Puy. Some details of organisation were agreed, such as the muster at Constantinople. In retrospect the central event occurred on 27 November at the end of the council held at Clermont in the Auvergne when Urban preached the Holy War to Jerusalem openly, apparently for the first time. However, there were other sermons, and some had reputedly vowed to undertake the eastern journey weeks earlier at Autun. Although his own exertions suggested Urban's intention to recruit as widely and extensively as possible, the overwhelming response proved difficult to control and probably exceeded what Alexius had envisaged, although in the event his preparations coped remarkably well with the influx of western forces between the summer of 1096, when the first contingents reached Byzantine provinces in the Balkans, and June 1097 when they left Greek lands in Asia Minor bound for Syria. Throughout, Alexius proved well informed and resourceful. Given the extraordinary popularity of Urban's message, he needed to be.

Although witnesses at the siege of Antioch in January 1098 insisted that the Christian host, despite severe losses in Asia Minor, still contained one hundred thousand armed troops, this is a more credible figure for the total number of original recruits: soldiers, women, children, non-combatants and hangers-on. It is likely that at most between fifty and seventy thousand fighting men reached Asia Minor at one time or another in 1096–7. Swelled by pilgrims using the military adventure as protection for their journey, this still represented a uniquely huge assembly when it finally gathered in one place outside Nicaea in June 1097, perhaps four or five times the size of William of Normandy's invasion force to England in 1066. Unprecedented in scale, the armies came from all parts of western Christendom, even though they increasingly became identified in western and Muslim sources alike as Franks, *Franci, al-ifranj.* The first contingents to embark east, as early as the spring and summer of 1096, included forces from Lombardy, that arrived in Byzantium by the summer of 1096, and from northern and eastern France, the Rhineland

and southern Germany, led by the Frenchmen Peter the Hermit and Walter of SansAvoir and the Germans Folkmar, the priest Gottschalk and Count Emich of Flonheim. After provoking and executing vicious anti-Jewish pogroms the length of the Rhineland in May and June 1096, the Franco-German armies moved east down the Danube. Although by no means the disorganised rabbles of legend and contemporary apologia, these armies found discipline hard to maintain, and those that struggled through to the Asiatic shore of the Bosporus in August 1096 met with annihilation at the hands of the Turks a month later. The fate, and therefore reputations, of the armies led by dukes and counts proved very different in outcome if not always in action.

There were five main such armies from beyond the Alps. Hugh of Vermandois, brother of Philip I of France, led troops from the royal territories in northern France. Godfrey of Bouillon, duke of Lower Lorraine, commanded the recruits from imperial lands in Flanders, the Low Countries and western Germany, and travelled with his younger landless brother Baldwin of Boulogne; their elder brother, Count Eustace III of Boulogne, journeyed separately. From southern Italy the troops raised embarked with Robert Guiscard's son, Bohemund of Taranto, and his nephew, the ambitious Tancred. The brothers-in-law Duke Robert of Normandy and Count Stephen of Blois began their march east with Count Robert II of Flanders, who left them behind in Italy in the winter of 1096–7 while he hurried on to Constantinople. And finally, the main contingent from Languedoc followed Count Raymond IV of Toulouse (often called the count of St Gilles), with whom Urban had negotiated directly in 1096, and the papal legate Adhemar of Le Puy. Arriving severally at Constantinople between November 1096 and June 1097, and, in some cases, not without violent coercion, each of the leaders was forced to offer an oath of fealty to Alexius* with the promise to restore to him territory once held by the Byzantines, a suitably vague formula that was to cause later difficulties. In return, Alexius pro-

* See below, pp. 76, 82–5, 101, 106–7.

vided the western host with money, provisions and a regiment of troops under the eunuch Taticius, an experienced Greek general.

Once Nicaea had been captured (19 June 1097) and Byzantine lands left behind, the campaign fell into four distinct phases: the march across Asia Minor to Syria (June to October 1097), including the major victory known as the battle of Dorylaeum (1 July 1097); the siege and defence of Antioch (October 1097 to June 1098); the occupation of north-western Syria (July 1098 to January 1099); and the march south, capture of Jerusalem (15 July) and defeat of an Egyptian relief army at Ascalon (January to August 1099). From at least November 1097, the Franks were joined in Syrian waters by fleets from Italy and northern Europe; throughout, new arrivals matched a constant stream of desertions, especially at the crisis of the campaign at Antioch. In September and October 1097, Tancred and Baldwin of Boulogne conducted raids into Cilicia; in February and March 1098, Baldwin managed to establish himself as ruler of the Armenian city of Edessa beyond the Euphrates. Adversity secured unity, notably on the battlefield; success, as at Antioch, threw up divisions. Bohemund took Antioch for himself,* encouraged by the failure of Alexius to come to the Franks' aid when they were facing catastrophe at the hands of a relief force before and after the city fell (June 1098). After the death of Adhemar of Le Puy (1 August 1098), tensions between the leaders rarely found easy resolution, and the final push towards the Holy City resulted from pressure by the rank and file, appalled at the squabbles of their commanders. Increasingly, as the privations multiplied and the odds against ultimate success lengthened, the Franks felt themselves to be instruments of divine providence. Reports of miracles and visions increased to provide a constant commentary and spur to action. Whatever else, the conquest of Antioch and Jerusalem introduced a new, unexpected and surprisingly durable element into the political calculations of the Near East, as well as leaving an indelible mark on the retina of history.

*

* See below, pp. 256–7.

THE SOURCES

The First Crusade generated an unprecedented flow of historical writing about one temporal event, as well as stimulating a whole series of vernacular verse epics and romances that continued to proliferate for the rest of the Middle Ages and beyond, from the twelfth-century cycles including the *Chanson d'Antioche* to Torquato Tasso's internationally popular *Gerusalemme Liberata* of 1580. The histories, many actually using the somewhat ambiguous word *historia* with its medieval overtones of story-telling rather than explanatory analysis, were written in Latin, and therefore by members of the educated élite. These texts circulated, if at all, among this same élite. However, some of the source material for these histories also found transmission into the vernacular epics, and some popular texts, such as that by Robert of Rheims, were later rendered in verse. With songs and oral story-telling, history and verse shared a common pool of accurate recall, memory, invention, interpretation and legend. This was true for even the earliest of accounts, none of which was other than didactic, designed to 'justify the ways of God to men', and all of which, at whatever remove, relied on the embroidered stories of old soldiers. The Latin histories divide into three overlapping groups: the accounts by participants in the expedition constructed shortly after the event; compilations of veterans' tales and versions of the eyewitness narratives composed by western intellectuals in the decade after 1099; and later descriptions based heavily on either or both of the first two categories and incorporated into larger historical projects by writers later in the twelfth century and beyond.

Three main accounts by participants survive: the anonymous *Gesta Francorum* (*Deeds of the Franks*, earliest extant version 1104, but much of it probably written by 1101); Fulcher of Chartres's *Historia Hierosolymitana*; and Raymond of Aguilers's *Historia Francorum* (also known as his *Liber*, i.e. book), all finished before 1105. A fourth *Historia*, completed by 1111 by Peter Tudebode, a veteran who lost two brothers on campaign, while containing some unique details, appears closely related to, if not heavily dependent upon, the anonymous *Gesta*. Raymond of Aguilers also seems to have used the *Gesta* for some details of the siege of Antioch, although he is, like Fulcher, essentially an independent source. Yet another separate version of events is provided by the sections of Albert of Aachen's *Historia* concerning the First Crusade, dating perhaps from as early as 1102. Albert did not go east but relied on the evidence of returning crusaders. Episodic and in places romantic, Albert, although not an eyewitness, preserves perhaps nearly as much authentic experience as the writers who saw the campaign for themselves. All these writers, and numerous other anonymous scribes such as the author of the *Historia Belli Sacri* or later panegyricists such as Ralph of Caen, whose *Gesta Tancredi* (*Deeds of Tancred*) dates from after 1112, worked in similar fashion. Each is a compilation, often collected over some time, of different sources or changing reflections. A number show close congruence with each other, suggesting a circulation and common dependency on some central accounts, notably the *Gesta Francorum*. None represents direct, unadorned memories. Each offers a view of how the expedition should be assessed and judged within a more or less explicit theological frame, even though a number were written by laymen, such as Pons of Balazun, a Provençal knight. For these reasons, the authenticity of the eyewitnesses lies in crafted invention as much as unadorned accuracy. Yet their testimony, taken with the surviving letters of the crusaders themselves,* and only slightly less prone to literacy device, muat stand as the closest reflection of what it was to be part of an expedition that was seen, by those present as well as later commentators, to have broken the historical mould, to have revealed God's immanent power in his redirection of Christian history.

All that being so, in the present volume the main narrative of the expedition is explored through the accounts of the three western writers who went on the expedition: Fulcher of Chartres,

---

* See below, p. xxxii.

Raymond of Aguilers and the anonymous author of the *Gesta Francorum*. Supplementing them, from a Greek perspective, is the *Alexiad* of Anna Comnena. While all contain material derived either from personal observation or the testimony of witnesses, all are literary compilations, not diaries or affidavits, and each has a particular relationship to the events described. Because of their importance in providing the main backbone of the story, these writers are discussed separately by way of introduction to the eyewitnesses.

The Narrative of the Gesta Francorum

The anonymous *Gesta Francorum* appears to have been written in 1101, certainly no later than 1103, although certain revisions concerning the role of Alexius Comnenus were inserted before 1105. One of the earliest literary accounts of the First Crusade, it was used by Raymond of Aguilers to check his memories and formed the basis for the histories by Robert of Rheims, Guibert of Nogent, Ekkehard of Aura and Baldric of Dol, as well as that of the crusade veteran Peter Tudebode. Although in general composed in a relatively unadorned style, certain overblown passages of romantic imagination, such as the account of dealings with Kerboga, atabeg of Mosul at Antioch, seem to have been interpolated. The first-hand accounts of military operations, such as the battle of Dorylaeum (1 July 1097) or the night commando raid that secured the fall of Antioch (3 June 1098), have prompted the suggestion that the author was a knight, although the text may equally well represent a compilation of field memories put together, perhaps at Jerusalem, by a cleric whose confidence in his knowledge of the Bible led him regularly to misquote where a layman might have checked. This possibility of later compilation may find support in the marked change of emphasis and focus after the siege of Antioch. For most of the narrative, the author's perspective is that of the southern Italian contingent led by Bohemund of Taranto. From the summer of 1098 (roughly from the siege of Antioch), while the personal witness remains as vivid as before, the action centres on the forces under the Limousin lord Raymond Pilet and the army of Raymond IV of Toulouse in their march southwards to Jerusalem, while Bohemund remained at Antioch. Whether or not this indicates a change of allegiance of a knightly author or the skilful manipulation of distinct eyewitness sources by a third party, the tone of the *Gesta* is immediate, the accounts of battles as lively and as confused as might be expected from a combatant. Running through the text is a fierce hostility to the Greeks, reinforced by later additions when Bohemund used the chronicle as propaganda during his recruitment in France of an anti-Greek expedition in 1104–5. Whatever else, the *Gesta* is not a diary. It was composed with the benefit of hindsight, however close. The bitterness towards Alexius must post-date the siege of Antioch, when the Byzantine emperor failed to bring aid. Nevertheless, whatever the exact circumstances of its composition, and for all its literary artifice and careful manipulation of fact and interpretation, the *Gesta* provides one of the most compelling of all histories of crusading.

The Narrative of Raymond of Aguilers

Raymond of Aguilers (or Aighuile in the Auvergne) was a canon of Notre Dame of Le Puy, the cathedral of Adhemar of Monteil, bishop of Le Puy and papal legate on the First Crusade. On the Jerusalem expedition Raymond accompanied Bishop Adhemar and Count Raymond IV of Toulouse, whose chaplain he became. In his distinctive southern French or Provençal view of events, he reflects in many instances, but significantly not all, the perspective of Count Raymond, who, by virtue of being of an older generation than the other leaders and speaking a different French vernacular from most of them (*langue d'oc* instead of *langue d'oïl*), often appeared isolated and was outvoted in council. Canon Raymond completed his *Historia* or *Liber* before 1105. He clearly had access to a version of the *Gesta Francorum* but had begun work on his book during the campaign itself, possibly at the siege of Antioch. Initially, Raymond collaborated with a Provençal knight, Pons of Balazun, who was killed during the siege of Arqah, near Tripoli (February–May 1099),* a connection which may explain Raymond's grasp of military tactics and the structure of the battles he described. Raymond is alert to the politics of the campaign's conduct and to the material conditions within the Provençal camp. He also appears firmly anti-Greek, in contrast with his employer, Count Raymond, who, after tetchy dealings with Alexius in Constantinople in the spring of 1097, tried to maintain consistently loyal and amicable relations with the Byzantine emperor. However, it is as chronicler of the manifestations of the spiritual *esprit de corps* of the self-proclaimed 'army of God' that Canon Raymond most clearly stands out, particularly in his descriptions of the visions and miracles that featured with increasing urgency at the siege of Antioch and during the final months of the campaign in 1099. In particular, Raymond championed the authenticity of the Holy Lance, discovered in Antioch by the Provençal Peter Bartholomew during the darkest days of June 1098, and which he personally had helped unearth. Raymond's position as an army chaplain may have encouraged this attention to the morale-boosting role of the miraculous and allowed him to be more sensitive to the spiritual mentalities of the mass of lay crusaders than the aloof academic account of Fulcher of Chartres or the secular-tinged *Gesta Francorum*. As an unabashed apologist for the Holy Lance, he was, by extension, also one for the honesty and integrity of the Provençal clergy who promoted it in the face of growing doubts and later outright disbelief. Yet, while paying a debt of respect to the dead Bishop Adhemar, Raymond did not flinch from recording the bishop's own initial scepticism over the Lance.† Throughout, professional credulity and critical judgement mix in a tone of seeming self-awareness that draws the reader into a narrative that retains clarity despite its detailed texture of information and scriptural allusion. For Raymond, as for his fellow historians, literal truth would have seemed banal even if at all

---

* See below, p. 284.   † See below, p. 210.

meaningful. In searching for the significance of events within a divine providential scheme, Raymond easily employed the rhetoric and language of the Bible. It was entirely appropriate to his and his companions' world view to describe the sack of Jerusalem in July 1099 in words from the Book of Revelation,* a natural as well as apt analogy for the culminating moments of an experience that from inception to fulfilment remained not wholly but centrally a religious exercise.

The Narrative of Fulcher of Chartres

By virtue of his education, probably at the great cathedral school of Chartres,† and his close proximity to a number of northern French leaders of the First Crusade, Fulcher of Chartres (1059–c.1128), while not free from errors and inventions, provides perhaps the clearest, coolest and best-organised account of the First Crusade. The first redaction of his *Historia* was probably begun in 1101 and completed before 1105; a second redaction was completed in 1124 which he continued to 1127. Initially attached to the armies of Count Stephen of Blois (also count of Chartres) and his brother-in-law Duke Robert of Normandy, for reasons unknown Fulcher left the main army on 17 October 1097 just south of Marash in northern Syria to go with Baldwin of Boulogne on his adventure eastwards to Tell Bashir and Edessa.‡ Fulcher stayed at Edessa until he accompanied Baldwin on his pilgrimage to Jerusalem at Christmas 1099. Thus Fulcher was not an eyewitness to the events at Antioch in 1097–8, the siege of Jerusalem§ or the battle of Ascalon (July–August 1099),¶ relying for his none the less detailed account of these events on other sources, including the *Gesta Francorum*, Raymond of Aguilers and other materials, including the letter apparently from the leaders of the crusade to the pope.** From November 1100,

* See below, p. 328.
† Thanks to a series of eminent scholar-bishops one of the intellectual power-houses of eleventh-century France.　　‡ See below, pp. 140–2.
§ See below, pp. 144–8, 329–33.　　¶ See below, pp. 345–8.
** See below, pp. 240–3.

when Baldwin of Boulogne arrived at Jerusalem to assume the rule of the kingdom after the death of his brother Godfrey the previous July, Fulcher lived in the Holy City, remaining as Baldwin I's chaplain until the king's death in 1118 and then possibly becoming prior of the Mount of Olives. Thus he was in a good position to check his details of the part of the crusade for which he was absent, as well as being well placed to describe the first generation of the new Latin kingdom of Jerusalem in the second and third books of his *Historia*.* Beside his didactic purpose shared with other histories of the Jerusalem campaign, Fulcher wrote from the perspective of a follower, first of Count Stephen and Duke Robert and then as an apologist for Baldwin and, by extension, his family, including his brothers Godfrey de Bouillon and Count Eustace of Boulogne. The sustained detail and precision of the dates Fulcher includes in his description of the northern princes' march through Italy and across the Balkans in 1096–7 may indicate that he kept some sort of diary or chronological *aide-mémoire*. If so, he may have already been contemplating a record of the expedition, perhaps at the invitation of his leaders. By the time he compiled his history after 1100, Fulcher also appeared eager to attract colonists to the beleaguered Frankish garrison in Jerusalem; this may colour his version of Urban II's Clermont address which avoids specific mention of the goal of Jerusalem but talks more generally about aiding the eastern Church. Partly because of this priority to make journeying east, as soldiers, pilgrims or settlers, appealing, Fulcher tended to gloss over certain conflicts that marked the First Crusade, such as the rows over the oath to Alexius and relations with the Greeks generally in 1097–8 or the divisions amongst the leadership over Antioch and the march into Palestine in 1098–9. This draining away of controversy to leave political blandness may arouse suspicion, especially when contrasted with the overt and robust partisanship of the *Gesta* and Raymond of Aguilers.

* See *An Eyewitness History of the Crusades: The Second Crusade* (Folio Society, London, 2004), pp. 5–59.

The Narrative of Anna Comnena

Anna Comnena (1083–1153) was the eldest child of Alexius I Comnenus, Byzantine emperor 1081–1118. Her encomiastic biography of her father, the *Alexiad*, incorporating an unfinished history by her husband Nicephorus Bryennius (d. *c.*1137), was not completed until the late 1140s, possibly even after the Second Crusade (1147–8) had once again disrupted Byzantine political life. Anna's obvious partisanship in favour of her father was matched by her disapproval of his successors, her younger brother John II (1118–43) and nephew Manuel I (1143–80), not least the latter's periodically pro-western policies. Shortly after John's accession she and her husband had been involved in a conspiracy to remove him, its failure leading to Anna's political exile in a convent; she later complained that she had been denied access to her father's friends for the next thirty years. Beneath a very traditional Greek literary style lurk political resentment and a fierce desire to exonerate her father's actions in tacit opposition to those of his heirs.

This is especially evident in her account of the First Crusade, which she may have seen passing through Constantinople in 1096–7 as a young teenage girl. Anna attempted to exonerate Alexius from all responsibility for a western military expedition that resulted in a long conflict over the ownership of Antioch and, in some eyes, led to sustained damage to Byzantine interests, authority and diplomacy in the eastern Mediterranean. If she wrote during or just after the Second Crusade, her strictures on the untrustworthiness of westerners would have been lent added resonance and topicality. For all her apparent fullness and sophistication, perhaps because of them, Anna is a most disingenuous and mendacious witness. Her main objective was to undermine the character and honesty of the Franks, treating them as at best misguided, childlike enthusiasts, and at worst deceitful, greedy barbarians, a permanent threat to the empire, in order to remove blame from her father for the débâcle at Antioch in 1098, when the emperor's failure to relieve the city was held by Bohemund and his successors to have dissolved the bond of fealty established between the crusaders and Alexius by the oaths exchanged at Constantinople in 1096–7. Throughout, Alexius is portrayed as wise, patient, long-suffering, compassionate and skilful, whereas it might be thought that he had miscalculated in summoning the crusaders in the first place and had thereafter been outmanoeuvred by Bohemund over Antioch. Instead of being a tribute to his power, the First Crusade exposed Alexius' limitations, which Anna wishes to disguise or conceal. Therefore Anna's account of the negotiations between the Franks and the emperor cannot be taken as other than special pleading.

In the main course of the campaign after the siege of Nicaea Anna is hardly interested, and her history of it descends into fragmented error once Antioch has been taken. Although the western sources demonstrate Bohemund's willingness to co-operate with Alexius at Constantinople, he is shown to harbour a thinly disguised hostile intent throughout, making him the epitome of the treacherous western barbarian. Yet western martial qualities had been highly fashionable at Alexius' court, a paradox Anna memorably captured in her justly famous description of Bohemund – whom as a girl she may have seen – inserted in her account of the treaty of Devol in 1108. Whether true to life or a vivid stereotype, the image is impressive:

Bohemund's appearance was, to put it briefly, unlike that of any other man seen in those days in the Roman world,* whether Greek or barbarian. The sight of him inspired admiration, the mention of his name terror. I will describe in detail the barbarian's characteristics. His stature was such that he towered almost a full cubit† over the tallest men. He was slender of waist and flanks, with broad shoulders and chest, strong in the arms; in general he was neither taper of form nor heavily built and fleshy, but perfectly proportioned. His hands were large, he had a good firm stance, and his neck and back were compact. If to the accurate and meticulous observer he appeared to stoop slightly, that was not caused by any weak-

---

* i.e. the Byzantine empire.   † The length of a forearm.

ness of the vertebrae of the lower spine, but presumably there
was some malformation there from birth. The skin all over his
body was very white, except for his face, which was both white
and red. His hair was lightish-brown and not as long as that of
other barbarians (that is, it did not hang on his shoulders); in
fact, the man had no great predilection for long hair, but cut
his short, to the ears. Whether his beard was red or of any
other colour I cannot say, for the razor had attacked it, leaving
his chin smoother than any marble. However, it *appeared* to
be red. His eyes were light blue and gave some hint of the
man's spirit and dignity. He breathed freely through nostrils
that were broad, worthy of his chest and a fine outlet for the
breath that came in gusts from his lungs. There was a certain
charm about him, but it was somewhat dimmed by the alarm
his person as a whole inspired; there was a hard, savage quality
in his whole aspect, due, I suppose, to his great stature and
his eyes; even his laugh sounded like a threat to others. Such
was his constitution, mental and physical, that in him both
courage and love were armed, both ready for combat. His
arrogance was everywhere manifest; he was cunning, too,
taking refuge quickly in any opportunism. His words were
carefully phrased and the replies he gave were regularly ambiguous. Only one man, the emperor, could defeat an adversary of such character, an adversary as great as Bohemund;
he did it through luck, through eloquence, and through the
other advantages that nature had given him.*

As an eyewitness, Anna leaves much to be desired. However,
her husband Nicephorus Bryennius had played an active part in
events at Constantinople in 1096–7;† she may have had access
to other reminiscences; her information on the campaign from
Nicaea to Antioch could conceivably have been derived from
Taticius or her father's friend, George Palaeologus, who certainly
provided her with information about Alexius and was with the

* *The Alexiad of Anna Comnena*, trans. E. R. A. Sewter (Penguin, 1969),
pp. 422–3.   † See below, pp. 78–86.

emperor at the time; and she seems to have used some imperial archives. Although not to be looked at for impartial accuracy, Anna's perspective remains an authentic representation of one strand of Byzantine response to the western incursions into the Greek sphere of influence produced by the unprecedentedly large and uncontrolled eruption of the First Crusade that, half a century later, retained the power to anger, alarm and astonish.

Other Sources

For specific episodes a wider circle of evidence is brought to bear in shorter extracts which are introduced and discussed as they appear in the general narrative. Thus letters of Urban II provide a frame for the preaching of 1095–6, as do those of the crusaders themselves for the attempts of those involved to understand what was happening to and around them. Other chronicle accounts, such as those of Robert of Rheims and Guibert of Nogent, contain direct evidence for only part of the story, such as the preparations of 1096, but, thereafter writing at second or third hand, do not compare with the four central narratives for the bulk of the enterprise. Albert of Aachen, also not a participant, relied on the evidence of veterans except for his vivid account of Peter the Hermit, the impact of whose preaching through country near Albert's home lingered in the local imagination. The experiences of the crusaders' victims find voice in a wholly different range of material, the Hebrew accounts of the Jewish massacres of 1096, the Syrian Arabic responses to the western invaders or the correspondence between the remnants of the Jerusalem Jewish community and their co-religionists in Egypt after the Holy War had run its violent course.* These corroborative, contradictory or unique sources expand and define the longer narratives of the four main accounts of what we call, but they did not, the First Crusade.

CHRISTOPHER TYERMAN

* See below, pp. 362–72.

Editorial Note

This book is based almost entirely upon the wealth of existing published translations of the major sources for the First Crusades. With such texts, taken from a plethora of languages and literary traditions – medieval Latin, Old French, Provençal, Byzantine Greek, Armenian, Syriac, Arabic, Hebrew – a certain degree of harmonisation is necessary if the average reader is not to be distracted or, worse, disorientated by stylistic discontinuities, especially in the treatment of names.

To this end, the names of western individuals have generally been standardised to their English forms. Byzantine names and other Greek terms conform to their traditional Latinate spellings. And all Turkish and Arabic names and words have been regularised to, at the least, recognisable variations on familiar forms, rather than in accordance with any strictly scholarly logic. The same is true of place-names: whichever of the various modern, medieval, western or eastern (or occasionally classical) forms has seemed most appropriate in context has been followed, and, if helpful, the variants identified in the accompanying footnotes and glosses.

In those few places where, for ease of reading, it has been necessary to make minor cuts within extracts, these have been done silently – as has the excision of chapter numbers and headings where they disrupt the narrative flow. However, all significant omissions have been marked with ellipses. Except for the substitution of the western calendar for dates originally given in the Islamic and Jewish ones, all substantive emendations or editorial interpolations within the source extracts are placed within square brackets.

CJT

Chronology

1095   *1–7 March*: Council of Piacenza

July: arrival of Pope Urban II in France

15 August: Pope Urban at Le Puy

18–28 November: Council of Clermont

27 November: crusade proclaimed by Pope Urban II

December: Peter the Hermit begins to preach the Cross

First outbreaks of persecution of Jews in France

1096   *23 December–6 January*: Pope Urban preaches the Cross at Limoges

6–12 January: Pope Urban preaches the Cross at Angers

11 February: King Philip of France confers on crusade with Hugh of Vermandois and the French magnates in Paris

c.1 March: Walter SansAvoir leaves for east

8 March: Peter the Hermit begins journey

16–22 March: synod at Tours at which Pope Urban presides over a ceremony of taking the Cross

Early April: Peter the Hermit at Trier

12–19 April: Peter the Hermit at Cologne

3 May: Emich of Flonheim's forces begin massacre of Jews at Speyer

18–20 May: Emich's followers massacre Jews at Worms

21 May: Walter SansAvoir enters Hungary

23 May: Jews at Regensburg forcibly baptised, probably by Peter the Hermit's followers

25–9 May: the destruction of the Jewish community at Mainz by Emich's forces

29 May: pogrom at Cologne begins

30 May: persecution of Jews at Prague, probably by followers of Folkmar

June: massacre of Jews around Cologne continues and is extended to Trier and Metz

End of June: Folkmar's army destroyed at Nitra

c.*1 July*: Gottschalk's army surrenders to the Hungarians at Pannonhalma

c.*3–4 July*: Peter the Hermit's army mauled at Nish

6–14 July: Cross preached by Pope Urban at the Council of Nîmes

c.*20 July*: Walter SansAvoir reaches Constantinople

1 August: Peter the Hermit reaches Constantinople

6–7 August: Peter the Hermit and Walter SansAvoir cross Bosporus

c.*11 August*: crusaders reach Cibotus

c.*15 August*: flight of Emich of Flonheim's forces from Wieselburg

mid-August: Godfrey of Bouillon leaves for east

September: Bohemund of Taranto and Tancred take Cross

September–October: Robert of Normandy, Robert of Flanders and Stephen of Blois leave for east

c.*24 September*: Italian and German crusaders establish base close to Nicaea

29 September: defeat and destruction of Italian and German crusaders

October: Hugh of Vermandois crosses Adriatic

21 October: remaining crusaders in Asia Minor defeated

c.*26 October*: Bohemund of Taranto leaves Italy

November: Hugh of Vermandois reaches Constantinople

23 December: Godfrey of Bouillon reaches Constantinople

1097 *December–January*: Raymond of St Gilles and Adhemar of Le Puy cross Dalmatia

c.*20 February*: Godfrey of Bouillon's force crosses Bosporus

c.*10 April*: Bohemund of Taranto reaches Constantinople

26 April: Bohemund's force crosses Bosporus

c.*27 April*: Raymond of St Gilles reaches Constantinople

6 May: Godfrey of Bouillon, Tancred, Robert of Flanders and Hugh of Vermandois arrive before Nicaea

14–28 May: Robert of Normandy and Stephen of Blois at Constantinople

16 May: Raymond of St Gilles reaches Nicaea

3 June: Robert of Normandy and Stephen of Blois reach Nicaea

19 June: surrender of Nicaea to the Greeks

26–9 June: departure of crusaders

1 July: battle of Dorylaeum

c.15 August: crusaders reach Iconium

c.10 September: crusaders reach Heraclea and defeat a Turkish army

c.14 September: Tancred and Baldwin of Boulogne leave for Cilicia

c.21 September: Tancred and Baldwin take Tarsus

c.27 September: main body of crusade reaches Caesarea

September–October: Tancred takes Adana and Misis

5–6 October: main body of crusade reaches Coxon

c.13 October: main body of crusade reaches Marash

c.15 October: Baldwin of Boulogne rejoins main army

c.17 October: Baldwin leaves main army

20–2 October: crusaders arrive before Antioch

c.17 November: Genoese fleet reaches St Simeon

30 December: earthquake at Antioch

1098 *c.20 January*: attempted flight of Peter the Hermit and William the Carpenter

20 February: arrival of Baldwin of Boulogne at Edessa

5 March: decision to construct siege castle of La Mahomerie before Antioch

10 March: Baldwin of Boulogne takes over government of Edessa

Before 29 March: Stephen of Blois elected commander-in-chief

2 June: Stephen of Blois leaves Antioch

3 June: Antioch taken by the crusaders

4–5 June: Kerboga's army begins to arrive before Antioch

10–11 June: night of panic among the crusaders and flight

11 June: visions of Stephen of Valence and Peter Bartholomew reported

14 June: discovery of the Holy Lance

c.*20 June*: Emperor Alexius hears erroneous reports of the situation in Antioch and decides to withdraw from Akshehir

27 June: embassy of Peter the Hermit to Kerboga

28 June: battle of Antioch

July–after 15 August: Raymond Pilet's expedition

July: al-Afdal captures Jerusalem from the Ortuqids

1 August: death of Adhemar of Le Puy

c.*25 September*: Raymond of St Gilles establishes Latin bishopric at al-Bara

27 November: investment of Ma'arrat al-Numan

11–12 December: fall and sack of Ma'arrat al-Numan

1099 c.*4 January*: conference in the Ruj at which Raymond of St Gilles proposes to take the other leaders into his service for pay

c.*5 January*: Raymond of St Gilles's followers dismantle the walls of Ma'arrat al-Numan

13 January: Raymond of St Gilles departs for the south

14 January: Robert of Normandy joins Raymond of St Gilles

2 February: remaining crusaders in Antioch decide to assemble at Latakiah

c.*14 February*: Raymond of St Gilles reaches Arqah

c.*25 February*: death of Anselm of Ribemont

c.*14 March*: Godfrey of Bouillon and Robert of Flanders join siege of Arqah

8 April: Peter Bartholomew undergoes ordeal

20 April: death of Peter Bartholomew

13 May: siege of Arqah raised

19 May: crusade reaches Beirut

23 May: crusade passes Tyre

3–6 June: crusaders at Ramleh; Latin bishopric of Ramleh-Lydda established

6 June: Tancred takes Bethlehem

7 June: crusaders arrive before Jerusalem

8 July: procession round Jerusalem

15 *July*: Jerusalem taken

22 *July*: election of Godfrey of Bouillon as ruler of Jerusalem

29 *July*: death of Pope Urban II

1 *August*: election of Arnulf of Chocques as Latin patriarch of Jerusalem

5 *August*: discovery of the True Cross

12 *August*: battle of Ascalon

End of August: bulk of crusaders leave for home

c.1 *December*: Pope Paschal II threatens to excommunicate crusaders who have not yet fulfilled their vows, and calls for aid for the Christians in Palestine*

* Chronology based on J. Riley-Smith, *The First Crusade and the Idea of Crusading* (Athlone, 1986). Reproduced by permission of Athlone, a Continuum imprint.

Maps

Europe and the Near East

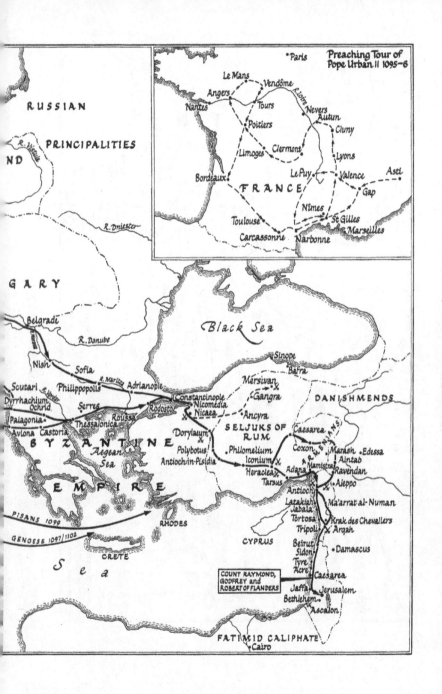

Preaching Tour of Pope Urban II 1095–6

Paris
Le Mans
Vendôme
Angers
Nantes
Tours
Nevers
R. Loire
Autun
Poitiers
Cluny
Lyons
Limoges
Clermont
Bordeaux
Le Puy
Valence
Asti
FRANCE
Gap
Nîmes
Toulouse
St Gilles
Marseilles
Carcassonne
Narbonne

RUSSIAN
PRINCIPALITIES
ND
R. Vistula

GARY
Belgrade
R. Danube
Black Sea
Nish
Sofia
Scutari
Philippopolis
R. Maritza
Adrianople
Sinope
Dyrrhachium
Serres
Rodosto
Mersivan
Ochrid
Palagonia
Rousa
Constantinople
Gangra
DANISHMENDS
Avlona
Castoria
Thessalonica
Nicomedia
Nicaea
Ancyra
BYZANTINE
Aegean
Dorylaeum
SELJUKS OF
Caesarea
Sea
Polybotus
RUM
Philomelium
Coxon
Marash
Edessa
Antioch-in-Pisidia
Iconium
Aintab
EMPIRE
Heraclea
Adana
Mamistra
Ravendan
Tarsus
Antioch
Aleppo
PISANS 1099
Latakiah
Ma'arrat al-Numan
Jabala
GENOESE 1097/1102
RHODES
Tortosa
Krak des Chevaliers
Tripoli
Arqah
CRETE
CYPRUS
Beirut
Damascus
Sidon
Sea
Tyre
Acre
COUNT RAYMOND,
Caesarea
GODFREY and
Jaffa
Jerusalem
ROBERT OF FLANDERS
Bethlehem
Ascalon
FATIMID CALIPHATE
Cairo

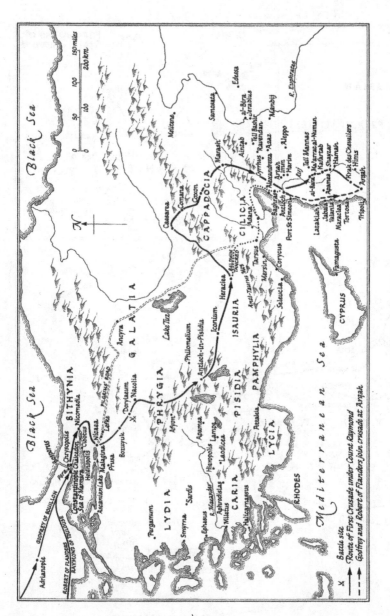

Asia Minor and Syria

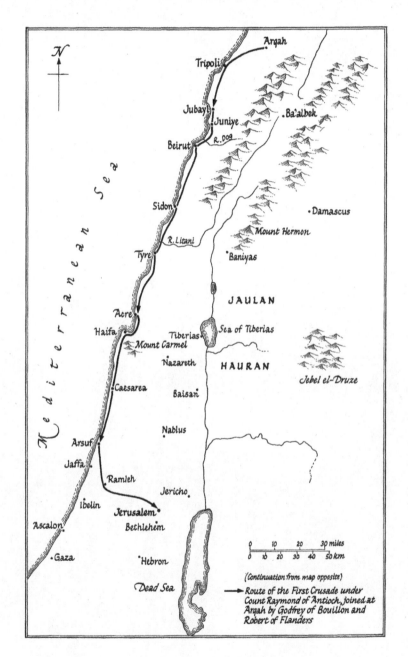

Palestine

I

The Call to Arms

March 1095–April 1096

At the end of the Council of Clermont, probably on 27 November 1095, Pope Urban II addressed the crowd gathered outside the cathedral. The event was carefully stage-managed. The bishop of Le Puy had been primed to come forward at the conclusion of the sermon to take the Cross, the new ceremony marking the adoption of this novel form of martial penance; the cries of Deus lo volt! *(God wills it!) were unlikely to have been entirely spontaneous. To be effective, ritual, ceremony and theatre need direction and planning. Of the five later contemporary accounts of what Urban actually said, none is reliable, each being composed after 1099, representing interpretations of what Urban could or should have said in the light of subsequent events and their theological exposition. However, two were composed by members of Urban's audience that November day in 1095, although this is very far from a guarantee of accuracy. One of these was written, probably before 1107, by Robert, a Benedictine monk whose scholarly achievements had led to his misguided appointment as abbot of St Remy in Rheims, in which capacity he attended the Council of Clermont. An unfailingly incompetent administrator, he was removed from his abbacy in 1097 and later from running the priory at Senuc a few months before his death in 1122. Judged by the number of surviving twelfth-century manuscripts, Robert's* Historia Hierosolymitana *proved easily the most popular account of the events of 1095–9, perhaps because of the clear interpretative gloss imposed by the author on his material, at least some of which derived from oral or written accounts of veterans.*

His version of Pope Urban's speech at Clermont follows.

'O race of Franks, race from across the mountains, race chosen and beloved by God – as shines forth in very many of your works – set apart from all nations by the situation of your country, as well as by your Catholic faith and the honour of the Holy Church! To you our discourse is addressed and for you our exhortation is intended. We wish you to know what a grievous cause has led us to your country, what peril threatening you and all the faithful has brought us.

'From the confines of Jerusalem and the city of Constantinople a horrible tale has gone forth and very frequently has been brought to our ears, namely, that a race from the kingdom of the Persians,* an accursed race, a race utterly alienated from God, a generation forsooth which has not directed its heart and has not entrusted its spirit to God, has invaded the lands of those Christians and has depopulated them by the sword, pillage and fire; it has led away a part of the captives into its own country, and a part it has destroyed by cruel tortures; it has either entirely destroyed the churches of God or appropriated them for the rites of its own religion. They destroy the altars, after having defiled them with their uncleanness. They circumcise the Christians, and the blood of the circumcision they either spread upon the altars or pour into the vases of the baptismal font. When they wish to torture people by a base death, they perforate their navels, and dragging forth the extremity of the intestines, bind it to a stake; then with flogging they lead the victim around until the viscera having gushed forth the victim falls prostrate upon the ground. Others they bind to a post and pierce with arrows. Others they compel to extend their necks and then, attacking them with naked swords, attempt to cut through the neck with a single blow. What shall I say of the abominable rape of the women? To speak of it is worse than to be silent. The kingdom of the Greeks is now dismembered by them and deprived of territory so vast in extent that it cannot be traversed in a march of two months. On whom therefore is

* i.e. Muslims or, specifically, the Seljuk Turks established in Iraq and Baghdad since the mid-eleventh century.

the labour of avenging these wrongs and of recovering this territory incumbent, if not upon you? You, upon whom above other nations God has conferred remarkable glory in arms, great courage, bodily activity, and strength to humble the hairy scalp of those who resist you.

'Let the deeds of your ancestors move you and incite your minds to manly achievements; the glory and greatness of King Charles the Great, and of his son Louis, and of your other kings,* who have destroyed the kingdoms of the pagans, and have extended in these lands the territory of the Holy Church. Let the Holy Sepulchre of the Lord our Saviour, which is possessed by unclean nations, especially incite you, and the Holy Places which are now treated with ignominy and irreverently polluted with their filthiness. Oh, most valiant soldiers and descendants of invincible ancestors, be not degenerate, but recall the valour of your progenitors.

'But if you are hindered by love of children, parents and wives, remember what the Lord says in the Gospel, "He that loveth father or mother more than me, is not worthy of me." "Everyone that hath forsaken houses, or brethren, or sisters, or father, or mother, or wife, or children, or lands for my name's sake shall receive a hundredfold and shall inherit everlasting life." Let none of your possessions detain you, no solicitude for your family affairs, since this land which you inhabit, shut in on all sides by the seas and surrounded by the mountain peaks, is too narrow for your large population; nor does it abound in wealth; and it furnishes scarcely food enough for its cultivators. Hence it is that you murder one another, that you wage war, and that frequently you perish by mutual wounds. Let therefore hatred depart from among you, let your quarrels end, let wars cease, and let all dissensions and controversies slumber. Enter upon the road to the Holy Sepulchre; wrest that land from the wicked race, and subject it to yourselves. That land which as the Scripture says "floweth

---

* Charlemagne (r. 768–814) and Louis the Pious (814–40) were increasingly figures of legend and portrayed as holy warriors against the infidel in vernacular epics, e.g. *The Song of Roland*.

with milk and honey", was given by God into the possession of the children of Israel.

'Jerusalem is the navel of the world; the land is fruitful above others, like another paradise of delights. This the Redeemer of the human race has made illustrious by his advent, has beautified by residence, has consecrated by suffering, has redeemed by death, has glorified by burial. This royal city, therefore, situated at the centre of the world, is now held captive by his enemies, and is in subjection to those who do not know God, to the worship of the heathens. She seeks therefore and desires to be liberated, and does not cease to implore you to come to her aid. From you especially she asks succour, because, as we have already said, God has conferred upon you above all nations great glory in arms. Accordingly undertake this journey for the remission of your sins, with the assurance of the imperishable glory of the kingdom of heaven.'

When Pope Urban had said these and very many similar things in his eloquent discourse, he so influenced to one purpose the desires of all who were present, that they cried out, 'It is the will of God! It is the will of God!' When the venerable Roman pontiff heard that, with eyes uplifted to heaven he gave thanks to God and, with his hand commanding silence, said:

'Most beloved brethren, today is manifest in you what the Lord says in the Gospel, "Where two or three are gathered together in my name there am I in the midst of them." Unless the Lord God had been present in your spirits, all of you would not have uttered the same cry. For, although the cry issued from numerous mouths, yet the origin of the cry was one. Therefore I say to you that God, who implanted this in your breasts, has drawn it forth from you. Let this then be your war-cry in combats, because this word is given to you by God. When an armed attack is made upon the enemy, let this one cry be raised by all the soldiers of God: "It is the will of God! It is the will of God!"

'And we do not command or advise that the old or feeble, or those unfit for bearing arms, undertake this journey; nor ought women to set out at all, without their husbands or brothers or legal guardians. For such are more of a hindrance than aid, more of a burden than advantage. Let the rich aid the needy; and according to their wealth, let them take with them experienced soldiers. The priests and clerks of any order are not to go without the consent of their bishop; for this journey would profit them nothing if they went without permission of these. Also, it is not fitting that laymen should enter upon the pilgrimage without the blessing of their priests.

'Whoever, therefore, shall determine upon this holy pilgrimage and shall make his vow to God to that effect and shall offer himself to him as a living sacrifice, holy, acceptable unto God, shall wear the sign of the Cross of the Lord on his forehead or on his breast. When, truly, having fulfilled his vow he wishes to return, let him place the Cross on his back between his shoulders. Such, indeed, by the twofold action will fulfil the precept of the Lord, as he commands in the Gospel, "He that taketh not his Cross and followeth after me, is not worthy of me." '

The other retrospective account of Urban's Clermont speech by one who was there was composed perhaps within ten years of the event by Fulcher of Chartres. While lacking the honed rhetoric of Robert of Rheims, Fulcher was none the less keen to portray a particular aspect of Urban's message, one determined by its outcome. As a resident of newly conquered Jerusalem and chaplain to King Baldwin I, Fulcher wished to emphasise the need for settlement in the east rather than stress the fate of Jerusalem; it was, when he wrote, already in Christian hands. His version of Urban's speech, therefore, as part of one general aim of his Historia *to recruit aid and settlers, chose to highlight the need to help the Church in the east, not the Holy City specifically.*

In the year 1095 after the Incarnation of Our Lord, while Henry the so-called emperor* was reigning in Germany and King Philip in France, evils of all kinds multiplied throughout Europe because of vacillating faith. Pope Urban II then ruled in the city

* Henry IV (1056–1106).

of Rome. He was a man admirable in life and habits who strove prudently and vigorously to raise the status of Holy Church ever higher and higher.

Moreover he saw the faith of Christendom excessively trampled upon by all, by the clergy as well as by the laity, and peace totally disregarded, for the princes of the lands were incessantly at war quarrelling with someone or other. He saw that people stole worldly goods from one another, that many captives were taken unjustly and were most barbarously cast into foul prisons and ransomed for excessive prices, or tormented there by three evils, namely hunger, thirst and cold, and secretly put to death, that Holy Places were violated, monasteries and villas consumed by fire, nothing mortal spared, and things human and divine held in derision.

When he heard that the interior part of Romania [Asia Minor] had been occupied by the Turks and the Christians subdued by a ferociously destructive invasion,* Urban, greatly moved by compassionate piety and by the prompting of God's love, crossed the mountains and descended into Gaul and caused a council to be assembled in Auvergne at Clermont, as the city is called. This council, appropriately announced by messengers in all directions, consisted of 310 members, bishops as well as abbots carrying the crozier.

On the appointed day† Urban gathered them around himself and in an eloquent address carefully made known the purpose of the meeting. In the sorrowing voice of a suffering Church he told of its great tribulation. He delivered an elaborate sermon concerning the many raging tempests of this world in which the faith had been degraded, as was said above.

Then as a suppliant he exhorted all to resume the powers of their faith and arouse in themselves a fierce determination to overcome the machinations of the devil, and to try fully to restore Holy Church, cruelly weakened by the wicked, to its honourable status as of old.

* Seljuk invasion of Anatolia after their victory at Manzikert, 1071.
† 27 November 1095.

'Dearest brethren,' he said, 'I, Urban, supreme pontiff and by the permission of God prelate of the whole world, have come in this time of urgent necessity to you, the servants of God in these regions, as a messenger of divine admonition. I hope that those who are stewards of the ministry of God shall be found to be good and faithful, and free from hypocrisy.

'For if anyone is devious and dishonest, and far removed from the moderation of reason and justice, and obstructs the law of God, then I shall endeavour with divine help to correct him. For the Lord has made you stewards over his household so that when the time comes you may provide it with food of modest savour. You will be blessed indeed if the Lord of the stewardship shall find you faithful.

'You are called shepherds; see that you do not do the work of hirelings. Be true shepherds, always holding your crooks in your hands; and sleeping not, guard on every side the flock entrusted to you.

'For if through carelessness or neglect a wolf carries off a sheep you will certainly not only lose the reward prepared for you by our Lord, but after first having been beaten by the rods of the lictor you will be summarily hurled into the abode of the damned.

'In the words of the Gospel, "You are the salt of the earth."* But if you fail how will the salting be accomplished? Oh, how many men must be seasoned! It is needful for you to salt with the corrective salt of your wisdom the ignorant who gape overmuch after the lusts of the world. Otherwise they will be putrefied by their transgression and be found unseasoned when the Lord speaks to them.

'For if he shall find in them worms, that is sins, because of your slothful performance of duty he will forthwith order them, despised, cast into the abyss of filth. And because you will not be able to restore such loss to him he will straightway banish you, damned in his judgement, from the presence of his love.

'But one that salteth ought to be prudent, far-seeing, modest,

* Matthew 5:13.

learned, peacemaking, truth-seeking, pious, just, equitable and pure. For how can the unlearned make others learned, the immodest others modest, and the impure others pure? If one hates peace how can one bring about peace? Or if one has soiled hands how can one cleanse those who are soiled of other pollution? For it is read, "If a blind man leads a blind man, both will fall into a pit."*

'Accordingly first correct yourselves so that then without reproach you can correct those under your care. If you truly wish to be the friends of God then gladly do what you know is pleasing to him.

'Especially see to it that the affairs of the Church are maintained according to its law so that simoniacal heresy in no way takes root among you. Take care that sellers and buyers, scourged by the lash of the Lord, be miserably driven out through the narrow gates to utter destruction.

'Keep the Church in all its ranks entirely free from secular power, cause a tithe of all the fruits of the earth to be given faithfully to God, and let them not be sold or retained.

'Whoever shall have seized a bishop, let him be accursed. Whoever shall have seized monks or priests or nuns, and their servants, or pilgrims and traders, and despoiled them, let him be accursed. Let thieves and burners of houses, and their accomplices, be banished from the Church and excommunicated.†

' "Thereafter we must consider especially", said Gregory, "how severely punished will be he who steals from another, if he is infernally damned for not being generous with his own possessions." For so it happened to the rich man in the familiar Gospel story.‡ He was not punished for stealing from another, but because having received wealth he used it badly.

'By these evils it has been said, dearest brethren, that you have seen the world disturbed for a long time and particularly in some

* Matthew 15:14, Luke 6:39.
† This refers to the decree establishing the Peace of God, under which infringement of Church property or rights was outlawed and local knights recruited to impose prevention and retribution.   ‡ Luke 16:19–31.

parts of your own provinces as we have been told. Perhaps due to your own weakness in administering justice scarcely anyone dares to travel on the road with hope of safety for fear of seizure by robbers by day or thieves by night, by force or wicked craft, indoors or out.

'Wherefore the truce commonly so called,* which was long ago established by the holy fathers, should be renewed. I earnestly admonish each of you to enforce it strictly in your own diocese. But if anyone, smitten by greed or pride, willingly infringes this truce, let him be anathema by virtue of the authority of God and by sanction of the decrees of this council.'

When these and many other matters were satisfactorily settled, all those present, clergy and people alike, spontaneously gave thanks to God for the words of the lord pope Urban and promised him faithfully that his decrees would be well kept. But the pope added at once that another tribulation not less but greater than that already mentioned, even of the worst nature, was besetting Christianity from another part of the world.

He said, 'Since, O sons of God, you have promised him to keep peace among yourselves and to sustain faithfully the rights of Holy Church more sincerely than before, there still remains for you, newly aroused by godly correction, an urgent task which belongs to both you and God, in which you can show the strength of your good will. For you must hasten to carry aid to your brethren dwelling in the east, who need your help for which they have often entreated.

'For the Turks, a Persian people, have attacked them, as many of you already know, and have advanced as far into Roman territory as that part of the Mediterranean which is called the Arm of St George.† They have seized more and more of the lands of the Christians, have already defeated them in seven times as many battles, killed or captured many people, have destroyed churches,

* The Truce of God specifying periods during which the Peace of God should be maintained and binding those who swore to the Truce to observe it.
† The Seljuks entered the Muslim world through Iran. The Arm of St George was the western name for the Bosporus and the Sea of Marmara.

and have devastated the kingdom of God. If you allow them to continue much longer they will conquer God's faithful people much more extensively.

'Wherefore with earnest prayer I, not I, but God exhorts you as heralds of Christ to urge repeatedly men of all ranks whatsoever, knights as well as foot-soldiers, rich and poor, to hasten to exterminate this vile race from our lands* and to aid the Christian inhabitants in time.

'I address those present; I proclaim it to those absent; moreover Christ commands it. For all those going thither there will be remission of sins if they come to the end of this fettered life while either marching by land or crossing by sea, or in fighting the pagans. This I grant to all who go, through the power vested in me by God.

'Oh, what a disgrace if a race so despicable, degenerate and enslaved by demons should thus overcome a people endowed with faith in Almighty God and resplendent in the name of Christ! Oh, what reproaches will be charged against you by the Lord himself if you have not helped those who are counted like yourselves of the Christian faith!

'Let those', he said, 'who are accustomed wantonly to wage private war against the faithful march upon the infidels in a war which should be begun now and be finished in victory. Let those who have long been robbers now be soldiers of Christ. Let those who once fought against brothers and relatives now rightfully fight against barbarians. Let those who have been hirelings for a few pieces of silver now attain an eternal reward. Let those who have been exhausting themselves to the detriment of body and soul now labour for a double glory. Yea, on the one hand will be the sad and the poor, on the other the joyous and the wealthy; here the enemies of the Lord, there his friends.

'Let nothing delay those who are going to go. Let them settle their affairs, collect money, and when winter has ended and

* A measure of attempts to see Christendom as one despite the breach between Rome and Constantinople in 1054; Urban actively promoted good relations with the eastern Church, and his crusade formed part of this strategy.

spring has come, zealously undertake the journey under the guidance of the Lord.'

After these words were spoken and the audience inspired to enthusiasm, many of them, thinking that nothing could be more worthy, at once promised to go and to urge earnestly those who were not present to do likewise. Among them was a certain bishop of Le Puy, Adhemar by name,* who afterwards acting as vicar apostolic prudently and wisely governed the entire army of God and vigorously inspired it to carry out the undertaking.

So when these matters which we have mentioned were decided in the council and firmly agreed upon by all, the blessing of absolution was given and all departed. After they had returned to their homes they told those who were not informed of what had been done. When the edict of the council had been proclaimed everywhere through the provinces, they agreed under oath to maintain the peace which is called the Truce [of God].

Indeed finally many people of varied calling, when they discovered that there would be remission of sins, vowed to go with purified soul whither they had been ordered to go.†

Oh, how fitting, and how pleasing it was to us all to see those crosses made of silk, cloth-of-gold or other beautiful material which these pilgrims, whether knights, other laymen or clerics sewed on the shoulders of their cloaks. They did this by command of Pope Urban once they had taken the oath to go. It was proper that the soldiers of God who were preparing to fight for his honour should be identified and protected by this emblem of victory. And since they thus decorated themselves with this emblem of their faith,‡ in the end they acquired from the symbol the reality itself. They clad themselves with the outward sign in order that they might obtain the inner reality.

The success of Urban's preaching campaign stunned observers. One of them, a northern French Benedictine scholar, Guibert of Nogent (1053–before 1125), recalled his impressions in his Gesta Dei per

---

* Adhemar of Monteil, from the Valentinois.
† For the decree see above, p. 10.   ‡ i.e. the Cross.

Francos (The Deeds of God through the Franks), *mainly compiled between 1104 and 1108. Using other written accounts, the memories of veterans such as Robert II, count of Flanders, and his own observations, as well as placing the events in a wide historical context, he perpetuated the rather misleading impression that the expedition had been the work specifically of the Franks (i.e. those living in the kingdom of the Franks, which could include Lorrainers as well as northern and southern Frenchmen).*

Pope Urban, whose name was Odo before becoming pope, was descended from a noble French family* from the area and parish of Rheims, and they say, unless the report is in error, that he was the first French pope. A cleric, he was made a monk of Cluny, after the abbot of glorious memory who aided Hugo;† not long afterwards he was made prior, and then, because of his abilities, he was appointed bishop of the city of Ostia, by order of Pope Gregory VII; finally, he was elected supreme pontiff of the apostolic see. His greatness of spirit was made manifest when he urged that the journey be undertaken, because when he first showed how it was to be done the whole world was astonished. His death, resplendent in miracles, attests to the state of his mind. According to what the bishop who succeeded him at Ostia wrote,‡ many signs were seen after he was dead and buried; a certain young man stood at his tomb, and swore by his own limbs that no sign had ever been given or might be given by the merit of Urban, who was called Odo. Before he could move a step, he was struck dumb, and paralysed on one side; he died the next day, offering testimony to the power of Urban. This great man, although honoured with great gifts, and even with prayers, by Alexius, prince of the Greeks, but driven much more by the danger to all of Christendom, which was diminished daily by pagan incursions (for he heard that Spain was steadily being torn apart by Saracen invasions), decided to make a journey to France, to recruit the people of his country. It was, to be sure, the ancient

* Of Lagery from Champagne.   † Abbot of Cluny, 1049–1109.
‡ Odo, nephew of Urban II.

custom for pontiffs of the apostolic see, if they had been harmed
by a neighbouring people, always to seek help from the French,
[as had] the pontiffs Stephen and Zacharias, in the time of Pepin
and Charles . . .* More respectful and humble than other nations
towards blessed Peter and pontifical decrees, the French, unlike
other peoples, have been unwilling to behave insolently against
God. For many years we have seen the Germans, particularly the
entire kingdom of Lotharingia, struggling with barbaric obsti-
nacy against the commands of St Peter and of his pontiffs.†
In their striving, they prefer to remain under a daily, or even eternal excommunication rather than submit. Last year while I was
arguing with a certain archdeacon of Mainz about a rebellion of
his people, I heard him vilify our king and our people, merely
because the king had given a gracious welcome everywhere in his
kingdom to His Highness Pope Paschal and his princes; he called
them not merely Franks, but, derisively, 'Francones'.‡ I said to
him, 'If you think them so weak and languid that you can deni-
grate a name known and admired as far away as the Indian
Ocean, then tell me upon whom did Pope Urban call for aid
against the Turks? Wasn't it the French? Had they not been
present, attacking the barbarians everywhere, pouring their
sturdy energy and fearless strength into the battle, there would
have been no help for your Germans, whose reputation there
amounted to nothing.' That is what I said to him. I say truly, and
everyone should believe it, that God reserved this nation for such
a great task. For we know certainly that, from the time that they
received the sign of faith that blessed Remigius§ brought to them
until the present time, they succumbed to none of the diseases of
false faith from which other nations have remained uncontami-
nated either with great difficulty or not at all. They are the ones
who, while still labouring under the pagan error, when they

* Popes Stephen II (752–7) and Zacharias (741–52) were helped by the Caro-
lingian king of the Franks, Pepin the Short (751–68).
† Referring to the Investiture Contest between Henry IV and Gregory VII.
‡ i.e. savages, like animals; Paschal II (1099–1118) visited France in 1107 while
Philip I was still on the throne.
§ St Remy, late fifth-century apostle to the Franks.

triumphed on the battlefield over the Gauls, who were Christians, did not punish or kill any of them, because they believed in Christ. Instead, those whom Roman severity had punished with sword and fire, native French generosity encased in gold and silver, covered with gems and amber. They strove to welcome with honour not only those who lived within their own borders, but they also affectionately cared for people who came from Spain, Italy or anywhere else, so that love for the martyrs and confessors, whom they constantly served and honoured, made them famous, finally driving them to the glorious victory at Jerusalem. Because it has carried the yoke since the days of its youth, it will sit in isolation, a nation noble, wise, warlike, generous, brilliant above all kinds of nations. Every nation borrows the name as an honorific title; do we not see the Bretons, the English, the Ligurians call men 'Frank' if they behave well? But now let us return to the subject.

When the pope crossed our borders, he was greeted with such great joy by crowds in the cities, towns and villages, because no one alive could remember when the bishop of the apostolic see had come to these lands. The year of the incarnate Word 1097 was hastening to its end,* when the bishop hastily convoked a council, choosing a city in Auvergne, Clermont. The council was even more crowded because of the great desire to see the face and to hear the words of such an excellent, rarely seen person. In addition to the multitudes of bishops and abbots, whom some, by counting their staves, estimated at approximately four hundred, learned men from all of France and the dependent territories flowed to that place. One could see there how he presided over them with serene gravity, with a dignified presence, and with what peppery eloquence the most learned pope answered whatever objections were raised. It was noted with what gentleness the most brilliant man listened gently to the most vehemently argued speeches, and how little he valued the social position of people, judging them only by God's laws.

Then Philip, king of the French, who was in the thirty-seventh

---

* An error for 1095.

year of his reign, having put aside his own wife, whose name was Berta, and having carried off Bertrada, the wife of the count of Anjou,* was excommunicated by the pope, who spurned both the attempts by important people to intercede for the king, and the offers of innumerable gifts. Nor was he afraid because he was now within the borders of the kingdom of France. In this council, just as he had planned before leaving Rome and seeking out the French for this reason, he gave a fine speech to those who were in attendance. Among other things which were said to exceed the memories of the listeners, he spoke about this project. His eloquence was reinforced by his literary knowledge; the richness of his speech in Latin seemed no less than that of any lawyer nimble in his native language. Nor did the crowd of disputants blunt the skill of the speaker. Surrounded by praiseworthy teachers, apparently buried by clouds of cases being pressed upon him, he was judged to have overcome, by his own literary brilliance, the flood of oratory and to have overwhelmed the cleverness of every speech. Therefore his meaning, and not his exact words, follow: 'If, among the churches scattered through the whole world, some deserve more reverence than others because they are associated with certain people and places, then, because of certain persons, I say, greater privileges are granted to apostolic sees; in the case of places, some privilege is granted to royal cities, as is the case with the city of Constantinople. We are grateful for having received from this most powerful Church the grace of redemption and the origin of all Christianity. If what was said by the Lord remains true, namely that "salvation is from the Jews", and it remains true that the Lord of the Sabbath has left his seed for us, lest we become like those of Sodom and Gomorrah, and that Christ is our seed, in whom lies salvation and blessing for all people, then the earth and the city in which he lived and suffered is called holy by the testimony of Scripture. If this land is the inheritance of God, and his holy temple, even before the Lord walked and suffered there, as the sacred and prophetic pages tell us, then what additional

* The same Count Fulk who met Pope Urban in 1096.

sanctity and reverence did it gain then, when the God of majesty took flesh upon himself there, was fed, grew up, and moving in his bodily strength walked here and there in the land? To abbreviate a matter that could be spun out at much greater length, this is the place where the blood of the Son of God, holier than heaven and earth, was spilled, where the body, at whose death the elements trembled, rested in its tomb. What sort of veneration might we think it deserves? If, soon after Our Lord's death, while the city was still in the possession of the Jews, the evangelist called it sacred, when he said, "Many bodies of the saints that have been asleep here have awoken, and come to the Holy City, and they have been seen by many,"* and it was said by the prophet Isaiah, "His tomb will be glorious,"† since this very sanctity, once granted by God the sanctifier himself, cannot be overcome by any evil whatsoever, and the glory of his tomb in the same way remains undiminished, then, O my dearly beloved brothers, you must exert yourselves, with all your strength, and with God leading you and fighting for you, to cleanse the holiness of the city and the glory of the tomb, which has been polluted by the thick crowd of pagans, if you truly aspire to the author of that holiness and glory, and if you love the traces that he has left on earth. If the Maccabees‡ once deserved the highest praise for piety because they fought for their rituals and their temple, then you too, O soldiers of Christ, deserve such praise, for taking up arms to defend the freedom of your country. If you think you must seek with such effort the thresholds of the apostles and of others, then why do you hesitate to go to see and to snatch up the Cross, the blood, and to devote your precious souls to rescuing them? Until now you have waged wrongful wars, often hurling insane spears at each other, driven only by greed and pride, for which you have deserved only eternal death and damnation. Now we propose for you battles which offer the gift

* Matthew 27:52–3.   † Isaiah 11:10.
‡ The central figures in two books of the Old Testament Apocrypha concerning second-century BC Jewish freedom fighters against the Hellenistic rulers of Palestine.

of glorious martyrdom, for which you will earn present and future praise. If Christ had not died and been buried in Jerusalem, had not lived there at all, if all these things had not taken place, surely this fact alone should be enough to drive you to come to the aid of the land and the city: that the law came from Sion and the word of God from Jerusalem. If all Christian preaching flows from the fountain of Jerusalem, then let the rivulets, wherever they flow over the face of the earth, flow into the hearts of the Catholic multitude, so that they may take heed of what they owe to this overflowing fountain. If "rivers return to the place whence they flow, so that they may continue to flow,"* according to the saying of Solomon, it should seem glorious to you if you are able to purify the place whence you received the cleansing of baptism and the proof of faith. And you should also consider with the utmost care whether God is working through your efforts to restore the Church that is the mother of churches; he might wish to restore the faith in some of the eastern lands, in spite of the nearness of the time of the Antichrist. For it is clear that the Antichrist makes war neither against Jews, nor against pagans, but, according to the etymology of his name, he will move against Christians. And if the Antichrist comes upon no Christian there, as today there are scarcely any, there will be no one to resist him, or any whom he might justly move among. According to Daniel and Jerome his interpreter, his tent will be fixed on the Mount of Olives, and he will certainly take his seat, as the apostle teaches, in Jerusalem, "in the temple of God, as though he were God",† and, according to the prophet, he will undoubtedly kill three kings pre-eminent for their faith in Christ, that is, the kings of Egypt, of Africa and of Ethiopia. This cannot happen at all, unless Christianity is established where paganism now rules. Therefore if you are eager to carry out pious battles, and since you have accepted the seedbed of the knowledge of God from Jerusalem, then you may restore the grace that was borrowed there. Thus through you the name of Catholicism will be propagated, and it will defeat the perfidy of the Antichrist and of the

* Ecclesiastes 1:7.   † 2 Thessalonians 2:4.

antichristians. Who can doubt that God, who surpasses every hope by means of his overflowing strength, may so destroy the reeds of paganism with your spark that he may gather Egypt, Africa and Ethiopia, which no longer share our belief, into the rules of his law, and "sinful man, the son of perdition",* will find others resisting him? See how the Gospel cries out that "Jerusalem will be trodden down by the Gentiles, until the time of the nations will be fulfilled."† "The time of nations" may be understood in two ways: either that they ruled at will over the Christians, and for their own pleasures have wallowed in the troughs of every kind of filth, and in all of these things have found no obstruction (for "to have one's time" means that everything goes according to one's wishes, as in "My time has not yet come, but your time is always ready,"‡ and one customarily says to voluptuaries, "You have your time"), or else the "time of nations" means the multitudes of nations who, before Israel is saved, will join the faith. These times, dearest brothers, perhaps will now be fulfilled, when, with the aid of God, the power of the pagans will be pushed back by you, and, with the end of the world already near, even if the nations do not turn to the Lord, because, as the apostle says, "there must be a falling away from faith."§ Nevertheless, first, according to the prophecies, it is necessary, before the coming of the Antichrist in those parts, either through you or through whomever God wills, that the empire of Christianity be renewed, so that the leader of all evil, who will have his throne there, may find some nourishment of faith against which he may fight. Consider, then, that Almighty Providence may have destined you for the task of rescuing Jerusalem from such abasement. I ask you to think how your hearts can conceive of the joy of seeing the Holy City revived by your efforts, and the oracles, the divine prophecies fulfilled in our own times. Remember that the voice of the Lord himself said to the Church, "I shall lead your seed from the east, and I shall gather you from the west."¶ The Lord has led our seed from the east, in

* 2 Thessalonians 2:3.   † Luke 21:24.   ‡ John 7:6.
§ 2 Thessalonians 2:3.   ¶ Isaiah 43:5.

that he brought forth for us in a double manner* out of the eastern land the early progeny of the Church. But out of the west he assembled us, for through those who last began the proof of faith, that is the westerners (we think that, God willing, this will come about through your deeds), Jerusalem's losses will be restored. If the words of Scripture and our own admonitions do not move your souls, then at least let the great suffering of those who wish to visit the Holy Places touch you. Think of the pilgrims who travel the Mediterranean; if they are wealthy, to what tributes, to what violence are they subjected; at almost every mile they are compelled to pay taxes and tributes; at the gates of the city, at the entrances of churches and temples, they must pay ransoms. Each time they move from one place to another they are faced with another charge, compelled to pay ransom, and the governors of the Gentiles commonly coerce with blows those who are slow to give gifts. What shall we say about those who have taken up the journey, trusting in their naked poverty, who seem to have nothing more than their bodies to lose? The money that they did not have was forced from them by intolerable tortures; the skin of their bones was probed, cut and stripped, in search of anything that they might have sewn within. The brutality of these evildoers was so great that, suspecting that the wretches had swallowed gold and silver, they gave them purgatives to drink, so that they would either vomit or burst their insides. Even more unspeakable, they cut their bellies open with swords, opening their inner organs, revealing with a hideous slashing whatever nature holds secret. Remember, I beg you, the thousands who died deplorably, and, for the sake of the Holy Places, whence the beginnings of piety came to you, take action. Have unshakeable faith that Christ will be the standard-bearer and inseparable advance guard before you who are sent to his wars.'

The superb man delivered this speech, and by the power of the blessed Peter absolved everyone who vowed to go, confirming this with an apostolic benediction, and establishing a sign of this honourable promise. He ordered that something like a soldier's

* Probably Sts Peter and Paul are indicated.

belt, or rather that for those about to fight for the Lord, something bearing the sign of the Lord's Passion, the figure of a Cross, be sewn on to the tunics and cloaks of those who were going. If anyone, after accepting this symbol, and after having made the public promise, then went back on his good intentions, either out of weak regretfulness, or out of domestic affection, such a person, according to the pope's decree, would be considered everywhere an outlaw, unless he came to his senses and fulfilled the obligation which he had foully laid aside. He also cursed with a horrible anathema all those who might dare to harm the wives, sons and possessions of those who took up God's journey for all of the next three years.

Finally, he entrusted the leadership of the expedition to the most praiseworthy of men, the bishop of the city of Le Puy (whose name, I regret, I have never discovered or heard*). He granted him the power to teach the Christian people as his representative, wherever they went, and therefore, in the manner of the apostles, he laid hands upon him and gave him his blessing as well. How wisely he carried out his commission the results of this wonderful effort demonstrate.

And so, when the council held at Clermont at the octave of blessed Martin in the month of November† was over, the great news spread through all parts of France, and whoever heard the news of the pontiff's decree urged his neighbours and family to undertake the proposed 'path of God' (for this was its epithet). The courtly nobility were already burning with desire, and the middle-level knights were bursting to set out, when lo, the poor also were aflame with desire, without any consideration for the scarcity of their resources, and without worrying about suitably disposing of their homes, vineyards and fields. Instead, each sold his assets at a price much lower than he would have received if he had been shut up in a painful prison and needed to pay an immediate ransom. At this time there was a general famine, with great poverty even among the very wealthy, since even though

* A peculiar lapse; the bishop of Le Puy was Adhemar of Monteil (d. 1098).
† 18–28 November 1095.

there were enough things, here and there, for sale for some people, they had nothing or scarcely anything with which those things could be bought. Masses of poor people learned to feed often on the roots of wild plants, since they were compelled by the scarcity of bread to search everywhere for some possible substitute. The misery that everyone was crying out about was clearly threatening to the powerful people as they watched, and, while each man, considering the anguish of the starving mob to be of little importance, became fastidiously parsimonious, fearing that he might squander the wealth for which he had worked hard by spending money too easily, the thirsty hearts of the avaricious, who rejoiced that the times smiled upon their brutal rates of interest, thought of the bushels of grain they had stored through the fertile years, and calculated how much their sale would add to their accumulating mountains of money. Thus, while some suffer terribly, and others swiftly go about their business, Christ, 'breaking the ships of Tarshish with a powerful wind',* resounded in everyone's ears, and he 'who freed those who were in adamantine chains'† broke the shackles of those desperate men whose hearts were ensnared by greed. Although, as I just said, hard times reduced everyone's wealth, nevertheless, when the hard times provoked everyone to spontaneous exile, the wealth of many men came out into the open, and what had seemed expensive when no one was moved was sold at a cheap price, now that everyone was eager for the journey. As many men were rushing to depart (I shall illustrate the sudden and unexpected drop in prices with one example of those things that were sold), seven sheep brought an unheard-of price of five pennies. The lack of grain became a surfeit, and each tried to get whatever money he could scrape together by any means; each seemed to be offering whatever he had, not at the seller's but at the buyer's price, lest he be late in setting out on the path of God. It was a miraculous sight: everyone bought high and sold low; whatever could be used on the journey was expensive, since they were in a hurry; they sold cheaply whatever items of value they

* Psalms 48:7.   † Psalms 68:6.

had piled up; what neither prison nor torture could have wrung from them just a short time before they now sold for a few paltry coins. Nor is it less absurd that many of those who had no desire to go, who laughed one day at the frantic selling done by the others, declaring that they were going on a miserable journey, and would return even more miserable, were suddenly caught up the next day, and abandoned all their goods for a few small coins, and set out with those at whom they had laughed.

Who can tell of the boys, the old men, who were stirred to go to war? Who can count the virgins and the weak, trembling old men? Everyone sang of battle, but did not say that they would fight. Offering their necks to the sword, they promised martyrdom. 'You young men', they said, 'will draw swords with your hands, but may we be permitted to earn this by supporting Christ.'*

Indeed they seemed to have a desire to emulate God, 'but not according to knowledge',† but God, who customarily turns many vain undertakings to a pious end, prepared salvation for their simple souls, because of their good intentions. There you would have seen remarkable, even comical things; poor people, for example, tied their cattle to two-wheeled carts, armed as though they were horses, carrying their few possessions, together with their small children, in the wagon. The little children, whenever they came upon a castle or a city, asked whether this was the Jerusalem to which they were going.

At that time, before people set out on the journey, there was a great disturbance, with fierce fighting, throughout the entire kingdom of the Franks. Everywhere people spoke of rampant thievery, highway robbery; endless fires burned everywhere. Battles broke out for no discernible reason, except uncontrollable greed. To sum up briefly, whatever met the eye of greedy men, no matter to whom it belonged, instantly became their prey. There-

---

* These lines, originally in verse, are apparently by Guibert himself.
† Romans 10:2.

fore the change of heart they soon underwent was remarkable and scarcely believable because of the heedless state of their souls, as they all begged the bishops and priests to give the sign prescribed by the above-mentioned pope, that is, the crosses. As the force of powerful winds can be restrained by the gentle rain, so all of the feuds of each against the other were put to rest by the aspiration embedded undoubtedly by Christ himself.

Whatever Urban said, the Council of Clermont issued a decree concerning the eastern expedition for those attending to take home with them to publicise the cause. The copy held by Lambert, bishop of Arras, is unequivocal about destination (Jerusalem), purpose (liberation of the eastern Church) and reward (pure motives attracting plenary remission of all penance for confessed sin): 'Whoever goes on the journey to free the Church of God in Jerusalem out of devotion alone, and not for the gaining of glory or money, can substitute the journey for all penance for sin.'*

The Clermont speech was only one of many delivered by Urban on his French tour in 1095–6. By February 1096, he was in Anjou and the Loire valley. The same year, the count of Anjou himself, Fulk Rechin ('the Sour', 1067–1109), described the pope's visit.

I wish to recall certain signs and prodigies which occurred during the last year of this period [1068–96] and which concerned not only our own land but the entire kingdom of Gaul, as the sequence of events later demonstrated. At this time stars fell from the heavens on to the earth like hailstones. This vision filled many people with wonder and struck them with a great terror. This sign was followed by a great wave of mortality throughout the kingdom of France and by a period of scarcity that was terrible. In our own city of Angers one hundred of our leading men perished and more than two thousand of the lesser folk.

Near the approach of Lent, the Roman pope Urban came to Angers and exhorted our people to go to Jerusalem in order to

* Quoted in E. Peters (ed.), *The First Crusade* (University of Pennsylvania Press, 1998), p. 37.

hunt the pagan people who had occupied this city and all of the lands of the Christians as far as Constantinople. For this reason the pope consecrated the church of St Nicholas on the day of Septuagesima [10 February 1096] and translated the body of my uncle Geoffrey from the chapter house into this church. This same apostolic man decided and ordained by a papal privilege that every year, on the day of the anniversary of the consecration which he had performed, a public feast would be celebrated and that the seventh part of the penances of those who attended would be remitted.

Departing, he went to Le Mans [14 February 1096] and from there to Tours. There he held a venerable council whose decrees were later published. During mid-Lent he was crowned and led a solemn procession from the church of St Maurice to that of St Martin [23 March 1096]. He gave me a golden flower which he held in his hand, and I decided that I and my successors would always carry that flower on the feast of Palm Sunday in memory and for my love of him. On the Palm Sunday that followed his departure, the church of St Martin burned down. The pope moved on to Saintes and celebrated the feast of Easter there.

Meanwhile Urban demonstrated sophisticated skills as promoter and propagandist, employing all available media: sermons; ceremonies; parades; legates; private conversation; and letters, a number of which survive indicating the main developing lines of the pope's thinking and aspirations.

Urban to the Faithful in Flanders, December 1095

Urban, bishop, servant of the servants of God, to all the faithful, both princes and subjects, waiting in Flanders; greeting, apostolic grace, and blessing.

Your brotherhood, we believe, has long since learned from many accounts that a barbaric fury has deplorably afflicted and laid waste the churches of God in the regions of the orient. More than this, blasphemous to say, it has even grasped in intolerable servitude its churches and the Holy City of Christ, glorified by his Passion and Resurrection. Grieving with pious concern at this calamity, we visited the regions of Gaul and devoted ourselves largely to urging the princes of the land and their subjects to free the churches of the east. We solemnly enjoined upon them at the Council of Auvergne [the accomplishment of] such an undertaking, as a preparation for the remission of all their sins. And we have constituted our most beloved son, Adhemar, bishop of Puy, leader of this expedition and undertaking in our stead, so that those who, perchance, may wish to undertake this journey should comply with his commands as if they were our own, and submit fully to his loosings or bindings, as far as shall seem to belong to such an office. If, moreover, there are any of your people whom God has inspired to this vow, let them know that he [Adhemar] will set out with the aid of God on the day of the Assumption of the Blessed Mary,* and that they can then attach themselves to his following.

Urban to His Supporters in Bologna, September 1096

Urban, bishop, servant of the servants of God, to his dear sons among the clergy and people of Bologna, greetings and apostolic benediction.

We give thanks for your goodness, that you remain always steadfast in the Catholic faith, situated as you are in the midst of schismatics and heretics† . . . and therefore we urge you, most beloved of the Lord, that you persist manfully along the path of truth and that your virtuous beginnings will lead to a better ending, since it is not he who begins a task, but he who perseveres in it until the end who will be saved . . . We have heard that some of you have conceived the desire to go to Jerusalem, and you should know that this is pleasing to us, and you should also know that if any among you travel, not for the desire of the goods of this

* 15 August.
† i.e. the supporters of the emperor Henry IV and his anti-pope Guibert of Ravenna.

world, but only those who go for the good of their souls and the liberty of the churches, they will be relieved of the penance for all of their sins, for which they have made a full and perfect confession, by the mercy of Almighty God and the prayers of the Catholic Church, as much by our own authority as that of all the archbishops and bishops in Gaul, because they have exposed themselves and their property to danger out of their love of God and their neighbour. To neither clerics nor monks, however, do we concede permission to go without the permission of their bishops or abbots. Let it be the bishops' duty to permit their parishioners to go only with the advice and provision of the clergy. Nor should young married men rashly set out on the journey without the consent of their spouses.

Urban to the Monks of the Congregation of Vallombrosa, 7 October 1096

We have heard that some of you want to set out with the knights who are making for Jerusalem with the good intention of liberating Christianity. This is the right kind of sacrifice, but it is planned by the wrong kind of person. For we were stimulating the minds of knights to go on this expedition, since they might be able to restrain the savagery of the Saracens by their arms and restore the Christians to their former freedom: we do not want those who have abandoned the world and have vowed themselves to spiritual warfare either to bear arms or to go on this journey; we go so far as to forbid them to do so. And we forbid religious – clerics or monks – to set out in this company without the permission of their bishops or abbots in accordance with the rule of the holy canons. The discretion of your religious profession must prevent you in this business from running the risk of either insulting the apostolic see or endangering your own souls. We have heard it said that your confrère, the abbot of the monastery of St Reparata, is considering leaving the Order shared by your congregation in common. And so in this present letter we send him an order, and by that we mean we forbid him to dare to rule the same monastery any longer without the permission of your common abbot, whom you call your major abbot. And if he does not obey, he or anyone else who perhaps dares to leave your congregation should be cut off with the sword of apostolic excommunication.

Given at Cremona on the seventh day of October. We want you to read this letter to the assembled monks and lay brothers and to let the other monasteries know its contents.*

Urban to the Counts of Besalú, Empurias, Roussillon, and Cerdaña and Their Followers, between January 1096 and July 1099

We beseech most carefully your lordships on behalf of the city or rather the Church of Tarragona† and we order you to make a vigorous effort to restore it in every possible way for the remission of sins. For you know what a great defence it would be for Christ's people and what a terrible blow it would be to the Saracens if, by the goodness of God, the position of that famous city were restored. If the knights of other provinces have decided with one mind to go to the aid of the Asian Church and to liberate their brothers from the tyranny of the Saracens, so ought you with one mind and with our encouragement to work with greater endurance to help a Church so near you resist the invasions of the Saracens. No one must doubt that if he dies on this expedition for the love of God and his brothers his sins will surely be forgiven and he will gain a share of eternal life through the most compassionate mercy of our God. So if any of you has made up his mind to go to Asia, it is here instead that he should try to fulfil his vow, because it is no virtue to rescue Christians from the Saracens in one place, only to expose them to the

---

* It is clear from other evidence that the problem of monks deserting their monasteries for the crusade was not uncommon.

† On the coast of Catalonia, south-west of Barcelona; Urban had been involved in the attempted establishment of a Christian diocese and outpost there for a decade. This letter is evidence of the easy application of the indulgences of the Jerusalem War to other theatres, although it seems from Urban's letter that many wished to go east none the less.

tyranny and oppression of the Saracens in another. May Almighty God arouse in your hearts a love of your brothers and
reward your bravery with victory over the enemy.

*The question of motive appears prominently in many analyses of the
First Crusade; it also preoccupied contemporary planners and commentators: only right intention, as the Clermont decree insisted,
could attract the offered spiritual privileges, the many setbacks on
the march being explained away as the consequence of sin. While on
any intimate personal level the thoughts of individuals are irrecov-
erable, publicly at least, in deals struck by departing crusaders with
monasteries to raise capital on property, letters and wills, there
runs a strong current of active piety. Much may represent the gloss
supplied by the clerical scribe or monkish adviser. However, given
the high cost of crusading in material terms, few could have had
many realistic expectations of purely mercenary profit. While acqui-
sition of temporal goods was intrinsic in the progress and survival
of any eleventh-century army, the journey to Jerusalem presented
unique difficulties, in its expense, physical effort, persistent dangers
and likelihood of death; most of those who embarked in 1096 neither
came back nor saw Jerusalem. The crusade was presented as an
armed pilgrimage, its temporal purpose of reconquest underpinned
by its spiritual imperative of penance.*

*Although by no means all surviving land charters echo peniten-
tial sentiments of a guilt-ridden yet pious military aristocracy, the
donation to the abbey of St Peter of Chartres by the local nobleman
Nivello in 1096 provides testimony of one man's burden that he
hoped the armed pilgrimage to Jerusalem would alleviate.*

Anyone who is the recipient of pardon through the grace of
heavenly atonement and who wants to be more completely freed
from the burden of his sins, whose weight oppresses the soul of
the sinner and prevents it from flying up to heaven, must look to
end his sins before they abandon him. And so I Nivello, raised in
a nobility of birth which produces in many people an ignobility
of mind, for the redemption of my soul and in exchange for a

great sum of money given me for this, renounce for ever in favour of St Peter* the oppressive behaviour resulting from a certain bad custom, handed on to me not by ancient right but from the time of my father, a man of little weight who first harassed the poor with this oppression. Thereafter I constantly maintained it in an atrociously tyrannical manner. I had harshly worn down the land of St Peter, that is to say Emprainville and the places around it, in the way that had become customary, by seizing the goods of the inhabitants there. This was the rough nature of this custom. Whenever the onset of knightly ferocity stirred me up, I used to descend on the aforesaid village, taking with me a troop of my knights and a crowd of my attendants, and against nature I would make over the goods of the men of St Peter for food for my knights.

And so since, in order to obtain the pardon for my crimes which God can give me, I am going on pilgrimage to Jerusalem which until now has been enslaved with her sons, the monks have given me 10 pounds in *denarii* towards the expenses of the appointed journey, in return for giving up this oppression; and they have given 3 pounds to my sister, called Comitissa, the wife of Hugh, viscount of Châteaudun, in return for her consent; 40 *solidi* to Hamelin my brother; with the agreement of my son Urso and my other relatives, whose names are written below. If in the course of time one of my descendants is tempted to break the strength of this concession and is convicted of such an act by the witnesses named below, may he, transfixed by the thunderbolt of anathema, be placed in the fires of hell with Dathan and Abiram, to be tormented endlessly. And so, to reinforce my confirmation of this, I make the sign of the Cross with my own hand and I pass the document over to my son called Urso and my other relatives and witnesses for them to confirm by making their signs. And everyone ought to note that I make satisfaction to St Peter for such abominable past injuries and that I will forever desist from causing this restless trouble, which is now stilled.

* i.e. the abbey of St Peter at Chartres.

II

The First Victims

April–September 1096

Unsurprisingly, the intentions of politicians and the response of their audiences often diverge. In 1095–6 the official line promoted a campaign against the infidels who, as enemies of Christ, had seized lands rightly belonging to Christians (the Holy Land) and were continuing to persecute the faithful and to threaten Christendom. The rhetoric deliberately focused on Christ and the scene of his life on earth, death and resurrection. There was nothing explicitly anti-Jewish in the papal programme. However, at a time of heightened communal excitement revolving around the image of Christ crucified and when large numbers of rural and urban property owners were seeking to realise their assets in order to pay for their journey east, where there existed significant established Jewish populations, as in many Rhineland cities, they risked becoming the object of ill-considered yet far from random hostility, more vulnerable because of the erosion of the power of their chief secular protector, the emperor Henry IV, and the pusillanimous behaviour of local bishops, to whom they looked for ecclesiastical defence. As 'enemies of the Christian faith', regarded by many Christians as responsible for Christ's death on the Cross, the Jews became the first of a long and bloody catalogue of victims of the new war of the Cross.

The massacres of 1096 may have begun at Cologne with the arrival there of Peter the Hermit in mid-April, but the main carnage was associated with the recruitment of Count Emich of Flonheim, whose forces, some weeks after the passage of Peter the Hermit, inspired atrocities of increasing ferocity as May progressed, at Speyer, Worms and Mainz, whence the infection spread north-wards to Cologne and the lower Rhine in late May and June, be-

yond the path of the crusaders who turned eastwards from Mainz to reach the Danube at Regensburg, where Peter the Hermit's army had already attempted forcible baptism of Jews in mid-May. With the departure of the crusaders from the region, the hysteria subsided and the violence ceased. The Jewish communities, shocked, wary but undisturbed for another half-century until the Second Crusade (1146–7), recuperated and revived. Some Christian observers, such as Albert in nearby Aachen, adopting the official theological line of disapproval of such attacks, condemned the excesses; his condemnation of cruelty is matched by his scorn at credulity, a moral he illustrated with the famous story of crusaders following a goose and a goat.

The trigger for these atrocities was the arrival in the Rhineland of the troops raised in the winter of 1095–6 by the charismatic preacher Peter the Hermit. The career and influence of Peter, controversial at the time, has remained a matter of debate. One tradition, deriving ultimately from Lorrainers, some of whom may have travelled east with Peter and later retold their experiences to the Rhineland chronicler Albert of Aachen or to one of his sources, credits Peter with being the primus auctor, *the chief instigator of the Jerusalem journey. Some straws in the wind suggest this impression cannot have been wholly fanciful or fictitious, even if elements of the tale are incredible as well as ignoring what can be reconstructed of the roles of Alexius and Urban. Peter did lead a substantial force east that set out from eastern France in March 1096, only four months after Clermont. All contemporary narrative accounts acknowledge his role in inciting the first military retinues to depart. Some prior collusion with the pope is possible, especially as Peter's preaching itinerary shadowed but never cut across Urban's. Peter remained a significant figure on the campaign even after the destruction of his forces in October 1096 and his subsequent attempt to desert the army at Antioch in January 1098. He was afforded status and respect by the emperor Alexius. The legend of Peter, which in outline was repeated in the history written by Alexius' daughter Anna Comnena, claimed a central role for the patriarch of Jerusalem; Patriarch Symeon had close contacts with Alexius' court and did indeed play a prominent part in the councils of the expedition when it arrived in Syria in the autumn of 1097. While the historiographically dominant 'French' tradition emphasises Urban's contribution, the distinct 'Lorraine' strand of memory found powerful and lasting expression not only in Albert of Aachen's independent and probably well-sourced version of events, the* Historia Hierosolymitana, *in which the account of 1095–9 may have been completed as early as 1102, but also in the vernacular verse cycle known as the* Chanson d'Antioche *and the highly influential and well-researched* Historia *of Archbishop William of Tyre (c.1184). On his return, Peter retired to a monastery he founded at Huy in the Meuse valley, not very far from Aachen where the chronicler Albert was a canon.*

Albert of Aachen's account, therefore, while in places hard to credit as literally accurate, and certainly fashioned to suit prevailing themes of religious interpretation, vividly preserves an exactly contemporary perception of the role played by Peter the Hermit.

Peter, a priest from Amiens in the western Frankish kingdom, who had at one time been a hermit, began his call for the expedition in Berry, a part of the kingdom, pleading with all his eloquence and using every sermon and address to preach it. His insistent advocacy won over bishops, abbots, priests and monks, laymen of the highest rank, princes of the kingdoms, all the people, the celibate, the unchaste, adulterers, murderers, thieves, perjurers, bandits. In short, all men of Christian faith were brought to repentance and joyfully assembled for the march.

What follows will explain the reason and purpose of Peter's preaching, which made him the chief instigator of the crusade.

Some years before the expedition set out, Peter had gone on pilgrimage to Jerusalem, and there, in the church of the Holy Sepulchre, had looked with horror on evil and forbidden practices. Grief-stricken and groaning in spirit, he prayed to God to avenge the wrongs he saw. He went to the patriarch of Jerusalem and asked how he could let infidels and godless men desecrate the Holy Places, plunder the offerings of the faithful and make the church a house of ill fame; how he could see Christians assaulted, holy pilgrims suffering unjust extortions and subjected at every turn to persecution.

The venerable patriarch and priest of the Holy Sepulchre replied: 'Most faithful of Christians, how can you thus upbraid and trouble a patriarch whose power and authority are like a tiny ant's before the overweening might of such enemies? My life is ransomed only by constant payments, without which I face torture and death. I fear the threats will grow daily unless Christendom sends help. You must be my envoy to summon it.'

Peter answered: 'Holy father, I have understood. I see how weak is the band of Christians living with you here, and what hardships you suffer at the hands of the heathen. So for God's love and to restore the honour of the saints, I shall go home, with God beside me for my safety, and I shall seek out first the pope, and then all Christian primates, the kings, the dukes, the counts, the rulers of the lands, and I shall tell them all of your wretched servitude, your unendurable hardships. The news of what is happening will soon be known to all.'

Meanwhile darkness covered earth and sky, and Peter went back to the Holy Sepulchre to pray. There, wearied with watching and supplication, he fell asleep. As he slept, the Lord Jesus appeared before him in majesty and addressed him, a weak mortal, in these words: 'Peter, most beloved Christian son, arise. Go to the patriarch, take from him a letter of appointment sealed with the sign of the Cross, and return with all speed to the land of your kinsmen. There make known the persecution and sufferings of my people and the wrongs done to the Holy Land. Rouse the hearts of the faithful to cleanse the Holy Places of Jerusalem and restore the service of the saints. Despite all perils and temptations, those who are called and chosen will find the gates of heaven opened to them.'

At this wondrous revelation of the power of God, when the vision ended Peter awoke, and in the first glimmerings of dawn he left the church. Going to the patriarch he told him that he had seen God, and requested a letter sealed with the Cross appointing him as his holy representative. This the patriarch gave gratefully, and by his leave Peter undertook the mission and started on his journey home. After a difficult crossing he landed at Bari and left at once for Rome. There he went to the pope and told him of the charge laid upon him by God and the patriarch to report the abomination of the heathen and their persecution of the saints and pilgrims. The pope listened readily and intently and promised in every particular to heed the bidding and the prayers of the saints . . .

At the beginning of summer in the same year [1096] in which Peter and Gottschalk,* after collecting an army, had set out, there assembled in like fashion a large and innumerable host of Christians from diverse kingdoms and lands; namely, from the realms of France, England, Flanders, and Lorraine . . . I know not whether by a judgement of the Lord, or by some error of mind, they rose in a spirit of cruelty against the Jewish people scattered throughout these cities and slaughtered them without mercy, especially in the kingdom of Lorraine, asserting it to be the beginning of their expedition and their duty against the enemies of the Christian faith. This slaughter of Jews was done first by citizens of Cologne. These suddenly fell upon a small band of Jews and severely wounded and killed many; they destroyed the houses and synagogues of the Jews and divided among themselves a very large amount of money. When the Jews saw this cruelty, about two hundred in the silence of the night began flight by boat to Neuss. The pilgrims and crusaders discovered them, and after taking away all their possessions, inflicted on them similar slaughter, leaving not even one alive.

Not long after this, they started upon their journey, as they had vowed, and arrived in a great multitude at the city of Mainz. There Count Emich,† a nobleman, a very mighty man in this region, was awaiting, with a large band of Teutons, the arrival of

* Gottschalk was a German crusade leader recruited by Peter the Hermit; his contingent surrendered to the Hungarians after a career of undisciplined rapine, c.1 July 1096.
† Count of Flonheim; not, as was once assumed, Leiningen.

the pilgrims who were coming thither from diverse lands by the king's highway.

The Jews of this city, knowing of the slaughter of their brethren, and that they themselves could not escape the hands of so many, fled in hope of safety to Bishop Ruthard. They put an infinite treasure in his guard and trust, having much faith in his protection, because he was bishop of the city. Then that excellent bishop of the city cautiously set aside the incredible amount of money received from them. He placed the Jews in the very spacious hall of his own house, away from the sight of Count Emich and his followers, that they might remain safe and sound in a very secure and strong place.

But Emich and the rest of his band held a council and, after sunrise, attacked the Jews in the hall with arrows and lances. Breaking the bolts and doors, they killed the Jews, about seven hundred in number, who in vain resisted the force and attack of so many thousands. They killed the women, also, and with their swords pierced tender children of whatever age and sex. The Jews, seeing that their Christian enemies were attacking them and their children, and that they were sparing no age, likewise fell upon one another, brothers, children, wives and sisters, and thus they perished at each other's hands. Horrible to say, mothers cut the throats of nursing children with knives and stabbed others, preferring them to perish thus by their own hands rather than to be killed by the weapons of the uncircumcised.

From this cruel slaughter of the Jews a few escaped; and a few because of fear, rather than because of love of the Christian faith, were baptised. With very great spoils taken from these people, Count Emich, Clarebold, Thomas, and all that intolerable company of men and women then continued on their way to Jerusalem, directing their course towards the kingdom of Hungary, where passage along the royal highway was usually not denied the pilgrims. But on arriving at Wieselburg,* the fortress of the king, which the rivers Danube and Leitha protect with marshes, the bridge and gate of the fortress were found closed by command

* Between Linz and Vienna on the Danube.

of the king of Hungary, for great fear had entered all the Hungarians because of the slaughter which had happened to their brethren . . .

But while almost everything had turned out favourably for the Christians, and while they had penetrated the walls with great openings, by some chance or misfortune, I know not what, such great fear entered the whole army that they turned in flight, just as sheep are scattered and alarmed when wolves rush upon them. And seeking a refuge here and there, they forgot their companions . . .

Emich and some of his followers continued in their flight along the way by which they had come. Thomas, Clarebold and several of their men escaped in flight towards Carinthia and Italy. So the hand of the Lord is believed to have been against the pilgrims, who had sinned by excessive impurity and fornication, and who had slaughtered the exiled Jews through greed of money, rather than for the sake of God's justice, although the Jews were opposed to Christ. The Lord is a just judge and orders no one unwillingly, or under compulsion, to come under the yoke of the Catholic faith.

There was another detestable crime in this assemblage of wayfaring people, who were foolish and insanely fickle. That the crime was hateful to the Lord and incredible to the faithful is not to be doubted. They asserted that a certain goose was inspired by the Holy Spirit, and that a she-goat was not less filled by the same Spirit. These they made their guides on this holy journey to Jerusalem; these they worshipped excessively; and most of the people following them, like beasts, believed with their whole minds that this was the true course. May the hearts of the faithful be free from the thought that the Lord Jesus wished the sepulchre of his most sacred body to be visited by brutish and insensate animals, or that he wished these to become the guides of Christian souls, which by the price of his own blood he deigned to redeem from the filth of idols!

There are two main Hebrew narratives devoted to the ghastly events of 1096. One, attributed to Solomon ben Simson, is a later-

twelfth-century compilation of sources for the massacres in Speyer, Worms, Mainz, Cologne and elsewhere. The other, known as The Narrative of the Old Persecutions, *was written much nearer the events by an anonymous author, possibly from Mainz.* It concentrates with devastating anecdotal detail on the pogroms carried out in three towns, Speyer, Worms and, especially, Mainz.*

I shall begin the narrative of past persecution – may the Lord protect us and all of Israel from future persecution.

In the year one thousand and twenty-eight† after the destruction of the Temple, this evil befell Israel. The noblemen and counts and the common people in the land of France united and decided to soar up like an eagle, to wage war and to clear a way to Jerusalem, the Holy City, and to come to the tomb of the crucified one, a rotting corpse that cannot avail and cannot save, being of no worth or significance.

They said to each other: 'Look now, we are going to a distant country to make war against mighty kings and are endangering our lives to conquer the kingdoms which do not believe in the crucified one, when actually it is the Jews who murdered and crucified him.' They stirred up hatred against us in all quarters and declared that either we should accept their abominable faith or else they would annihilate us all, even infants and sucklings. The noblemen and common people placed an evil symbol – a vertical line over a horizontal one – on their garments and special hats on their heads.

When the communities in the land of France heard this, they were gripped by fear and trembling, and they resorted to the custom of their ancestors.‡ They wrote letters and despatched messengers to all communities around the River Rhine, bidding them to proclaim fast-days and seek mercy from God, that he might save them from the hands of the enemy. When the letters reached the saints, the men of renown, the pillars of the universe

---

* Hence the other title by which it is often known, the *Mainz Anonymous*.
† 1096; medieval rabbinical tradition dated the destruction of the Temple to AD 68, not 70.   ‡ Prayer, charity and repentance.

in Mainz, they wrote to the land of France, saying: 'All the communities have decreed a fast-day. We have done our duty. May the Omnipresent One save us and you from all the trouble and affliction. We are greatly concerned about your well-being. As for ourselves, there is no great cause for fear. We have not heard a word of such matters, nor has it been hinted that our lives are threatened by the sword.'

When the errant ones started arriving in this land [Rhineland], they sought money to buy bread. We gave it to them, applying to ourselves the verse: 'Serve the king of Babylon, and live.'* All this, however, did not avail us. Because of our sins, whenever the errant ones arrived at a city, the local burghers would harass us, for they were at one with them in their intention to destroy vine and root all along their way to Jerusalem.

When the errant ones came, battalion after battalion like the army of Sennacherib, some of the noblemen in this kingdom declared: 'Why do we sit? Let us join them, for every man who goes on this path and clears the way to the unholy grave of the crucified one will be fully qualified and ready for hell.' The errant ones gathered, the nobles and the commoners from all provinces, until they were as numerous as the sands of the sea. A proclamation was issued: 'Whosoever kills a Jew will receive pardon for all his sins.'† There was a Count Dithmar‡ there who said that he would not depart from this kingdom until he had slain one Jew; only then would he proceed on his journey.

When the holy community of Mainz learned of this, they decreed a fast-day and cried out loudly to the Lord. Young and old alike fasted day and night, reciting prayers of lamentation in the morning and evening. Despite all of this, however, our God did not withhold his wrath from us. For the errant ones came with their insignia and banners before our homes, and, upon seeing one of us, they would pursue and pierce him with their lances – till we became afraid even to step on the thresholds of our homes.

* Jeremiah 27:17.
† Perhaps a distortion of Urban's Clermont indulgences.
‡ Folkmar, leader of German crusaders, May–June 1096.

On 3 May, on the sabbath, the measure of justice began to fall upon us. The errant ones and the burghers first plotted against the holy men, the saints* of the Most High, in Speyer, and they planned to seize all of them together in the synagogue. Told of this, the saints arose on sabbath morning, prayed quickly, and departed from the synagogue. When the enemy saw that their plot to take them all captive together had been frustrated, they rose up against them and slew eleven of them. This was the beginning of the persecution, fulfilling the biblical verse: 'And at my sanctuary shall you begin.'

When Bishop John heard of this, he came with a large army and whole-heartedly aided the community, taking them indoors and rescuing them from the enemy. The bishop then took some of the burghers and cut off their hands, for he was a righteous man among the Gentiles, and the Omnipresent One used him as a means for our benefit and rescue.†

Rabbi Moshe, son of Rabbi Yekuthiel, stood in the breach. He endangered himself for his fellow Jews.‡ As a result of his efforts, all those who had been forcibly converted and had survived in Henry's domain by fleeing to various places were enabled to return.§ And through the aid of the king, Bishop John enabled the remnant of the community of Speyer to take refuge in his fortified towns.

The Lord had mercy upon them for the sake of his great name, and the bishop concealed them until the enemies of the name had passed. The Jews engaged in fasting, weeping and lamentation, and began to despair greatly, for day after day the errant ones and the Gentiles and Emich, may his bones be ground to dust, and the common people all gathered against

* i.e. future martyrs.
† In orthodox Christian teaching, as Jews are mentioned in the Book of Revelation, they are to be protected by the Church until such Final Judgement; this could also serve clerical commercial and fiscal interests. Forced baptism also ran against canon law.
‡ Rabbi Moshe bar Yekuthiel, a Talmudic scholar, figured prominently in the Speyer community, being one of the recipients of an imperial privilege in 1090.
§ This was only granted by Henry IV in 1097 on his return from Italy.

them to capture and annihilate them. Through the efforts of Rabbi Moshe, Bishop John saved them, for the Lord had moved him to keep them alive without taking a bribe – for it was the Lord's doing to grant us a vestige and a remnant by the bishop's hand.

When the bad tidings reached Worms that some of the community of Speyer had been murdered, the Jews of Worms cried out to the Lord and wept in great and bitter lamentation. They saw that the decree had been issued in heaven and that there was no escape and no recourse. The community then was divided into two groups: some fled to the bishop and sought refuge in his castles; others remained in their homes, for the burghers had given them false promises, which, like broken reedstaffs, cause harm and do no good. For the burghers were in league with the errant ones in their intention to wipe out our people's name and remnant. So they offered us false solace: 'Do not fear them, for anyone who kills one of you – his life will be forfeit for yours.' The Jews had nowhere to flee, as the Jewish community had entrusted all their money to their non-Jewish neighbours. It was for this very reason that their neighbours handed them over to the enemy.

On 5 May, a Monday, they cunningly plotted against the Jews.* They took a rotting corpse of theirs, which had been buried thirty days previously, and bore it into the city, saying: 'Look what the Jews have done to one of us. They took a Gentile, boiled him in water, and poured the water into our wells in order to poison us to death!' When the errant ones and burghers heard this, they cried out. They all assembled, anyone capable of drawing and bearing a sword, big and small, and declared: 'Behold, the time has come to avenge him who was nailed to the wood, whom their forefathers slew. Now, let no remnant or vestige of them be allowed to escape, not even a babe or a suckling in the cradle.'

* This is an early variant on what became the two standard medieval libels that Jews systematically poisoned Christian water supplies and that they ritually butchered Christians.

The enemy came and smote those who had remained at home – handsome lads, pretty and pleasant girls, old men and old women – all extended their necks in martyrdom. Manumitted servants and maids* were also slain in sanctification of the eternally awesome and sublime name of him who rules above and below, who was and will be, whose name is Lord of Hosts, and who is crowned with the graces of the seventy-two names, he who created the Torah 974 generations before the creation of the world; and there were twenty-six generations between the creation and Moses, father of the prophets, through whom the Torah was given – the same Moses who wrote in this Torah: 'It is the Lord whom you have chosen today,' etc. It was for him and his Torah that they were slain like oxen, and dragged through the market-places and streets like sheep to be slaughtered, and lay naked in the streets, for the foe stripped them and left them naked.

When the survivors saw their brethren lying naked and the chaste daughters of Israel naked – under this great duress they yielded to the foe. For the errant ones had said that they would not leave a single survivor. So some of the Jews said: 'Let us do their will for the time being, and then go and bury our brethren and also save our children from them.' For the enemy had already seized the few remaining children, thinking that perhaps they would be gained for their erroneous faith. But the children did not turn away from their Creator, and their hearts did not stray after the crucified one; but they clung to God on High.

Those of the community who had remained within the bishop's chambers sent garments so that the dead might be clothed by those rescued, for the survivors were charitable people. The heads of the community remained there [in the bishop's palace], and most of the community were spared initially. They sent words of comfort to the forced converts: 'Do not fear and do not take to heart what you have done. If the Blessed

---

* Manumission implies the existence of slaves acting as servants within the Jewish community; not uncommon in many parts of eleventh-century Christendom.

Holy One saves us from our enemies, then we shall be with you in death and in life. But do not turn away from the Lord.'

On 18 May the errant ones and the burghers said: 'Let us also take vengeance against those who have remained in the court-yard and chambers of the bishop.' People assembled from all the surrounding villages, together with the errant ones and the burghers, and they besieged and fought against them. A great battle was fought between the two groups until they captured the chambers where the children of the Sacred Covenant were shel-tered. When they saw that the war was on every side by decree of the King of Kings, they justified heaven's judgement upon them, placed their trust in their Creator, and offered true sacrifices, taking their children and whole-heartedly slaughtering them in witness to the oneness of the venerated and awesome name. The notables of the community were slain there.

There was a man there by the name of Meshullam, son of Isaac, and he called out in a great voice to his beloved wife Mis-tress Zipporah and to all those present: 'Hear me, adults and children! God gave me this son; my wife Zipporah bore him in her advanced age. His name is Isaac. I shall now offer him up as a sacrifice as our Father Abraham did his son Isaac.' His wife Zip-porah said to him: 'My lord, my lord, wait, do not yet move your hand towards the boy whom I have raised and brought up, whom I bore in my old age. Slaughter me first and let me not see the death of the child.'* He replied: 'I shall not tarry even for a second. He who gave him to us shall take him as his share and place him in the bosom of our father Abraham.' He bound Isaac, his son, and took the knife in his hand to slaughter him, reciting the blessing for ritual slaughter. The boy responded: 'Amen.' And he slaughtered the boy. He took his shrieking wife and together they left the room. The errant ones then slew them.

'Wilt thou restrain thyself for these things, O Lord?' Yet, with all this, his great wrath did not turn away from us!

There was a lad there named Isaac, son of Daniel. They [the Christians] asked him: 'Do you wish to exchange your God for a

* A clear reference to the story of Abraham and Isaac, Genesis 21:16.

disgusting idol?' He replied, 'God forbid that I should deny him. In him I shall place my trust and I shall even yield up my soul to him.' They put a rope around his neck and dragged him through the entire city in the muddy streets to the house of their idolatry. There was still some life in his frame when they said to him: 'You can still be saved if you agree to change your religion.' Having already been strangled, he could not utter a word from his mouth, so he gestured with his finger to say: 'Cut off my head.' And they slit his throat.

There was yet another youth there [in Worms], by the name of Simha ha-Cohen, son of our master Isaac ha-Cohen, whom they sought to contaminate with their putrid water. They said to him: 'Look, they have all been killed already and are lying naked.' The youth cleverly answered: 'I will do all that you ask of me if you take me to the bishop.' So they took him and brought him to the bishop's courtyard. The bishop's nephew was there, too, and they began to invoke the name of the foul and disgusting scion and then left him in the bishop's courtyard. The youth drew his knife, then gnashed his teeth, like a lion worrying his prey, at the noble-man, the bishop's kinsman; then he dashed at him and plunged the knife into his belly, and the man fell dead. Turning from there, he stabbed yet another two, until the knife broke in his hand. They fled in all directions. When they saw that his knife had broken, they attacked him and slew him. There was slain the youth who had sanctified the name, doing what the rest of the community had not done – slaying three uncircumcised ones with his knife.

The rest devotedly fasted daily and then endured martyrdom. They had wept for their families and their friends to the point of exhaustion, so that they were unable to fight against the enemy. They declared: 'It is the decree of the King. Let us fall into the hand of the Lord, and let us go and behold the great light.' There they all fell attesting the oneness of the name.

A distinguished woman, named Mistress Mina, found refuge below the ground in a house outside the city. The people of the city gathered outside her hiding-place and called: 'Behold, you are a woman of valour. Perceive that God is no longer concerned with saving you, for the slain are lying naked in the open streets with no one to bury them. Yield to baptism.' They fell all over themselves entreating her, as they did not wish to slay her, for her fame had travelled far because the notables of her city and the nobles of the land used to frequent her company. But she answered by saying: 'Heaven forfend that I should deny God on high. Slay me for him and his holy Torah, and do not tarry any longer.' There she was slain, she who was praised in the gates. They all were slain sanctifying the name whole-heartedly and willingly, slaughtering one another: young men and maidens, old men and women, and babes, too, were sacrificed in sanctification of the name.

Those specifically mentioned by name acted thus, and the others not mentioned by name even surpassed them in valour. What they did had never been witnessed by the eye of man. It is of them and the likes of them that it was said: 'From mortals, by your hand, O Lord; from mortals of this world, whose portion is in this life . . .' 'Neither hath the eye seen a God beside thee, who workest for him that waiteth for him.' They all fell by the hand of the Lord and returned to their rest, to the great light in the Garden of Eden. Behold, their souls are bound up till the time of the end in the bond of life with the Lord God, who created them.

When the saints, the pious ones of the Most High, the holy community of Mainz, heard that some of the community of Speyer had been slain and that the community of Worms had been attacked a second time, their spirits failed and their hearts melted and became as water. They cried out to the Lord: 'Alas, O Lord God! Will you completely annihilate the remnant of Israel? Where are all your wonders which our forefathers related to us, saying: "Did You not bring us up from Egypt, O Lord?" But now you have forsaken us, delivering us into the hands of the Gentiles to destroy us!'

All the Jewish community leaders assembled and came before the bishop with his officers and servants, and said to them: 'What shall we do about the news we have received regarding the slaughter of our brethren in Speyer and Worms?' They [the bishop and his followers] replied: 'Heed our advice and bring all your money into our treasury and into the treasury of the bishop. And you, your wives, sons and all your belongings shall come into the courtyard of the bishop. Thus will you be saved from the errant ones.' Actually, they gave this advice so as to herd us together and hold us like fish that are caught in an evil net and then turn us over to the enemy. The bishop assembled his ministers, servants and great noblemen in order to rescue us from the errant ones, for at first it had been his desire to save us, but in the end he turned against us.*

One day a Gentile woman came, bringing a goose which she had raised since it was new-born. The goose would accompany the Gentile woman wherever she went, and the woman would call to all passers-by, saying: 'Look, the goose understands my intention to go straying and he desires to accompany me.'† The errant ones and burghers then gathered against us and said to us: 'Where is he in whom you place your trust? How will you be saved? See the wonders which the crucified one works for us.' And they all came with swords and lances to destroy us, but some of the burghers came and prevented them. At this point, the errant ones all united and battled the burghers on the bank of the River Rhine, until a crusader was slain.

Seeing this the crusaders cried out: 'The Jews have caused this,' and nearly all of them reassembled.

When the holy people [the Jews] saw this, their hearts melted. The foe reviled and derided them, with the intention of falling upon them. Upon hearing their words, the Jews, old and young alike, said: 'Would that our death might be by the hand of the Lord, so that we should not perish at the hands of the enemies of the Lord; for he is a merciful God, the sole sovereign of the universe.'

They abandoned their houses; neither did they go to the

---

* Bishop Ruthard's ambivalence is confirmed by other Jewish sources; it is not unlikely.

† This has echoes of Albert of Aachen's goose story; see above, p. 36.

synagogue save on the sabbath.* That was the final sabbath
before the evil decree befell us, when a small number of them
entered the synagogue to pray; Rabbi Judah, son of Rabbi Isaac,
also came there to pray on that sabbath. They wept exceedingly,
to the point of exhaustion, for they saw that it was a decree of
the King of Kings.

A venerable student, Baruch, son of Isaac, was there, and he
said to us: 'Know that this decree has been issued against us in
truth and honesty, and we cannot be saved; for this past night I
and my son-in-law Judah heard the souls praying here [in the
synagogue] in a loud voice, like weeping. When we heard the
sound, we thought at first that perhaps some of the community
had come back from the court of the bishop to pray in the synagogue at midnight because of their anguish and bitterness of
heart. We ran to the door of the synagogue, but it was closed.
We heard the sound, but we understood nothing. We returned
frightened to our house, for it was close to the synagogue. Upon
hearing this, we cried out: "Alas, O Lord God! Will you completely annihilate the remnant of Israel?" ' Then they went and
reported the occurrence to their brethren who were concealed in
the court of the count and in the bishop's chambers. Thereupon,
they, too, wept exceedingly.

On 25 May, the wicked Emich, may his bones be ground to
dust between iron millstones, arrived outside the city with a
mighty horde of errant ones and peasants, for he, too, had said: 'I
desire to follow the stray course.' He was the chief of all our
oppressors. He showed no mercy to the aged or youths, or maidens, babes or sucklings – not even the sick; and he made the
people of the Lord like dust to be trodden underfoot, killing their
young men by the sword and disembowelling their pregnant
women.

They [the crusaders] encamped outside the city for two days.
The leaders of the community now said: 'Let us send him money
and give him letters of safe conduct, so that the [Jewish] communities along the route will honour him. Perhaps the Lord will

* Probably 24 May 1096.

intercede in his abundant grace.' For they had already given away their money, giving the bishop, the count, his officers and servants, and the burghers about 400 halves [marks] to aid them [the Jews]. But it was of no avail whatever.

We were not even comparable to Sodom and Gomorrah, for in their case they were offered reprieve if they could produce at least ten righteous people, whereas in our case not twenty, not even ten, were sought.

On 27 May, the day on which Moses said: 'Be ready against the third day' – on that day the diadem of Israel fell. The students of the Torah fell, and the outstanding scholars passed away; ended was the glory of the Torah, and the radiance of wisdom came to an end. 'He hath cast down from heaven unto the earth the splendour of Israel.' Humility and the fear of sin ceased. Gone were the men of virtuous deed and purity, nullifiers of evil decrees and placators of the wrath of their Creator. Diminished were the ranks of those who give charity in secret, gone was truth; gone were the explicators of the word and the law; fallen were the people of eminence, while the number of the shameless and insolent increased. Alas that they are gone! For since that day on which the Second Temple was destroyed, their like had not arisen, nor shall there be their like again. They sanctified the name with all their heart and with all their soul and with all their might; happy are they.

At midday, the evil Emich, may his bones be ground to dust, came with his entire horde. The townspeople opened the gate to him, and the enemies of the Lord said to one another: 'Look, the gate has opened by itself; this the crucified one has done for us in order that we may avenge his blood on the Jews.' They then came with their banners to the bishop's gate, where the people of the Sacred Covenant were assembled – a vast horde of them, as the sand upon the sea-shore. When the saints, the fearers of the Most High, saw this great multitude, they placed their trust in their Creator and clung to him. They donned their armour and their weapons of war, adults and children alike, with Rabbi Calonymus, son of Rabbi Meshullam, at their head.

There was a pious man there, one of the great men of the generation, Rabbi Menaham, son of Rabbi David, the Levite. He said to the entire community: 'Sanctify the venerable and awesome name with a willing heart.' They all answered as did the sons of our father Jacob when he wished to reveal the time of the final redemption to his children but was prevented from doing so because the divine presence departed from him. Jacob then said: 'Perhaps I have been found to have a defect, just like Abraham, my grandfather, or like my father Isaac.' And like our fathers, who, when they received the Torah at Mount Sinai at this season, promptly declared: 'We shall do and obey,' so did the martyrs now declare in a great voice: 'Hear, O Israel, the Lord is our God, the Lord is one.'

And they all advanced towards the gate to fight against the errant ones and the burghers. The two sides fought against each other around the gate, but as a result of their transgressions the enemy overpowered them and captured the gate. The bishop's people, who had promised to help them, being as broken reed-staffs, were the first to flee, so as to cause them to fall into the hands of the enemy.

The enemies now came into the courtyard and found Rabbi Isaac, son of Rabbi Moses, whom they smote with a stroke of the sword, slaying him. However, fifty-three souls fled with Rabbi Calonymus via the bishop's chambers, entered a long chamber called the sacristy, and remained there. The enemy entered the courtyard on 27 May, the third day of the week, a day of darkness and gloom, a day of clouds and thick darkness – let darkness and the shadow of death claim it for their own, let God not enquire after it from above, nor let the light shine upon it. O sun and moon! Why did you not withhold your light? O stars, to whom Israel has been compared, and the twelve constellations, like the number of the tribes of Israel, the sons of Jacob – why was your light not withheld from shining for the enemy who sought to eradicate the name of Israel? Enquire and seek: was there ever such a mass sacrificial offering since the time of Adam?

When the people of the Sacred Covenant saw that the heavenly decree had been issued and that the enemy had defeated them, they all cried out, young and old men, maidens, girls, children, menservants and maids, and wept for themselves and for their lives, saying: 'Let us bear the yoke of the holy creed, for now the enemy can slay us but by the lightest of the four deaths, which is the sword, and we shall then merit eternal life, and our souls will abide in the Garden of Eden, in the speculum of the great luminary.' They all then said with gladness of heart and with willing soul: 'After all things, there is no questioning the ways of the Holy One, blessed be he and blessed be his name, who has given us his Torah and has commanded us to allow ourselves to be killed and slain in witness to the oneness of his holy name. Happy are we if we fulfil his will, and happy is he who is slain or slaughtered and who dies attesting the oneness of his name. Such a one will not only be worthy of entering the world-to-come and of sitting in the realm of the saints who are the pillars of the universe, he will also exchange a world of darkness for one of light, a world of sorrow for one of joy, a transitory world for an eternal world.'

And in a great voice they all cried out as one: 'We need tarry no longer, for the enemy is already upon us. Let us hasten to offer ourselves as a sacrifice to our Father in heaven. Anyone possessing a knife should slaughter us in sanctification of the one name of the everlasting one. Then this person should thrust his sword into either his throat or his stomach, slaughtering himself.' They all arose, man and woman alike, and slew one another. The young maidens, the brides and the bridegrooms looked out through the windows and cried out in a great voice: 'Look and behold, O Lord, what we are doing to sanctify thy great name, in order not to exchange thy divinity for a crucified scion who was despised, abominated and held in contempt in his own generation, a bastard son conceived by a menstruating and wanton woman.' They were all slaughtered, and the blood of the slaughter streamed into the chambers where the children of the Sacred Covenant had taken refuge. They lay in rows, babes and aged men together, gurgling in their throats in the manner of slaughtered sheep.

'Wilt thou restrain thyself for these things, O Lord?' Avenge the spilt blood of thy servants! Let one and all behold – has the like of this ever occurred? For they all vied with one another, each with his fellow, saying: 'I shall be the first to sanctify the name of the supreme King of Kings.' The saintly women threw their money outside in order to delay the enemy, until they had slaughtered their children. The hands of compassionate women strangled their children in order to do the will of their master, and they turned the faces of their tender, lifeless children towards the Gentiles.

When the enemy came into the chambers, they smashed the doors and found the Jews writhing and rolling in blood; and the enemy took their money, stripped them naked, and slew those still alive, leaving neither a vestige nor a remnant. Thus they did in all the chambers where children of the Sacred Covenant were to be found. But one room remained which was somewhat difficult to break into, and the enemy fought over it till nightfall.

When the saints saw that the enemy was prevailing over them, they rose up, men and women alike, and slaughtered the children, and then slaughtered one another. Some of them fell upon their swords and perished, and others were slaughtered with their own swords or knives. The righteous women hurled stones from the windows on the enemy, and the enemy threw rocks back at them. The women were struck by the stones, and their bodies and faces were completely bruised and cut. They taunted and reviled the errant ones with the name of the crucified, despicable and abominable son of harlotry, saying: 'In whom do you place your trust? In a putrid corpse!' The misled ones then approached to smash the door.

There was a distinguished young woman there named Mistress Rachel, daughter of Isaac, son of Asher, who said to her friend: 'Four children have I. Have no mercy on them either, lest those uncircumcised ones come and seize them alive and raise them in their ways of error. In my children, too, shall you sanctify the holy name of God.' One of her friends came and took the knife. When Rachel saw the knife, she cried loudly and bitterly and smote her face, crying and saying: 'Where is thy grace, O Lord?' She [the friend] then took Rachel's little son Isaac, who was a delightful boy, and slaughtered him. She [Rachel] said to her friend: 'Upon your life do not slaughter Isaac before Aaron.' The lad Aaron, upon seeing that his brother had been slaughtered, cried: 'Mother, mother, do not slaughter me,' and fled, hiding under a box. Rachel then took her two daughters, Bella and Madrona, and sacrificed them to the Lord God of Hosts, who commanded us not to depart from his pure doctrine, and to remain whole-hearted with him.

When this pious woman had completed sacrificing three of her children to our Creator, she raised her voice and called to her son Aaron: 'Aaron, where are you? I will not spare you either, or have mercy on you.' She drew him out by his feet from under the box where he had hidden, and slaughtered him before the exalted and lofty God. Rachel then placed them in her two sleeves, two children on one side and two on the other, beside her stomach, and they quivered beside her until finally the errant ones captured the chamber and found her sitting and lamenting over them. They said to her: 'Show us the money you have in your sleeves'; but when they saw the slaughtered children, they smote and killed her upon them.

It is of her that it was said: 'The mother was dashed in pieces with her children.' She perished with them as did that righteous woman who perished with her seven sons,* and it is of her that it was said: 'The mother of the children rejoices.'

The errant ones slew all those who were inside and stripped them naked as they still quivered and writhed in their blood. 'See, O Lord, and behold, how abject I am become.' Then they threw them out of the rooms, through the windows, naked, creating mounds upon mounds, heaps upon heaps, until they appeared as a high mountain. Many of the children of the Sacred Covenant were still alive when they were thus thrown, and they gestured with their fingers: 'Give us water to drink.' When the

* Hannah and her seven sons, 2 Maccabees 7; an ironic use of a book so frequently employed by contemporary crusading apologists.

errant ones saw this, they asked: 'Is it your desire to defile your-selves?' The victims shook their heads in refusal and gazed upwards to their Father in heaven, thus saying no, and pointed with their fingers to the blessed Holy One, whereupon the errant ones slew them.

Such were the deeds of those that have been cited by name. As for the rest of the community, how much more did they do to attest the oneness of the holy name, and all of them fell into the hand of the Lord.

The errant ones then began to rage tumultuously in the name of the crucified one. They raised their banner and proceeded to the remainder of the community, in the courtyard of the count's fortress. They besieged them, too, and warred against them until they had taken the gatehouse of the courtyard and slew some of them as well. A man was there, named Moses, son of Helbo. He called his two sons and said to them: 'My sons, Helbo and Simon, at this hour Gehenna is open and the Garden of Eden is open. Which of the two do you desire to enter?' They replied, saying: 'Lead us into the Garden of Eden.' They extended their throats, and the enemy smote them, father and sons together.

There was also a Torah scroll in the room; the errant ones came into the room, found it, and tore it to shreds. When the holy and pure women, daughters of kings, saw that the Torah had been torn, they called in a loud voice to their husbands: 'Look, see, the holy Torah – it is being torn by the enemy!' And they all said, men and women together: 'Alas, the holy Torah, the perfection of beauty, the delight of our eyes, to which we used to bow in the synagogue, kissing and honouring it! How has it now fallen into the hands of the impure uncircumcised ones?'

When the men heard the words of these pious women, they were moved with zeal for the Lord, our God, and for his holy and precious Torah. One young man, by the name of David, son of our master Rabbi Menahem, said to them: 'My brothers, rend your garments for the honour of the Torah!' They then rent their garments in accordance with the instructions of our sages.

They found an errant one in one of the rooms, and all of

them, men and women, threw stones at him till he fell dead. When the burghers and the errant ones saw that he had died, they fought against them. They went up on the roof of the house in which the children of the Covenant were; they shattered the roof, shot arrows at them, and pierced them with spears.

There was a man [there] by the name of Jacob, son of Sullam, who was not of distinguished lineage and whose mother was not of Jewish origin. He called out in a loud voice to all those that stood about him: 'All my life, until now, you have scorned me, but now I shall slaughter myself.' He then slaughtered himself in the name of him who is called mighty of mighties, whose name is Lord of hosts.

Another man was there, Samuel the elder, son of Mordecai. He, too, sanctified the name. He took his knife and plunged it into his stomach, spilling his innards on to the ground. He called to all those standing about him and declared: 'Behold, my brothers, what I shall do for the sanctification of the eternally living one.' Thus did the elder perish, attesting the oneness of God's name and in sanctification of God-fear.

The errant ones and the burghers now departed from there and entered the city, and they came to a certain courtyard where David, son of Nathaniel, was hiding together with his wife, children and his entire household – the courtyard of a certain priest. The priest said to him: 'Behold, not a vestige or remnant has survived in the bishop's courtyard or the count's. They have all been slain, cast away and trampled underfoot in the streets – except for the few who were profaned. Do as they did, so that you may be saved – you, your money and your entire household – from the errant ones.'

The God-fearing man replied: 'Go to the errant ones and to the burghers and tell them all to come to me.' When the priest heard the words of Master David, he rejoiced greatly, for he thought: 'Such a distinguished Jew has consented to give heed to our words.' He ran to them and related the words of the righteous man. They, too, rejoiced greatly and gathered about the house by the thousands and myriads. When the righteous man saw them, he placed his trust in his Creator and called out to them, saying: 'Alas, you are children of whoredom, believing as you do in one born of whoredom. As for me – I believe in the eternally living God who dwells in the lofty heavens. In him have I trusted to this day and in him will I trust until my soul departs. If you slay me, my soul will abide in the Garden of Eden – in the light of life. You, however, descend to the deep pit, to eternal obloquy, condemned together with your deity – the son of promiscuity, the crucified one!'

Upon hearing the words of the pious man, they flew into a rage. They raised their banners and encamped around the house and began to cry out and shout in the name of the crucified one. They advanced towards him and slew him, his pious wife, his sons, his son-in-law, and his entire household and kin – all of them were slain there in sanctification of the name. There the righteous man fell, together with the members of his household.

Then they turned and came to the house of Samuel, son of Naaman; he, too, sanctified the holy name. They gathered around his house, for he alone of the entire community had remained at home. They asked him to allow himself to be defiled with their putrid and profane water. He placed his trust in his Creator, he and all those with him, and they did not give heed to them [the crusaders]. The enemy slew them all and cast them out through the windows.

Those who have been cited by name performed these acts. As to the rest of the community and their leaders – I have no knowledge to what extent they attested the oneness of the name of the King of Kings, the Holy One, blessed be he and blessed be his name, like Rabbi Akiba and his companions.* May the Lord rescue us from this exile.

After leaving the Rhineland blood-bath behind, the misleadingly named Peasants' or People's Crusade proceeded in various contingents across central Europe down the Danube and across the Balkans towards Constantinople during June and July 1096. Some

* Jewish scholars martyred by Emperor Hadrian AD 132–4.

*groups, such as those led by Gottschalk or Folkmar, were destroyed
by local opposition in Hungary; others, like Count Emich's, turned
back in the Balkans. But the armies of Walter SansAvoir and Peter
the Hermit reached Constantinople between 20 July and 1 August
1096, their travails reported by the disapproving Guibert of Nogent.*

While the leaders, who needed to spend large sums of money for
their great retinues, were preparing like careful administrators,
the common people, poor in resources but copious in number,
attached themselves to a certain Peter the Hermit, and they
obeyed him as though he were the leader, as long as the matter
remained within our own borders. If I am not mistaken, he was
born in Amiens, and, it is said, led a solitary life in the habit of a
monk in I do not know what part of upper Gaul, then moved on,
I don't know why, and we saw him wander through cities and
towns, spreading his teaching, surrounded by so many people,
given so many gifts, and acclaimed for such great piety, that I
don't ever remember anyone equally honoured. He was very generous to the poor with the gifts he was given, making prostitutes
morally acceptable for husbands, together with generous gifts,
and, with remarkable authority, restoring peace and treaties
where there had been discord before. Whatever he did or said
seemed like something almost divine. Even the hairs of his mule
were torn out as though they were relics, which we report not as
truth, but as a novelty loved by the common people. Outdoors he
wore a woollen tunic, which reached to his ankles, and above it a
hood; he wore a cloak to cover his upper body, and a bit of his
arms, but his feet were bare. He drank wine and ate fish, but
scarcely ever ate bread. This man, partly because of his reputation, partly because of his preaching, had assembled a very large
army, and decided to set out through the land of the Hungarians.
The restless common people discovered that this area produced
unusually abundant food, and they went wild with excess in
response to the gentleness of the inhabitants. When they saw
the grain that had been piled up for several years, as is the custom
in that land, like towers in the fields, which we are accustomed

to call *metas** in everyday language, and although supplies of various meats and other foods were abundant in this land, not content with the natives' decency, in a kind of remarkable madness, these intruders began to crush them. While the Hungarians, as Christians to Christians, had generously offered everything for sale, our men wilfully and wantonly ignored their hospitality and generosity, arbitrarily waging war against them, assuming that they would not resist, but would remain entirely peaceful. In an accursed rage they burned the public granaries we spoke of, raped virgins, dishonoured many marriage beds by carrying off many women, and tore out or burned the beards of their hosts. None of them now thought of buying what he needed, but instead each man strove for what he could get by theft and murder, boasting with amazing impudence that he would easily do the same against the Turks. On their way they came to a castle that they could not avoid passing through. It was sited so that the path allowed no divergence to the right or left. With their usual insolence they moved to besiege it, but when they had almost captured it, suddenly, for a reason that is no concern of mine, they were overwhelmed; some died by the sword, others were drowned in the river, others, without any money, in abject poverty, deeply ashamed, returned to France. And because this place was called Moisson, and when they returned they said that they had been as far as Moisson, they were greeted with great laughter everywhere.†

When he was unable to restrain this undisciplined crowd of common people, who were like prisoners and slaves, Peter, together with a group of Germans and the dregs of our own people, whose foresight had enabled them to escape, reached the city of Constantinople on the calends of August [1 August 1096]. But a large army of Italians, Ligurians, Langobards, together with men from parts of countries beyond the Alps, had preceded him, and had decided to wait for his army and the armies of the

* Classical Latin for a conical column.
† *Moisson* in French means harvest; the place may have been Semlin on the Hungarian frontier or Wieselburg between Linz and Vienna.

other Frankish leaders, because they did not think that they had a large enough army to go beyond the province of the Greeks and attack the Turks.

Further details of the march come from Albert of Aachen.

In the year of the Incarnation of the Lord 1096, in the fourth indiction, in the thirteenth year of the reign of Henry IV, third august emperor of the Romans, and in the forty-third year of the empire, in the reign of Pope Urban II, formerly Odoard, on the eighth day of March, Walter, surnamed the Penniless,* a well-known soldier, set out, as a result of the preaching of Peter the Hermit, with a great company of Frankish foot-soldiers and only about eight knights. On the beginning of the journey to Jerusalem he entered into the kingdom of Hungary. When his intention and the reason for his taking this journey became known to Lord Coloman, most Christian king of Hungary, he was kindly received and was given peaceful transit across the entire realm, with permission to trade. And so without giving offence, and without being attacked, he set out even to Belgrade, a Bulgarian city, passing over to Malevilla,† where the realm of the king of Hungary ends. Thence he peacefully crossed the Morava river.

But sixteen of Walter's company remained in Malevilla, that they might purchase arms. Of this Walter was ignorant, for he had crossed long before. Then some of the Hungarians of perverse minds, seeing the absence of Walter and his army, laid hands upon those sixteen and robbed them of arms, garments, gold and silver and so let them depart, naked and empty-handed. Then these distressed pilgrims, deprived of arms and other things, hastened on their way to Belgrade, which has been mentioned before, where Walter with all his band had pitched tents

* Walter II of Poissy was lord of Boissy SansAvoir in the Ile de France; he was far from penniless.
† Possibly Semlin on the Hungarian–Bulgarian border; King Coloman I was king of Hungary 1095–1114.

for camp. They reported to him the misfortune which had befallen them, but Walter heard this with equanimity, because it would take too long to return for vengeance.

On the very night when those comrades, naked and empty-handed, were received, Walter sought to buy the necessaries of life from a chief of the Bulgarians and the magistrate of the city; but these men, thinking it a pretence, and regarding them as spies, forbade the sale of anything to them. Wherefore, Walter and his companions, greatly angered, began forcibly to seize and lead away the herds of cattle and sheep, which were wandering here and there through the fields in search of pasture. As a result, a serious strife arose between the Bulgarians and the pilgrims who were driving away the flocks, and they came to blows. However, while the strength of the Bulgarians was growing even to 140, some of the pilgrim army, cut off from the multitude of their companions, arrived in flight at a chapel. But the Bulgarians, their army growing in number, while the band of Walter was weakening and his entire company scattered, besieged the chapel and burned sixty who were within; on most of the others, who escaped from the enemy and the chapel in defence of their lives, the Bulgarians inflicted grave wounds.

After this calamity and the loss of his people, and after he had passed eight days as a fugitive in the forests of Bulgaria, Walter, leaving his men scattered everywhere, withdrew to Nish, a very wealthy city in the midst of the Bulgarian realm. There he found the duke and prince of the land and reported to him the injury and damage which had been done him. From the duke he obtained justice for all; nay, more, in reconciliation the duke bestowed upon him arms and money, and the same lord of the land gave him peaceful conduct through the cities of Bulgaria, Sofia, Philippopolis and Adrianople, and also licence to trade.

He went down with all his band, even to the imperial city, Constantinople, which is the capital of the entire Greek empire. And when he arrived there, with all possible earnestness and most humble petition he implored from the lord emperor himself permission to delay peacefully in his kingdom, with licence to buy the necessaries of life, until he should have as his companion Peter the Hermit, upon whose admonition and persuasion he had begun this journey. And he also begged that, when the troops were united, they might cross in ships over the arm of the sea called the Strait of St George,* and thus they would be able to resist more safely the squadrons of the Turks and the Gentiles. The outcome was that the requests made of the lord emperor, Alexius by name, were granted.

Not long after these events, Peter and his large army, innumerable as the sands of the sea – an army which he had brought together from the various realms of the nations of the Franks, Swabians, Bavarians and Lotharingians – were making their way to Jerusalem. Descending on that march into the kingdom of Hungary, he and his army pitched their tents before the gate of Oedenburg . . .

Peter heard this report and, because the Hungarians and Bulgarians were fellow Christians, absolutely refused to believe so great a crime of them, until his men, coming to Malevilla, saw hanging from the walls the arms and spoils of the sixteen companions of Walter who had stayed behind a short time before, and whom the Hungarians had treacherously presumed to rob. But when Peter recognised the injury to his brethren, at the sight of their arms and spoils, he urged his companions to avenge their wrongs.

These sounded the trumpet loudly, and with upraised banners they rushed to the walls and attacked the enemy with a hail of arrows. In such quick succession and in such incredible numbers did they hurl them in the face of those standing on the walls that the Hungarians, in no wise able to resist the force of the besieging Franks, left the walls, hoping that within the city they might be able to withstand the strength of the Gauls. Godfrey, surnamed Burel – a native of the city Etampes, master and standard-bearer of two hundred foot-soldiers, himself a foot-soldier, and a man of great strength – seeing the flight of the

* The westerners' name for the Bosporus and Sea of Marmara; see map p. xliv.

Hungarians away from the walls, then quickly crossed over the walls by means of a ladder he chanced to find there. Reinald of Broyes, a distinguished knight, clad in helmet and coat of mail, ascended just after Godfrey; soon all the knights, as well as the foot-soldiers, hastened to enter the city. The Hungarians, seeing their own imminent peril, gathered seven thousand strong for defence; and, having passed out through another gate which looked towards the east, they stationed themselves on the summit of a lofty crag, beyond which flowed the Danube, where they were invincibly fortified. A very large part of these were unable to escape quickly through the narrow passage, and they fell before the gate. Some who hoped to find refuge on the top of the mountain were cut down by the pursuing pilgrims; still others, thrown headlong from the summit of the mountain, were buried in the waves of the Danube, but many escaped by boat. About four thousand Hungarians fell there, but only a hundred pilgrims, not counting the wounded, were killed at that same place.

This victory won, Peter remained with all his followers in the same citadel five days, for he found there an abundance of grain, flocks of sheep, herds of cattle, a plentiful supply of wine and an infinite number of horses . . .

When Peter learned of the wrath of the king and his very formidable gathering of troops, he deserted Malevilla with all his followers and planned to cross the Morava with all spoils and flocks and herds of horses. But on the whole bank he found very few boats, only 150, in which the great multitude must pass quickly over and escape, lest the king should overtake them with a great force. Hence many who were unable to cross in boats tried to cross on rafts made by fastening poles together with twigs. But driven hither and thither in these rafts without rudders, and at times separated from their companions, many perished, pierced with arrows from the bows of the Patzinaks, who inhabited Bulgaria. As Peter saw the drowning and destruction which was befalling his men, he commanded the Bavarians, the Alemanni and the other Teutons, by their promise of obedience to come to the aid of their Frankish brethren. They were carried to that place by seven rafts; then they sank seven small boats of the Patzinaks with their occupants, but took only seven men captive. They led these seven captives into the presence of Peter and killed them by his order.

When he had thus avenged his men, Peter crossed the Morava river and entered the large and spacious forests of the Bulgarians with supplies of food, with every necessary, and with the spoils from Belgrade. And after a delay of eight days in those vast woods and pastures, he and his followers approached Nish, a city very strongly fortified with walls. After crossing the river before the city by a stone bridge, they occupied the field, pleasing in its verdure and extent, and pitched their tents on the banks of the river . . .

Peter, obedient to the mandate of the emperor, advanced from the city of Sofia and withdrew with all his people to the city of Philippopolis. When he had related the entire story of his misfortune in the hearing of all the Greek citizens, he received, in the name of Jesus and in fear of God, very many gifts for him. Next, the third day after, he withdrew to Adrianople, cheerful and joyful in the abundance of all necessaries. There he tarried in camp outside the walls of the city only two days, and then withdrew after sunrise on the third day. A second message of the emperor was urging him to hasten his march to Constantinople, for, on account of the reports about him, the emperor was burning with desire to see this same Peter. When they had come to Constantinople, the army of Peter was ordered to encamp at a distance from the city, and licence to trade was fully granted . . .

Small in stature but mighty in heart and speech, Peter, accompanied only by Fulcher,* was brought by the imperial officers into the presence of the emperor, who wished to see if he was as his reputation reported. As he entered, Peter boldly greeted the emperor in the name of the Lord Jesus Christ, and told him in detail how by the love and grace of Christ himself he had left his country to visit the Holy Sepulchre, briefly recounting the

* One of the leading knights in Peter's army from the Chartrain region of northern France.

hardships he had borne. Mighty men, he said, earls and the greatest dukes, would shortly follow in his steps, having resolved like him, with hearts on fire, to take the road to Jerusalem. Seeing Peter and hearing his words, the emperor acknowledged the purpose in his heart, and asked what he would have that he could give. Peter begged for alms of the emperor's mercy to sustain him and his people, telling him of the great losses he had suffered by his men's heedlessness and disobedience. His humility moved the emperor to pity, and he commanded that 200 Byzantine *aurei* should be given him, and distributed a quarter-bushel of *tartara* [a denomination of money] to his army.

The subsequent destruction in Asia Minor in September and October 1096 of the assembled armies of Walter and Peter, alongside a force that had arrived at Constantinople directly from Lombardy, proved a source of moral disapproval alike for western and eastern observers. The grisly fate of the 'People's Crusade' supplied a powerful introduction to the author of the Gesta Francorum,* *who described events for much of the crusade from the perspective of the army of Bohemund of Taranto, the Norman leader from southern Italy.*

When that time had already come, of which the Lord Jesus warns his faithful people every day, especially in the Gospel where he says, 'If any man will come after me, let him deny himself, and take up his cross, and follow me,'† there was a great stirring of heart throughout all the Frankish lands, so that if any man, with all his heart and all his mind, really wanted to follow God and faithfully to bear the Cross after him, he could make no delay in taking the road to the Holy Sepulchre as quickly as possible. For even the pope [Urban II] set out across the Alps as soon as he could, with his archbishops, bishops, abbots and priests, and he began to deliver eloquent sermons and to preach, saying, 'If any man wants to save his soul, let him have no hesitation in taking the way of the Lord in humility, and if he lacks money, the divine

* See above, pp. xxiv–xxv.   † Matthew 16:24.

mercy will give him enough.' The lord pope said also, 'Brothers, you must suffer for the name of Christ many things, wretchedness, poverty, nakedness, persecution, need, sickness, hunger, thirst and other such troubles, for the Lord says to his disciples, "You must suffer many things for my name,"* and "Be not ashamed to speak before men, for I will give you what you shall say," and afterwards "Great will be your reward." ' And when these words had begun to be rumoured abroad through all the duchies and counties of the Frankish lands, the Franks, hearing them, straightway began to sew the Cross on the right shoulders of their garments, saying that they would all with one accord follow in the footsteps of Christ, by whom they had been redeemed from the power of hell. So they set out at once from their homes in the lands of the Franks.

The Franks ordered themselves in three armies. One, which entered into Hungary, was led by Peter the Hermit and Duke Godfrey, Baldwin his brother and Baldwin, count of Hainault.† These most valiant knights and many others (whose names I do not know) travelled by the road which Charlemagne, the heroic king of the Franks, had formerly caused to be built to Constantinople.‡

The aforesaid Peter was the first to reach Constantinople on 1 August, and many Germans came with him. There they found men from northern and southern Italy and many others gathered together. The emperor [Alexius I Comnenus] ordered such provisions as there were in the city to be given to them, and he said, 'Do not cross the Hellespont until the great army of the Christians arrives, for there are not enough of you to fight

---

* The author misquotes Acts 9:16, which might indicate he was a layman relying on faulty aural memory or a cleric too confident to check his references.

† Godfrey of Bouillon, duke of Lower Lorraine; Baldwin of Boulogne his younger brother; and Baldwin, count of Mons in Hainault. For the first two, see Appendix, pp. 375–6.

‡ The traditional pilgrim route via the Danube, Morava and Maritza valleys had become associated with an entirely legendary journey to Jerusalem by Charlemagne, who had been refashioned to suit the aspirations of the late eleventh century.

against the Turks.' But those Christians behaved abominably, sacking and burning the palaces of the city, and stealing the lead from the roofs of the churches and selling it to the Greeks, so that the emperor was angry, and ordered them to cross the Hellespont. After they had crossed they did not cease from their misdeeds, and they burned and laid waste both houses and churches. At last they reached Nicomedia, where the Italians and Germans broke away from the Franks,* because the Franks were intolerably proud. The Italians chose a leader called Rainald; the Germans also chose a leader, and they all went into [Asia Minor] and travelled for four days' journey beyond the city of Nicaea, where they found a deserted castle named Xerigordus which they took, finding therein plenty of corn and wine and meat and abundance of all good things. But when the Turks heard that the Christians were in the castle, they came and besieged it. Before its gate was a well, and beneath its walls a spring, where Rainald went out to lay an ambush for the Turks, but when they arrived on Michaelmas Day they caught Rainald and his company, and killed many of them. The survivors fled into the castle, which the Turks at once besieged, cutting off the water supply. Our men were therefore so terribly afflicted by thirst that they bled their horses and asses and drank the blood; others let down belts and clothes into a sewer and squeezed out the liquid into their mouths; others passed water into one another's cupped hands and drank; others dug up damp earth and lay down on their backs, piling the earth upon their chests because they were so dry with thirst. The bishops and priests encouraged our men and told them not to despair. This miserable state of affairs went on for eight days. Then the leader of the Germans made an agreement to betray his comrades to the Turks, and pretending that he was going out to fight he fled to them, and many men went with him. Of the remainder, those who would not renounce God were killed; others, whom the Turks captured alive, were divided among their captors like sheep, some were put up as targets and shot with arrows, others sold and given away as if they were brute beasts. Some of the

* Here meaning Frenchmen, not all westerners.

Turks took their prisoners home to Khorasan,* Antioch or Aleppo or wherever they happened to live. These men were the first to endure blessed martyrdom for the name of our Lord Jesus.

Afterwards, when the Turks heard that Peter the Hermit and Walter the Penniless† were in Cibotus, which is beyond the city of Nicaea, they came thither full of glee intending to kill them and their comrades, and when they had come they found Walter and his men, and killed them at once. Peter the Hermit, however, had gone off to Constantinople a little before this happened, for he could not control such a mixed company of people who would not obey him or listen to what he said. The Turks fell upon his men and killed most of them – some they found asleep, others naked, and all these they slaughtered. Among the rest they found a priest saying mass, and they killed him at once upon the altar. Those who managed to escape fled to Cibotus. Some leapt into the sea, and others hid in the woods and mountains. The Turks chased some of our men into the castle, and piled up wood so that they could burn them and the castle together, but the Christians in the castle set fire to the pile of wood, and the flames were blown back against the Turks and burned some of them, but God delivered our men from that fire. At last the Turks took them alive and apportioned them as they had done with the others, sending them away through all the neighbouring lands, some to Khorasan and some to Persia. All this happened in October.‡ When the emperor heard that the Turks had inflicted such a defeat on our men he rejoiced greatly, and gave orders for the survivors to be brought back over the Hellespont. When they had crossed over he had them completely disarmed.

The eruption of pious militancy from the west allowed the daughter of the Greek emperor Alexius, Anna Comnena, to draw a convenient veil over her father's involvement in summoning what proved to be very awkward allies as well as to highlight her themes of the violence, barbarism, intemperance, untrustworthiness and

---

* Signifying the Muslim heartlands of Iraq and Iran.
† See above, p. 57n.   ‡ 21 October 1096.

uncontrolled enthusiasm of the westerners, themes that coloured her whole picture of the crusaders and their expedition.

[Alexius] had no time to relax before he heard a rumour that countless Frankish armies were approaching. He dreaded their arrival, knowing as he did their uncontrollable passion, their erratic character and their irresolution, not to mention the other peculiar traits of the Celts,* with their inevitable consequences: their greed for money, for example, which always led them, it seemed, to break their own agreements without scruple for any chance reason. He had consistently heard this said of them and it was abundantly justified. So far from despairing, however, he made every effort to prepare for war if need arose. What actually happened was more far-reaching and terrible than rumour suggested, for the whole of the west and all the barbarians who lived between the Adriatic and the Straits of Gibraltar migrated in a body to Asia, marching across Europe country by country with all their households. The reason for this mass movement is to be found more or less in the following events. A certain Celt, called Peter, with the surname Cucupetrus,† left to worship at the Holy Sepulchre and after suffering much ill treatment at the hands of the Turks and Saracens who were plundering the whole of Asia, he returned home with difficulty. Unable to admit defeat, he wanted to make a second attempt by the same route, but realising the folly of trying to do this alone (worse things might happen to him) he worked out a clever scheme. He decided to preach in all the Latin countries. A divine voice, he said, commanded him to proclaim to all the counts in France that all should depart from their homes, set out to worship at the Holy Shrine and with all their soul and might strive to liberate Jerusalem from the Agarenes.‡ Surprisingly, he was successful. It was as if he had inspired every heart with some divine oracle. Celts assembled from all parts, one after another, with arms and

* Anna's typically archaic description of western Europeans.
† Perhaps a play on the Picard *chtou*, little. Otherwise Peter the Hermit.
‡ Muslims; derived from the sons of Hagar, supposed ancestor of the Arabs.

horses and all the other equipment for war. Full of enthusiasm and ardour they thronged every highway, and with these warriors came a host of civilians, outnumbering the sand of the seashore or the stars of heaven, carrying palms and bearing crosses on their shoulders. There were women and children, too, who had left their own countries. Like tributaries joining a river from all directions they streamed towards us in full force, mostly through Dacia.* The arrival of this mighty host was preceded by locusts, which abstained from the wheat but made frightful inroads on the vines. The prophets of those days interpreted this as a sign that the Celtic army would refrain from interfering in the affairs of Christians but bring dreadful affliction on the barbarian Ishmaelites, who were the slaves of drunkenness and wine and Dionysus. The Ishmaelites are indeed dominated by Dionysus and Eros; they indulge readily in every kind of sexual licence, and if they are circumcised in the flesh they are certainly not so in their passions. In fact, the Ishmaelites are nothing more than slaves – trebly slaves – of the vices of Aphrodite. Hence they reverence and worship Astarte and Ashtaroth, and in their land the figure of the moon and the golden image of Chobar are considered of major importance.† Corn, because it is not heady and at the same time is most nourishing, has been accepted as the symbol of Christianity. In the light of this the diviners interpreted the references to vines and wheat. So much for the prophecies. The incidents of the barbarians' advance followed in the order I have given, and there was something strange about it, which intelligent people at least would notice. The multitudes did not arrive at the same moment, nor even by the same route – how could they cross the Adriatic *en masse* after setting out from different countries in such great numbers? – but they made the voyage in separate groups, some first, some in a second party and others after them in order, until all had arrived, and then they began their march across Epirus. Each army, as I have said, was preceded by a plague of locusts, so that everyone, having

* Hungary and the Danube basin, another archaism.
† This is fantasy; Islam is the most monotheistic of religions.

observed the phenomenon several times, came to recognise locusts as the forerunners of Frankish battalions. They had already begun to cross the Straits of Lombardy [Otranto] in small groups when the emperor summoned certain leaders of the Roman forces and sent them to the area round Dyrrhachium [Durazzo] and Avlona, with instructions to receive the voyagers kindly and export from all countries abundant supplies for them along their route; then to watch them carefully and follow, so that if they saw them making raids or running off to plunder the neighbouring districts, they could check them by light skirmishes. These officers were accompanied by interpreters who understood the Latin language; their duty was to quell any incipient trouble between natives and pilgrims. I would like here to give a clearer and more detailed account of the matter.

The report of Peter's preaching spread everywhere, and the first to sell his land and set out on the road to Jerusalem was Godfrey [of Bouillon]. He was a very rich man, extremely proud of his noble birth, his own courage and the glory of his family. (Every Celt desired to surpass his fellows.) The upheaval that ensued as men and women took to the road was unprecedented within living memory. The simpler folk were in very truth led on by a desire to worship at Our Lord's tomb and visit the Holy Places, but the more villainous characters (in particular Bohemund and his like) had an ulterior purpose, for they hoped on their journey to seize the capital itself, looking upon its capture as a natural consequence of the expedition. Bohemund disturbed the morale of many nobler men because he still cherished his old grudge against the emperor. Peter, after his preaching campaign, was the first to cross the Lombardy Straits, with eighty thousand infantry and one hundred thousand horsemen. He reached the capital via Hungary.* The Celts, as one might guess, are in any case an exceptionally hotheaded race and passionate, but let them once find an inducement and they become irresistible.

The emperor knew what Peter had suffered before from the Turks and advised him to wait for the other counts to arrive, but

* Peter arrived 1 August 1096.

he refused, confident in the number of his followers. He crossed the Sea of Marmara and pitched camp near a small place called Helenopolis. Later some Normans, ten thousand in all, joined him but detached themselves from the rest of the army and ravaged the outskirts of Nicaea, acting with horrible cruelty to the whole population; they cut in pieces some of the babies, impaled others on wooden spits and roasted them over a fire; old people were subjected to every kind of torture. The inhabitants of the city, when they learnt what was happening, threw open their gates and charged out against them. A fierce battle ensued, in which the Normans fought with such spirit that the Nicaeans had to retire inside their citadel. The enemy therefore returned to Helenopolis with all the booty. There an argument started between them and the rest (who had not gone on the raid) – the usual quarrel in such cases – for the latter were green with envy. That led to brawling, whereupon the daredevil Normans broke away for a second time and took Xerigordus by assault. The sultan's reaction was to send Elkhanes with a strong force to deal with them. He arrived at Xerigordus and captured it; of the Normans some were put to the sword and others taken prisoner. At the same time Elkhanes made plans to deal with the remainder, still with Cucupetrus. He laid ambushes in suitable places, hoping that the enemy on their way to Nicaea would fall into the trap unawares and be killed. Knowing the Celtic love of money, he also enlisted the services of two determined men who were to go to Peter's camp and there announce that the Normans, having seized Nicaea, were sharing out all the spoils of the city. This story had an amazing effect on Peter's men; they were thrown into confusion at the words 'share' and 'money'; without a moment's hesitation they set out on the Nicaea road in complete disorder, practically heedless of military discipline and the proper arrangement which should mark men going off to war. As I have said before, the Latin race at all times is unusually greedy for wealth, but when it plans to invade a country, neither reason nor force can restrain it. They set out helter-skelter, regardless of their individual companies. Near the Dracon they fell into the Turkish ambuscade and were miserably slaughtered. So great a multitude of Celts and Normans died by the Ishmaelite sword that when they gathered the remains of the fallen, lying on every side, they heaped up, I will not say a mighty ridge or hill or peak, but a mountain of considerable height and depth and width, so huge was the mass of bones. Some men of the same race as the slaughtered barbarians later, when they were building a wall like those of a city, used the bones of the dead as pebbles to fill up the cracks. In a way the city became their tomb. To this very day it stands with its encircling wall built of mixed stones and bones.* When the killing was over, only Peter with a handful of men returned to Helenopolis. The Turks, wishing to capture him, again laid an ambush, but the emperor, who had heard of this and indeed of the terrible massacre, thought it would be an awful thing if Peter also became a prisoner. Constantine Euphorbenus Catacalon was accordingly sent with powerful contingents in warships across the Straits to help him. At his approach the Turks took to their heels. Without delay Catacalon picked up Peter and his companions (there were only a few) and brought them in safety to Alexius, who reminded Peter of his foolishness in the beginning and added that these great misfortunes had come upon him through not listening to his advice. With the usual Latin arrogance Peter disclaimed responsibility and blamed his men for them, because (said he) they had been disobedient and followed their own whims. He called them brigands and robbers, considered unworthy therefore by the Saviour to worship at his Holy Sepulchre. Some Latins, after the pattern of Bohemund and his cronies, because they had long coveted the Roman empire† and wished to acquire it for themselves, found in the preaching of Peter an excuse and caused this great upheaval by deceiving more innocent people. They sold their lands on the pretence that they were leaving to fight the Turks and liberate the Holy Sepulchre.‡

* Picaresque denouement for the massacred of September and October 1096.
† An article of Anna's faith, much exaggerated by her; encouraged by the Norman attacks of the early 1080s led by, among others, Bohemund.
‡ The classic Greek propagandist view.

III

The Journey to the East

December 1096–June 1097

*Between August and October 1096 the larger, wealthier, more dis-
ciplined armies embarked eastwards. The anonymous author of the*
Gesta Francorum *who travelled with Bohemund of Taranto, or
based his account on the memories of those who did, described the
process, beginning with Godfrey of Bouillon's departure from Lorraine in mid-August, before recounting a rather fancifully dramatic
account of Bohemund's recruitment to the cause of the Cross in
September.*

Our second army came through the Dalmatian lands, and it was
led by Raymond count of St Gilles, and the bishop of Le Puy.*
The third came by way of the old Roman road.† In this band
were Bohemund and Richard of the Principality, Robert count of
Flanders, Robert the Norman, Hugh the Great, Everard of Puiset,
Achard of Montmerle, Isoard of Mouzon‡ and many others.
Some of them came to the port of Brindisi, others to Bari or
Otranto. Hugh the Great and William son of the marquis§ em-
barked at Bari and sailed to Durazzo, but the governor of that

---

* Raymond IV, count of Toulouse, and Adhemar, bishop of Le Puy.
† The Via Egnatia running from Durazzo to Constantinople.
‡ Bohemund of Taranto, son of Robert Guiscard, ruler of Apulia; Richard,
son of Count William of the principality of Salerno; Robert II, count of Flan-
ders; Robert II, duke of Normandy, eldest son of William the Conqueror;
Hugh, count of Vermandois, brother of King Philip I of France; Everard III of
Le Puiset, viscount of Chartres; Achard, castellan of Montmerle in Burgundy;
Isoard of Mouzon in the Ardennes.
§ William, son of Emma, Bohemund's sister, and brother of Tancred; jour-
neyed east with Hugh of Vermandois.

place, hearing that warriors of such experience were arriving, immediately devised a treacherous plan, and he arrested them and sent them under guard to the emperor at Constantinople, so that they might swear fealty to him.

After this Duke Godfrey was the first of all our leaders to reach Constantinople with a great army, and he arrived two days before Christmas, and encamped outside the city until that wretch of an emperor gave orders that quarters were to be assigned to him in the suburbs. When the duke had settled in, he sent his squires out each day, quite confidently, to get straw and other things necessary for the horses; but, when they thought that they could go out freely wherever they liked, the wretched Emperor Alexius ordered his Turcopuli and Patzinaks to attack and kill them.* So Baldwin [of Boulogne], the duke's brother, hearing of this, lay in ambush, and when he found the enemy killing his men he attacked them bravely and by God's help defeated them. He took sixty prisoners, some of whom he killed and others he presented to the duke his brother. When the emperor heard of this he was very angry, and the duke, realising this, led his men out of the suburb and encamped outside the walls. Late that evening the miserable emperor ordered his men to attack the duke and the Christian army, but our unconquered leader with his Christian knights drove back the imperial troops, killing seven men and driving the rest to the gates of the city. Afterwards he came back to his camp and stayed there for five days, until he came to an agreement with the emperor, who told him to cross the Hellespont and promised that he would have as good provision there as he had in Constantinople; moreover the emperor promised to give alms to the poor so that they could live.

As for Bohemund, that great warrior, he was besieging Amalfi when he heard that an immense army of Frankish crusaders had arrived, going to the Holy Sepulchre and ready to fight the pagans. So he began to make careful enquiries as to the arms they carried, the badge which they wore in Christ's pilgrimage and

* The Turcopole – i.e. Turkish – and Pecheneg mercenaries were regularly employed by the Greeks.

the war-cry which they shouted in battle. He was told, 'They are well armed, they wear the badge of Christ's Cross on their right arm or between their shoulders, and as a war-cry they shout all together "God's will, God's will, God's will!" ' Then Bohemund, inspired by the Holy Ghost, ordered the most valuable cloak which he had to be cut up forthwith and made into crosses, and most of the knights who were at the siege began to join him at once, for they were full of enthusiasm, so that Count Roger* was left almost alone, and when he had gone back to Sicily he grieved and lamented because he had lost his army.† My lord Bohemund went home to his own land‡ and made careful preparations for setting out on the way to the Holy Sepulchre. Thereafter he crossed the sea with his army, and with him went Tancred son of the marquis, Richard of the Principality and Ranulf his brother, Robert of Anse, Herman of Cannes, Robert of Sourdeval, Robert Fitz-Toustan, Humphrey Fitz-Ralph, Richard son of Count Ranulf, the count of Russignolo and his brothers, Boel of Chartres, Aubré of Cagnano and Humphrey of Monte Scaglioso.§ All these crossed at Bohemund's expense, and reached

* Count Roger the Great, brother of Robert Guiscard and conqueror of Sicily after 1060.
† September 1096. This is a fanciful story. Bohemund had close contacts with Urban II whom he had met on a number of occasions. It is inconceivable that Bohemund knew nothing of Urban's plans, still less of Alexius' invitation a year after the pope began his visit to France and eighteen months after the Greek embassy to Piacenza. This story is a conveniently uplifting fiction; it also lets Bohemund escape any suggestion of prior collusion with the Greeks.
‡ Taranto in the heel of Italy.
§ Tancred, Bohemund's nephew and later successor as prince of Antioch; Richard and Ranulf of the principality of Salerno; Robert of Ansa, former rebel, loyal to Bohemund and Tancred on crusade; Hermann of Canne, son of Duke Humphrey of Apulia; Robert of Sourdeval, originally from the Cotentin in Normandy, vassal of Count Roger of Sicily; Robert Fitz-Toustan of the Norman family of the counts of Molise; Humphrey FitzRalph, vassal of Bohemund's brother Roger Borsa, duke of Apulia; Richard, son of Count Rainulf of Caiazzo; Count Godfrey of Ruscinolo; Boel of Chartres, vassal of Roger Borsa; Aubrey of Cagnano, killed at Harenc, October 1097; Humphrey, probably actually Godfrey of Monte Scaglioso, related to Robert Guiscard; his aunt later married Robert II of Normandy. Details from E. Jamison, 'Some Notes on the *Anonymi Gesta Francorum*', in *Studies in French Language and*

western Macedonia, where they found plenty of corn and wine and other things to eat, and going down into the valley of Andronopolis,* they waited for their men, until all had crossed over. Then Bohemund called a council to encourage his men, and to warn them all to be courteous and refrain from plundering that land, which belonged to Christians, and he said that no one was to take more than sufficed for his food.

Anna Comnena, aged only thirteen at the time, supplied from the perspective of half a century later a vividly anecdotal and partisan account of the early arrivals of the western armies in Constantinople in the winter of 1096–7.

A certain Hugh, brother of the king of France, with all the pride of a Navatus in his noble birth and wealth and power, as he was about to leave his native country (ostensibly for a pilgrimage to the Holy Sepulchre) sent an absurd message to the emperor proposing that he [Hugh] should be given a magnificent reception: 'Know, emperor, that I am the king of kings, the greatest of all beneath the heavens. It is my will that you should meet me on my arrival and receive me with the pomp and ceremony due to my noble birth.' When this letter reached Alexius, John the son of Isaac the sebastocrator† happened to be duke of Dyrrhachium, and Nicholas Mavrocatacalon, commander of the fleet, had anchored his ships at intervals round the harbour there. From this base he made frequent voyages of reconnaissance to prevent pirate ships sailing by unnoticed. To these two men the emperor now sent urgent instructions: the duke was to keep watch by land and sea for Hugh's arrival and inform Alexius at once when he came; he was also to receive him with great pomp; the admiral was exhorted to keep a constant vigil – there must be no relaxation or negligence whatever. Hugh reached the coast of Lombardy safely and forthwith despatched envoys to the duke of

---

Mediaeval Literature Presented to Professor M. K. Pope by Pupils, Colleagues and Friends (University of Manchester Press, 1939).   * The river Drim or Drino.
† Highest Byzantine honoric title, invented by Alexius I for his brother Isaac.

Dyrrhachium. There were twenty-four of them in all, armed with breastplates and greaves of gold and accompanied by Count William the Carpenter and Elias (who had deserted from the emperor at Thessalonica).* They addressed the duke as follows: 'Be it known to you, duke, that our Lord Hugh is almost here. He brings with him from Rome the golden standard of St Peter.† Understand, moreover, that he is supreme commander of the Frankish army. See to it then that he is accorded a reception worthy of his rank and yourself prepare to meet him.' While the envoys were delivering this message, Hugh came down via Rome to Lombardy, as I have said, and set sail for Illyricum from Bari, but on the crossing he was caught by a tremendous storm. Most of his ships, with their rowers and marines, were lost. Only one ship, his own, was thrown up on the coast somewhere between Dyrrhachium and a place called Pales, and that was half-wrecked. Two coastguards on the look-out for his arrival found him, saved by a miracle. They called to him, 'The duke is anxiously waiting for your coming. He is very eager to see you.' At once he asked for a horse and one of them dismounted and gave him his own gladly. When the duke saw him, saved in this way, and when he had greeted him, he asked about the voyage and heard of the storm which had wrecked his ships. He encouraged Hugh with fine promises and entertained him at a magnificent banquet. After the feasting Hugh was allowed to rest, but he was not granted complete freedom. John the duke had immediately informed the emperor of the Frank's adventures and was now awaiting further instructions. Soon after receiving the news Alexius sent Butumites‡ to Epidamnus (which we have on numerous occasions called Dyrrhachium) to escort Hugh, not by the direct route but on a detour through Philippopolis to the capital. He

* Hugh, count of Vermandois, or 'the Great', was the brother of King Philip I of France. Elias served in the early 1080s during the Balkan War with Robert Guiscard; William was viscount of Melun.

† If so, he was not alone; Raymond of Toulouse also probably bore a papal banner. Such emblems were favourite tools of the eleventh-century papacy; William of Normandy carried one on his invasion of England in 1066.

‡ Manuel Butumites, Greek admiral.

was afraid of the armed Celtic hordes coming on behind him. Hugh was welcomed with honour by the emperor, who soon persuaded him by generous largess and every proof of friendship to become his liege-man and take the customary oath of the Latins.

This affair was merely the prelude. Barely fifteen days later Bohemund made the crossing to the coast of Cabalium. Hard on his heels came Count Richard of the Principate.* He too when he reached the Lombardy coast wanted to cross over to Illyricum. A three-masted pirate vessel of large tonnage was hired for 6,000 gold staters. She carried two hundred rowers and towed three ship's boats. Richard did not make for Avlona, as the other Latin armies had done, but after weighing anchor changed direction a little and with a favourable wind sailed straight for Chimara (he was fearful of the Roman fleet). However, in escaping the smoke he fell into the fire: he avoided the ships lying in wait at different points in the Lombardy straits but crossed the path of the commander-in-chief of the whole Roman fleet, Nicholas Mavrocatacalon himself.† The latter had heard of this pirate vessel some time before and had detached biremes, triremes and some fast cruisers from the main force; with these he moved from his base at Ason to Cabalium and there took up station. The so-called 'second count' was sent with his own galley (*Excussatum*‡ to the ordinary seamen) to light a torch when he saw the rowers loose the stern cables of the enemy ship and throw them into the sea. Without delay the order was carried out and Nicholas, seeing the signal, hoisted sail on some of his ships, while others were rowed with oars – they looked like millipedes – against Richard, who was now at sea. They caught him before he had sailed three stades from the land, eager to reach the opposite coast by Epidamnus. He had 1,500 soldiers on board, plus eighty horses belonging to the nobles. The helmsman, sighting Nicholas, reported to the Frank: 'The Syrian fleet is on us. We're in danger of being killed by dagger and sword.' The count at

* *c.*26 October 1096; for Richard of the principate of Salerno see above, p. 71n.
† Experienced Greek admiral in the Balkans in the 1080s and after.
‡ Latin *excussatum*, a boat apparently reserved for the second-in-command.

once ordered his men to arm and put up a good fight. It was midwinter – the day sacred to the memory of Nicholas, greatest of pontiffs* – but there was a dead calm and the full moon shone more brightly than in the spring. As the winds had fallen completely the pirate ship could no longer make progress under sail; it lay becalmed on the sea. At this point in the history I should like to pay tribute to the exploits of Marianus [Mavrocatacalon]. He immediately asked the duke of the fleet, his father, for some of the lighter vessels and then steered straight for Richard's ship. He fell upon the prow and tried to board her. The marines soon rushed there when they saw that he was fully armed for battle, but Marianus, speaking in their language, told the Latins there was no need for alarm; he urged them not to fight against fellow Christians. Nevertheless one of them fired a crossbow and hit his helmet. The arrow drove clean through the top of it without touching a hair on his head – providence thwarted it. Another arrow was quickly fired at the count, striking him on the arm; it pierced his shield, bored through his breastplate of scale-armour and grazed his side. A certain Latin priest who happened to be standing in the stern with twelve other fighting-men saw what had occurred and shot several times with his bow at Marianus. Even then Marianus refused to give up; he fought bravely himself and encouraged his men to follow his example, so that three times the priest's comrades had to be relieved because of wounds or fatigue. The priest, too, although he had been hit again and again and was covered with streams of blood from his wounds, still was undaunted. After a bitter contest which went on from evening till the next midday the Latins yielded much against their will to Marianus, when they had asked for and obtained an amnesty from him. The warrior-priest, however, even when the armistice was being arranged, did not cease from fighting. After emptying his quiver of arrows, he picked up a sling-stone and hurled it at Marianus, who protected his head with a shield, but that was broken into four and his helmet was shattered. The blow stunned him; he lost consciousness at once and for some time lay

* 6 December 1096.

speechless, just as the famous Hector lay almost at his last gasp when struck by Ajax's stone. With difficulty he recovered his senses, pulled himself together and firing arrows against his enemy wounded him three times. The polemarch (he was more that than a priest) was far from having had his fill of battle, although he had exhausted the stones and arrows and was at a loss what to do and how to defend himself against his adversary. He grew impatient, on fire with rage, gathering himself for the spring like a wild animal. He was ready to use whatever came to hand and when he found a sack full of barley-cakes, he threw them like stones, taking them from the sack. It was as if he were officiating at some ceremony or service, turning war into the solemnisation of sacred rites. He picked up one cake, hurled it with all his might at Marianus' face and hit him on the cheek. So much for the story of the priest, the ship and its marines.* As for Count Richard, he put himself in the hands of Marianus, together with his ship and her crew, and thereafter gladly followed him. When they reached land and were disembarking, the priest kept on making enquiries about Marianus; he did not know his name, but described him by the colour of his garments. When at last he found him, he threw his arms round him and with an embrace boasted, 'If you had met me on dry land, many of you would have died at my hands.' He drew out a large silver cup, worth 130 staters, and as he gave it to Marianus and uttered these words, he died.

It was at this time that Count Godfrey made the crossing with some other counts and an army of ten thousand horsemen and seventy thousand infantry. When he reached the capital he quartered his men in the vicinity of the Propontis [Sea of Marmara], from the bridge nearest the Cosmidium as far as the church of St Phocas. But when the emperor urged him to go over to the far side of the Propontis he put off the decision from day to day; the crossing was deferred with a series of excuses. In fact, of course, he was waiting for Bohemund and the rest of the counts to

* Anna is shocked at a priest fighting – a common enough western phenomenon at the time.

arrive. Peter had in the beginning undertaken his great journey to worship at the Holy Sepulchre, but the others (and in particular Bohemund) cherished their old grudge against Alexius and sought a good opportunity to avenge the glorious victory which the emperor had won at Larissa.* They were all of one mind and in order to fulfil their dream of taking Constantinople they adopted a common policy. I have often referred to that already: to all appearances they were on pilgrimage to Jerusalem; in reality they planned to dethrone Alexius and seize the capital. Unfortunately for them, he was aware of their perfidy, from long experience. He gave written orders to move the auxiliary forces with their officers from Athyra to Philea *en masse* (Philea is a place on the coast of the Black Sea). They were to lie in wait for envoys from Godfrey on their way to Bohemund and the other counts coming behind him, or vice versa; all communications were thus to be intercepted. Meanwhile the following incident took place. Some of the counts who accompanied Godfrey were invited by the emperor to meet him. He intended to give them advice: they should urge Godfrey to take the oath of allegiance. The Latins, however, wasted time with their usual verbosity and love of long speeches, so that a false rumour reached the Franks that their counts had been arrested by Alexius. Immediately they marched in serried ranks on Byzantium [Constantinople], starting with the palaces near the Silver Lake;† they demolished them completely. An assault was also made on the city walls, not with *helepoleis*‡ (because they had none), but trusting in their great numbers they had the effrontery to try to set fire to the gate below the palace,§ near the sanctuary of St Nicholas. The vulgar mob of Byzantines, who were utterly craven, with no experience of war, were not the only ones to weep and wail and beat their breasts in impotent fear when they saw the Latin ranks; even more alarmed were the emperor's loyal adherents. Recalling the Thursday on which the city was captured, they were afraid that on that day (because of what had occurred

* Over the Normans in 1083 in the Balkans.   † Unidentified.
‡ Movable siege engines.   § The palace of Blachernae.

then)* vengeance might be taken on them. All the trained soldiers hurried to the palace in disorder, but the emperor remained
calm: there was no attempt to arm, no buckling on of scaled
cuirass, no shield, no spear in hand, no girding on of his sword.
He sat firmly on the imperial throne, gazing cheerfully on them,
encouraging and inspiring the hearts of all with confidence, while
he took counsel with his kinsmen and generals about future
action. In the first place he insisted that no one whatever should
leave the ramparts to attack the Latins, for two reasons: because
of the sacred character of the day (it was the Thursday of Holy
Week, the supreme week of the year, in which the Saviour suffered an ignominious death on behalf of the whole world); and
secondly because he wished to avoid bloodshed between Christians. On several occasions he sent envoys to the Latins advising
them to desist from such an undertaking. 'Have reverence,' he said,
'for God on this day was sacrificed for us all, refusing neither the
Cross, nor the nails, nor the spear – proper instruments of punishment for evildoers – to save us. If you must fight, we too shall be
ready, but after the day of the Saviour's resurrection.' They, far
from listening to his words, rather reinforced their ranks, and so
thick were the showers of their arrows that even one of the emperor's retinue, standing near the throne, was struck in the chest.
Most of the others ranged on either side of the emperor, when
they saw this, began to withdraw, but he remained seated and un-
ruffled, comforting them and rebuking them in a gentle way – to
the wonder of all. However, as he saw the Latins brazenly approaching the walls and rejecting sound advice, he took active
steps for the first time. His son-in-law Nicephorus (my Caesar)
was summoned.† He was ordered to pick out the best fighters,
expert archers, and post them on the ramparts; they were to fire
volleys of arrows at the Latins, but without taking aim and mostly
off-target, so as to terrify the enemy by the weight of the attack, but
at all costs to avoid killing them. As I have remarked, he was fearful of desecrating that day and he wished to prevent fratricide.

* 2 April 1097; the reference is to the capture of the city by Alexius in 1081.
† Nicephorus Bryennius, later Anna's husband.

Other picked men, most of them carrying bows, but some wielding long spears, he ordered to throw open the gate of St Romanus and make a show of force with a violent charge against the enemy; they were to be drawn up in such a way that each lancer had two peltasts [foot-soldiers] to protect him on either side. In this formation they would advance at a walking pace, but send on ahead a few skilled archers to shoot at the Celts from a distance and alter direction, right or left, from time to time; when they saw that the space between the two armies had been reduced to a narrow gap, then the officers were to signal the archers accompanying them to fire thick volleys of arrows at the horses, not at the riders, and gallop at full speed against the enemy. The idea was partly to break the full force of the Celtic attack by wounding their mounts (they would not find it easy to ride in this condition) and partly (this was more important) to avoid the killing of Christians. The emperor's instructions were gladly followed. The gates were flung open; now the horses were given their head, now reined in. Many Celts were slain, but few of the Romans on that day were wounded. We will leave them and return to the Caesar, my lord. Having taken his practised bowmen, he set them on the towers and fired at the barbarians. Every man had a bow that was accurate and far-shooting. They were all young, as skilled as Homer's Teucer in archery. The Caesar's bow was truly worthy of Apollo. Unlike the famous Greeks of Homer he did not 'pull the bowstring until it touched his breast and draw back the arrow so that the iron tip was near the bow';* he was making no demonstration of the hunter's skill, like them. But like a second Hercules he shot deadly arrows from deathless bows and hit the target at will. At other times, when he took part in a shooting contest or in a battle, he never missed his aim: at whatever part of a man's body he shot, he invariably and immediately inflicted a wound there. With such strength did he bend his bow and so swiftly did he let loose his arrows that even Teucer and the two Ajaxes were not his equal in archery. Yet, despite his skill, on this occasion he respected the holiness of the

* The Caesar was Nicephorus Bryennius; the quotation is from *Iliad*, IV.123.

day and kept in mind the emperor's instructions, so that when he saw the Franks recklessly and foolishly coming near the walls, protected by shield and helmet, he bent his bow and put the arrow to the bowstring, but purposely shot wide, shooting sometimes beyond the target, sometimes falling short. Although, for the day's sake, he refrained from shooting straight at the Latins, yet whenever one of them in his foolhardiness and arrogance not only fired at the defenders on the ramparts, but seemingly poured forth a volley of insults in his own language as well, the Caesar did bend his bow. 'Nor did the dart fly in vain from his hand,' but pierced the long shield and cleft its way through the corselet of mail, so that arm and side were pinned together. 'Straightway he fell speechless to the ground,' as the poet says, and a cry went up to heaven as the Romans cheered their Caesar and the Latins bewailed their fallen warrior. The battle broke out afresh, their cavalry and our men on the walls both fighting with courage; it was a grim, dour struggle on both sides. However, when the emperor threw in his guards, the Latin ranks turned in flight. On the next day Hugh advised Godfrey to yield to the emperor's wish, unless he wanted to learn a second time how experienced a general Alexius was. He should take an oath, he said, to bear his true allegiance. But Godfrey rebuked him sternly. 'You left your own country as a king,' he said, 'with all that wealth and a strong army; now from the heights you've brought yourself to the level of a slave. And then, as if you had won some great success, you come here and tell me to do the same.' 'We ought to have stayed in our own countries and kept our hands off other peoples',' replied Hugh. 'But since we've come thus far and need the emperor's protection, no good will come of it unless we obey his orders.' Hugh was sent away with nothing achieved. Because of this and reliable information that the counts coming after Godfrey were already near, the emperor sent some of his best officers with their troops to advise him once more, even to compel him to cross the Straits. No sooner were they in sight when the Latins, without a moment's hesitation, not even waiting to ask them what they wanted, launched an attack and began to fight them. In this fierce engagement many on both sides fell and all the emperor's men who had attacked with such recklessness were wounded. As the Romans showed greater spirit the Latins gave way. Thus Godfrey not long after submitted; he came to the emperor and swore on oath as he was directed that whatever cities, countries or forts he might in future subdue, which had in the first place belonged to the Roman empire, he would hand over to the officer appointed by the emperor for this very purpose. Having taken the oath he received generous largess, was invited to share Alexius' hearth and table, and was entertained at a magnificent banquet, after which he crossed over to Pelecanum and there pitched camp.* The emperor then gave orders that plentiful supplies should be made available for his men.

In the wake of Godfrey came Count Ralph,† with fifteen thousand cavalry and foot-soldiers. He encamped with his attendant counts by the Propontis near the patriarch's monastery; the rest he quartered as far as Sosthenium along the shore. Following Godfrey's example he procrastinated, waiting for the arrival of those coming after him, and the emperor who dreaded it (guessing what was likely to happen) used every means, physical and psychological, to hurry them into crossing the Straits. For instance, Opus‡ was summoned – a man of noble character, unsurpassed in his knowledge of things military – and when he presented himself before the emperor he was despatched overland with other brave men to Ralph. His instructions were to force the Frank to leave for the Asian side. When it was clear that Ralph had no intention of going, but in fact adopted an insolent and quite arrogant attitude to the emperor, Opus armed himself and set his men in battle order, maybe to scare the barbarian. He thought this might persuade him to set sail. But the Celtic reaction was immediate: with his available men he accepted the challenge, 'like a lion who rejoices when he has found a huge prey'. There and then he started a violent battle. At this moment

* Godfrey crossed *c*.20 February 1097.   † Nothing is known of his origins.
‡ Opus was another experienced Greek general.

Pegasius* arrived by sea to transport them to the other side and when he saw the fight on land and the Celts throwing themselves headlong at the Roman ranks, he disembarked and himself joined in the conflict, attacking the enemy from the rear. In this fight many men were killed, but a far greater number were wounded. The survivors, under the circumstances, asked to be taken over the Straits; reflecting that if they joined Godfrey and told him of their misfortunes he might be stirred to action against the Romans, the emperor prudently granted their request; he gladly put them on ships and had them transported to the Saviour's tomb, especially since they themselves wanted this. Friendly messages, offering great expectations, were also sent to the counts whom they were awaiting. Consequently, when they arrived, they willingly carried out his instructions. So much for Count Ralph. After him came another great contingent, a numberless heterogeneous host gathered together from almost all the Celtic lands with their leaders (kings and dukes and counts and even bishops). The emperor sent envoys to greet them as a mark of friendship and forwarded politic letters. It was typical of Alexius: he had an uncanny prevision and knew how to seize a point of vantage before his rivals. Officers appointed for this particular task were ordered to provide victuals on the journey – the pilgrims must have no excuse for complaint for any reason whatever. Meanwhile they were eagerly pressing on to the capital. One might have compared them for number to the stars of heaven or the grains of sand poured out over the shore; as they hurried towards Constantinople they were indeed 'numerous as the leaves and flowers of spring' (to quote Homer). For all my desire to name their leaders, I prefer not to do so. The words fail me, partly through my inability to make the barbaric sounds – they are so unpronounceable – and partly because I recoil before their great numbers. In any case, why should I try to list the names of so enormous a multitude, when even their contemporaries became indifferent at the sight of them? When they did finally arrive in the capital, on the

* Greek naval commander.

emperor's orders they established their troops near the monastery of St Cosmas and St Damian. It was not nine heralds, after the old Greek custom, who 'restrained them with cries', but a considerable number of soldiers who accompanied them and persuaded them to obey the emperor's commands. With the idea of enforcing the same oath that Godfrey had taken, Alexius invited them to visit him separately. He talked with them in private about his wishes and used the more reasonable among them as intermediaries to coerce the reluctant. When they rejected advice – they were anxiously waiting for Bohemund to come – and found ingenious methods of evasion by making new demands, he refuted their objections with no difficulty at all and harried them in a hundred ways until they were driven to take the oath.* Godfrey himself was invited to cross over from Pelecanum to watch the ceremony. When all, including Godfrey, were assembled and after the oath had been sworn by every count, one nobleman dared to seat himself on the emperor's throne. Alexius endured this without a word, knowing of old the haughty temper of the Latins, but Count Baldwin went up to the man, took him by the hand and made him rise. He gave him a severe reprimand: 'You ought never to have done such a thing, especially after promising to be the emperor's liege-man. Roman emperors don't let their subjects sit with them. That's the custom here and sworn liege-men of His Majesty should observe the customs of the country.' The man said nothing to Baldwin, but with a bitter glance at Alexius muttered some words to himself in his own language: 'What a peasant! He sits alone while generals like these stand beside him!' Alexius saw his lips moving and calling one of the interpreters who understood the language asked what he had said. Being told the words he made no comment to the man at the time, but kept the remark to himself. However, when they were all taking their leave of him, he sent for the arrogant, impudent fellow and asked who he was, where he came from and what his lineage was. 'I am a pure Frank', he replied, 'and of noble birth. One thing I know: at

* A sign of the importance of the oath to Alexius' view of the enterprise.

a crossroads in the country where I was born is an ancient shrine;* to this anyone who wishes to engage in single combat goes, prepared to fight; there he prays to God for help and there he stays awaiting the man who will dare to answer his challenge. At that crossroads I myself have spent time, waiting and longing for the man who would fight – but there was never one who dared.' Hearing this the emperor said, 'If you didn't get your fight then, when you looked for it, now you have a fine opportunity for many. But I strongly recommend you not to take up position in the rear of the army, nor in the van; stand in the centre with the *hemilochitae* [junior officers]. I know the enemy's methods. I've had long experience of the Turk.' The advice was not given to him alone, but as they left he warned all the others of the manifold dangers they were likely to meet on the journey. He advised them not to pursue the enemy too far, if God gave them the victory, lest falling into traps set by the Turkish leaders they should be massacred.

The role of Bohemund on crusade proved to be most controversial. For the laudatory author of the Gesta Francorum, *Bohemund was a hero traduced and betrayed by an unscrupulous and treacherous Emperor Alexius. In what is almost a mirror image, Anna Comnena's apologia for her father's policy ascribed nefarious intent to Bohemund, who came to represent all that was deceitful, ambitious and dangerous about western warlords. In the trading of blame and exoneration, Bohemund's stay at Constantinople in April 1097 became a central moment in respective demonologies and eulogies. First, the* Gesta Francorum *gives its account of Bohemund's journey to and stay in Constantinople.*

Then we† set out and travelled through very rich country from one village to another, and from one city to another and from one castle to another, until we came to Castoria, where we held the feast of Christmas and stayed for some days trying to buy

* Possibly at Soissons.
† Note the personal touch, not necessarily to be taken literally.

provisions, but the inhabitants would sell us none, because they were much afraid of us, taking us to be no pilgrims but plunderers come to lay waste the land and to kill them. So we seized oxen, horses and asses, and anything else we could find, and leaving Castoria we went into Monastir where there was a castle of heretics.* We attacked this place from all sides and it soon fell into our hands, so we set fire to it and burnt the castle and its inhabitants together. After this we reached the River Vardar, and my lord Bohemund crossed over with some of his men, but not all, for the count of Russignolo and his brothers stayed behind. The emperor's army came up and attacked the count and his brothers and all their men, so when Tancred heard of this he went back and, diving into the river, he swam across to the others, with two thousand men following him. They found Turcopuli and Patzinaks fighting with our men, so they made a sudden and gallant attack and, since they were men of experience, they defeated the enemy and took many prisoners whom they bound and led before my lord Bohemund. He said to them, 'You scoundrels, why do you kill Christ's people and mine? I have no quarrel with your emperor!' They answered, 'We cannot do anything else. We are at the emperor's command, and whatever he orders, that we must do.' Bohemund let them go scot-free. This battle was fought on the fourth day of the week, which was Ash Wednesday.† Blessed be God in all his works!

The wretched‡ emperor commanded one of his own men, who was very dear to him and whom they call the *kyriopalatios*,§ to accompany our messengers so that he might guide us safely through his country until we came to Constantinople. Whenever we passed by any of their cities this man used to tell the people of the land to bring us provisions, as those whom we have

---

* Perhaps Manichaean heretics, supposedly not uncommon in the Balkans at the time.   † 18 February 1097.
‡ Note the pejorative epithet applied to Alexius.
§ Lord of the imperial palace.

mentioned before used to do. It was clear that they were so much afraid of my lord Bohemund's strong army* that they would not allow any of our men to go inside the walls of the cities. Our men wanted to attack one of the castles and take it, because it was full of goods of all kinds, but the valiant Bohemund would not allow this, for he wished to treat the country justly and to keep faith with the emperor, so he was furious with Tancred and all the others. This happened one evening, and next morning the inhabitants of the castle emerged in procession, carrying crosses in their hands, and came into the presence of Bohemund, who received them with joy and let them also go away rejoicing. After this we reached a town called Serres, where we encamped and had provisions good enough for Lent. While we were there Bohemund made an agreement with two of the *kyriopalatioi*, and because of his friendship with them and his desire to treat the country justly he ordered all the animals which our men had stolen and kept to be given back. Thereafter we reached the city of Rusa.† The Greek inhabitants came out and approached my lord Bohemund rejoicing, bringing us plenty of provisions, so we pitched our tents there on the Wednesday in Holy Week.‡ While we were there Bohemund left his army, and went ahead to Constantinople with a few knights to take counsel with the emperor. Tancred stayed behind with the army of Christ, and when he saw that the pilgrims were buying food he had the idea of turning aside from the road and bringing the people where they could live in plenty; so that he went into a certain valley full of all kinds of things which are good to eat, and there we kept the festival of Easter with great devotion.

When the emperor had heard that Bohemund, that most distinguished man, had come, he ordered him to be received with proper ceremony, but took care to lodge him outside the city. After Bohemund had settled in, the emperor sent to invite him to a secret conference. Duke Godfrey and his brother [Baldwin of Boulogne] were also present, and the count of St Gilles [Ray-

---

* Actually Bohemund's was probably one of the smallest of the leaders' contingents.   † Unidentified place west of the River Maritza.   ‡ 1 April 1097.

mond IV, count of Toulouse] was near the city. Then the emperor, who was troubled in mind and fairly seething with rage, was planning how to entrap these Christian knights by fraud and cunning, but by God's grace neither he nor his men found place or time to harm them. At last all the elders of Constantinople, who were afraid of losing their country, took counsel together and devised a crafty plan of making the dukes, counts and all the leaders of our army swear an oath of fealty to the emperor. This our leaders flatly refused to do, for they said, 'Truly, this is unworthy of us, and it seems unjust that we should swear to him any oath at all.'

Perhaps, however, we were fated to be misled often by our leaders, for what did they do in the end? They may say that they were constrained by need, and had to humble themselves willy-nilly to do what that abominable emperor wanted.

Now the emperor was much afraid of the gallant Bohemund, who had often chased him and his army from the battlefield, so he told Bohemund that he would give him lands beyond Antioch, fifteen days' journey in length and eight in width, provided that he would swear fealty with free consent, and he added this promise, that if Bohemund kept his oath faithfully he would never break his own. But why did such brave and determined knights do a thing like this? It must have been because they were driven by desperate need.*

The emperor for his part guaranteed good faith and security to all our men, and swore also to come with us, bringing an army and a navy, and faithfully to supply us with provisions both by land and sea, and to take care to restore all those things which we had lost. Moreover he promised that he would not cause or permit anyone to trouble or vex our pilgrims on the way to the Holy Sepulchre.

The count of St Gilles was encamped outside the city in the suburbs, and his army had stayed behind, so the emperor ordered

* Compare the other accounts that provide very different explanations for Bohemund's behaviour. These are examined by J. Shepard, 'When Greek Meets Greek', *Byzantine and Modern Greek Studies*, xii (1988).

him to do homage and swear fealty as the others had done; but when the emperor sent him this message the count was planning how to revenge himself on the imperial army. Duke Godfrey and Robert, count of Flanders, and the other leaders, however, told him that it would be improper to fight against fellow Christians, and the valiant Bohemund said that if Count Raymond did any injustice to the emperor, or refused to swear fealty to him, he himself would take the emperor's part. Therefore the count took the advice of his friends and swore that he would respect the life and honour of Alexius, and neither destroy them nor permit any-one else to do so; but when he was asked to do homage he said that he would not, even at the peril of his life.* After this my lord Bohemund's army came up to Constantinople.

Anna Comnena describes the meeting between Norman warrior and Byzantine emperor.

Knowing that he himself was not of noble descent, with no great military following because of his lack of resources, [Bohemund] wished to win the emperor's good will, but at the same time to conceal his own hostile intentions against him. With only ten Celts he hurried to reach the capital before the rest.† Alexius understood his schemes – he had long experience of Bohe-mund's deceitful, treacherous nature – and desired to talk with him before his companions arrived; he wanted to hear what Bohemund had to say and while he still had no chance of corrupting the rest (they were not far away now) he hoped to persuade him to cross over to Asia. When Bohemund came into his presence, Alexius at once gave him a smile and enquired about his journey. Where had he left the counts? Bohemund replied frankly and to the best of his knowledge to all these ques-tions, while the emperor politely reminded him of his daring deeds at Larissa and Dyrrhachium;‡ he also recalled Bohe-mund's former hostility. 'I was indeed an enemy and foe then,'

---

* For Raymond of Aguilers's fuller explanation, see below, pp. 106–7.
† Bohemund reached Constantinople *c.*10 April 1097.   ‡ In 1082–3 and 1085.

said Bohemund, 'but now I come of my own free will as Your Majesty's friend.' Alexius talked at length with him, in a somewhat discreet way trying to discover the man's real feelings, and when he concluded that Bohemund would be prepared to take the oath of allegiance, he said to him, 'You are tired now from your journey. Go away and rest. Tomorrow we can discuss matters of common interest.' Bohemund went off to the Cosmidium, where an apartment had been made ready for him and a rich table was laid full of delicacies and food of all kinds. Later the cooks brought in meat and flesh of animals and birds, uncooked. 'The food, as you see, has been prepared by us in our customary way,' they said, 'but if that does not suit you here is raw meat which can be cooked in whatever way you like.' In doing and saying this they were carrying out the emperor's instructions. Alexius was a shrewd judge of a man's character, cleverly reading the innermost thoughts of his heart, and knowing the spiteful, malevolent nature of Bohemund, he rightly guessed what would happen. It was in order that Bohemund might have no suspicions that he caused the uncooked meat to be set before him at the same time, and it was an excellent move. The cunning Frank not only refused to taste any of the food, but would not even touch it with his fingertips; he rejected it outright, but divided it all up among the attendants, without a hint of his own secret misgivings. It looked as if he was doing them a favour, but that was mere pretence: in reality, if one considers the matter rightly, he was mixing them a cup of death. There was no attempt to hide his treachery, for it was his habit to treat servants with utter indifference. However, he told his own cooks to prepare the raw meat in the usual Frankish way. On the next day he asked the attendants how they felt. 'Very well,' they replied and added that they had suffered not the slightest harm from it. At these words he revealed his hidden fear: 'For my own part,' he said, 'when I remembered the wars I have fought with him, not to mention the famous battle, I was afraid he might arrange to kill me by putting a dose of poison in the food.' Such were the actions of Bohemund. I must say I have never seen an evil man who in all his deeds and words did not depart far from the path of right; whenever a man leaves the middle course, to whatever extreme he inclines he takes his stand far from virtue. Bohemund was summoned then and required, like the others, to take the customary Latin oath. Knowing what his position was he acquiesced gladly enough, for he had neither illustrious ancestors nor great wealth (hence his forces were not strong – only a moderate number of Celtic followers).* In any case Bohemund was by nature a liar. After the ceremony was over, Alexius set aside a room in the palace precincts and had the floor covered with all kinds of wealth: clothes, gold and silver coins, objects of lesser value filled the place so completely that it was impossible for anyone to walk in it. He ordered the man deputed to show Bohemund these riches to open the doors suddenly. Bohemund was amazed at the sight. 'If I had had such wealth,' he said, 'I would long ago have become master of many lands.' 'All this', said the man, 'is yours today – a present from the emperor.' Bohemund was overjoyed. After accepting the gift and thanking him for it, he went off to rest at his lodging-place. Yet when the things were brought to him, although he had expressed such admiration before, he changed. 'I never thought I should be so insulted by the emperor,' he said. 'Take them away. Give them back to the sender.' Alexius, familiar with the Latins' characteristic moodiness, quoted a popular saying: 'His mischief shall return upon his own head.' Bohemund heard about this, and when he saw the servants carefully assembling the presents to carry them away, he changed his mind once more; instead of sending them off in anger he smiled on them, like a sea-polypus which transforms itself in a minute. The truth is that Bohemund was a habitual rogue, quick to react to fleeting circumstance; he far surpassed all the Latins who passed through Constantinople at that time in rascality and courage, but he was equally inferior in wealth and resources. He was the supreme mischief-maker. As for inconstancy, that followed automatically – a trait common to all

* A reference to the origins of Bohemund's father, Robert Guiscard, a younger son of a minor aristocratic family of Hauteville in Normandy.

Latins. It was no surprise then that he should be overjoyed to receive the money he had formerly refused. When he left his native land, he was a soured man, for he had no estates at all. Apparently he left to worship at the Holy Sepulchre, but in reality to win power for himself – or rather, if possible, to seize the Roman empire itself, as his father had suggested. He was prepared to go to any length, as they say, but a great deal of money was required. The emperor, aware of the man's disagreeable, ill-natured disposition, cleverly sought to remove everything that contributed to Bohemund's secret plans. When therefore Bohemund demanded the office of domestic of the east, he was not granted his request; he could not 'out-Cretan the Cretan', for Alexius was afraid that once possessed of authority he might use it to subjugate all the other counts and thereafter convert them easily to any policy he chose. At the same time, because he did not wish Bohemund to suspect in any way that his plans were already detected, he flattered him with fine hopes. 'The time for that is not yet ripe, but with your energy and loyalty it will not be long before you have even that honour.' After a conversation with the Franks and after showing his friendship for them with all kinds of presents and honours, on the next day he took his seat on the imperial throne. Bohemund and the others were sent for and warned about the things likely to happen on their journey. He gave them profitable advice. They were instructed in the methods normally used by the Turks in battle; told how they should draw up a battle line, how to lay ambushes; advised not to pursue far when the enemy ran away in flight. In this way, by means of money and good advice, he did much to soften their ferocious nature. Then he proposed that they should cross the Straits. For one of them, Raymond, the count of St Gilles, Alexius had a deep affection, for several reasons: the count's superior intellect, his untarnished reputation, the purity of his life. He knew moreover how greatly Raymond valued the truth: whatever the circumstances, he honoured truth above all else. In fact, St Gilles outshone all Latins in every quality, as the sun is brighter than the stars. It was for this that Alexius detained him for some time.* Thus, when all the others had taken their leave of him and made the journey across the Straits of the Propontis to Damalium, and when he was now relieved of their troublesome presence, he sent for him on many occasions. He explained in more detail the adventures that the Latins must expect to meet with on their march; he also laid bare his own suspicions of their plans. In the course of many conversations on this subject he unreservedly opened the doors of his soul, as it were, to the count; he warned him always to be on his guard against Bohemund's perfidy, so that if attempts were made to break the treaty he might frustrate them and in every way thwart Bohemund's schemes. St Gilles pointed out that Bohemund inherited perjury and guile from his ancestors – it was a kind of heirloom. 'It will be a miracle if he keeps his sworn word,' he said. 'As far as I am concerned, however, I will always try to the best of my ability to observe your commands.' With that he took his leave of the emperor and went off to join the whole Celtic army.† Alexius would have liked to share in the expedition against the barbarians, too, but he feared the enormous numbers of the Celts. He did think it wise, though, to move to Pelecanum.‡ Making his permanent headquarters near Nicaea, he could obtain information about their progress and at the same time about Turkish activities outside the city, as well as about the condition of the inhabitants inside. It would be shameful, he believed, if in the mean time he did not himself win some military success. When a favourable opportunity arose, he planned to capture Nicaea himself; that would be preferable to receiving it from the Celts (according to the agreement already made with them). Nevertheless he kept the idea to himself. Whatever dispositions he made, and the reasons for them, were known to himself alone, although he did entrust this task to Butumites (his sole confi-

---

* In fact Raymond had caused the most difficulty in swearing an oath; only later did relations warm between him and Alexius. Anna reverses the responses of Raymond and Bohemund at Constantinople.
† Count Raymond reached Nicaea on 16 May 1097.
‡ On the Asiatic side of the Sea of Marmara; see map p. xliv.

dant). Butumites was instructed to suborn the barbarians in Nicaea by all kinds of guarantees and the promise of a complete amnesty, but also by holding over them the prospect of this or that retribution – even massacre – if the Celts took the city. He had long been assured of Butumites' loyalty and he knew that in such matters he would take energetic measures. The history of the foregoing events has been set out in chronological order from the beginning.

The last to arrive at Constantinople were the forces of Duke Robert II of Normandy and his brother-in-law Count Stephen of Blois. Setting out from northern France in September or October 1096 with Count Robert II of Flanders, they travelled via Italy. While Robert of Flanders, who had old family ties with the Greek emperor, hastened across the Adriatic, Duke Robert and Count Stephen wintered in Italy before embarking for Byzantium, arriving at the imperial capital only in mid-May 1097 when most of the host had already assembled at the siege of Nicaea.* With Count Stephen travelled Fulcher of Chartres who kept a careful record of the journey for inclusion in his Historia.

In the year 1096 of the Lord's Incarnation and in the month of March following the council, which, as has been said, Pope Urban held during November in Auvergne, some who were more speedy in their preparation than others began to set out on the holy journey. Others followed in April or May, in June or in July, or even in August or September or October as they were able to secure the means to defray expenses.†

In that year peace and a very great abundance of grain and wine existed in all countries by the grace of God, so that there was no lack of bread on the trip for those who had chosen to follow him with their crosses in accordance with his commands.

Since it is fitting to remember the names of the leaders of the pilgrims at that time I mention Hugh the Great, the brother of

* See below, p. 108.
† Urban set 15 August as the departure date; see above, p. 25.

King Philip of France, the first of the heroes to cross the sea. Hugh landed with his men near Durazzo, a city in Bulgaria,* but rashly advancing with a small force was captured there by the citizens and conducted to the emperor at Constantinople. Here he stayed for some time, being not entirely free.

After him Bohemund of Apulia, a son of Robert Guiscard, of the nation of the Normans, passed with his army over the same route. Next Godfrey, duke of Lorraine, travelled through Hungary with a large force. Raymond, count of the Provençals, with Goths and Gascons, and also Adhemar, bishop of Le Puy, crossed through Dalmatia.

A certain Peter the Hermit, having gathered to himself a crowd of people on foot but only a few knights, was the first to pass through Hungary. Afterwards Walter the Penniless, who was certainly a very good soldier, was the commander of these people. Later he was killed with many of his companions between Nicomedia and Nicaea by the Turks.†

In the month of October, Robert, count [i.e. duke] of the Normans, a son of William, king of the English, began the journey, having collected a great army of Normans, English and Bretons. With him went Stephen, the noble count of Blois, his brother-in-law, and Robert, count of the Flemings, with many other nobles.‡

Therefore since such a multitude came from all western countries, little by little and day by day the army grew while on the march from a numberless host into a group of armies. You could see a countless number from many lands and of many languages. However, they were not gathered into a single army until we reached the city of Nicaea.§

What then shall I say? The islands of the seas and all the kingdoms of the earth were so moved that one believed the prophecy of David fulfilled, who said in his psalm, 'All the nations whom thou hast made shall come and worship before thee, O Lord',¶

---

* The Balkans; October 1096.   † 21 October 1096.
‡ Stephen, count of Blois and Chartres; Robert II, count of Flanders.
§ Robert of Normandy and Count Stephen were the last to reach Nicaea, 3 June 1097.   ¶ Psalms 86:9.

and what those who arrived later deservedly said, 'We shall worship in the place where His feet have stood.'* Of this journey moreover we read much more in the prophets which it would be tedious to repeat.

Oh, what grief there was! What sighs, what weeping, what lamentation among friends when husband left his wife so dear to him, his children, his possessions however great, his father and mother, brothers and other relatives!

But however many tears those remaining shed for departing friends and in their presence, none flinched from going because for love of God they were leaving all that they possessed, firmly convinced that they would receive a hundredfold what the Lord promised to those who loved him.

Then husband told wife the time he expected to return, assuring her that if by God's grace he survived he would come back home to her. He commended her to the Lord, kissed her lingeringly, and promised her as she wept that he would return. She, though, fearing that she would never see him again, could not stand but swooned to the ground, mourning her loved one whom she was losing in this life as if he were already dead. He, however, like one who had no pity – although he had – and as if he were not moved by the tears of his wife nor the grief of any of his friends – yet secretly moved in his heart – departed with firm resolution.

Sadness was the lot of those who remained, elation, of those who departed. What then can we say further? 'This is the Lord's doing, and it is marvellous in our eyes.'†

Then we western Franks crossed Gaul and travelling through Italy came to Lucca, a most famous city. Near there we met Pope Urban; and Robert the Norman, Count Stephen of Blois, and others of us who desired talked with him. After we had received his blessing we went on to Rome rejoicing.‡

When we entered the basilica of the blessed Peter we found the men of Guibert, that stupid pope, in front of the altar. With

---

* Psalms 132:7.   † Psalms 118:23.

‡ Note the first person, implying Fulcher's presence.

swords in hand they wickedly snatched the offerings placed there on the altar. Others ran along the rafters of the monastery itself and threw stones at us as we lay prostrate in prayer. For when they saw anyone faithful to Urban they straightway wished to kill him.

Moreover in one tower of the basilica were the men of the Lord Urban. They were guarding it well and faithfully and as far as possible were resisting his adversaries. For that we grieved when we saw such an outrage committed there. But we heartily desired that nothing be done except as vengeance by the Lord. Many who had come thus far with us hesitated no longer but returned to their homes, weakened by cowardice.

We, however, travelled through the middle of Campania and reached Bari, a very wealthy city situated by the side of the sea. There in the church of the blessed Nicholas we prayed fervently to God, and then we went down to the harbour hoping to cross at once. But because the seamen objected, saying that fortune was perverse and the winter season was coming, which would expose us to dangers, Count Robert of Normandy was obliged to withdraw into Calabria and spent the entire winter there. But Robert, count of Flanders, crossed with his whole force at once.*

At that time many of the common people who were left [to their own resources] and who feared privation in the future sold their weapons and again took up their pilgrims' staves, and returned home as cowards. For this reason they were regarded as despicable by God as well as by mankind, and it redounded to their shame.

In the year of our Lord 1097, with the return of spring in March, the Norman count and Count Stephen of Blois with all of his followers, for Stephen likewise had been awaiting an opportune time for the crossing, again turned towards the sea. When the fleet was ready in the nones of April which then happened to be on the holy day of Easter,† they embarked at the port of Brindisi.

'How unsearchable are the judgements of God, how in-

* Early December 1096.   † 5 April 1097.

scrutable His ways!'* For among all these ships we saw one near the shore which suddenly cracked through the middle for no apparent reason. Consequently, four hundred of both sexes perished by drowning, but concerning them joyous praise at once went up to God. For when those standing round about had collected as many bodies of the dead as possible, they found crosses actually imprinted in the flesh of some of them, between the shoulders. For it was fitting that this same symbol of victory, which they had worn on their clothes while living, should remain by the will of God as a token of faith upon those thus occupied in his service. At the same time it was also proper that such a miracle should show those who witnessed it that the dead had now attained by the mercy of God the peace of eternal life. Thus it was most certainly manifest that the scriptural prophecy had been fulfilled: 'The just, though they shall be taken prematurely by death, shall be in peace.'†

Of the others now struggling with death but few survived. Their horses and mules were swallowed up by the waves, and much money was lost. At the sight of this disaster we were much afraid; so much so that many faint-hearted who had not yet embarked returned to their homes, giving up the pilgrimage and saying that never again would they entrust themselves to the treacherous sea.

We, however, relying implicitly on Almighty God, put out to sea in a very gentle breeze with sails hoisted and to the sound of many trumpets. For three days we were detained at sea by the lack of wind. On the fourth day‡ we reached land near the city of Durazzo, about ten miles distant I judge. Our fleet entered two harbours. Then joyfully indeed we set foot on dry land and crossed over in front of the aforementioned city.

And so we passed through the lands of the Bulgars in the midst of steep mountains and desolate places. Then we all came to a swift stream called the River of the Demon by the local inhabitants and justly so.§ For we saw many people of the common sort

* Romans 11:33.   † Wisdom 4:7.
‡ 9 April 1097.   § The River Skumbi.

perish in this river, people who hoped to wade across step by step but who were suddenly engulfed by the strong force of the current. Not one of the onlookers was able to save any of them. Wherefore we shed many tears from compassion. Many of the foot-soldiers would have lost their lives in the same manner had not the knights with their trained horses brought aid to them. Then we pitched camp near the shore and spent one night. On all sides were great mountains which were uninhabited.

At daybreak the trumpets sounded, and we began to climb the mountain which is called Bagora. After we had crossed the mountain and passed through the cities of Ochrida, Monastir, Edessa and Stella we reached a river called the Vardar. Although it was customary to cross this river only by boat we joyfully waded across with the aid of God. The following day we camped in front of the city of Thessalonica [Salonica], a city rich in goods of all kinds.

After a stop of four days* we travelled across Macedonia through the valley of Philippi [Angista] and through Crisopolis, Christopolis [Kavalla], Praetoria [Peritheorion, Jenidscheh], Messinopolis [Mosynopolis], Macra [Makri], Traianopolis [Orichova], Neapolis, Panadox [Panidos], Rodosto [Tekirdagh], Heraclea [Ereghli], Salumbria [Silivri], and Natura [Athyra, Buyukcekmece] and thus reached Constantinople. We pitched our tents before this city and rested fourteen days.†

But we did not try to enter the city because it was not agreeable to the emperor (for he feared that possibly we would plot some harm to him). Therefore it was necessary for us to buy our daily supplies outside the walls. These supplies the citizens brought to us by order of the emperor. We were not allowed to enter the city except at the rate of five or six each hour. Thus while we were leaving, others were entering to pray in the churches.

Oh, what a noble and beautiful city is Constantinople! How many monasteries and palaces it contains, constructed with wonderful skill! How many remarkable things may be seen in the principal avenues and even in the lesser streets! It would be very

* 22–6 April 1097.   † 14–28 May 1097.

tedious to enumerate the wealth that is there of every kind, of gold, of silver, of robes of many kinds, and of holy relics. Merchants constantly bring to the city by frequent voyages all the necessities of man. About twenty thousand eunuchs, I judge, are always living there.

After we were sufficiently rested our leaders, after taking counsel, made under oath an agreement with the emperor at his insistence. Bohemund and Duke Godfrey who had preceded us had already agreed to it. But Count Raymond refused to subscribe.* However, the count of Flanders took the oath as did the others. For it was essential that all establish friendship with the emperor since without his aid and counsel we could not easily make the journey, nor could those who were to follow us by the same route. To them [the princes] indeed the emperor himself offered as many *numisma*† and garments of silk as pleased them, and the horses and money which they needed for making such a journey.

When this was done we crossed the sea which is called the Arm of St George, and then hurried on to the city of Nicaea.‡ Lord Bohemund, Duke Godfrey, Count Raymond and the count of Flanders had already been besieging it since the middle of May. It was then in the possession of the Turks, a valiant race from the east skilled with the bow. They had crossed the Euphrates river from Persia fifty years before and had subjugated the whole Roman land as far as the city of Nicomedia.§

Oh, how many severed heads and how many bones of the slain we found lying in the fields near the sea around Nicomedia! In that year the Turks had annihilated our people, who were ignorant of the arrow and new to its use. Moved by pity at this sight we shed many tears.¶

* More complicated than that; see Raymond of Aguilers, below, pp. 106–7.
† Greek gold coin.   ‡ 3 June 1097.
§ The Seljuks, who had penetrated Iraq in the 1050s and Anatolia in the 1070s.
¶ Refers to the slaughter of the followers of Peter the Hermit and others killed in the area September–October 1096.

Only a fortnight before Duke Robert and Count Stephen reached Nicaea on 3 June, the Provençal army under Raymond IV, count of Toulouse and St Gilles, and Urban II's chosen legate, Bishop Adhemar of Le Puy, had arrived to join the siege. Their journey from southern France had been dogged with problems. Avoiding the sea-crossing of the Adriatic, either because of numbers, expense or the wintry weather, the Provençals found themselves struggling down the Dalmatian coast at the bitter turn of the year 1096–7 before the long march across the Balkans, only reaching Constantinople in late April and, after tetchy negotiations over the oath of allegiance demanded by Alexius, Nicaea on 16 May. The often painful passage of the Provençal army east was described in occasionally resentful detail by Count Raymond's chaplain, Raymond of Aguilers.*

Following its departure, the army entered Slavonia and underwent many privations during the winter season.† Truly, Slavonia is a forsaken land, both inaccessible and mountainous, where for three weeks we saw neither wild beasts nor birds. The barbarous and ignorant natives would neither trade with us nor provide guides, but fled from their villages and strongholds and, as though they had been badly injured by our infirm stragglers, slew these poor souls – the debilitated, the old women and men, the poor and the sick – as if they were slaughtering cattle. Because of the familiarity of the Slavs with the countryside, it was difficult for our heavily armed knights to give chase to these unarmed robbers through the midst of rugged mountains and very dense forests. Yet our army endured these marauders because our soldiers could neither fight them in the open nor avoid skirmishes with them.

We break our story at this point to relate a glorious encounter of the count which occurred one day along the route when Raymond and his band, upon finding themselves hedged in by the Slavs, rushed and captured some six of them. The count, now

* See above, pp. xxv–xxvii.
† The Provençals were in Slavonia, which roughly corresponds to modern Dalmatia, December 1096 to January 1097.

sorely pressed by their menacing comrades, realised that he must break through to his army, and so gave a command to snatch out the eyes of some of his captives, to cut off the feet of others, and to mangle the nose and hands of yet others and abandon them. Thus, he and his comrades fled to safety while the enemy were horror-stricken by the gruesome sight of their mutilated friends and paralysed by grief. In such manner he was freed from the agony of death and this perilous place by God's goodness.

Actually, we find it difficult to report the bravery and judgement displayed by Raymond in Slavonia. For almost forty days we journeyed in this land, at times encountering such clouds of fog that we could almost touch these vapours and shove them in front of us with our bodies. In the midst of these dangers the count always protected his people by fighting in the rearguard and by being the last one to reach his quarters. Some might return to camp in the middle of the day or at sundown, but not Raymond, who frequently arrived at his tent in the middle of the night or at the cock's crow.

We passed through Slavonia without losses from starvation or open conflict largely through God's mercy, the hard work of the count, and the counsel of Adhemar. This successful crossing of the barbarous lands leads us to believe that God wished his host of warriors to cross through Slavonia in order that brutish, pagan men, by learning of the strength and long-suffering of his soldiers, would at some time recover from their savageness or as unabsolved sinners be led to God's doom.

Upon our arrival at Scutari* after our strenuous passage across Slavonia, the count affirmed brotherhood and bestowed many gifts upon the king of the Slavs so that the crusaders could buy in peace and look for the necessities of life.† But this was only an illusion, for we sorely regretted our trust in the sham peace when the Slavs took advantage of the occasion, went berserk as was their custom, slew our people and snatched what they could from the unarmed. You may well believe we prayed

---

* Shkodër in Albania; late January 1097.
† Possibly a local magnate called Bodin.

for a refuge and not for revenge; but why should we continue this dreary account of Slavonia?

On our encampment at Durazzo* we were confident that we were in our land, because we believed that Alexius and his followers were our Christian brothers and confederates. But truly, with the savagery of lions they rushed upon peaceful men who were oblivious of their need for self-defence. These brigands, operating by night, slew our people in groves and places far from camp and stole what they could from them. While the Greeks acted thus without restraint, their leader, John Comnenus,† promised peace; but during such a truce they killed Pontius Rainaud and fatally wounded his brother, Peter, two most noble princes.‡ We had a chance for vengeance, but we renewed our march in preference to vindicating our injustices. *En route*, we had letters concerning security and brotherhood, and I may say of filiation, from the emperor; but these were empty words, for before and behind, to the right and to the left Turks, Cumans, Uzes and the tenacious peoples – Pechenegs and Bulgars – were lying in wait for us.§

To add to our troubles, one day we were in the valley of Monastir¶ when the Pechenegs captured the bishop of Le Puy, who had wandered a short time from camp looking for a comfortable lodging. They threw him from his mule, stripped him, and struck him heavily upon the head. But one of the fellow Pechenegs, while seeking gold from Adhemar, saved him from his fellow brigands; and so the great bishop, indispensable to God's justice, was spared to mankind because of God's compassion. When the commotion was heard in camp, the attacking crusaders saved the bishop from the Pechenegs, who had been slow in despatching him.

Thus, surrounded by treacherous imperial soldiers, we came to a fort, Bucinat, where Raymond heard that the Pechenegs lay in ambush for us in the defiles of a nearby mountain.** The

* Early February 1097.   † Alexius' nephew.
‡ Pontius Rainard and his brother Peter, Provençal knights.
§ The Provençals took the Via Egnatia across the Balkan peninsula.
¶ Mid-February 1097.   ** Bucinat not identified.

count turned the tables by lying in ambush for them, and, along with his knights, took these mercenaries by surprise in a sudden attack, killing many and routing the others. In the midst of these events mollifying despatches from Alexius arrived; yet still the enemy encircled us, and on all sides we were confronted with the emperor's deceit.

Soon thereafter we arrived at Rusa, a town where the open contempt of its citizens so strained our customary forbearance that we seized arms, broke down the outer walls, captured great booty, and received the town in surrender.* We then left after we had raised our banner over the town and shouted *Tolosa*, the rallying cry of the count. Our march took us thence to Rodosto [Tekirdagh],† where mercenary troops of Alexius, anxious to avenge the Rusa defeat, attacked us; but we slew a number of these hirelings and took some loot.

Now our agents returned to us at Rodosto from the court of Alexius where we had sent them. They brought rosy reports of Byzantine promises largely because the emperor bribed them; thus the following events need no further comment. Byzantine and crusader envoys urged Raymond to abandon his army and, unarmed with a few followers, to hurry to the court of the *basileus* [emperor]. They reported that Bohemund, the duke of Lorraine, the count of Flanders, and other princes besought Raymond to make a pact concerning the crusade with Alexius, who might take the Cross and become leader of God's army.‡ They added that Alexius was willing to transact all affairs beneficial to the trip with the count in matters pertaining to him and to others. They further stated that the absence of such a great man's advice on the eve of combat would be unfortunate. Therefore, they pressed Raymond to come to Constantinople with a small force so that upon completion of arrangements with Alexius there would be no delay of the march. Raymond followed this advice, left a garrison in camp, and preceded the army on

* Keshan in Thrace, 12 April 1097.
† Count Raymond met Greek envoys there 18 April 1097.
‡ For these negotiations see above and below, pp. 82–5, 101, 106–7.

this mission, going alone and unarmed to Constantinople.

Thus far, the recording of these deeds, deeds marked by both a joyous and prosperous course, has been an agreeable task to the writer. However, the story is now pressed so with the burden of harshness and grief that it wearies me that I began what I have sworn to complete. Frankly, I do not know how to record these events in their importance. Shall I write of the most fraudulent and abominable treachery of the emperor's counsel? Or shall I record the most infamous escape of our army and its unimaginable helplessness? Or by relating the deaths of such great princes, shall I leave a memorial of eternal grief? To the contrary, let whoever wishes to know enquire from others rather than from us.

However, we shall report this very important occurrence. While all of our people dreamed of leaving camp, fleeing, forsaking their comrades, and giving up all which they had carried from faraway lands, they were led back to such a steadfast strength through the saving grace of repentance and fasting that only their former ignominy of desperation and desire for flight strongly embarrassed them. But we shall tarry no longer with this sad account.

Upon the most honourable reception of Raymond by Alexius and his princes,* the *basileus* demanded from the count homage and an oath which the other princes had sworn to him. Raymond responded that he had not taken the Cross to pay allegiance to another lord or to be in the service of any other than the one for whom he had abandoned his native land and his paternal goods. He would, however, entrust himself, his followers and his effects to the emperor if he would journey to Jerusalem with the army. But Alexius temporised by excusing himself from the march on the grounds that he was afraid that the Germans, Hungarians, Cumans and other fierce people would plunder his empire if he undertook the march with the pilgrims.

In the mean time the count, after learning of the rout and death of his men, believed that he had been misled and through

* Raymond reached Constantinople *c*.27 April 1097.

the services of some of our leaders summoned the emperor on charges of betraying the crusaders. But Alexius replied that he himself had been unaware that our troops had plundered his kingdom and that his people had borne many wrongs, and that he knew of no legal grounds for the count's investigation unless it was that while Raymond's army in its accustomed way was ravaging villages and walled towns his men fled at the sight of the imperial army. Yet he promised he would make amends to the count, and he gave Bohemund as a hostage of his pledge. They came to judgement, and the count, contrary to justice, was compelled to free his hostage.

Meanwhile, our army arrived in Constantinople and after it came the bishop with his brother, whom he had left ill in Durazzo. Alexius sent word again and again promising that he would reward the count handsomely if he would pay the same homage as the other princes; but Raymond brooded over revenge for unjust treatment of himself and his men and sought means to remove the shame of such ill fame. However, the duke of Lorraine and the count of Flanders and other princes deplored such thoughts, saying that it was the height of folly for Christians to fight Christians when the Turks were near at hand. Bohemund, in fact, pledged his support to Alexius in case Raymond took action against him or if the count longer excused himself from homage and an oath. At this juncture, following consultation with his Provençals, the count swore that he would not, either through himself or through others, take away from the emperor life and possessions. When he was cited concerning homage, he replied that he would not pay homage because of the peril to his rights. We may add that Alexius gave him little of worldly goods because of his intransigence.*

---

* Raymond's conditional oath may have been modelled on Provençal custom, but it scarcely altered the relationship and obligations to Alexius that all the leaders shared.

IV

The First Victories

May–October 1097

The siege of Nicaea (6 May–19 June 1097), capital of the Seljuk sultan of Rum, Kilij Arslan I, saw the western host assembled together for the first time. Although it bore the brunt of the action and the attempts to break the siege by Kilij Arslan, it failed to storm the city, whose surrender was eventually negotiated by Alexius I using his fleet to impose a complete blockade by land and water. Many crusaders appeared disgruntled at the consequent lack of booty, for which Alexius soon compensated by showering the commanders with gifts. The siege tested the crusaders' mettle as soldiers and as allies, in their relations both with one another and of the whole army with Alexius. On those scores, the challenge was well met, the westerners displaying the ordered adaptability and ingenuity of tactics and military methods that came to characterise the rest of the long campaign. The four main narrators supplied their own distinctive accounts, reflecting their different loyalties and, in part, for the three western writers, the actual contrast in their personal experience of the siege.

The Gesta Francorum

Tancred and Richard of the Principality crossed the Hellespont secretly, because they did not want to take the oath to the emperor, and nearly all Bohemund's forces went with them. Soon afterwards the count of St Gilles approached Constantinople, and he stayed on there with his forces. Bohemund stayed with the emperor in order to consult him about the supply of provisions to the people who had gone on beyond Nicaea, so

Duke Godfrey was the first to go to Nicomedia, taking with him Tancred and all the others. They stayed there for three days, and when the duke saw that there was no road by which he could lead these people to Nicaea (for there were so many of them that they could not go by the route which the other [crusaders]* had followed) he sent ahead three thousand men with axes and swords so that they could go on and hack open a route for our pilgrims as far as the city of Nicaea. This route led over a mountain, steep and very high, so the pathfinders made crosses of metal and wood, and put them upon stakes where our pilgrims could see them. Eventually we came to Nicaea, which is the capital of Rum,† on Wednesday, 6 May, and there we encamped. Before my lord the valiant Bohemund came to us we were so short of food that a loaf cost 20 or 30 pence, but after he came he ordered plenty of provisions to be brought to us by sea, so goods poured in by both land and sea, and all Christ's army enjoyed great abundance.

On Ascension Day‡ we began to lay siege to the town, and to build siege engines and wooden towers by means of which we could knock down the towers on the wall. We pressed the siege so bravely and fiercely for two days that we managed to undermine the wall of the city, but the Turks who were inside sent messengers to the others who had come to their help, telling them that they might come and enter, fearlessly and safely, by way of the south gate, for there was no one there to stand in their way or attack them. This gate, however, was blocked on that very day (the Saturday after Ascension Day) by the count of St Gilles and the bishop of Le Puy. The count, who came from the other side of the city with a very strong army, trusting in God's protection and glorious in his earthly weapons, found the Turks coming towards the gate against our men. Protected on all sides by the sign of the Cross, he made a fierce attack upon the enemy and defeated them so that they took to flight and many of them were killed. The survivors rallied with the help of other Turks and

* Peter the Hermit's followers (*alii*, i.e. 'others', in the Latin text).
† Seljuk sultanate of Rum or, more generally, Asia Minor.   ‡ 14 May 1097.

came in high spirits, exulting in their certainty of victory, bringing with them ropes with which to lead us bound into Khorasan. They came along gleefully and began to descend a little way from the top of the mountain, but as many as came down had their heads cut off by our men, who threw the heads of the slain into the city by means of a sling, in order to cause more terror among the Turkish garrison.

After this the count of St Gilles and the bishop of Le Puy took counsel together how they could undermine a tower which stood over against their camp, so they set men to sap it, with arbalests and archers to protect them. The sappers dug down to the foundations of the wall and inserted beams and pieces of wood, to which they set fire, but because all this was done in the evening it was already night when the tower fell, and since it was dark our men could not fight with the defenders. That night the Turks arose in haste and rebuilt the wall so strongly that at daybreak there was no chance of defeating them at that point.

Soon afterwards Robert, count of Normandy, and Count Stephen* arrived with many others, and Roger of Barneville† followed them. Then Bohemund took up his station in front of the city, with Tancred next to him, then Duke Godfrey and the count of Flanders, next to whom was Robert of Normandy, and then the count of St Gilles and the bishop of Le Puy. The city was therefore so closely besieged by land that no one dared go out or in. Our men were all, for the first time, collected together in this place, and who could count such a great army of Christians? I do not think that anyone has ever seen, or will ever again see, so many valiant knights.

On one side of the city was a great lake, on which the Turks launched boats, and they went in and out bringing fodder and wood and many other things, so our leaders took counsel together and sent messengers to Constantinople to ask the emperor

* Stephen, count of Blois and Chartres, husband of Adela, daughter of William the Conqueror, and so Duke Robert's brother-in-law.
† Vassal of Count Roger of Sicily; died heroically at Antioch 4 June 1098; later a hero of vernacular *chansons*.

to have boats brought to Cibotus, where there is a harbour, and to have oxen collected to drag these boats over the mountains and through the woods until they reached the lake. The emperor had this done immediately, and sent his Turcopuli with them. His men would not launch the boats at once on the day on which they arrived, but they put out on the lake at nightfall, with the boats full of Turcopuli who were well armed. At daybreak there were the boats, all in very good order, sailing across the lake towards the city. The Turks, seeing them, were surprised and did not know whether it was their own fleet or that of the emperor, but when they realised that it was the emperor's they were afraid almost to death, and began to wail and lament, while the Franks rejoiced and gave glory to God. Then the Turks, realising that their armies could do no more to help them, sent a message to the emperor saying that they would surrender the city to him if he would let them go free with their wives and children and all their goods. The emperor, who was a fool as well as a knave, told them to go away unhurt and without fear; he had them brought to him at Constantinople under safe conduct, and kept them carefully so that he could have them ready to injure the Franks and obstruct their crusade.

We besieged this city for seven weeks and three days, and many of our men suffered martyrdom there and gave up their blessed souls to God with joy and gladness, and many of the poor starved to death for the name of Christ. All these entered heaven in triumph, wearing the robe of martyrdom which they have received, saying with one voice, 'Avenge, O Lord, our blood which was shed for thee, for thou art blessed and worthy of praise for ever and ever. Amen.'

Raymond of Aguilers

We hastened to Nicaea, where Godfrey, Bohemund and other leaders, who were in the vanguard, besieged Nicaea, a city well protected by natural terrain and clever defences.* Its natural

* Count Raymond arrived 16 May 1097.

fortifications consisted of a great lake lapping at its walls and a ditch, brimful of run-off water from nearby streams, blocking entrance on three sides. Skilful men had enclosed Nicaea with such lofty walls that the city feared neither the attack of enemies nor the force of any machine. The *ballistae** of the nearby towers were so alternately faced that no one could move near them without peril, and if anyone wished to move forward, he could do no harm because he could easily be struck down from the top of a tower.

In short, as we have said, Bohemund besieged the town from the north, the duke and the Germans from the east, the count and the bishop of Le Puy from the south; and for the record the count of Normandy was absent.† At this time we must record the following event. While the count of Toulouse wished to encamp there, the Turks marched down from the mountains in two bodies and fell upon our army. Doubtless they had made their plans with the hope that while one contingent fought Godfrey and the Germans encamped to the east, the other group of Turks would enter Nicaea through the south gate and go out by another gate and thereby easily rout our unsuspecting forces. But God, the customary scourge of wicked counsel, ruined their schemes so that it seems that he planned the battle according to the following outcome. God caused the count, who at that moment was about to make camp with his men, to attack that body of Turks which at the very same time was on the point of entering Nicaea. In the first charge Raymond routed and killed many of the Turks and then chased the remaining ones to a nearby mountain, while at the same time the Turks who had planned to rush the Germans were likewise put to flight and crushed.

Following this success, we built machines and stormed the wall, all to no purpose. The wall was almost impregnable, and the courageous defence with arrows and machines was frustrating. Finally, after five weeks of fruitless siege, through God's will some troops of the entourage of Adhemar and Raymond after a skirmish pushed forward at great peril to the foot of a tower.

* Often crossbow-like artillery.   † Robert of Normandy arrived 3 June 1097.

Under the protection of a *testudo* [siege shelter] they sapped, undermined, and toppled it to the ground. The coming of night prevented the capture of Nicaea. By the next morning our efforts proved futile, because under the cover of darkness the defenders had restored the walls. Nicaea, gripped by fear, surrendered in great part because Greek ships which had been drawn overland now floated on the lake. Consequently, the Turks, isolated from their friends by this act, bowed to Alexius as they no longer hoped for help while they daily watched the Frankish army grow, a fact accented even more by the arrival of the count of Normandy.

Alexius had pledged to the princes and the Frankish people that he would hand over to them all of the gold, silver, horses and effects of all kinds which were in Nicaea; and he further stated that he would found there a Latin monastery and hospice for needy Franks. He also promised to give so much to every person in the army that every soldier would wish to serve him at all times. The Franks trusted these sincere words and praised the surrender. But once in possession of Nicaea, Alexius acted as such an ingrate to the army that as long as he might live people would ever revile him and call him traitor.

At this time we learned that when Peter the Hermit and his peasant hordes had arrived in Constantinople months before the main crusading force, Alexius had betrayed him by forcing Peter and his followers, unfamiliar with both the locale and the art of war, to cross the Straits with no defence against the Turks. So the Nicene Turks, sensing an easy kill, rapidly and easily butchered sixty thousand peasants and missed only the survivors who escaped their swords by taking refuge in a fortress. The victors, emboldened and made arrogant by their success, sent the captured weapons and crusaders to their noblemen and to Saracen leaders in distant places, and wrote throughout their lands that the Franks were unwarlike.*

---

* These crusaders had been destroyed September/October 1096.

Fulcher of Chartres

When they who were besieging Nicaea heard, as has been said, of the arrival of our leaders, the count of Normandy and Stephen of Blois, they joyfully came out to meet us and escorted us to a place south of the city where we pitched our tents.

Once before,* the Turks had gathered in force hoping to drive the besiegers away from the city if possible or else to defend it with their own soldiers more effectively. But they were fiercely thrown back by our men, nearly two hundred of them being killed. Moreover when they saw that the Franks were so inspired and so strong in military valour they retreated in haste into the interior of Romania [Anatolia] until such time as they should feel the occasion opportune for attacking again.

It was the first week in June when we, the last to arrive, reached the siege. At that time a single army was formed from the many that were there. Those skilled at reckoning estimated it to number six hundred thousand men accustomed to war. Of these, one hundred thousand were protected by coats of mail and helmets. In addition there were those not bearing arms, viz. the clerics, monks, women and children.†

What further then? If all who departed from their homes to undertake the holy journey had been present there doubtless would have been six million fighting men. But from Rome, from Apulia, from Hungary or from Dalmatia, some, unwilling to undergo the hardships, had returned to their homes. In many places thousands had been killed, and some of the sick who went on with us finally died. You could see many graves along the roads and in the fields where our pilgrims had been publicly buried.

It should be explained that for as long as we besieged the city of Nicaea food was brought in by ocean ships with the consent of the emperor. Then our leaders ordered machines of war to be made, battering-rams, *scrofae*, wooden towers and *petrariae*.

---

* 16 May 1097.
† The figures are greatly inflated but the nature of the host is accurate.

Arrows were shot from bows and stones hurled from *tormenta.**
Our enemies and our own men fought back and forth with all
their might. We often assailed the city with our machines, but
because there was a strong wall facing us the assault would be
brought to naught. Turks struck by arrows or stones often perished and Franks likewise.

Truly you would have grieved and sobbed in pity when the
Turks killed any of our men in any way near the wall, for they
lowered iron hooks by means of ropes and snatched up the body
to plunder it. None of our men dared or were able to wrest such a
corpse from them. After stripping the bodies the Turks would
throw them outside [the walls].

Then with the aid of oxen and ropes we dragged some small
boats from Cibotus over the land to Nicaea and launched them
in the lake to guard the approach to the city lest the place be supplied with provisions.†

But after we had worn down the city by five weeks of siege and
had often terrified the Turks with our attacks, they meantime
held a council and, through intermediaries to the emperor,
secretly surrendered the city to him, a city already hard-pressed
by our power and skill.

Then the Turks admitted into it Turcopoles sent thither by the
emperor. These latter took possession of the city with all the
money in it in the name of the emperor just as he had commanded. Wherefore after all this money was seized the emperor
ordered gifts to be presented to our leaders, gifts of gold and silver and raiment; and to the foot-soldiers he distributed copper
coins which they call *tartara*. On that day when Nicaea was
seized or surrendered in this manner the month of June had
reached the solstice.‡

*Anna Comnena's detailed account of the siege of Nicaea, with her
description of how her father engineered its successful conclusion,*

* *Scrofa* ('sow') was a shed protecting sappers; *petrariae* and *tormenta* threw
stones.   † The boats were launched on the night of 17–18 June 1097.
‡ It was in fact taken on 19 June 1097, not on the solstice (20 June).

stands in marked contrast to the perfunctory record of the next crisis of the crusade at the battle of Dorylaeum (1 July). Once the western army marched out of Byzantine-held territory in the last days of June 1097, Anna's interest and possibly knowledge flagged, reviving briefly but unreliably when she considered events at Antioch in 1097–8.

Bohemund and all the counts met at a place from which they intended to sail across to Cibotus, and with Godfrey they awaited the arrival of St Gilles who was coming with the emperor. Thus with their forces united they would set out along the road to Nicaea. However, their numbers were so immense that further delay became impossible – the food supplies were deficient. So they divided their army in two: one group drove on through Bithynia and Nicomedia towards Nicaea; the other crossed the strait to Cibotus and assembled in the same area later. Having approached Nicaea in this manner they allotted towers and intervening battlements to certain sections. The idea was to make the assault on the walls according to these dispositions; rivalry between the various contingents would be provoked and the siege pressed with greater vigour. The area allotted to St Gilles was left vacant until he arrived. At this moment the emperor reached Pelecanum, with his eye on Nicaea (as I have already pointed out). The barbarians inside the city meanwhile sent repeated messages to the sultan [Kilij Arslan I] asking for help, but he was still wasting time and as the siege had already gone on for many days, from sunrise right up to sunset, their condition was obviously becoming extremely serious. They gave up the fight, deciding that it was better to make terms with the emperor than to be taken by the Celts. Under the circumstances they summoned Butumites, who had often promised in a never-ending stream of letters that this or that favour would be granted by Alexius, if only they surrendered to him. He now explained in more detail the emperor's friendly intentions and produced written guarantees. He was gladly received by the Turks, who had despaired of holding out against the overwhelming strength of their enemies; it was wiser, they thought, to cede Nicaea voluntarily to Alexius and share in his gifts, with honourable treatment, than to become the victims of war to no purpose. Butumites had not been in the place more than two days before St Gilles arrived, determined to make an attempt on the walls without delay; he had siege engines ready for the task. Meanwhile a rumour spread that the sultan was on his way. At this news the Turks, inspired with courage again, at once expelled Butumites. As for the sultan, he sent a detachment of his forces to observe the Frankish offensive, with orders to fight if they met any Celts. They were seen by St Gilles's men from a distance and a battle took place – but it went ill for the Turks, for the other counts and Bohemund himself, learning of the engagement, set aside up to two hundred men from each company, thus making up a considerable army, and sent them immediately to help. They overtook the barbarians and pursued them till nightfall. Nevertheless, the sultan was far from downcast at this setback; at sunrise the next morning he was in full armour and with all his men occupied the plain outside the walls of Nicaea. The Celts heard about it and they too armed themselves for battle. They descended on their enemies like lions. The struggle that then ensued was ferocious and terrible. All through the day it was indecisive, but when the sun went down the Turks fled. Night had ended the contest.* On either side many fell and most of them were killed; the majority of the fighters were wounded. So the Celts won a glorious victory. The heads of many Turks they stuck on the ends of spears and came back carrying these like standards, so that the barbarians, recognising afar off what had happened and being frightened by this defeat at their first encounter, might not be so eager for battle in future. So much for the ideas and actions of the Latins. The sultan, realising how numerous they were and after this onslaught made aware of their self-confidence and daring, gave a hint to the Turks in Nicaea: 'From now on do just what you consider best.' He already knew that they preferred to deliver up the city to Alexius than to become prisoners of the

* 16 May 1097.

Celts. Meanwhile St Gilles, setting about the task allotted to him, was constructing a wooden tower, circular in shape; inside and out he covered it with leather hides and filled the centre with intertwined wickerwork. When it was thoroughly strengthened, he approached the so-called Gonatas Tower. His machine was manned by soldiers whose job was to batter the walls and also by expert sappers, equipped with iron tools to undermine them from below; the former would engage the defenders on the ramparts above, while the latter worked with impunity below. In place of the stones they prised out, logs of wood were put in and when their excavations reached the point where they were nearly through the wall and a gleam of light could be seen from the far side, they set light to these logs and burned them. After they were reduced to ashes, Gonatas inclined even more, and merited its name [kneeling] even more than before. The rest of the walls were surrounded with a girdle of battering-rams and 'tortoises'; in the twinkling of an eye, so to speak, the outer ditch was filled with dust, level with the flat parts on either side of it. Then they proceeded with the siege as best they could.

The emperor, who had thoroughly investigated Nicaea, and on many occasions, judged that it could not possibly be captured by the Latins, however overwhelming their numbers. In his turn he constructed *helepoleis** of several types, but mostly to an unorthodox design of his own which surprised everyone. These he sent to the counts. He had, as we have already remarked, crossed with the available troops and was staying at Pelecanum near Mesampeli, where in the old days a sanctuary was built in honour of George, the great martyr. Alexius would have liked to accompany the expedition against the godless Turks, but abandoned the project after carefully weighing the arguments for and against: he noted that the Roman [Byzantine] army was hopelessly outnumbered by the enormous host of the Franks; he knew from long experience, too, how untrustworthy the Latins were. Nor was that all: the instability of these men and their treacherous nature might well sweep them again and again from one extreme to the other;

* Siege engines.

through love of money they were ready to sell their own wives and children for next to nothing. Such were the reasons which prevented him then from joining the enterprise. However, even if his presence was unwise, he realised the necessity of giving as much aid to the Celts as if he were actually with them. The great strength of its walls, he was sure, made Nicaea impregnable; the Latins would never take it. But when it was reported that the sultan was bringing strong forces and all necessary food supplies across the [Ascanian] lake,* with no difficulty at all, and these were finding their way into the city, he determined to gain control of the lake. Light boats, capable of sailing on its waters, were built, hoisted on wagons and launched on the Cibotus side. Fully armed soldiers were put on board, under the command of Manuel Butumites. Alexius gave them more standards than usual – so that they might seem far more numerous than they really were – and also trumpets and drums. He then turned his attention to the mainland. He sent for Taticius and Tzitas. With a force of brave peltasts, two thousand in all, they were despatched to Nicaea; their orders were to load their very generous supply of arrows on mules as soon as they disembarked and seize the fort of St George; at a good distance from the walls of Nicaea they were to dismount from their horses, go on foot straight for the Gonatas Tower and there take up position; they were then to form ranks with the Latins and acting under their orders assault the walls. Obedient to the emperor's instructions Taticius reported to the Celts that he had arrived with his army, whereupon everyone put on armour and attacked with loud shouts and war-cries. Taticius' men fired their arrows in great volleys while the Celts made breaches in the walls and kept up a constant bombardment of stones from their catapults. On the side of the lake the enemy were panic-stricken by the imperial standards and the trumpets of Butumites, who chose this moment to inform the Turks of the emperor's promises. The barbarians were reduced to such straits that they dared not even peep over the battlements of Nicaea. At the same time they gave up all hope of the sultan's coming. They decided it was better to hand

* See map p. xliv.

over the city and start negotiations with Butumites to that end. After the usual courtesies Butumites showed them the chryso-bull* entrusted to him by Alexius, in which they were not only guaranteed an amnesty, but also a liberal gift of money and honours for the sister and wife of the sultan. These offers were extended to all the barbarians in Nicaea without exception. With confidence in the emperor's promises the inhabitants allowed Butumites to enter the city. At once he sent a message to Taticius: 'The quarry is now in our hands. Preparations must be made for an assault on the walls. The Celts must be given that task too, but leave nothing to them except the wall-fighting round the ramparts. Invest the city at all points, as necessary, and make the attempt at sunrise.' This was in fact a trick to make the Celts believe that the city had been captured by Butumites in fighting; the drama of betrayal carefully planned by Alexius was to be concealed, for it was his wish that the negotiations conducted by Butumites should not be divulged to the Celts. On the next day the call to battle was sounded on both sides of the city: on one, from the mainland, the Celts furiously pressed the siege; on the other Butumites, having climbed to the battlements and set up there the imperial sceptres and standards, acclaimed the emperor to the accompaniment of trumpets and horns. It was in this way that the whole Roman force entered Nicaea. Nevertheless, knowing the great strength of the Celts, as well as their fickle nature and passionate, impulsive whims, Butumites guessed that they might well seize the fort if they once got inside. The Turkish satraps in Nicaea, moreover, were capable, if they wished, of throwing into chains and massacring his own force – in comparison with the Romans they were numerous. Therefore he took possession of the keys of the city gate at once. There was at this time only one gate allowing people to enter or leave, the others having been closed through fear of the Celts just beyond the walls. With the keys of this particular gate in his hands, he determined to reduce the number of satraps by a ruse. It was essential to have them at his mercy, if he was himself to avoid a catastrophe. He sent for them

* Literally 'golden bull', i.e. imperial proclamation.

and advised a visit to the emperor, if they wanted to receive from
him large sums of money, to be rewarded with high distinctions
and to find their names on the lists of annual pensioners. The
Turks were persuaded and during the night the gate was opened;
they were let out, a few at a time and at frequent intervals, to make
their way across the nearby lake to Rodomer and the half-caste
Monastras, who were stationed by St George's fort.* Butumites'
orders were that the satraps should be forwarded to the emperor
immediately they disembarked; not even for a brief moment were
they to be detained, lest uniting with the Turks sent on behind
them they might plot some mischief against the Romans. This was
in fact a simple prediction, an intuitive remark which could only
be attributed to the man's long experience, for as long as the new
arrivals were quickly sent on to Alexius the Romans were secure
and no danger whatever hung over them; but when Rodomer and
Monastras relaxed their vigilance they found themselves in peril
from the barbarians whom they kept back. The Turks, as their
numbers grew, planned to take one of two courses: either in the
night they would attack and kill the Romans, or they would bring
them as prisoners to the sultan. The latter was unanimously
decided to be the better idea. They did attack in the night and took
them away as their captives. The place they made for was the
hilltop of Azala . . .† stades from the walls of Nicaea. Having arrived there they naturally dismounted to rest their horses. Now
Monastras was a half-caste and understood the Turkish dialect;
Rodomer, too, having been captured by the Turks long ago and
having lived with them for a considerable time, was himself not
unacquainted with their language. They tried hard to move their
captors with persuasive arguments. 'Why are you mixing a lethal
potion for us, as it were, without deriving the slightest benefit for
yourselves? When the others without exception are enjoying great
rewards from the emperor and having their names enrolled for
annual pensions, you will be cutting yourselves off from all these
privileges. Well now, don't be such fools, especially when you can

* Rodomer the Bulgarian was a cousin of Anna; Monastras, half Greek, half
Turk, was a widely experienced general.   † Gap in text.

live in safety without interference and return home exulting in riches. You may perhaps acquire new territory. Don't throw yourselves into certain danger. Maybe you'll meet Romans lying in ambush over there,' pointing to mountain streams and marshy parts; 'if you do, you'll be massacred and lose your lives for nothing. There are thousands of men lying in wait for you, not only Celts and barbarians, but a multitude of Romans as well. Now if you take our advice, you will turn your horses' heads and come to the emperor with us. We swear, as God is our witness, that you will enjoy countless gifts at his hands, and then, when it pleases you, you will leave as free men, without hindrance.' These arguments convinced the Turks. Pledges were exchanged and both parties set out on their way to Alexius. On their arrival at Pelecanum, all were received with a cheerful smile (although inwardly he was very angry with Rodomer and Monastras). For the present they were sent off to rest, but on the next day all those Turks who were eager to serve him received numerous benefits; those who desired to go home were permitted to follow their own inclination – and they too departed with not a few gifts. It was only later that Alexius severely reprimanded Rodomer and Monastras for their folly, but seeing that they were too ashamed to look him in the face, he altered his attitude and with words of forgiveness strove to conciliate them. We will leave Rodomer and Monastras there. Let us come back to Butumites. When he was promoted duke of Nicaea at that time by the emperor, the Celts asked him for permission to enter the city: they desired to visit the sacred churches there and worship. Butumites, as I have already remarked, was well aware of the Celtic disposition and a visit *en masse* was refused. However, he did open the gates for groups of ten.

The emperor was still in the vicinity of Pelecanum. He wished those counts who had not yet sworn allegiance to give him their pledges in person. Written instructions were issued to Butumites to advise all counts not to begin the march to Antioch before doing homage to the emperor; this would be an opportunity for them to accept even greater gifts. Hearing of money and gifts,

Bohemund was the first to obey Butumites' advice. He immediately counselled all of them to return. Bohemund was like that
– he had an uncontrollable lust for money. The emperor welcomed them with great splendour at Pelecanum. He was most
sedulous in promoting their welfare. Finally he called them
together and spoke: 'Remember the oath you have all sworn to
me and if you really intend not to transgress it, advise any others
you know, who have not sworn, to take this same oath.' They at
once sent for these men and all, with the exception of Tancred,
Bohemund's nephew, assembled to pay homage. Tancred, a man
of independent spirit, protested that he owed allegiance to one
man only, Bohemund, and that allegiance he hoped to keep till
his dying day. He was pressed by the others, including even the
emperor's kinsmen. With apparent indifference, fixing his gaze
on the tent in which the emperor held the seat of honour (a tent
more vast than any other in living memory), he said, 'If you fill it
with money and give it to me, as well as the sums you have given
to all the other counts, then I too will take the oath.' Palaeologus,
zealous on the emperor's behalf and finding Tancred's words
insufferable and hypocritical, pushed him away with contempt.*
Tancred recklessly darted towards him, whereupon Alexius rose
from his throne and intervened. Bohemund, for his part, calmed
down his nephew, telling him it was improper to behave with
disrespect to the emperor's relatives. Tancred, ashamed now of
acting like a drunken lout before Palaeologus and to some extent
convinced by the arguments of Bohemund and the others, took
the oath. When all had taken their leave of the emperor, Taticius
and the forces under his command were ordered to join the
Franks; Taticius' duty would be to help and protect them on all
occasions and also to take over from them any cities they captured, if indeed God granted them that favour.† Once more
therefore the Celts made the crossing on the next day and all set

* George Palaeologus, a Comnenan loyalist, friend of Alexius, was later one of
Anna's sources.
† Taticius had experience of leading western troops against the Pechenegs in
the Balkans in the early 1090s.

out for Antioch. Alexius assumed that not all their men would necessarily follow the counts; he accordingly notified Butumites that all Celts left behind were to be hired to guard Nicaea. Taticius, with his forces, and all the counts, with their numberless hosts, reached Lefke in two days. At his own request Bohemund was in charge of the vanguard, while the rest followed in column of march at a slow pace. When some Turks saw him moving rather fast on the plain of Dorylaeum* they thought they had chanced upon the whole Celtic army and treating it with disdain they at once attacked. That crazy idiot, Latinus, who had dared to seat himself on the imperial throne, forgetting the emperor's advice stupidly rode out in front of the rest (he was on the extreme end of Bohemund's line). Forty of his men were killed then and he himself was seriously wounded. He turned in flight and hurried back to the centre – visible proof, although he would not admit it in words, of Alexius' wise counsel. Bohemund, seeing the ferocity of the Turks, sent for reinforcements, which quickly arrived. From then on the battle was hotly contested, but the terrible conflict ended in a victory for the Romans and Celts.† After that the march continued, but with the contingents in touch with one another. They were met near Hebraice‡ by the sultan Tanisman§ and Hasan, who alone commanded eighty thousand fully armed infantry. It was a hard-fought battle, not only because of the vast numbers involved, but also because neither side would give way. However, the Turks were fighting with more spirit and Bohemund, commanding on the right wing, realised this. So, detaching himself from the rest of the army, he made a headlong onslaught on Kilij Arslan himself, charging 'like a lion exulting in his might', as the poet says. This had a terrifying effect on the enemy and they fled. The Celts, remembering the emperor's instructions, did not pursue them very far, but they

* 1 July 1097.
† Notice the prominence given to the Greeks not mentioned in western sources; Taticius was in the vanguard with Bohemund on the march from Nicaea.   ‡ Heraclea; some confusion by Anna here.
§ Perhaps Malik Ghazi Gumushtigin, the Danishmend leader.

occupied the Turkish entrenchment and rested there for a short time. They again fell in with the Turks near Augustopolis,* attacked and routed them completely. After that the barbarians faded away. The survivors from the battle were scattered in all directions, leaving behind their women and children and making certain of their own safety in flight; in future they had not even the strength to look the Latins in the face.

The battle of Dorylaeum (1 July 1097) tested the western army almost to destruction. Fought, as scholars now convincingly propose, some thirty miles north of Dorylaeum (Eskisehir), the narrow escape at the hands of the Turks under Kilij Arslan I demonstrated certain crucial military truths. The western army's columns were spread over many miles, marching up to two days apart. The vanguard, under Bohemund, Tancred, Robert of Normandy and Stephen of Blois, became detached from the rest. Entering a narrow valley, they were ambushed by the Turks who almost overran the Christians as they desperately attempted to defend a hastily constructed armed camp next to a marsh. Only determined and skilled leadership by Bohemund in particular held the line together long enough for the rest of the crusader forces under Count Raymond, Bishop Adhemar, Hugh of Vermandois and Godfrey of Bouillon to arrive on the field and, by an outflanking manoeuvre, to turn the tide of battle so decisively that the Turks fled, leaving their own camp to be plundered by the Christians at will. The lessons taken from this alarming and, as the accounts suggest, frightening encounter included the understanding of the need for closer formation on the march; recognition of the outstanding ability of Bohemund as a field commander; and awareness of the Turkish tactics of harrying, ambush and the feint by their lightly armed cavalry. Quickly the westerners learned to adapt to local military as well as physical conditions. But the whole enterprise had almost fallen at its second hurdle. Of the three eyewitness accounts, the Gesta *author (with Bohemund) and Fulcher of Chartres (with Robert of Normandy and Stephen of Blois) viewed the battle from the perspective of the*

---

* North-west of Iconium; unlikely.

beleaguered vanguard, while Raymond of Aguilers – whose account is notable for omitting a description of the privations experienced in central Anatolia – reflects the Provençal army's relief operation that finally swung the battle the crusaders' way.

The Gesta Francorum

When the city had surrendered, and the Turks had been taken to Constantinople, the emperor was exceedingly glad because the city was put under his authority, and he ordered alms to be distributed bountifully to our poor pilgrims. On the first day after we left the city we came to a bridge, and there we stayed for two days. On the third day, before dawn, our men arose, and because it was dark they could not see to keep together, but divided into two bands, and thus they travelled for two days. In one band were the brave Bohemund, Robert the Norman and the gallant Tancred, with many others; in the other were the count of St Gilles and Duke Godfrey, the bishop of Le Puy, Hugh the Great and the count of Flanders, with many others.

On the third day the Turks made a fierce and sudden attack upon Bohemund and his comrades.* These Turks began, all at once, to howl and gabble and shout, saying with loud voices in their own language some devilish word which I do not understand. The valiant Bohemund saw that there were innumerable Turks some distance off, howling and shouting like demons, so he ordered all the knights to dismount at once and to pitch camp quickly. Before the camp was pitched he said to all the knights, 'Gentlemen, most valiant soldiers of Christ, you can see that we are encircled and that the battle will be hard, so let the knights go out to fight bravely, while the foot-soldiers are careful and quick in pitching the camp.'

After we had set ourselves in order the Turks came upon us from all sides, skirmishing, throwing darts and javelins and

---

* Battle of Dorylaeum, 1 July 1097; for site, probably thirty miles north of Dorylaeum (Eskisehir), see J. France, *Victory in the East* (Cambridge University Press, 1994), pp. 170–81.

shooting arrows from an astonishing range. Although we had no
chance of withstanding them or of taking the weight of the
charge of so many foes we went forward as one man. The women
in our camp were a great help to us that day, for they brought up
water for the fighting men to drink, and gallantly encouraged
those who were fighting and defending them. The valiant Bohemund made haste to send a message to the others (the count of
St Gilles and Duke Godfrey, Hugh the Great and the bishop of Le
Puy, with all the rest of the Christian knights) telling them to
hurry and come to the battlefield with all speed, and saying, 'If
any of you wants to fight today, let him come and play the man.'
So Duke Godfrey, who was reckless and brave, with Hugh the
Great, came first and arrived together, with their forces, and the
bishop of Le Puy followed them with his, and the count of St
Gilles came next with a great force.

Our men could not understand whence could have come
such a great multitude of Turks, Arabs, Saracens and other
peoples whose names I do not know, for nearly all the mountains and hills and valleys, and all the flat country within and
without the hills, were covered with this accursed folk. For our
part, we passed a secret message along our line, praising God
and saying, 'Stand fast all together, trusting in Christ and in the
victory of the Holy Cross. Today, please God, you will all gain
much booty.'*

Our line of battle formed up at once. On the left wing were the
valiant Bohemund, Robert the Norman, the gallant Tancred,
Robert of Anse and Richard of the Principality. The bishop of Le
Puy came round by the other mountain, so that he could take
those misbelieving Turks in the rear, and Raymond, count of St
Gilles and a very gallant knight, rode also on the left wing. On the
right wing were Duke Godfrey and the count of Flanders, who
was very eager to fight, and Hugh the Great with many others
whose names I do not know.

As soon as our knights charged, the Turks, Arabs, Saracens,

* A much-repeated passage indicating an army's need for plunder to survive
rather than deep-seated crusader mercenary motives.

Agulani* and all the rest of the barbarians took to their heels and fled through the mountain passes and across the plains. There were 360,000 Turks, Persians, Paulicians,† Saracens and Agulani, with other pagans, not counting the Arabs, for God alone knows how many there were of them. They fled very fast to their camp, but they were not allowed to stay there long, so they continued their flight and we pursued them, killing them, for a whole day, and we took much booty, gold, silver, horses, asses, camels, oxen, sheep and many other things about which we do not know. If God had not been with us in this battle and sent us the other army quickly, none of us would have escaped, because the fighting went on from the third hour until the ninth, but Almighty God, who is gracious and merciful, delivered his knights from death and from falling into the hands of the enemy and sent us help speedily. Yet two distinguished knights were killed, Godfrey of Monte Scaglioso‡ and William son of the marquis, Tancred's brother, together with other knights and foot-soldiers whose names I do not know.

What man, however experienced and learned, would dare to write of the skill and prowess and courage of the Turks, who thought that they would strike terror into the Franks, as they had done into the Arabs and Saracens, Armenians, Syrians and Greeks, by the menace of their arrows? Yet, please God, their men will never be as good as ours. They have a saying that they are of common stock with the Franks, and that no men, except the Franks and themselves, are naturally born to be knights. This is true, and nobody can deny it, that if only they had stood firm in the faith of Christ and holy Christendom, and had been willing to accept One God in Three Persons, and had believed rightly and faithfully that the Son of God was born of a virgin mother, that he suffered, and rose from the dead and ascended in the sight of his disciples into heaven, and sent them in full measure

---

* Possibly Albanians, but generally an exotic name used for effect, not analysis.
† Another exoticism; Paulicians followed the heresy of Paul of Samosata and denied the Orthodox divinity of Christ. The author is unlikely to have known this.   ‡ See above, p. 73n.

the comfort of the Holy Ghost, and that he reigns in heaven and earth, you could not find stronger or braver or more skilful soldiers; and yet by God's grace they were beaten by our men. This battle was fought on 1 July.

Fulcher of Chartres

When our barons received permission from the emperor to depart, we left Nicaea on the third day before the calends of July [29 June] to go into the interior parts of Romania. But when we had been on our way for two days, it was reported to us that the Turks had laid a trap for us in the plains through which they thought we would have to pass and that there they expected to do battle.*

When we heard this we did not lose courage.† But that evening when our scouts saw many of the Turks a long distance away, they at once notified us of it. Therefore that night we had our tents protected on all sides by watchmen. Early in the morning, which was on the calends of July,‡ we took up our arms and at the sound of the trumpet divided into battle wings with the tribunes and centurions skilfully leading the cohorts and centuries. With banners flying we began to advance in good order.

Then at the second hour of the day [7–8 a.m.], lo, their scouts approached our sentries! When we heard this we pitched our tents near a marsh and took off our pack-saddles in order that we would be better able to fight.

After this was done, behold! there were the Turks, those pagan Persians whose amir and prince was that Suleiman§ who had held the city of Nicaea and the country of Romania in his power. They had at Suleiman's command collected about him, having come to his aid for a distance of more than thirty days. There were present with him many amirs or princes, viz. Amircaradigum,

* 30 June 1097.
† Fulcher was with Bohemund, Robert of Normandy and the advance guard that was trapped by the Turks.
‡ 1 July 1097.   § i.e. Kilij Arslan I, sultan of Rum.

Miriathos and many others.* Altogether they numbered 360,000 fighters, that is to say, bowmen, for it was their custom to be armed in that manner. All were mounted. On the other hand we had both footmen and bowmen.

At that time Duke Godfrey, Count Raymond and Hugh the Great had been absent from us for two days. They had for some reason, I know not what, separated from us with a large number of men at a place where the road divided.† For that reason we suffered [in the ensuing battle] an irreparable loss because as many of our men were slain as there were Turks who escaped death or capture. Because those who were separated from us received our messengers late, they were tardy in coming to our aid.

Meanwhile the Turks were howling like wolves and furiously shooting a cloud of arrows. We were stunned by this. Since we faced death and since many of us were wounded we soon took to flight. Nor is this remarkable because to all of us such warfare was unknown.

And now from the other side of the marsh a dense mass of the enemy fiercely forced its way as far as our tents. The Turks entered some of these tents and were snatching our belongings and killing some of our people when by the will of God the advance guard of Hugh the Great, Count Raymond and Duke Godfrey came upon this disaster from the rear. Because our men had retreated to our tents those of the enemy who had entered fled at once thinking that we had suddenly returned to attack them. What they took for boldness and courage was, if they could have known, really great fear.

What shall I say next? We were all indeed huddled together like sheep in a fold, trembling and frightened, surrounded on all sides by enemies so that we could not turn in any direction. It was clear to us that this happened because of our sins. For luxury had defiled some of us, and avarice and other vice had corrupted others. A great clamour rose to the sky, not only from our men

* Garbled; possibly invented for generic exotic effect.
† At Lefke, south-east of Nicaea. See map p. xliv.

and our women and children but also from the pagans rushing upon us. By now we had no hope of surviving.

We then confessed that we were defendants at the bar of justice and sinners, and we humbly begged mercy from God. The bishop of Le Puy, our patron, and four other bishops were there, and a great many priests also, vested in white. They humbly besought God that he would destroy the power of our enemy and shed upon us the gifts of his mercy. Weeping they sang and singing they wept. Then many people fearing that death was nigh ran to the priests and confessed their sins.*

Our leaders, Count Robert of Normandy and Stephen, count of Blois, and Robert, count of Flanders, and Bohemund also, resisted the Turks as far as they were able and often tried to attack them. They were also strongly assailed by the Turks.

The Lord does not give victory to splendour of nobility nor brilliance in arms but lovingly helps in their need the pure in heart and those who are fortified with divine strength. Therefore he, perhaps appeased by our supplications, gradually restored our strength and more and more weakened the Turks. For when we saw our comrades hastening to our aid from the rear† we praised God and regained our courage and formed into troops and cohorts and strove to resist the enemy.

Oh, how many of our men straggling behind us on the road did the Turks kill that day! From the very first hour of the day until the sixth, as I have said, difficulties hampered us.‡ However, little by little our spirits revived as our comrades reinforced us and as divine grace was miraculously present, and then as if by sudden impulse the Turks all turned their backs in flight.

Shouting fiercely we followed them over the mountains and through the valleys. We did not cease pursuing them until our swiftest men had reached their tents. Then some of our men loaded many of the camels and horses of the Turks with their

* In fact Adhemar took an active role in leading the decisive pincer movement on the Turks' left flank.
† The main force of Godfrey, Raymond and Hugh.
‡ 6–7 a.m. to 11 a.m. to 12 noon; cf. the *Gesta* account above, pp. 126–9.

possessions and even with the tents abandoned there in panic. Others followed the fleeing Turks until nightfall. Because our horses were famished and exhausted we kept a few of theirs.

It was a great miracle of God that during the next and the third days the Turks did not cease to flee although no one, unless God, followed them further.

Gladdened by such a victory we all gave thanks to God. He had willed that our journey should not be brought entirely to naught but that it should be prospered more gloriously than usual for the sake of that Christianity which was his own. Wherefore from east to west the tidings shall resound forever.

Then indeed we continued our journey carefully. One day we suffered such extreme thirst that some men and women died from its torments. The Turks, fleeing before us in confusion, sought hiding-places for themselves throughout Romania.

Raymond of Aguilers

Following these events, we left Nicaea bound for Romania [Anatolia]; and on the march the next day Bohemund and some of the princes indiscreetly parted from the count, the bishop and the duke.* On the third day of Bohemund's diversionary march, as he was considering making camp, his soldiers beheld 150,000 men approaching in battle formation. While he formed his battle ranks according to circumstance and made ready for the fight, he lost many stragglers; and so as the skirmish heightened Bohemund summoned to his aid the count and the duke, who were only two miles distant. The help was not slow in coming. The crusaders donned their armour, mounted their steeds, and galloped off to fight the enemy shortly after Bohemund's messenger brought the news.

The sight of the onrushing knights chilled the hopes of Kilij Arslan, the attacking leader, and he fled precipitately. It seems to

* At Lefke, 27 June 1097; the advance guard contained Bohemund, Robert of Normandy and Taticius' Greeks; the rearguard was led by Count Raymond, Adhemar of Le Puy and Duke Godfrey of Lower Lorraine.

us that it was poetic justice that Kilij Arslan, who had seized captives and many tents from Bohemund, now through God's power abandoned his goods.* Although we did not see it, some recounted a remarkable miracle in which two handsome knights in flashing armour, riding before our soldiers and seemingly invulnerable to the thrusts of Turkish lances, menaced the enemy so that they could not fight. Although we learned this from apostate Turks now in our ranks, we can certify from evidence that for two days on the march we saw dead riders and dead horses.

Following the defeat and repulsion of the Turks, we rapidly crossed through Romania in peace although an illness of Raymond retarded the march a bit. Distasteful as the following may be to scoffers, it should be made a matter of public record because it is an account of the miracle-working of divine mercy. A Saxon count in our army, claiming to be a legate of St Gilles, said that he had been urged twice to command the count: 'Relax, you will not die of this infirmity because I have secured a respite for you from God and I shall always be at hand.' Although the count was most credulous, he was so weakened by the malady that when he was taken from his bed and placed upon the ground, he scarcely had a breath of life. So [William] the bishop of Orange read the office as if he were dead; but divine compassion, which had made him leader of his army, immediately raised him from death and returned him safe and sound.†

Between the battle on 1 July and the arrival of the main crusader force before Antioch on 20–2 October lay some of the most arduous and painful marching of the entire expedition. Casualties, especially among non-combatants, were high, through exhaustion, dehydration, malnutrition, disease and, in the long detour the main army took across the Anti-Taurus Mountains (September–October 1097), accident and hypothermia. The only concerted Turkish resistance

* Raymond of Aguilers was with the rearguard, unlike Fulcher or the author of the *Gesta*, who record events from the vanguard's perspective.
† Raymond of Aguilers is notable for omitting a description of the privations experienced during the passage of central Anatolia.

was brushed aside at Heraclea (Ereghli) c.10 September. There the army split; Tancred and Baldwin of Boulogne raided southwards through Cilicia, often in hostile competition with each other, capturing or liberating (many of the locals were Armenian Christians) Tarsus, Adana and Mamistra, before rejoining the main column in northern Syria in mid-October. Meanwhile, the bulk of the western force had headed north-east from Heraclea so as to come down on Antioch from the north through potentially friendly Armenian regions. Though costly in men and equipment, this circuitous march served the dual function of gaining allies and cutting Antioch off from a supportive hinterland. The Gesta Francorum *describes what happened.*

After the Turks, who are enemies of God and holy Christendom, were altogether defeated, they fled wildly for four days and nights. It happened that Suleiman their leader, son of old Suleiman,* was fleeing from Nicaea when he met ten thousand Arabs who thus accosted him, 'O unhappy man, more miserable than all our people, why are you fleeing in terror?' Suleiman answered them weeping, 'Because when I had just (as I thought) defeated all the Franks and bound them as captives – in fact I wanted to have them bound together in pairs – I happened to look back, and saw such an innumerable army of their men that if you or anyone else had been there you would have thought that all the mountains and hills and valleys and all the plains were full of them. So when we saw them we were terribly afraid and took to flight at once, barely escaping from their hands, and that is why we are still terror-stricken. If you will believe me and trust my words, be off, because if they but know that you are here, hardly one of you will escape with his life.'† The Arabs, having heard such a tale, turned back and went in scattered bands throughout Rum. Meanwhile we were coming in pursuit of those abominable Turks, who were fleeing before us every day, and when they came

* Kilij Arslan I, sultan of Rum, son of Kilij Arslan (d. 1086); the author is oddly well informed.
† Typical of the fantastical rhetoric the author ascribes to Muslim leaders.

to castles or cities they used to deceive and mislead the inhabitants, saying, 'We have defeated and conquered all the Christians so that none of them will ever dare to oppose us again, so let us come in.' Once inside, they used to loot the churches and houses and other places, and carry off horses, asses, mules, gold and silver and anything else they could find. They also kidnapped Christian children, and burned or destroyed everything that might be helpful or useful to us, as they fled in great terror at our approach. We therefore pursued them through a land which was deserted, waterless and uninhabitable,* from which we barely emerged or escaped alive, for we suffered greatly from hunger and thirst, and found nothing at all to eat except prickly plants which we gathered and rubbed between our hands. On such food we survived wretchedly enough, but we lost most of our horses, so that many of our knights had to go on as foot-soldiers, and for lack of horses we had to use oxen as mounts, and our great need compelled us to use goats, sheep and dogs as beasts of burden.

At last we began to reach fertile country, full of good and delicious things to eat and all sorts of provisions, and finally we reached Iconium,† where the inhabitants of that country gave us advice, warning us to carry skins full of water, for it is very scarce for a day's journey from that city. So we did this, and came at last to a river where we encamped for two days, and then our scouts took the road before us until they came to Heraclea, in which a large Turkish garrison was waiting in ambush to attack the Christian knights. Our knights, trusting in Almighty God, found these Turks and attacked them boldly, so on that day our enemies were defeated and fled as quickly as an arrow, shot by a strong hand, flies from the bowstring. Our men entered the city at once, and we stayed there for four days.

While we were there Tancred son of the marquis and Count Baldwin, Duke Godfrey's brother, went off together and entered the valley of Botrenthro.‡ Tancred and his knights struck out by

* The desert of the central Anatolian plateau.
† Iconium, after Nicaea the capital of Rum.
‡ Leading south towards the coast of Cilicia; *c.*14 September 1097.

themselves and came to Tarsus, where the Turks sallied from the city and came against them in one band, ready to fight with the Christians, so our men attacked them and fought with them and put them to flight, and they rushed back to the city as fast as they could. Tancred the knight of Christ galloped up and encamped before the city gate. The noble Count Baldwin came up with his army from the other direction and asked Tancred to make a friendly agreement about sharing the city, but Tancred said, 'I flatly refuse to make this pact with you.' When night fell, all the Turks fled away together, for they were terrified, and thereupon the inhabitants of the city came out in the dark, shouting at the tops of their voices, 'Come on, unconquered Franks, come on! The Turks have all gone because they are so much afraid of you!'

At dawn the chief men of the city came and surrendered it, saying to Tancred and Baldwin, who were quarrelling over it, 'Sirs, let be. We desire and seek to have for our ruler and lord the man who yesterday fought so gallantly against the Turks.' Count Baldwin, a man with great achievements to his credit, went on arguing and quarrelling with Tancred, saying, 'Let us go in together and sack this city, and whoever can get most, let him keep it, and whoever can take most, let him take it.' The most valiant Tancred replied, 'Far be this from me. I have no wish to plunder Christians. The men of this city have chosen me, and they want me to be their lord.' At last, however, brave as he was, he could not stand up to Count Baldwin because of the strength of his forces.* And so, willy-nilly, he left the city and boldly led his men away. Two fine cities, Athena [Adana] and Manustra [Mamistra], together with many castles, surrendered to him directly.

The main army, led by Raymond, count of St Gilles and the most excellent Bohemund, Duke Godfrey and many others, entered the land of the Armenians, thirsting and craving for the blood of the Turks. They came at last to a castle which was so strong that they could not prevail against it. They had with them a man called Simeon, who was born in that country, and he asked for this place, so that he could defend it from the hands of

---

* Tarsus was taken *c*.21 September 1097.

the Turkish enemies. Our leaders granted it to him, and he stayed there with his people. We, however, went on and had a good journey to Caesarea in Cappadocia, and when we left Cappadocia we came to a city of great splendour and wealth* which the Turks had been besieging for three weeks a little before our arrival, but they could not take it. When we came the city surrendered to us at once with great rejoicing. A knight called Peter d'Aups† asked our leaders to let him hold it in fealty to God and the Holy Sepulchre, and to our leaders and the emperor, and this they freely granted to him with a very good will. During the next night Bohemund heard that great numbers of the Turks who had been besieging the city were just ahead of us, so he and his own knights got ready to attack them wherever they were, but he could not find them.

After this we came to a city called Coxon, in which there were plentiful supplies of provisions of which we were badly in need. The Christians who lived in that city surrendered it at once, and we stayed there, very comfortably, for three days, and our men were much recovered. Count Raymond, hearing that the Turkish garrison of Antioch had made off, held a council and decided to send thither some of his knights, so that they could take charge of it. Those whom he appointed for this mission were Peter the seneschal of Castillon, William of Montpellier, Peter of Roaix, Peter Raymond of Hautpoul and five hundred knights. These men came into a valley near Antioch and reached a castle held by the Paulicians, where they heard that the Turks were in the city and were preparing to defend it in strength. Peter of Roaix left the others and approached Antioch on the following night, entering the valley of Ruj where he found Turks and Saracens whom he attacked, killing many of them and driving the others into headlong flight. When the Armenians who lived in this country saw that he had been so brave in defeating the pagans they surrendered to him at once, and he

* Probably Comana.
† Peter d'Aupis or Aliphas was a southern Italian Norman who entered Greek service after 1085. He founded a prominent twelfth-century Byzantine dynasty.

immediately occupied the city of Rusa and many castles.

We, who stayed at Coxon, set out and began to cross a damnable mountain,* which was so high and steep that none of our men dared to overtake another on the mountain path. Horses fell over the precipice, and one beast of burden dragged another down. As for the knights, they stood about in a great state of gloom, wringing their hands because they were so frightened and miserable, not knowing what to do with themselves and their armour, and offering to sell their shields, valuable breastplates and helmets for threepence or fivepence or any price they could get. Those who could not find a buyer threw their arms away and went on. When we had crossed that accursed mountain we came to a city called Marash. The peasants came out of that city to meet us, rejoicing and bringing plenty of merchandise, and there we had all kinds of provisions, and waited for the arrival of my lord Bohemund. So at last our knights came into the valley where stands the royal city of Antioch,† capital of Syria, which was granted to blessed Peter, prince of the apostles, to restore it to the holy faith, by Our Lord Jesus who liveth and reigneth with God the Father in the unity of the Holy Ghost, One God, world without end. Amen.

Before Antioch could be invested, however, Baldwin of Boulogne set off eastwards with a small retinue of knights towards and across the Euphrates where, at Edessa in February and March, he established himself as military governor. In his company went Fulcher of Chartres who provided the closest, if partial and sympathetic, account of Baldwin's not always respectable ascent to power, the first Frankish commander of the First Crusade to establish his own principality in the Near East.

Then we came to Antioch, which they call the Lesser, in the province of Pisidia, and then to Iconium. In these regions we very often were in need of bread and other food. For we found Romania, a land which is excellent and very fertile in products

* Anti-Taurus mountains.   † Lost by the Byzantines to the Turks in 1084.

of all kinds, terribly wasted and depopulated by the Turks.*

Often, however, you could see many people much revived from the products of the scattered farms which we found from time to time throughout the country. This was with the help of that God who with five loaves and two fishes fed five thousand people. Wherefore we were well content, and rejoicing we acknowledged that these were gifts of the mercy of God.

Then indeed you would have laughed, or perhaps wept from pity, because many of our people, who lacked beasts of burden since many of their own had died, loaded wethers, she-goats, sows and dogs with their possessions, viz. clothing, food or whatever baggage was necessary for pilgrims. We saw the backs of these small beasts chafed by the weight of this baggage. And sometimes even armed knights used oxen as mounts.

And whoever heard of such a mixture of languages in one army? There were present Franks, Flemings, Frisians, Gauls, Allobroges, Lotharingians, Alemanni, Bavarians, Normans, English, Scots, Aquitanians, Italians, Dacians, Apulians, Iberians, Bretons, Greeks and Armenians. If any Briton or Teuton wished to question me I could neither reply nor understand.†

But though we were of different tongues we seemed, however, to be brothers in the love of God and to be of nearly one mind. For if anyone lost any of his property he who found it would keep it very carefully for many days until by enquiry he found the loser and returned what was found. This was indeed proper for those who were piously making the pilgrimage.

When we reached the city of Heraclea, we beheld a certain sign in the sky which appeared in brilliant whiteness in the shape of a sword with the point towards the east.‡ What it portended for the future we did not know, but we left the present and the future to God.

* Late July–August 1097.
† Significant admission of linguistic, national and regional diversity and potential divisiveness.
‡ Comet seen in Europe 30 September to 14 October when the crusaders were more probably at Caesarea; they were at Heraclea 10–14 September 1097.

We then came to a certain flourishing city which is called Marash. We rested quietly there for three days.* But when we had marched a day's journey from there and were now not further than three days from Antioch of Syria, I, Fulcher, withdrew from the [main] army and with the lord Count Baldwin, brother of Duke Godfrey, turned into the country to the left.†

Baldwin was indeed a most capable knight. Previously he had left the army with those men whom he had brought with him and had taken with great boldness the city which is called Tarsus of Cilicia. He took it away from Tancred, who had introduced his own men with the consent of the Turks. Leaving guards in it Baldwin had returned to the [main] army.‡

And so trusting in the Lord and in his own strength, Baldwin collected a few knights and set out towards the Euphrates. There he took many towns by force as well as by strategy. Among them was the most desirable, called Turbezel.§ The Armenians who dwelled there gave it up peacefully to him, and many other towns were also subjected to him.

When the report of this had circulated far and wide, the prince of the city of Edessa sent a delegation to Baldwin.¶ This city is very famous and is in a most fertile area. It is in Syrian Mesopotamia about twenty miles beyond the above-mentioned Euphrates and about a hundred miles or more from Antioch.**

Baldwin was asked by the duke to go there so that they could become mutual friends, like father and son, as long as they both should live. And if by chance the duke of Edessa should die Baldwin was to possess the city and all the duke's territory immediately as a permanent inheritance just as if he were the latter's

* 13–16 October 1097; see map p. xliv.

† 17 October 1097; thereafter Fulcher was no longer an eyewitness of the events of the main crusade.

‡ The Cilician raid lasted from mid-September to mid-October 1097.

§ Tell Bashir; see map p. xliv.

¶ The governor of Edessa was the Armenian Thorus, claiming authority from Byzantium but effectively independent.

** Edessa was in fact forty-five miles east of the Euphrates and c.160 miles from Antioch; see map p. xliv.

own son. Since the duke had neither son nor daughter and since he was unable to defend himself against the Turks, this Greek wished that he and his territory should be defended by Baldwin. He had heard that Baldwin and his knights were very formidable fighting men.

As soon as Baldwin heard this offer and had been persuaded of its truth under oath by the deputies from Edessa, he with his little army of eighty knights proceeded to cross the Euphrates. After we had crossed this river we went on very hastily all night and, very much afraid, passed between the Saracen towns which were scattered about.

When the Turks who were in the fortified town of Samosata heard this, they set ambushes for us on the way through which they thought we would go. But on the following night a certain Armenian carefully sheltered us in his castle. He warned us to guard against these snares of the enemy, and for this reason we hid there for two days.*

But on the third day the Turks, irked by such delay, rushed down upon us from their place of hiding and with flags flying galloped in front of the castle in which we were located and before our eyes drove off as plunder the livestock which they found in the pastures.

We went out against them, but because we were few we were unable to contend with them. They shot arrows but wounded none of us. However, they left one of their men, killed by a lance, on the field. His horse was kept by the man who unseated him. Then the enemy left, but we remained there.

On the following day we resumed our journey. When we were passing by the towns of the Armenians, you would have been amazed to see them coming humbly to meet us, carrying crosses and banners, and kissing our feet and garments for the love of God because they had heard that we were going to pro-tect them against the Turks under whose yoke they had been long oppressed.†

* *c*.15 February 1098.
† The Turks had captured Edessa in 1087; Thorus in 1094.

At length we reached Edessa where the aforesaid prince of the city and his wife, together with the citizens, joyfully received us and fulfilled their promises to Baldwin without delay.

After we had been there for fifteen days the citizens wickedly plotted to slay their prince because they hated him and to elevate Baldwin to the palace to rule the land. This was suggested and it was done. Baldwin and his men were much grieved because they were not able to obtain mercy for him.*

As soon as Baldwin had accepted as a gift from the citizens the princely position of this man, who had been wickedly murdered, he began a war against the Turks who were in the country. Many times he defeated or killed them. However, it happened also that many of our men were killed by the Turks.

I, Fulcher of Chartres, was the chaplain of this same Baldwin.†

---

* Fulcher glosses over Baldwin's complicity in this shady and dishonourable transfer of power.

† Except for his description of Jerusalem, below, pp. 309–11, Fulcher is not an eyewitness again until below, pp. 344–8.

V

The Siege of Antioch

October 1097–June 1098

The siege of Antioch rapidly assumed legendary status in the experience of the participants and then in the memory of Christendom. From late October 1097 until early June 1098 the crusaders, never enough to surround the city completely, laboured unsuccessfully to starve or coerce Antioch, the key to northern Syria, into surrender. Two significant relief forces were repulsed: the first, led by Duqaq of Damascus, in late December with difficulty; the second, under Duqaq's estranged brother Ridwan of Aleppo, with surprising conclusiveness at the battle of Lake Antioch early in February. The lack of unity among the squabbling Turkish warlords of Syria and the Jazira almost certainly saved the western host from annihilation, despite a now steady stream of reinforcements arriving from the west mainly by sea at the ports of Antioch, Latakiah and St Simeon.

Such were the constant anxieties and privations, notably a persistent shortage of food, that many tried to desert, including, abortively, Peter the Hermit in January 1098. However, force of hostile circumstance and mounting casualties acted as much to unite as to undermine. A common fund was created to pay for the construction of forts; the high command began habitually to co-operate in military operations. By the end of March the leadership had appointed Stephen of Blois as some sort of co-ordinator of their activities (ductor).

However, at some point Taticius, the Greek general assigned by Alexius I to accompany the crusade, departed, possibly to gather aid although later western opinion accused him of cowardice and treachery. More alarming were the reports in late May of the approach of a third and larger relieving army under Kerboga of

Mosul which, although vitally held up for a few weeks at Edessa, threatened to catch the Christian host in the open, pinned between a Muslim field army and an unconquered garrison in Antioch. Unsurprisingly, panic spread. On 2 June a bout of hysteria hit the crusaders' camp with many fleeing for the coast, including Stephen of Blois, who never entirely lived down the shame. Yet that very night (2–3 June), aided by an inside contact, Bohemund led a spectacular commando raid that gave the crusaders entry into the city, although the Muslim garrison still held out in the citadel high above the city. Antioch had been taken not a moment too soon: within hours the outriders of Kerboga's massive army began to appear around the walls of the city. It must have seemed to the soldiers of the Cross that they had been saved by a miracle; to survive they were to need a few more.

Fulcher of Chartres

In the month of October the Franks came to Antioch in Syria, a city founded by Seleucus, son of Antiochus. Seleucus made it his capital. It was previously called Reblata. Moreover it lay on the other side of the river which they called the Orontes. Our tents were ordered pitched before the city between it and the first milestone. Here afterwards battles were very frequently fought which were most destructive to both sides. When the Turks rushed out from the city they killed many of our men, but when the tables were turned they grieved to find themselves beaten.

Antioch is certainly a very large city, well fortified and strongly situated. It could never be taken by enemies from without provided the inhabitants were supplied with food and were determined to defend it.* There is in Antioch a much-renowned church dedicated to the honour of Peter the apostle where he, raised to the episcopate, sat as bishop after he had received from the Lord Jesus the primacy of the Church and the keys to the kingdom of heaven.

There is another church too, circular in form, built in honour

---

* Fulcher visited Antioch in October 1100.

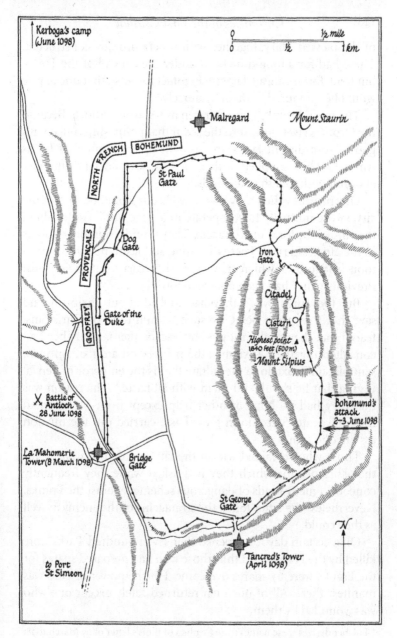

The siege of Antioch, October 1097–June 1098

of the blessed Mary, together with others fittingly constructed. These had for a long time been under the control of the Turks, but God, foreseeing all, kept them intact for us so that one day he would be honoured in them by ourselves.

The sea is, I think, about thirteen miles from Antioch. Because the Orontes river flows into the sea at that point, ships filled with goods from distant lands are brought up its channel as far as Antioch. Thus supplied with goods by sea and land, the city abounds with wealth of all kinds.

Our princes, when they saw how hard it would be to take the city, swore mutually to co-operate in a siege until, God willing, they took it by force or stratagem. They found a number of boats in the aforesaid river. These they took and fashioned into a pontoon bridge over which they crossed to carry out their plans. Previously they had been unable to ford the river.

But the Turks, when they had looked about anxiously and saw that they were beset by such a multitude of Christians, feared that they could not possibly escape them. After they had consulted together, Aoxianus, the prince and amir of Antioch, sent his son Sanxado to the sultan, that is the emperor of Persia, urging that he should aid them with all haste.* The reason was that they had no hope of other help except from Muhammad their advocate. Sanxado in great haste carried out the mission assigned to him.

Those who remained within the city guarded it, waiting for the assistance for which they had asked while they frequently concocted many kinds of dangerous schemes against the Franks. Nevertheless the latter foiled the stratagems of the enemy as well as they could.

On a certain day it happened that seven hundred Turks were killed by the Franks, and thus those who had prepared snares for the Franks were by snares overcome. For the power of God was manifest there. All of our men returned safely except one who was wounded by them.

* Fulcher derives these names from Stephen of Blois's letter of 29 March 1098; see below, pp. 183–5.

Oh, how many Christians in the city, Greeks, Syrians and Armenians, did the Turks kill in rage and how many heads did they hurl over the walls with *petrariae* and *fundibula* [stone-throwing machines] in view of the Franks! This grieved our men very much. The Turks hated these Christians, for they feared that somehow the latter might assist the Franks against a Turkish attack.

After the Franks had besieged the city for some time and had scoured the country round about in search of food for themselves and were unable to find even bread to buy, they suffered great hunger. For this reason all were very much discouraged, and many secretly planned to withdraw from the siege and to flee by land or by sea.

But they had no money on which to live. They were even obliged to seek their sustenance far away and in great fear by separating themselves forty or fifty miles from the siege, and there in the mountains they were often killed by the Turks in ambush.

We felt that misfortunes had befallen the Franks because of their sins and that for this reason they were not able to take the city for so long a time. Luxury and avarice and pride and plunder had indeed vitiated them. Then the Franks, having again consulted together, expelled the women from the army, the married as well as the unmarried, lest perhaps defiled by the sordidness of riotous living they should displease the Lord. These women then sought shelter for themselves in neighbouring towns.*

The rich as well as the poor were wretched because of starvation as well as the slaughter, which daily occurred. Had not God, like a good pastor, held his sheep together, without doubt they would all have fled thence at once in spite of the fact that they had sworn to take the city. Many, though, because of the scarcity of food, sought for many days in neighbouring villages what was necessary for life; and they did not afterwards return to the army but abandoned the siege entirely.

---

* This scapegoating of women and sex for failure was a common theme of crusader campaigns; crusading, as a penitential exercise, and sex sat uneasily together in the minds of clerical arbiters of morality and diviners of God's will.

At that time we saw a remarkable reddish glow in the sky and besides felt a great quake in the earth, which rendered us all fearful. In addition many saw a certain sign in the shape of a cross, whitish in colour, moving in a straight path towards the east.*

Raymond of Aguilers

Thereafter as we approached Antioch, many princes proposed that we postpone the siege, especially since winter was close and the army, already weakened by summer heat, was now dispersed throughout strongholds.† They further argued that the crusaders should wait for imperial forces as well as for reported reinforcements *en route* from France, and so advised us to go into winter quarters until spring. Raymond, along with other princes standing in opposition, made a counter-proposal: 'Through God's inspiration we have arrived, through his loving kindness we won the highly fortified city, Nicaea, and through his compassion, have victory and safety from the Turks as well as peace and harmony in our army; therefore, our affairs should be entrusted to him. We ought not to fear kings or leaders of kings, and neither dread places nor times since the Lord has rescued us from many perils.' The counsel of the latter prevailed and we arrived and encamped near Antioch so that the defenders firing from the heights of their towers wounded both our men in their tents and our horses.

We now take this opportunity to describe Antioch and its terrain so that our readers who have not seen it may follow the encounters and attacks. Nestled in the Lebanon mountains is a plain in width one day's journey and in length one and a half day's journey. The plain is bounded by a marsh; to the east a river which flows around a portion of this plain runs back to the edge of the mountains situated in the region to the south so that there

---

* 30 December 1097.
† 20–2 October 1097; there were serious debates as to whether to invest Antioch closely or create a wider perimeter to assist supplies and forage; a close siege was decided.

is no crossing between the mountains and the river, and thence it winds its way to the nearby Mediterranean. Antioch is so located in these straits made by the stream cutting through the above-mentioned mountains that the western flow of the river past the lower wall forms the land between it and the city in the shape of an arrow. Actually the city, lying a bit to the east, rises high in that direction and within its enclosure embraces the tops of three mountains. The mountain situated to the north is so cut off from the others by a great cliff that only a most difficult approach is possible from one to another. The northern hill boasts a fortress and the middle hill another which in the Greek language is called Colax, but the third hill has only towers. Furthermore, this city extends two miles in length and is so protected with walls, towers and breastworks that it may dread neither the attack of machine nor the assault of man even if all mankind gathered to besiege it.

In short, the Frankish army of one hundred thousand armed men encamped along a line to the north of the described Antioch was content to remain there without making a frontal assault. Despite the fact that there were in the city only two thousand first-rate knights, four or five thousand ordinary knights and ten thousand or more footmen, Antioch was safe from attack as long as the gates were guarded because a valley and marshes shielded the high walls. Upon our arrival we took our positions helter-skelter, posted no watches, and acted so stupidly that the enemy, had they known, could have overrun any sector of our camp.

At this time regional castles and nearby cities fell to us largely because of fear of us and a desire to escape Turkish bondage. Our knights, ignoring public interest, left Antioch in the selfish hopes of acquiring some of these material benefits. Even those who stayed in camp enjoyed the high life so that they ate only the best cuts, rump and shoulders, scorned brisket and thought nothing of grain and wine.

In these good times only watchmen along the walls reminded us of our enemies concealed within Antioch, but the Turks soon discovered that the Christians openly and unarmed laid waste villages and fields. Although I am poorly informed of the

Turkish movements, our foes shortly emerged from Antioch or came from Aleppo, some two days' journey away, and killed our scattered and defenceless foragers. These countermeasures lessened our easy life, and the new opportunities for slaughter and pillage encouraged the Saracens to patrol their roads more consistently.

News of these events stirred the crusaders to pick Bohemund to lead a counter-attack. Although he could muster only 150 knights Bohemund, accompanied by the counts of Flanders and Normandy and prompted by shame of backing out of the venture, finally set out largely because of God's admonition. They located, followed and drove the enemy to death in the Orontes.* Then the Christians returned happily with booty to the camp. At the same time Genoese ships docked on the coast at Port St Simeon some ten miles away.† During this time the enemy gradually slipped out of Antioch, killed squires and peasants who pastured their horses and cattle across the river, and returned with plunder into the city.

We now pause in our narrative to describe the setting so as to clarify coming events. Our tents stood close to the river and a pontoon bridge, made of boats found there, spanned it.‡ Antioch also had a bridge at the lower western corner and a hill opposite us upon which were two mosques and a chapel of tombs. In returning to our account we note again that our often outnumbered troops dared to tangle with the emboldened opposition. But the Turks, often dispersed and routed, renewed the fight partly because they were lightly armed with bows and were very agile on horseback, and partly because they could race back across their aforementioned bridge. They also liked to shower down arrows from their hill. I remind you that their bridge was almost a mile from ours, and on the plain between the bridges daily and incessant skirmishes took place. Because of their encampment near the banks of the river, Raymond and Adhemar bore the brunt of the raids. These hit-and-run attacks

* A foraging raid began just after Christmas 1097.
† *c.*17 November 1097.   ‡ See map p. 145.

cost the above leaders all of their horses because the Turks, unskilled in the use of lances and swords, fought at a distance with arrows and so were dangerous in pursuit or flight.

In the third month of the siege when the count of Normandy was absent, Godfrey ill, and prices sky-high, Bohemund and the count of Flanders were selected to conduct a foraging expedition into Hispania while Raymond and Adhemar garrisoned the camp.* News of these developments caused the besieged to renew their usual sallies. In turn, Raymond moved against them in his customary way, put his footmen in battle order, and then accompanied by a few knights gave chase to the Turks. In the ensuing mêlée he captured and killed two of the assailants on the hill's slope and drove the others across their bridge into Antioch. The sight was too much for the footmen, who broke ranks, dropped their standards, and ran pell-mell to the bridge. In their false security, they threw rocks and other missiles against the bridge defenders. The Turks regrouped and made a counter-attack by the way of the bridge and a lower ford.

At this time our knights galloped towards our bridge in pursuit of a runaway horse made riderless by them. The footmen mistook this to be a flight of the knights and fled in a hurry from the Turkish charge. In the clash the Turks relentlessly butchered the fugitives. The Frankish knights, who stopped to fight, found themselves grabbed by the fleeing rabble, who snatched their arms, the manes and tails of their horses, and pulled them from their mounts. Other knights followed along in the push out of a sense of mercy and regard for the safety of their people. The Turks hurriedly and pitilessly chased and massacred the living and robbed the dead. It was not disgraceful enough for our men to throw down their weapons, to run away, to forget all sense of shame; no, they even jumped into the river to be hit by stones or arrows or to be drowned. Only the strong and skilful swimmers crossed the river and came to friendly quarters.

* Hispania is the valley of Ruj to the south-east of Antioch; see map p. xliv. The raid occurred in late December 1097.

In the running fight from their bridge to our bridge, the Turks killed up to fifteen knights and around twenty footmen. The standard-bearer of the bishop of Le Puy and a noble young man, Bernard of Béziers, lost their lives there, and Adhemar's standard was taken.* We hope that our account of the shamelessness of our army will bring neither blame nor anger of God's servants against us, because really God on the one hand brought adulterous and pillaging crusaders to repentance and on the other cheered our army in Hispania [Ruj].

Gossip of the flourishing affairs and a sensational victory of Raymond's troops spread from our camp to Bohemund, and as a result raised morale there. During an attack on a village Bohemund heard a few of his peasants take to heel and yell for help, and a force despatched to investigate the disorder soon saw a body of Turks and Arabs in hot pursuit. Among the auxiliary group were the count of Flanders and some Provençals, a name applied to all those from Burgundy, Auvergne, Gascony and Gothia [Guienne]. I call to your attention that all others in our army are called Franks, but the enemy make no distinction and use Franks for all. But I must return to the story. The count of Flanders rashly reined his horse against the Turks rather than suffer the disgrace of withdrawing to report the enemy's approach. The Turks, unfamiliar with the use of swords in close battle, sought safety in flight, yet the count of Flanders did not lay down his sword until he had killed one hundred of his foes.

As the count of Flanders returned victoriously to Bohemund, he discovered twelve thousand Turks approaching his rearguard and he saw to his left a great number of footmen standing on a hill not far away. Following consultations with the rest of his army, he returned with reinforcements and took the offensive while Bohemund, with the other crusaders, trailed at some distance and thus shielded the rear lines. The Turks have a customary method of fighting, even when outnumbered, of attempting to surround their enemies; so in this encounter they

* Bernard of Béziers was in Count Raymond's entourage.

did likewise, but the good judgement of Bohemund forestalled their tricks.*

The Turkish and Arabic attackers of the count of Flanders fled when they realised the ensuing fight would be waged hand to hand with swords rather than at a distance with arrows. The count of Flanders then pursued the foe for two miles and the living could see the slain lying all along the way like sheaves of grain in the field at harvest time. During this encounter Bohemund struck the ambushing forces, scattered and routed them, but could not prevent the previously mentioned mob of enemy footmen from sneaking away through places impassable on horseback.

I dare say, if I were not modest, I would rate this battle before the Maccabaean war, because Maccabaeus with three thousand struck down forty-eight thousand of his foes while here four hundred knights routed sixty thousand pagans. But we neither disparage the courage of Maccabaeus nor boast of the bravery of our knights; however, we proclaim God, once wonderful to Maccabaeus, was even more so to our army.

Our response to the attackers' flight was such a diminution of bravery that the crusaders failed to follow the fleeing Turks. Our victorious army consequently came back to camp without provisions,† and the ensuing famine drove prices so high that 2 *solidi* scarcely had purchasing power equal to one day's bread ration for one man, and other things were equally high. The poor along with the wealthy, who wished to save their goods, deserted the siege, and those who remained because of spiritual strength endured the sight of their horses wasting away from starvation. Straw was scarce and 7 or 8 *solidi* did not buy an adequate amount of grain for one night's provender for one horse.

To add to our misfortunes, Bohemund, now famous for his brilliant service in Hispania, threatened to depart, adding that honour had brought him to his decision because he saw his

---

* The foraging party had stumbled upon a relief army under Duqaq of Damascus.

† This suggests the foraging raid had been a failure, despite the author's gloss.

men and horses dying from hunger; moreover, he stated that he was a man of limited means whose personal wealth was inadequate for a protracted siege. We learned afterwards that he made these statements because ambition drove him to covet Antioch.

In the mean time there was an earth tremor on the calends of January and we also saw a very miraculous sign in the sky.* On the night's first watch a red sky in the north made it appear as if the sun rose on a new day. Although God had so scourged his army in order that we might turn to the light which arose in the darkness, yet the minds of certain ones were so dense and headstrong that they were recalled from neither riotous living nor plundering. Then Adhemar urged the people to fast three days, to pray, to give alms and to form a procession; he further ordered the priests to celebrate masses and the clerks to repeat psalms. Thus the blessed Lord, mindful of his loving kindness, delayed his children's punishment lest it increase the pride of the pagans.

I turn now to one whom I had almost forgotten because he had been consigned to oblivion. This man, Taticius, accompanied our army in place of Alexius; he had a disfigured nose and lacked any redeeming qualities.† Daily, Taticius quietly admonished the princes to retire to nearby fortresses and drive out the besieged with numerous sallies and ambushes. But when all these things were disclosed to the count, who had been ill from the day of his forced flight near the bridge, he convened his princes and the bishop of Le Puy. Then at the conclusion of the council Raymond distributed 500 marks to the group on the terms that, if any one of the knights lost his horse, it would be replaced from the 500 marks and other funds which had been granted to the brotherhood.‡

* 1 January 1098; possibly more correctly 30 December 1097.

† The author chooses to blacken Taticius and the Greeks for what he probably saw as their treachery and cowardice over Antioch. The reality was more complex; see above, p. 89n.

‡ This implies the existence of a sworn fraternity among the crusade leaders with a common fund.

This agreement of the brotherhood was very useful at that time because the poor people of the army, who wished to cross to the other side of the river to forage, dreaded the ceaseless attacks of the Turks; and few wished to fight them since the horses of the Provençals, scarcely numbering one hundred, were scrawny and feeble. I hasten to state that the same situation existed in the camp of Bohemund and other leaders.

Following the action of the brotherhood, our knights boldly attacked the enemy because those who had worthless and worn-out horses knew they could replace their lost steeds with better ones. Oh, yes! another fact may be added; all the princes with the exception of the count offered Antioch to Bohemund in the event that it was captured. So with this pact Bohemund and other princes took an oath that they would not abandon the siege of Antioch for seven years unless it fell sooner.*

While these affairs were conducted in camp, an unconfirmed story spread that the army of the emperor was approaching, an army composed, it was said, of many races, Slavs, Pechenegs, Cumans and Turcopoles.† Turcopoles were so named because they were either reared with Turks or were the offspring of a Christian mother and of a Turkish father. They feared to associate with us because of their bad treatment of us along the journey. Actually Taticius, that disfigured one, anxious for an excuse to run away, not only fabricated the above lie but added to his sins with perjury and betrayal of friends by hastening away in flight after ceding to Bohemund two or three cities, Tursol, Mamistra and Adana. Therefore, under the pretence of joining the army of Alexius, Taticius broke camp, abandoned his followers, and left with God's curse; by this dastardly act, he brought eternal shame to himself and his men.‡

* Perhaps a confusion with the oath sworn on the evening of the city's capture on 2–3 June 1098.
† An accurate reflection on Greek dependence on foreign mercenaries for their army.
‡ Taticius' departure, for whatever reason, proved highly convenient for Bohemund's ambition to acquire Antioch; see above, p. 89n.

The Gesta Francorum

When we drew near to the bridge over the Orontes our scouts, who used always to go ahead of us, found barring their way a great number of Turks who were hurrying to reinforce Antioch, so they attacked the Turks with one heart and mind and defeated them. The barbarians were thrown into confusion and took to flight, leaving many dead in that battle, and our men who by God's grace overcame them took much booty, horses, camels, mules and asses laden with corn and wine. Afterwards, when our main forces came up, they encamped on the bank of the river, and the gallant Bohemund came at once with four thousand knights to guard the city gate, so that no one could go out or come in secretly by night. Next day, Wednesday, 21 October, the main army reached Antioch about noon, and we established a strict blockade on three gates of the city, for we could not besiege it from the other side because a mountain, high and very steep, stood in our way.* Our enemies the Turks, who were inside the city, were so much afraid of us that none of them tried to attack our men for nearly a fortnight. Meanwhile we grew familiar with the surroundings of Antioch, and found there plenty of provisions, fruitful vineyards and pits full of stored corn, apple-trees laden with fruit and all sorts of other good things to eat.

The Armenians and Syrians who lived in the city came out and pretended to flee to us, and they were daily in our camp, but their wives were in the city. These men spied on us and on our power, and reported everything we said to those who were besieged in the city. After the Turks had found out about us, they began gradually to emerge and to attack our pilgrims wherever they could, not on one flank only but wherever they could lay ambush for us, either towards the sea or towards the mountain.

Not far off there stood a castle called Aregh, manned by many of the bravest of the Turks, who often used to make attacks on our men. When our leaders heard that such things were happening, they were very troubled and sent some of our knights to

* Mount Silpius; see map p. 145.

reconnoitre the place where the Turks had established themselves. When our knights, who were looking for the Turks, found the place where they used to hide, they attacked the enemy, but had to retreat a little way to where they knew Bohemund to be stationed with his army. Two of our men were killed there in the first attack. When Bohemund heard of this he went out, like a most valiant champion of Christ, and his men followed him. The barbarians fell upon our men because they were few, yet they joined battle in good order and many of our enemies were killed. Others, whom we captured, were led before the city gate and there beheaded, to grieve the Turks who were in the city.

There were others who used to come out of the city and climb upon a gate, whence they shot arrows at us, so that the arrows fell into my lord Bohemund's camp, and a woman was killed by a wound from one of them.*

Thereafter all our leaders met together and summoned a council. They said, 'Let us build a castle on top of Mount Malregard,† so that we can stay here safe and sound, without fear of the Turks.' The castle was built and fortified, and all our leaders took turns in guarding it.

By and by, before Christmas, corn and all foodstuffs began to be very dear, for we dared not go far from the camp and we could find nothing to eat in the land of the Christians. (No one dared to go into the land of the Saracens except with a strong force.) Finally our leaders held a council to decide how they should provide for so many people, and in this council they determined that one part of our army should go and do its best to get supplies and to protect the flanks of our forces, while the other part should stay behind, faithfully to guard the non-combatants. Then Bohemund said, 'Gentlemen and most gallant knights, if you wish, and if it seems to you a good plan, I will go on this expedition, with the count of Flanders.' So when we had celebrated Christmas with great splendour these two set out on Monday the second day of the week,‡ and with them went others, more than twenty

* A reminder of the diversity of people in the army.
† A hill north of the city; see map p. 145.   ‡ 28 December 1097.

thousand knights and foot-soldiers in all, and they entered, safe and sound, into the land of the Saracens. Now it happened that many Turks, Arabs and Saracens had come together from Jerusalem and Damascus and Aleppo and other places* and were approaching to relieve Antioch, so when they heard that a Christian force had been led into their country they prepared at once for battle, and at daybreak they came to the place† where our men were assembled. The barbarians split up their forces into two bands, one before and one behind, for they wanted to surround us on all sides, but the noble count of Flanders, armed at all points with faith and with the sign of the Cross (which he bore loyally every day), made straight for the enemy with Bohemund at his side, and our men charged them in one line. The enemy straightway took to flight, turning tail in a hurry; many of them were killed and our men took their horses and other plunder. Others, who remained alive, fled quickly and went into 'the wrath fitted for destruction', but we came back in great triumph, and praised the glorified God the Three in One, who liveth and reigneth now and eternally. Amen.

While this was going on the Turks (enemies of God and holy Christendom) who were acting as garrison to the city of Antioch heard that my lord Bohemund and the count of Flanders were not with the besieging army, so they sallied from the city and came boldly to fight with our men, seeking out the places where the besiegers were weakest, for they knew that some very valiant knights were away, and they found that on the Tuesday‡ they could withstand us and do us harm. Those wretched barbarians came up craftily and made a sudden attack upon us, killing many knights and foot-soldiers who were off their guard. On that grievous day the bishop of Le Puy lost his seneschal, who was carrying his banner and guarding it, and if there had not been a river between us and them they would have at-

---

* Led by Duqaq of Damascus (1095–1104).
† Al-Bara; this great foraging raid of December 1097 was not a success; see Raymond of Aguilers's account below, p. 150.   ‡ 29 December 1097.

tacked us more often and done very great harm to our people.

Just then the valiant Bohemund arrived with his army from the land of the Saracens, and he came over Tancred's mountain* thinking that he might find something which could be carried off, for our men had pillaged all the land. Some of his followers had found plunder, but others were coming back empty-handed. Then the gallant Bohemund shouted at the fugitives from our camp, 'You wretched and miserable creatures! You scum of all Christendom! Why do you want to run away so fast? Stop now, stop until we all join forces, and do not rush about like sheep without a shepherd. If our enemies find you rushing all over the place they will kill you, for they are on the watch day and night to catch you without a leader or alone, and they are always trying to kill you or to lead you into captivity.' When he had said this he returned to his camp together with his men, but more of them were empty-handed than carrying plunder.

The Armenians and Syrians, seeing that our men had come back with scarcely any supplies, took counsel together and went over the mountains by paths which they knew, making careful enquiries and buying up corn and provisions which they brought to our camp, in which there was a terrible famine, and they used to sell an ass's load for 8 *hyperperi*, which is 120 shillings in our money. Many of our people died there, not having the means to buy at so dear a rate.

Because of this great wretchedness and misery William the Carpenter and Peter the Hermit fled away secretly.† Tancred went after them and caught them and brought them back in disgrace. (They gave him a pledge and an oath that they were willing to return to the camp and give satisfaction to the leaders.) William spent the whole of the night in my lord Bohemund's tent, lying on the ground like a piece of rubbish. The following

* The hill to the south of the city. Tancred fortified it in April 1098; see map p. 145.
† About 20 January 1098; William, viscount of Melun, was nicknamed the Carpenter for the manner in which he despatched his enemies in battle, not for any practical hobby.

morning, at daybreak, he came and stood before Bohemund, blushing for shame. Bohemund said to him, 'You wretched disgrace to the whole Frankish army – you dishonourable blot on all the people of Gaul! You most loathsome of all men whom the earth has to bear, why did you run off in such a shameful way? I suppose that you wanted to betray these knights and the Christian camp, just as you betrayed those others in Spain?'* William kept quiet, and never a word proceeded out of his mouth. Nearly all the Franks assembled and humbly begged my lord Bohemund not to allow him to suffer a worse punishment. He granted their request without being angry, and said, 'I will freely grant this for the love I bear you, provided that the man will swear, with his whole heart and mind, that he will never turn aside from the path to Jerusalem, whether for good or ill, and Tancred shall swear that he will neither do, nor permit his men to do, any harm to him.' When Tancred heard these words he agreed, and Bohemund sent the Carpenter away forthwith; but afterwards he sneaked off without delay, for he was greatly ashamed.†

God granted that we should suffer this poverty and wretchedness because of our sins. In the whole camp you could not find a thousand knights who had managed to keep their horses in really good condition.

While all this was going on, our enemy Taticius,‡ hearing that the Turkish army had attacked us, admitted that he had been afraid that we had all perished and fallen into the hands of the enemy. So he told all sorts of lies, and said, 'Gentlemen and most gallant knights, you see that we are here in great distress and that no reinforcements can reach us from any direction. Let me therefore go back to the country of Rum, and I will guarantee without delay to send by sea many ships, laden with corn, wine, barley, meat, flour, cheese and all sorts of provisions which we need; I

* In 1087, William had deserted from the siege of Tudela amid accusations of Muslim bribery.   † During the night of 10–11 June 1098.

‡ Experienced Byzantine general assigned to the crusade after Nicaea; he had marched in the vanguard with Bohemund; for this incident see Shepard, 'When Greek Meets Greek', above, p. 89n.

will also have horses brought here to sell, and will cause goods to be brought hither by land under the emperor's safe conduct. See, I will swear faithfully to do all this, and I will attend to it myself. Meanwhile my household and my pavilion shall stay in the camp as a firm pledge that I will come back as soon as I can.'

So that enemy of ours made an end of his speech. He left all his possessions in the camp; but he is a liar, and always will be. We were thus left in direst need, for the Turks were harrying us on every side, so that none of our men dared to go outside the encampment. The Turks were menacing us on the one hand, and hunger tormented us on the other, and there was no one to help us or bring us aid. The rank and file, with those who were very poor, fled to Cyprus or Rum or into the mountains. We dared not go down to the sea for fear of those brutes of Turks, and there was no road open to us anywhere.

Anna Comnena tried hard to counter western apologists' exploit-ation of Taticius' departure to vilify the Greeks by blaming it on a trick by Bohemund.

What happened then, you ask. Well, the Latins with the Roman army reached Antioch by what is called the 'Quick Route'.* They ignored the country on either side. Near the walls of the city a ditch was dug, in which the baggage was deposited, and the siege of Antioch began. It lasted for three lunar months.† The Turks, anxious about the difficult position in which they found them-selves, sent a message to the sultan of Khorasan,‡ asking him to supply enough men to help them defend the people of Antioch and chase away the besieging Latins. Now it chanced that a cer-tain Armenian§ was on a tower of the city, watching that part of the wall allotted to Bohemund. This man often used to lean over

---

* Hardly; the route chosen over the Anti-Taurus mountains was twice as long as the direct route through Cilicia: see map p. xliv.
† 21 October 1097 to 3 June 1098.
‡ Probably Kerboga, atabeg of Mosul, rather than Berkyaruk, sultan of Bagh-dad.   § Firuz; did he and Bohemund converse in Greek? See above, p. 89n.

the parapet and Bohemund, by flagrant cajolery and a series of attractive guarantees, persuaded him to hand over the city. The Armenian gave his word: 'Whenever you like to give some secret sign from outside, I will at once hand over to you this small tower. Only make sure that you, and all the men under you, are ready. And have ladders, too, all prepared for use. Nor must you alone be ready: all the men should be in armour, so that as soon as the Turks see you on the tower and hear you shouting your war-cries, they may panic and flee.' However, Bohemund for the time being kept this arrangement to himself. At this stage of affairs a man came with the news that a very large force of Agarenes was on the point of arriving from Khorasan; they would attack the Celts. They were under the command of Kerboga. Bohemund was informed and being unwilling to hand over Antioch to Taticius (as he was bound to do if he kept his oaths to the emperor) and coveting the city for himself, he devised an evil scheme for removing Taticius involuntarily.* He approached him. 'I wish to reveal a secret to you', he said, 'because I am concerned for your safety. A very disturbing report has reached the ears of the counts – that the sultan has sent these men from Khorasan against us at the emperor's bidding. The counts believe the story is true and they are plotting to kill you. Well, I have now done my part in forewarning you: the danger is imminent. The rest is up to you. You must consult your own interests and take thought for the lives of your men.' Taticius had other worries apart from this: there was a severe famine (an ox-head was selling for 3 gold staters) and he despaired of taking Antioch. He left the place, therefore, boarded the Roman ships anchored in the harbour of Soudi [St Simeon] and sailed for Cyprus.

Muslim observers were no less transfixed by the epic struggle for Antioch. Abu Yala Hamza ibn Asad al-Tamimi (c.1073–1160), known, from his family's name, as Ibn al-Qalanisi ('son of the Hatter'), wrote a history of his native city, Damascus, for the years 974

* Crucial to Anna's defence of her father.

to 1160. A prominent public official in Damascus, well educated and a poet as well as lawyer and administrator, Ibn al-Qalanisi supplies an exactly contemporary account of the irruption of the Franks into Syria written by someone who was already adult when the crusaders burst into Syria in the winter of 1097–8. Written before the fashion for an almost obligatory gloss of jihad rhetoric, Ibn al-Qalanisi's description is generally factual and dispassionate without minimising the effect of the western invasion. Unlike many Muslim writers, who saw Syria as a peripheral backwater, Ibn al-Qalanisi is of interest because he is portraying his own region rather than attempting the more common Arabic literary exercise of a universal history.

In this year [1097] there began to arrive a succession of reports that the armies of the Franks had appeared from the direction of the sea of Constantinople with forces not to be reckoned for multitude. As these reports followed one upon the other, and spread from mouth to mouth far and wide, the people grew anxious and disturbed in mind. The king, Daud ibn Suleiman ibn Qutulmish,* whose dominions lay nearest to them, having received confirmation of these statements, set about collecting forces, raising levies and carrying out the obligation of Holy War. He also summoned as many of the Turkmens [Turkish freebooters] as he could to give him assistance and support against them, and a large number of them joined him along with the askar [military entourage] of his brother. His confidence having been strengthened thereby, and his offensive power rendered formidable, he marched out to the fords, tracks and roads by which the Franks must pass, and showed no mercy to all of them who fell into his hands. When he had thus killed a great number, they turned their forces against him, defeated him and scattered his army, killing many and taking many captive, and plundered and enslaved. The Turkmens, having lost most of their horses, took to flight. The king of the Greeks bought a great many of those whom they had enslaved, and

* Kilij Arslan I of Rum.

had them transported to Constantinople. When the news was received of this shameful calamity to the cause of Islam, the anxiety of the people became acute and their fear and alarm increased. The date of this battle was 4 July 1097.*

At the end of July the amir Yaghi Sayan, lord of Antioch, accompanied by the amir Sukman ibn Ortuq† and the amir Kerboga, set out with his askar towards Antioch, on receipt of news that the Franks were approaching it. Yaghi Sayan therefore hastened to Antioch, and despatched his son to al-Malik Duqaq at Damascus, to Janah al-Dawla at Hims, and to all the other cities and districts, appealing for aid and support, and inciting them to hasten to the Holy War, while he set about fortifying Antioch and expelling its Christian population. On 12 September the Frankish armies descended on Baghras and developed their attack upon the territories of Antioch, whereupon those who were in the castles and forts adjacent to Antioch revolted and killed their garrisons except for a few who were able to escape from them. The people of Artah did likewise, and called for reinforcements from the Franks. During July–August a comet appeared in the west; it continued to rise for a space of about twenty days, and then disappeared.

Meanwhile, a large detachment of the Frankish army, numbering about thirty thousand men, had left the main body and set about ravaging the other districts, in the course of which they came to al-Bara, and slaughtered about fifty men there. Now the askar of Damascus had reached the neighbourhood of Shayzar, on their way to support Yaghi Sayan, and when this detachment made its descent on al-Bara, they moved out against it. After a succession of charges by each side, in which a number of their men were killed, the Franks returned to al-Ruj, and thence proceeded towards Antioch.‡ Oil, salt and other necessaries became dear and unprocurable in Antioch, but so much was smuggled into the city that they became cheap again. The Franks dug a

---

* Actually 1 July 1097.
† With his brother Il-Ghazi, rulers of Jerusalem until 1098, when it was captured by the Egyptians.   ‡ Late December 1097.

trench between their position and the city, owing to the frequent sallies made against them by the army of Antioch.

Now the Franks, on their first appearance, had made a covenant with the king of the Greeks, and had promised him that they would deliver over to him the first city which they should capture. They then captured Nicaea, and it was the first place they captured, but they did not carry out their word to him on that occasion, and refused to deliver it up to him according to the stipulation.* Subsequently they captured on their way several frontier fortresses and passes.

The attitude in the Christian army, at once fearful yet optimistic of God's favour, is captured in two letters written from the crusader camp outside Antioch early in 1098.

The Patriarch of Jerusalem to the Church in the West, Antioch, January 1098

The patriarch of Jerusalem and the bishops, Greek as well as Latin, and the whole army of God and the Church to the Church of the west; fellowship in celestial Jerusalem, and a portion of the reward of their labour.

Since we are not unaware that you delight in the increase of the Church, and we believe that you are concerned to hear matters adverse as well as prosperous, we hereby notify you of the success of our undertaking. Therefore, be it known to your delight that God has triumphed in forty important cities and in two hundred fortresses of his Church in Romania [Asia Minor], as well as in Syria, and that we still have one hundred thousand men in armour, besides the common throng, though many were lost in the first battles. But what is this? What is one man in a thousand? Where we have a count, the enemy have forty kings; where we have a company, the enemy have a legion; where we have a knight, they have a duke; where we have a foot-soldier, they have a count; where we have a camp, they have a kingdom.

* Not so.

However, confiding not in numbers, nor in bravery, nor in any presumption, but protected by justice and the shield of Christ, and with St George, Theodore, Demetrius and Basil, soldiers of Christ, truly supporting us, we have pierced, and in security are piercing, the ranks of the enemy. On five general battlefields, God conquering, we have conquered.

But what more? In behalf of God and ourselves, I, apostolic patriarch, the bishops and the whole order of the Lord, urgently pray, and our spiritual mother Church calls out: 'Come, my most beloved sons, come to me, retake the crown from the hands of the sons of idolatry, who rise against me – the crown from the beginning of the world predestined for you.' Come, therefore, we pray, to fight in the army of the Lord at the same place in which the Lord fought, in which Christ suffered for us, leaving to you an example that you should follow his footsteps. Did not God, innocent, die for us? Let us therefore also die, if it be our lot, not for him, but for ourselves, that by dying on earth we may live for God. Yet it is [now] not necessary that we should die, nor fight much, for we have [already] sustained the more serious trials, but the task of holding the fortresses and cities has been heavily reducing our army. Come, therefore, hasten to be repaid with the twofold reward – namely, the land of the living and the land flowing with milk and honey and abounding in all good things. Behold, men, by the shedding of our blood the way is open everywhere. Bring nothing with you except only what may be of use to us. Let only the men come; let the women, as yet, be left. From the home in which there are two, let one, the one more ready for battle, come. But those, especially, who have made the vow, [let them come]. Unless they come and discharge their vow, I, apostolic patriarch, the bishops and the whole order of the Orthodox, do excommunicate them and remove them utterly from the communion of the Church. And do you likewise, that they may not have burial among Christians, unless they are staying for suitable reasons. Come, and receive the twofold glory! This, therefore, also write.

Anselm of Ribemont to Manasses II, Archbishop of Rheims, Antioch, 10 February 1098

To his reverend lord M., by God's grace archbishop of Rheims, A. of Ribemont, his vassal and humble servant – greeting.

Inasmuch as you are our lord and as the kingdom of France is especially dependent upon your care, we tell to you, our father, the events which have happened to us and the condition of the army of the Lord. Yet, in the first place, although we are not ignorant that the disciple is not above his master, nor the servant above his lord, we advise and beseech you in the name of our Lord Jesus to consider what you are and what the duty of a priest and bishop is. Provide therefore for our land, so that the lords may keep peace among themselves, the vassals may in safety work on their property, and the ministers of Christ may serve the Lord, leading quiet and tranquil lives. I also pray you and the canons of the holy mother church of Rheims, my fathers and lords, to be mindful of us, not only of me and of those who are now sweating in the service of God, but also of the members of the army of the Lord who have fallen in arms or died in peace.

But passing over these things, let us return to what we promised. Accordingly after the army had reached Nicomedia, which is situated at the entrance to the land of the Turks, we all, lords and vassals, cleansed by confession, fortified ourselves by partaking of the body and blood of our Lord, and proceeding thence beset Nicaea on the second day before the nones of May.* After we had for some days besieged the city with many machines and various engines of war, the craft of the Turks, as often before, deceived us greatly. For on the very day on which they had promised that they would surrender, Suleiman† and all the Turks, collected from neighbouring and distant regions, suddenly fell upon us and attempted to capture our camp. However, the count of St Gilles, with the remaining Franks, made an attack upon them and killed an innumerable multitude. All the others

* 6 May 1097.　　† Kilij Arslan I.

fled in confusion. Our men, moreover, returning in victory and bearing many heads fixed upon pikes and spears, furnished a joyful spectacle for the people of God. This was on the seventeenth day before the calends of June.*

Beset moreover and routed in attacks by night and day, they surrendered unwillingly on the thirteenth day before the calends of July.† Then the Christians, entering the walls with their crosses and imperial standards, reconciled the city to God, and both within the city and outside the gates cried out in Greek and Latin, 'Glory to thee, O God.' Having accomplished this, the princes of the army met the emperor who had come to offer them his thanks, and having received from him gifts of inestimable value, some withdrew, with kindly feelings, others with different emotions.

We moved our camp from Nicaea on the fourth day before the calends of July‡ and proceeded on our journey for three days. On the fourth day the Turks, having collected their forces from all sides, again attacked the smaller portion of our army, killed many of our men and drove all the remainder back to their camps. Bohemund, count of the [Normans], Count Stephen [of Blois] and the count of Flanders commanded this section. When these were thus terrified by fear, the standards of the larger army suddenly appeared. Hugh the Great and the duke of Lorraine were riding at the head, the count of St Gilles and the venerable bishop of Le Puy followed. For they had heard of the battle and were hastening to our aid. The number of the Turks was estimated at 260,000. All of our army attacked them, killed many and routed the rest. On that day I returned from the emperor, to whom the princes had sent me on public business.

After that day our princes remained together and were not separated from one another. Therefore, in traversing the countries of Asia Minor and Armenia we found no obstacle, except that after passing Iconium, we, who formed the advance guard, saw a few Turks. After routing these, on the twelfth day before

* 16 May 1097.   † 19 June 1097.   ‡ 28 June 1097.

the calends of November,* we laid siege to Antioch, and now we captured the neighbouring places, the cities of Tarsus and Latakiah and many others, by force. On a certain day, moreover, before we besieged the city, at the 'Iron Bridge'† we routed the Turks, who had set out to devastate the surrounding country, and we rescued many Christians.‡ Moreover, we led back the horses and camels with very great booty.

While we were besieging the city, the Turks from the nearest redoubt daily killed those entering and leaving the army. The princes of our army, seeing this, killed four hundred of the Turks who were lying in wait, drove others into a certain river and led back some as captives. You may be assured that we are now besieging Antioch with all diligence, and hope soon to capture it. The city is supplied to an incredible extent with grain, wine, oil and all kinds of food.

I ask, moreover, that you and all whom this letter reaches pray for us and for our departed brethren. Those who have fallen in battle are: at Nicaea, Baldwin of Ghent, Baldwin Chalderuns, who was the first to make an attack upon the Turks and who fell in battle on the calends of July,§ Robert of Paris, Lisiard of Flanders, Hilduin of Mazingarbe, Anseau of Caien, Manasses of Clermont, Laudunensis.

Those who died from sickness: at Nicaea, Guy of Vitreio, Odo of Vernolio [Verneuil (?)], Hugh of Rheims; at the fortress of Sparnum, the venerable abbot Roger, my chaplain; at Antioch, Alard of Spiniaeco, Hugh of Calniaco.

Again and again I beseech you, readers of this letter, to pray for us, and you, my lord archbishop, to order this to be done by your bishops. And know for certain that we have captured for the Lord two hundred cities and fortresses. May our mother, the western Church, rejoice that she has begotten such men,

---

* 21 October 1097.
† Bridge over the Orontes, north of Antioch ('Iron' being a pun on Fernus, the Latin name for the river, not the material of the bridge); taken 20 October 1097.   ‡ Probably local Christians, Greek or Armenian.
§ 1 July 1097, at Dorylaeum.

who are acquiring for her so glorious a name and who are so wonderfully aiding the eastern Church. And in order that you may believe this, know that you have sent to me a tapestry by Raymond 'de Castello'. Farewell.

The siege continued with little sign of an immediate end.

Raymond of Aguilers

News now came that the commander of the caliph at the head of a large army from Khorasan was bringing aid to Antioch.* Following a council of war in Adhemar's house, footmen were ordered to defend the camp and knights to ride out against the new force. This decision came because it was likely that the unfit and timid ones in the ranks of the footmen would show more cowardice than bravery if they saw a large force of Turks. The expeditionary group left under the cover of night and hid in some hills two leagues away from camp so that the defenders could not send word of their departure. Now I beseech those who have attempted to disparage our army in the past to hear this; indeed may they hear so that when they understand God's example of mercy on our behalf, they may hasten to give satisfaction with penitential wailing.

God increased the size of the six units of the knights so that each one seemed to grow from scarcely seven hundred men to more than two thousand. Certainly, it taxes me to know what to say of the bravado of the army whose knights actually sang warlike songs so joyously that they seemed to look upon the approaching battle as if it were a sport. It is to be observed here that the site of the coming fight was near the place where the river flowed within a mile of the marsh and thereby prohibited the Turkish customary encircling movements which depended upon the dispersion of their forces. Furthermore, God, who had offered the above-mentioned advantages, now offered us six adjoining valleys by which our troops could move to battle; con-

* In fact Ridwan of Aleppo, February 1098.

sequently, within one hour we had marched out and occupied the field. Thus as the sun shone brightly on our arms and buck-lers, the battle began with our men at first gradually pushing forward while the Turks ran to and fro, shot their arrows, and slowly retreated.*

Nevertheless, our troops suffered heavy losses until the first line of the Turks was driven against the rear echelons. Deserters later informed us that there were at least twenty-eight thousand Turkish cavalrymen in this encounter. When the hostile lines finally milled together, the Franks prayed to God and rushed for-ward. Without delay the ever-present Lord 'strong and mighty in battle' shielded his children and cast down the pagans. Thereafter the Franks chased them almost ten miles from the battle site to their highly fortified fortress. Upon the sight of this débâcle the occupants of the castle burned it and took to flight.† This outcome caused joy and jubilation in the camp, because we con-sidered the burning of the fortification as another victory.

At the same time fighting broke loose everywhere in the direc-tion of Antioch because our foes planned a two-pronged attack – one from the besieged and one from the unexpected auxiliary troops. God showed no favourites and battled along with the footmen while he smiled upon the knights, so that the victory of the footmen over the besieged was no less than the knights' repulse of the reinforcements. With the battle and booty won, we carried the heads of the slain to camp and stuck them on posts as grim reminders of the plight of their Turkish allies and of future woes for the besieged. Now as we reflect upon it, we have con-cluded that this was God's command because the Turks had formerly disgraced us by fixing the point of the captured banner of the blessed Mary in the ground. Thus God disposed that the sight of lifeless heads of friends supported by pointed sticks would ban further taunts from the defenders of Antioch.

Ambassadors of the king of Babylon [Egypt] were present dur-ing these events, and upon viewing the miracles which God performed through his servants, praised Jesus, son of the Virgin

* Battle of Lake Antioch, 9 February 1098.   † Harim, east of Antioch.

Mary, who through these wretched beggars trampled under foot the most powerful tyrants.* In addition, they promised friendship and favourable treatment, and reported benevolent acts of their king to Egyptian Christians and our pilgrims. Consequently, our envoys, charged with entering into a friendly pact, departed with them.

Contemporaneous with these events our princes decided to fortify an area on a hill which commanded the tents of Bohemund and thereby to thwart any and all possible enemy attacks against our tents.† Upon completion of this work our fortifications were so strengthened that we were to all intents and purposes in an enclosed city made strong by work and natural terrain. Thus this new fortress, lying to our east, as well as the walls of Antioch and the nearby protecting marsh, guarded our camp and restricted attacks from the besieged to areas near the gates. Moreover, a river flowed to the west, and to the north an old wall wound its way down the mountain to the river. The plan of strengthening another fortification on the little mountain situated above the Turkish bridge also met with public approval, but siege machines which were built in camp proved useless.

In the fifth month of the investment at the time our ships carrying provisions docked in port, the besieged began to block the way to the sea and to kill supply crews.‡ At first the Turks threatened at all times largely because the indisposition of our leaders to retaliate emboldened them. To counter these dangers we finally decided to fortify the camp near the bridge. In view of the absence of many of our forces at the port, the count and Bohemund were elected to guard the absentees' return as well as to carry back mattocks and other tools necessary for construction of the new fort. Upon learning of the mission of Raymond and Bohemund, the besieged began their usual attacks. In turn, our

* For the negotiations with the Egyptians see below, p. 179n. The author delights in portraying the crusaders as 'beggars' – a good moral if not historical point about spiritual value and reward.

† La Mahomerie, 5 March 1098; see map p. 145.

‡ More and more ships from the west, both Italy and northern Europe, were arriving in Syrian waters providing vital access to supplies, e.g. in Cyprus.

troops both unwary and disorderly advanced only to be shamefully scattered and routed.

When on the fourth day as the count and Bohemund with a
great multitude, secure as they thought in this rabble, returned
from port, they were spied upon by the Turks. But why make a
longer story of it? There was a fight, our troops fled and we lost
almost three hundred men and no one knows how much in
spoils and arms. While we, like cattle in the mountains and crags,
were being killed and dashed down, aid from the camp moved
against the Turks, who then turned from the slaughter of the
fugitives. Lord God, why these tribulations? Our forces within
the camp and those without who had the services of the two
greatest leaders in your army – Raymond and Bohemund – were
overcome and vanquished. Shall we flee to the camp or shall the
guardians of the camp flee to us? 'Arise, O Lord. Help us in honour of thy name.'* If the report of the defeat of the princes had
been heard in the camp, or if by chance we had learned of the
rout of the army contingents, then collectively we would have
fled. Now at the right moment the Lord aided us and incited
those whom he had formerly cowed to be foremost in battle.

Upon viewing our stolen goods and his victory as well as the
rashness of a few Christians, Yaghi Sayan,† commander of Antioch, sent his knights and footmen from the city. Confident of
success, he commanded the gates of Antioch to be closed after
them, thereby demanding that his soldiers win the fight or perish.
In the mean time the crusaders, as ordered, moved forward gradually, but the Turks ran hither and thither, fired arrows, and boldly
attacked our men. Our soldiers, unchecked by Turkish manoeuvres, suffered but awaited the time for a mass assault. The
flowing tears and plaintive prayers made one think that God's
compassion must be in the offing.

When the time for the encounter came, a very noble Provençal knight, Isoard of Ganges, accompanied by 150 footmen,
knelt, invoked the aid of God, and stirred his comrades to action

---

* Ambush probably 6 March 1098.
† Yaghi Sayan, Turkish governor of Antioch.

by shouting, 'Charge! Soldiers of Christ!' Thereupon he hurled himself against the Turks, and as our troops rushed to the attack, the haughtiness of the enemy was shattered. The gate was closed, the bridge was strait, but the river was very broad. What then? The panicky Turks were either smashed to the ground and slaughtered or crushed with stones in the river, for flight lay open to no one. Peace would have come to Antioch on this day had not Yaghi Sayan swung open the gate. I myself heard from many participants that they knocked twenty or more Turks into the river with bridge railings. There Godfrey distinguished himself greatly, for he blocked the Turks scrambling to enter the gate and forced them to break into two ranks as they ascended the steps.

Following a religious service, the happy victors marched back to camp with great spoils and many horses. Oh! How we wish you fellow Christians who follow us in your vows could have seen this noteworthy event! Namely, a horseman, fearful of death, hurriedly plunged into the deep waters of the river only to be grabbed by his fellow Turks, thrown from his horse, and drowned in the stream along with the mob which had seized him. The hardships of the encounter were rewarded by the sight of the returning masses. Some running back and forth between the tents on Arabian horses were showing their new riches to their friends, and others, sporting two or three garments of silk, were praising God, the bestower of victory and gifts, and yet others, covered with three or four shields, were happily displaying these mementoes of their triumph. While they were able to convince us with these tokens and other booty of the greatness of their battle prowess, they could give no exact information on the number of dead because the Turkish rout ended at night, and consequently the heads of the fallen enemy had not been brought to camp.

However, on the following day at the site of a proposed fortification in front of their bridge, the bodies of some of our foes were discovered in a ditch close to a mountain which served as a Saracen cemetery. Excited by the sight of Turkish spoils, the poor violated all of the tombs and so, having disinterred the

Turkish cadavers, there remained no doubt of the extent of the victory. The dead numbered around fifteen hundred, and I remain silent on both those buried in the city and those dragged under the waters of the river. But the corpses were hurled into the Orontes lest the intolerable stench interfere with construction of the fort.

Indeed, the sailors who in the flight of the count and Bohemund had been routed and wounded were still terror-stricken and sceptical of the outcome. But, as if strengthened by the sight of the great number of dead, they began to praise God, who is accustomed to chastening and cheering his children. So, by God's decree it happened that the Turks, who killed the food porters along the coast and river banks and left them to the beasts and birds, in turn made food in that place for the same beasts and birds.

Following acknowledgement of victory and attendant festivities as well as completion of the fort, Antioch was besieged from the north and south. Then debate ensued over the choice of a prince as guardian of the new fort, since a community affair is often slighted because all believe it will be attended to by others.* While some of the princes, desirous of pay, solicited the vote of their peers for the office, the count, contrary to the wishes of his entourage, grabbed control, partly in order to excuse himself from the accusation of sloth and avarice and partly to point the way of force and wisdom to the slothful.

During the preceding summer Raymond had been weakened by a grave and long illness and consequently was so debilitated during the winter that it was reported he was disposed neither to fight nor to give. Although he had performed great services, he was considered an unimportant person because the people believed he was capable of more effort. He bore such enmity from the doubt cast upon his Christian strength that he was almost alienated from the Provençals. Meanwhile, the count disregarded these insults, trusting that the besieged Antiochenes,

* La Mahomerie, commissioned 5 March, probably completed by 20 March 1098; see map p. 145.

for the most part overcome, would flee; but, on the contrary, he was surrounded by his foes one morning at daybreak.

A great miracle of God's protection manifested itself when sixty of our men withstood the assault of seven thousand Saracens; and even more marvellous, on the preceding day a torrent of rain drenched the fresh earth and thus filled the fosse around the castle. As a result no obstacles but the strength of the Lord hindered the enemy. Yet I think that it is not the time to ignore the great courage of several knights who, as guards of the bridge, were now isolated and found themselves unable to flee since a distance of an arrow's flight lay between them and their fortress. Pushing forward against the Saracens in a circular formation, these knights advanced to the corner of a nearby house where they met courageously and intrepidly the enveloping attack, both the fury of the arrows and the cloud of rocks.

At the same time the noise of combat attracted our forces, and as a result the fort was saved from its attackers; however, despite the fact that the Turks gave up their drive at the sight of approaching reinforcements, those in the rearguard were destroyed although their bridge was close by. Again the ditch and the walls of the fortress were repaired so that the carriers of food could go and return safely from port. Consequently, the envy suffered by the count calmed to the extent that he was called father and defender of our army, and following these events Raymond's reputation rose because single-handed he had met the onslaughts of the enemy. After the blockade of the bridge and the bridge gate, the Turks made sorties from another gate located to the south and near the river. From here they led their horses to a nook, which afforded an excellent pasture between the mountains and the river.

After reconnoitring and setting a time, some of our men circled around the city by crossing a rough mountain while others forded the river, and the combined party led away two thousand horses from the pasture. This number did not count mules and she-mules which were retaken. It is to be noted that formerly many she-mules *en route* from the sea to Antioch had been stolen by the Turks, and these animals now recovered were given back to their owners on proper identification.

Soon afterwards Tancred fortified a monastery situated on the other side of the river, and in view of its importance in blockading the city the count of Toulouse gave Tancred 100 marks of silver, and other princes contributed according to their means.* Thus it pleases me to note that, although we were fewer in numbers, God's grace made us much stronger than the enemy. At this time arriving couriers often reported enemy reinforcements; and, in fact, these rumours spread not only from Armenians and Greeks but also from residents of Antioch. I call to your attention that the Turks occupied Antioch fourteen years before [1084] and, in the absence of servants, had used Armenians and Greeks as such and had given wives to them. They, nevertheless, were disposed to flee to us with horses and arms as soon as escape was possible. Many timid crusaders along with the Armenian merchants took flight as rumours spread, but on the other hand able knights from various fortresses returned and also brought, adjusted and repaired their arms. When the waning cowardice disappeared sufficiently, and boldness – sufficient at all times to brave all perils with and for brothers – returned, one of the besieged Turks [Firuz] confided in our princes that he would deliver Antioch to us.

The Gesta Francorum

Now when my lord Bohemund heard rumours that an immense force of Turks† was coming to attack us, he thought the matter over and came to the other leaders, saying, 'Gentlemen and most valiant knights, what are we to do? We have not sufficient numbers to fight on two fronts. Do you know what we might do? We could divide our forces into two, the foot-soldiers staying here in

* Fort at the church of St George south of the city, commissioned 5 April 1098; see map p. 145.
† Led by Ridwan of Aleppo (1095–1113), brother of Duqaq of Damascus. The battle of Lake Antioch was fought on 9 February 1098.

a body to guard the tents and to contain, so far as possible, those who are in the city. The knights, in another band, could come out with us against our enemies, who are encamped not far off, at the castle of Aregh beyond the Orontes bridge.'

That evening the valiant Bohemund went out from the camp with other very gallant knights, and took up his position between the river and the lake. At dawn he ordered his scouts to go out forthwith and to discover the number of Turkish squadrons, and where they were, and to make sure what they were doing. The scouts went out and began to make careful enquiries as to where the army of the Turks was hidden, and they saw great numbers of the enemy coming up from the river in two bands, with the main army following them. So the scouts returned quickly, saying, 'Look, look, they are coming! Be ready, all of you, for they are almost upon us!' The valiant Bohemund said to the other leaders, 'Gentlemen and unconquered knights, draw up your line of battle!' They answered, 'You are brave and skilful in war, a great man of high repute, resolute and fortunate, and you know how to plan a battle and how to dispose your forces, so do you take command and let the responsibility rest with you. Do whatever seems good to you, both for your own sake and for ours.' Then Bohemund gave orders that each commander should arrange his own forces in line of battle. This was done, and they drew up in six lines. Five of them together charged the enemy, while Bohemund held his men a little in reserve. Our army joined battle successfully and fought hand-to-hand; the din arose to heaven, for all were fighting at once and the storm of missiles darkened the sky. After this the main army of the Turks, which was in reserve, attacked our men fiercely, so that they began to give back a little. When Bohemund, who was a man of great experience, saw this, he groaned, and gave orders to his constable, Robert Fitz-Gerard, saying, 'Charge at top speed, like a brave man, and fight valiantly for God and the Holy Sepulchre, for you know in truth that this is no war of the flesh, but of the spirit. So be very brave, as becomes a champion of Christ. Go in peace, and may the Lord be your defence!' So Bohemund, protected on all sides by the sign of the Cross, charged the Turkish forces, like a lion which has been starving for three or four days, which comes roaring out of its cave thirsting for the blood of cattle, and falls upon the flocks careless of its own safety, tearing the sheep as they flee hither and thither. His attack was so fierce that the points of his banner were flying right over the heads of the Turks.

The other troops, seeing Bohemund's banner carried ahead so honourably, stopped their retreat at once, and all our men in a body charged the Turks, who were amazed and took to flight. Our men pursued them and massacred them right up to the Orontes bridge. The Turks fled in a hurry back to their castle, picked up everything they could find, and then, having thoroughly looted the castle, they set fire to it and took to flight. The Armenians and Syrians, knowing that the Turks had been completely defeated, came out and laid ambushes in passes, killing or capturing many men.

Thus, by God's will, on that day our enemies were overcome. Our men captured plenty of horses and other things of which they were badly in need, and they brought back a hundred heads of the dead Turks to the city gate, where the ambassadors of the amir of Cairo* (for he had sent them to our leaders) were encamped. The men who had stayed in the camp had spent the whole day in fighting with the garrison before the three gates of the city. This battle was fought on Shrove Tuesday, 9 February, by the power of Our Lord Jesus Christ, who with the Father and the Holy Ghost liveth and reigneth, One God, world without end. Amen.

Our men, by God's will, came back exulting and rejoicing in the triumph which they had that day. Their conquered enemies, who were totally defeated, continued to flee, scurrying and wandering hither and thither, some into Khorasan and some into the land of the Saracens. Then our leaders, seeing that our enemies

* Al-Afdal, an Armenian who had risen in Fatimid service to become vizier of Egypt; for these protracted negotiations, see J. France, *Victory in the East* (Cambridge University Press, 1994), esp. pp. 165–6, 251–3, 325–7.

who were in the city were constantly harrying and vexing us, by day and night, wherever they might do us harm, met in council and said, 'Before we lose all our men, let us build a castle at the mosque which is before the city gate where the bridge stands, and by this means we may be able to contain our enemies.' They all agreed and thought that it was a good plan. The count of St Gilles was the first to speak, and he said, 'Help me to build this castle, and I will fortify and hold it.' 'If you wish it,' replied Bohemund, 'and if the other leaders approve, I will go with you to St Simeon* and give safe conduct to the men who are there, so that they can construct this building.† The people who are to stay here must keep watch on all sides so as to defend themselves.'

The count and Bohemund therefore set out for St Simeon's Port. We who stayed behind gathered together, and were beginning to build the castle, when the Turks made ready and sallied out of the city to attack us. They rushed upon us and put our men to flight, killing many, which was a great grief to us.

Next day the Turks, realising that some of our leaders were away, and that they had gone to the port on the previous day, got ready and sallied out to attack them as they came back from the port. When they saw the count and Bohemund coming back and escorting the builders, they began to gnash their teeth and gabble and howl with very loud cries, wheeling round our men, throwing darts and shooting arrows, wounding and slaughtering them most brutally. Their attack was so fierce that our men began to flee over the nearest mountain, or wherever there was a path. Those who could get away quickly escaped alive, and those who could not were killed. On that day more than a thousand of our knights or foot-soldiers suffered martyrdom, and we believe that they went to heaven and were clad in white robes and received the martyr's palm.

Bohemund did not follow the same route which they had followed, but came more quickly with a few knights to where we were gathered together, and we, angry at the loss of our com-

* Port of Antioch; the castle in question is called La Mahomerie, opposite the Bridge Gate; see map p. 145.   † 6 March 1098.

rades, called on the name of Christ and put our trust in the pilgrimage to the Holy Sepulchre and went all together to fight the Turks, whom we attacked with one heart and mind. God's enemies and ours were standing about, amazed and terrified, for they thought that they could defeat and kill us, as they had done with the followers of the count and Bohemund, but Almighty God did not allow them to do so. The knights of the true God, armed at all points with the sign of the Cross, charged them fiercely and made a brave attack upon them, and they fled swiftly across the middle of the narrow bridge to their gate. Those who did not succeed in crossing the bridge alive, because of the great press of men and horses, suffered there everlasting death with the devil and his imps; for we came after them, driving them into the river or throwing them down, so that the waters of that swift stream appeared to be running all red with the blood of Turks, and if by chance any of them tried to climb up the pillars of the bridge, or to reach the bank by swimming, he was stricken by our men who were standing all along the river bank. The din and the shouts of our men and the enemy echoed to heaven, and the shower of missiles and arrows covered the sky and hid the daylight. The Christian women who were in the city came to the windows in the walls, and when they saw the wretched fate of the Turks they clapped their hands secretly. (The Armenians and Syrians who were under the command of Turkish leaders had to shoot arrows at us, whether they liked it or not.) Twelve amirs of the Turkish army suffered death in body and soul in the course of that battle, together with fifteen hundred more of their bravest and most resolute soldiers, who were the best in fighting to defend the city. The survivors no longer had the courage to howl and gabble day and night, as they used to do. Darkness alone separated the two sides, and night put an end to the fighting with darts, spears and arrows. Thus our enemies were defeated by the power of God and the Holy Sepulchre, so that henceforth they had less courage than before, both in words and works. On that day we recouped ourselves very well, with many things of which we were badly in need, as well as horses.

Next day, at dawn, other Turks came out from the city and collected all the stinking corpses of the dead Turks which they could find on the river bank, except those that were concealed in the actual river bed, and buried them at the mosque which is beyond the bridge before the gate of the city, and together with them they buried cloaks, gold bezants, bows and arrows, and other tools the names of which we do not know. When our men heard that the Turks had buried their dead, they made ready and came in haste to that devil's chapel, and ordered the bodies to be dug up and the tombs destroyed, and the dead men dragged out of their graves. They threw all the corpses into a pit, and cut off their heads and brought them to our tents (so that they could count the number exactly), except for those which they loaded on to four horses belonging to the ambassadors of the amir of Cairo and sent to the sea coast. When the Turks saw this, they were very sad and grieved almost to death, for they lamented every day and did nothing but weep and howl. On the third day* we combined together, with great satisfaction, to build the castle already mentioned, with stones we had taken from the tombs of the Turks. When the castle was finished, we began to press hard from every side upon our enemies whose pride was brought low. But we went safely wherever we liked, to the gate and to the mountains, praising and glorifying our Lord God, to whom be honour and glory, world without end. Amen.

Stephen, Count of Blois and Chartres, presents one of the First Crusade's most enigmatic figures. Hen-pecked by his redoubtable bluestocking wife, Adela, daughter of William the Conqueror, Stephen acquitted himself well prior to the siege of Antioch. There, his talents were recognised by his being appointed ductor of the whole expedition, a reflection of the growing institutional ties that the leaders imposed on themselves to enhance their chances of success. Yet less than ten weeks later Stephen fled on the night of 2 June 1098, only hours before the city fell. After a concerted campaign of domestic humiliation by his ashamed wife, he returned to

* Possibly 8 March 1098.

*the Near East with the ill-fated 1101 expedition only to be killed at
the battle of Ramleh in 1102, his reputation partly restored.**

Stephen, Count of Blois and Chartres, to His Wife, Adela, Antioch, 29 March 1098

Count Stephen to Adela, his sweetest and most amiable wife,† to
his dear children, and to all his vassals of all ranks – his greeting
and blessing.

You may be very sure, dearest, that the messenger whom I sent
to give you pleasure left me before Antioch safe and unharmed,
and through God's grace in the greatest prosperity. And already
at that time, together with all the chosen army of Christ, endowed
with great valour by him, we had been continuously advancing for
twenty-three weeks towards the home of our Lord Jesus. You may
know for certain, my beloved, that of gold, silver and many other
kind of riches I now have twice as much as your love had assigned
to me when I left you. For all our princes, with the common consent
of the whole army, against my own wishes, have made me up to the
present time the leader, chief and director of their whole expedition.

You have certainly heard that after the capture of the city of
Nicaea we fought a great battle with the perfidious Turks and by
God's aid conquered them. Next we conquered for the Lord all
Asia Minor and afterwards Cappadocia. And we learned that
there was a certain Turkish prince Assam,‡ dwelling in Cappadocia; thither we directed our course. All his castles we
conquered by force and compelled him to flee to a certain very
strong castle situated on a high rock. We also gave the land of
that Assam to one of our chiefs and in order that he might conquer
the above-mentioned Assam, we left there with him many soldiers
of Christ. Thence, continually following the wicked Turks, we

---

* See *An Eyewitness History of the Crusades: The Second Crusade* (Folio Society,
London, 2004), pp. 26–7.
† A formal endearment; contemporaries portrayed the formidable Adela,
daughter of William the Conqueror, as neither sweet nor amiable, at least to
her browbeaten husband.   ‡ Possibly of the Danishmends.

drove them through the midst of Armenia, as far as the great river Euphrates. Having left all their baggage and beasts of burden on the bank, they fled across the river into Arabia.

The bolder of the Turkish soldiers, indeed, entering Syria, hastened by forced marches night and day, in order to be able to enter the royal city of Antioch before our approach. The whole army of God learning this gave due praise and thanks to the omnipotent Lord. Hastening with great joy to the aforesaid chief city of Antioch, we besieged it and very often had many conflicts there with the Turks; and seven times with the citizens of Antioch and with the innumerable troops coming to its aid, whom we rushed to meet, we fought with the fiercest courage, under the leadership of Christ. And in all these seven battles, by the aid of the Lord God, we conquered and most assuredly killed an innumerable host of them. In those battles, indeed, and in very many attacks made upon the city, many of our brethren and followers were killed and their souls were borne to the joys of paradise.

We found the city of Antioch very extensive, fortified with incredible strength and almost impregnable. In addition, more than five thousand bold Turkish soldiers had entered the city, not counting the Saracens, Publicans,* Arabs, Turcopuli, Syrians, Armenians and other different races of whom an infinite multitude had gathered together there. In fighting against these enemies of God and of our own we have, by God's grace, endured many sufferings and innumerable evils up to the present time. Many also have already exhausted all their resources in this very holy passion. Very many of our Franks, indeed, would have met a temporal death from starvation, if the clemency of God and our money had not succoured them. Before the above-mentioned city of Antioch, indeed, throughout the whole winter we suffered for our Lord Christ from excessive cold and enormous torrents of rain. What some say about the impossibility of bearing the heat of the sun throughout Syria is untrue, for the winter there is very similar to our winter in the west.

* i.e. Paulicians, technically a small eastern heretical sect, but here merely indicating local non-Catholic Christians.

When truly Yaghi Sayan, the amir of Antioch – that is, prince and lord – perceived that he was hard-pressed by us, he sent his son, Shams al-Dawla by name, to the prince who holds Jerusalem, and to the prince of Calep, Ridwan, and to Duqaq ibn Tutush, prince of Damascus. He also sent into Arabia to Bolianuth and to Carathania to Hamelnuth. These five amirs with twelve thousand picked Turkish horsemen suddenly came to aid the inhabitants of Antioch. We, indeed, ignorant of all this, had sent many of our soldiers away to the cities and fortresses. For there are 165 cities and fortresses throughout Syria which are in our power. But a little before they reached the city, we attacked them at three leagues' distance with seven hundred soldiers, on a certain plain near the 'Iron Bridge'. God, however, fought for us, his faithful, against them. For on that day, fighting in the strength that God gives, we conquered them and killed an innumerable multitude – God continually fighting for us – and we also carried back to the army more than two hundred of their heads, in order that the people might rejoice on that account.* The emperor of Babylon [Egypt] also sent Saracen messengers to our army with letters, and through these he established peace and concord with us.†

I love to tell you, dearest, what happened to us during Lent. Our princes had caused a fortress to be built before a certain gate which was between our camp and the sea.‡ For the Turks, daily issuing from this gate, killed some of our men on their way to the sea. The city of Antioch is about five leagues' distance from the sea. For this reason they sent the excellent Bohemund and Raymond, count of St Gilles, to the sea with only sixty horsemen, in order that they might bring mariners to aid in this work. When, however, they were returning to us with those mariners, the Turks collected an army, fell suddenly upon our two leaders and forced them to a perilous flight. In that unexpected flight we lost more than five hundred of our foot-soldiers – to the glory of God. Of our horsemen, however, we lost only two, for certain.

* Battle of Lake Antioch, 9 February 1098.   † See above, p. 179n.
‡ La Mahomerie, 5–20 March 1098.

Hours after Count Stephen deserted, the city fell, a result of Bohemund's imaginative diplomacy with a disaffected defender, possibly an Armenian called Firuz, who held one section of the eastern wall where, thanks to the bravery of a small contingent of troops in a daring commando night attack (2–3 June 1098), the Christians effected an entry into the city. Its capture was recorded by Raymond of Aguilers.

Following a common council, the princes despatched Bohemund and Godfrey as well as the count of Flanders to test this offer. Upon their arrival at a hill of Antioch in the middle of the night, a messenger from the traitorous Turk commanded, 'Do not move until a lamp passes by.'*

It was customary for three or four men carrying lamps to pass along the walls, waking and cautioning sentinels. When the lights passed, our men in the shadows of the wall set a ladder and started to climb. A Frank, named Fulcher and undoubtedly the brother of Budellus of Chartres, fearlessly mounted the wall and was followed closely by the count of Flanders, who ordered Bohemund and the duke to follow. However, in the hasty ascent the ladder broke, but those who were already atop the wall lowered themselves into the city and broke open a gate. Entering by this means the crusaders killed all whom they met, and at daybreak they cried out in such terrifying screams that the whole city was thrown into confusion and women and children wept.

Some of the Christians in the nearby fort of Raymond, awakened by the tumult, repeated, 'Enemy reinforcements have come.' But others replied, 'The cries of anguish are not the voices of rejoicing.'

Now as dawn broke our standards flew atop the southern hill of Antioch. Panicked by the sight of our troops on the overhanging hill, some of the Antiochians rushed through the gates while others leaped from the walls. The Lord threw them into such chaos that not a single one stood and fought. After many months

* The night of 2–3 June 1098.

of arduous siege this happy scene now unfolded for us, a scene in which the long-time defenders of Antioch could neither escape from the city nor avoid death in daring flight.

An agreeable and charming occurrence for us took place there when some Turks, attempting to escape unobserved through the crags separating the hill from the north, met a group of crusaders. Forced to retreat, the thwarted Turks spurred their steeds so hurriedly that all plunged together from the rocky cliffs. The fatal plunge of the Turks was indeed a pleasant spectacle for us, but we were saddened by the loss of more than three hundred horses dashed to death there.*

We shall not comment upon the amount of booty, but you may believe whatever comes to mind and compute more. We cannot estimate the number of slain Turks and Saracens, and it would be sadistic to relate the novel and varied means of death. In the mean time the defenders of the citadel, situated on a middle hill, observed the slaughter of their comrades and the cessation of the battle, and consequently chose to defend their fort. But Yaghi Sayan, fleeing by way of one of the gates, was seized and decapitated by Armenian peasants, who in turn presented us with his head. Yaghi Sayan, who had decapitated many Armenians, was, I think because of God's inexpressible will, in turn beheaded by their countrymen.

The city of Antioch fell on 3 June, but it had been under attack from around 22 October of the preceding year. Our troops refrained from attacking the citadel while they examined and took inventory of the spoils; and further oblivious of God, the bestower of so many favours, they gormandised sumptuously and splendidly as they gave heed to dancing girls.

The author of the Gesta Francorum *gives the impression that he was in the party of knights that scaled the walls that night.*

By this time all the paths were shut and blocked against the

---

* This refers to the desperate dependence on the supply of horses to make the western knights effective.

Turks, except for that by the river, where there was a castle and also a monastery.* If we could have succeeded in fortifying this castle in strength, none of the enemy would have dared to go out of the city gate. So our men held a council, and agreed unanimously, saying, 'Let us choose one of our number who can hold that castle strongly, and keep our enemies from the mountains and the plain, and prevent them from going into and out of the city.' Then Tancred was the first to stand forward among the others, and he said, 'If I may know what reward I shall have, I will guard the castle carefully with only my own followers, and I will do all that a man may to cut the path by which our enemies most often launch their cruel attacks.' The council immediately offered him 400 marks of silver,† so he made no delay, but arose at once with his best knights and followers, and forthwith blocked the paths against the Turks, so that none of them dared to go out of the city gate, either for fodder, wood or anything else which they needed, because they were very much afraid of him. Tancred stayed there with his men and began to blockade the city closely. That same day a very large number of Armenians and Syrians came confidently down from the mountains, carrying provisions for the Turks, to help those who were besieged in the city. Tancred met them and captured both them and all their loads – corn, wine, barley, oil and other such things. He was so forceful and so lucky that he managed to keep all the paths barred and blocked against the Turks until Antioch was taken.

I cannot tell you all the things which we did before the city fell, for there is in this land neither clerk nor layman who could write down the whole story or describe it as it happened, but I will tell you a little of it.

There was a certain amir of Turkish race called Firuz,‡

---

* Monastery of St George.

† Evidence for collective action based probably on a common fund established by the council of leaders.

‡ Possibly a renegade Armenian Christian; he knew Greek; see below, pp. 190–1 and note.

who had struck up a great friendship with Bohemund. Bohemund used often to send messengers to him, sounding him as to whether he would receive him, in friendship's name, into the city, and promising in return that he would willingly have Firuz christened, and would cause riches and great honour to be bestowed on him. Firuz agreed, and accepted the promised benefits, saying, 'I am warden of three towers, which I freely promise to Bohemund, and I will receive him into them at whatever time he shall choose.' So when Bohemund was sure that he could enter the city he was glad, and came coolly, looking pleased with himself, to the council of leaders, and said to them jokingly, 'Most gallant knights, you see that we are all, both great and less, in dire poverty and misery, and we do not know whence better fortune will come to us. If, therefore, you think it a good and proper plan, let one of us set himself above the others, on condition that if he can capture the city or engineer its downfall by any means, by himself or by others, we will all agree to give it to him.' The other leaders all refused and denied him, saying, 'This city shall not be granted to anyone, but we will all share it alike; as we have had equal toil, so let us have equal honour.' When Bohemund heard these words he looked less pleased, and went straight off.

Not long afterwards we heard news of an army of our enemies, drawn from the Turks, Paulicians, Agulani,* Azymites† and many other peoples. All our leaders came together at once and held a council, saying, 'If Bohemund can take this city, either by himself or by others, we will thereafter give it to him gladly, on condition that if the emperor comes to our aid and fulfils all his obligations which he promised and vowed, we will return the city to him as it is right to do. Otherwise Bohemund shall take it into his power.' So Bohemund now began to send a tactful request to his friend every day, making the most flattering, extensive and tempting promises, saying, 'See, now we have a chance

---

* Paulicians and Agulani were eastern Christian heretics, but the terms are not used precisely here (cf. p. 184n).
† A fanciful name for Armenians. These rumours concerned the approach of Kerboga, atabeg (i.e. military governor) of Mosul, with a new relief army.

of doing whatever good deed we want to do; so now, friend Firuz, give me your help.' Firuz was pleased by the message, and said that he would give Bohemund all the help that he was bound to provide, and the next night he secretly despatched his son to Bohemund, as a pledge to give him greater confidence that he should enter the city. He also sent word that on the morrow the whole Frankish army should be summoned, and should pretend to go out and plunder the land of the Saracens, but that afterwards it should return quickly by the western mountain.* 'And I', he said, 'will watch out for these troops very carefully, and I will admit them into the towers which I have in my power and keeping.' Then Bohemund sent quickly for one of his followers, nicknamed 'Bad-crown', and told him to go out as a herald to summon a great force of Franks to make faithful preparations to go into the land of the Saracens, and this Bad-crown did. Bohemund confided his plan to Duke Godfrey and the count of Flanders, the count of St Gilles and the bishop of Le Puy, telling them, 'God willing, this night shall Antioch be betrayed to us.'

All the preparations were thus made. The knights went by the plain and the foot-soldiers by the mountain, and they rode and marched all night until towards dawn, when they began to approach the towers of which Firuz, who had been watching all night, was warden. Then Bohemund dismounted at once and said to his men, 'Go on, strong in heart and lucky in your comrades, and scale the ladder into Antioch, for by God's will we shall have it in our power in a trice.' The men came to the ladder, which was already set up and lashed firmly to the battlements of the city, and nearly sixty of them went up it and occupied the towers which Firuz was guarding. But when Firuz saw that so few of our men had come up, he began to be afraid, fearing lest he and they should fall into the hands of the Turks and he said (in Greek), Μικροὺς Φράγκους ἔχομεν (which means 'We have few Franks'). 'Where is the hero Bohemund? Where is that unconquered soldier?' Meanwhile a certain soldier from southern Italy went back down the ladder and ran as

* See map p. 145.

fast as he could to Bohemund, crying out, 'Why are you stand-ing here, sir, if you have any sense? What did you come to get? Look! We have taken three towers already!'* Bohemund and the others bestirred themselves, and they all came rejoicing to the ladder. When those who were in the towers saw them, they began to call out cheerfully, 'God's will!' and we called back the same words. Now an amazing number of men began to climb; they went up and ran quickly to the other towers. Whomsoever they found there they put to death at once, killing the brother of Firuz among them. Meanwhile the ladder, up which our men had climbed, happened to break, so that we were plunged in great despair and grief. However, although the ladder was broken, there was a gate not far from us to the left, but it was shut and some of us did not know where it was, for it was still dark. Yet by fumbling with our hands and poking about we found it, and all made a rush at it, so that we broke it down and entered.†

At this moment the shrieks of countless people arose, making an amazing noise throughout the city. Bohemund did not waste time on this account, but ordered his glorious banner to be car-ried up to a hill opposite the citadel. All the people in the city were screaming at once. At dawn,‡ our men who were outside in the tents heard an overpowering din break out in the city, so they hurried out and saw Bohemund's banner aloft on the hill. They all came running as fast as they could and entered the city gates, killing all the Turks and Saracens whom they found there except for those who fled up to the citadel. Some other Turks got out through the gates and saved their lives by flight. Yaghi Sayan,§ their leader, who was much afraid of the Franks, took to flight headlong with many companions, and as they fled they came into Tancred's land not far from the city. Their horses were tired

* This suggests mutual understanding of Greek, possibly shared by Bohe-mund, whose baptismal name, Mark, was Greek. Bohemund was a nickname after a legendary giant.
† The immediacy of this account has suggested to some the presence of the author on this raid.   ‡ 3 June 1098.
§ Governor of Antioch since 1086/7, in 1097–8 an ally of Ridwan of Aleppo.

out, so they entered one of the villages and hid in a house. When the people who lived on that mountain (they were Syrians and Armenians) knew who the fugitive was, they captured him at once and cut off his head, which they took to my lord Bohemund as the price of their freedom. His belt and scabbard were worth 60 bezants.

All this happened on 3 June, which was a Thursday. All the streets of the city on every side were full of corpses, so that no one could endure to be there because of the stench, nor could anyone walk along the narrow paths of the city except over the corpses of the dead.

Ibn al-Qalanisi recorded the fate of the city and its governor.

At the beginning of June 1098 the report arrived that certain of the men of Antioch among the armourers in the train of the amir Yaghi Sayan had entered into a conspiracy against Antioch and had come to an agreement with the Franks to deliver the city up to them, because of some ill usage and confiscations which they had formerly suffered at his hands. They found an opportunity of seizing one of the city bastions which they sold to the Franks, and thence admitted them into the city during the night.* At daybreak they raised the battle-cry, whereupon Yaghi Sayan took to flight and went out with a large body, but not one person amongst them escaped to safety. When he reached the neighbourhood of Armanaz, an estate near Ma'arrat Masrin, he fell from his horse to the ground. One of his companions raised him up and remounted him, but he could not maintain his balance on the back of the horse, and after falling repeatedly he died. As for Antioch, the number of men, women and children killed, taken prisoner and enslaved from its population is beyond computation. About three thousand men fled to the citadel and fortified themselves in it, and some few escaped for whom God had decreed escape.

* 2–3 June 1098.

Anselm of Ribemont provided his own account of the end of the siege.

In the name of the Lord!

To his lord and father, Manasses, by the grace of God venerable archbishop of Rheims, Anselm of Ribemont, his loyal vassal and humble servant; greeting.

Let Your Eminence, reverend father and lord, know that, even though absent and not present, we are daily asking aid in our hearts from you – not only from you, but, also, from all the sons of the holy mother church of Rheims, in whom we have the greatest faith. Likewise, inasmuch as you are our lord, and the counsel of the whole kingdom of France is especially dependent upon you, we are keeping you, father, informed of whatever happy and adverse events have happened to us. Let the others, moreover, be informed through you, that you may share equally in our sufferings, and rejoice with us in our success.

We have informed you how we fared in the siege and capture of Nicaea, in our departure thence and our journey through all Romania and Armenia. It now remains for us to tell you a little about the siege of Antioch, the many kinds of danger we there tasted, and the innumerable battles which we fought against the king of Aleppo, the king of Damascus, and against the adulterous king of Jerusalem.*

Antioch has been besieged by the army of the Lord since the thirteenth day before the calends of November† with exceeding valour and courage beyond words. What unheard of battles you might have perceived there at a certain gateway to the west! How marvellous it would seem to you, were you present, to see them daily rushing forth through six gates – both they and ourselves fighting for safety and life! At that time our princes, seeking to enclose the city more and more closely, first besieged the eastern gate, and Bohemund, having built a fort there, stationed a part

* Ridwan, Duqaq and, probably, Sukman ibn Ortuq of Jerusalem.
† 19 October 1097.

of his army in it. However, since our princes then felt somewhat elated, God, who chasteneth every son whom he loveth, so chastened us that hardly seven hundred horses could be found in our army; and thus, not because we lacked proven and valiant men, but from lack of horses, or food, or through excessive cold, almost all were dying. The Turks, moreover, supplied with horses and all necessities in abundance, were wont daily to ride around our camp, a certain stream which lay between serving as a wall. There was likewise a castle of the Turks almost eight miles away; and these Turks were daily killing many of our men, who were going back and forth from our army. Our princes went out against them and with God's help put them to flight and killed many of them. Therefore the ruler of Antioch, seeing himself afflicted, called the king of Damascus to his aid. By God's providence, this king met Bohemund and the count of Flanders, who had gone to find food with a part of our army, and, God's help prevailing, he was defeated and routed by them.* The ruler of Antioch, still concerned about his safety, sent to the king of Aleppo and aroused him with promises of very great wealth, to the end that he should come with all his forces. Upon his arrival, our princes went forth from camp, and that day, God being their helper, with seven hundred knights and a few foot-soldiers they defeated twelve thousand Turks with their king, put them to flight, and killed many of them.† Our men regained not a few horses from that battle, and returned rejoicing with victory. Growing stronger and stronger, therefore, from that day our men took counsel with renewed courage as to how they might besiege the western gate which cut off access to the sea, wood and fodder. By common agreement, therefore, Bohemund and the count of St Gilles went to the coast to fetch those who were staying there.‡ Meanwhile, those who had remained to look after the possessions, seeking to

---

* The foraging raid's encounter with Duqaq late December 1097; a misleading verdict on the battle which left the crusaders empty-handed even if the Muslims withdrew.　　† Battle of Lake Antioch, 9 February 1098.
‡ 5 March 1098.

acquire a name for themselves, went out incautiously one day after breakfast, near that western gate, from which they were ingloriously repulsed and put to flight. On the third day after this, Bohemund and the count of St Gilles, on their way back, sent word to the princes of the army to meet them, [intending] together to besiege the gate. However, since the latter delayed for a short time, Bohemund and the count of St Gilles were beaten and put to flight. Therefore all our men, grieving and bewailing their disgrace, as well, for a thousand of our men fell that day, formed their lines and defeated and put to flight the Turks, who offered great resistance. On this day, moreover, almost fourteen hundred of the enemy perished both by weapons and in the river, which was swollen with winter rains.

And so, when this had been accomplished, our men began to build the fortress, which they strengthened, also, with a double moat and a very strong wall, as well as with two towers. In it they placed the count of St Gilles with machine men and bowmen.* Oh, with what great labour we established the fortress! One part of our army served the eastern front, another looked after the camp, while all the rest worked on this fortress. Of the latter, the machine men and bowmen kept watch on the gate; the rest, including the princes themselves, did not stop in the work of carrying stones and building the wall. Why recount the trials of many kinds, which, even if passed over in silence, are sufficiently evident in themselves – hunger, intemperate weather and the desertion of faint-hearted soldiers? The more bitter they were, the more ready our men were in enduring them. Yet, indeed, we think that we should by no means pass in silence the fact that on a certain day the Turks pretended that they would surrender the city and carried the deception so far as to receive some of our men among them, and several of their men came out to us. While this was going on in this manner, they, like the faithless people that they were, set a trap for us in which Walo, the constable, and others of them as well as

* The fort of La Mahomerie.

of us were destroyed. A few days after this, moreover, it was announced to us that Kerboga, chief of the army of the king of the Persians, had sworn to our death. God, however, who does not desert those who place their trust in him, did not abandon his people, but on the nones of June* compassionately gave to us the city of Antioch, which three of its citizens betrayed. We, however, devastated the city, and on that same day killed all the pagans in it, except some who were holding out in the castle of the city.

* 5 June; in fact 2–3 June.

VI

The Holy Lance

June 1098

The arrival of Kerboga of Mosul plunged the Christian army into its worst crisis as the elation at finally entering Antioch turned to hopeless despair at the sight of the huge Muslim relief force and the consequent rapid deterioration of supplies and morale. The combination of famine, danger and the prospect of violent death produced a new wave of desertions (10–11 June). The problem for the leadership lay in the difficulty of raising the spirits of the army sufficiently to attempt a break-out, seemingly the only chance of survival. The Gesta Francorum describes the crusaders' plight.

Now Kerboga* was commander-in-chief of the army of the sultan of Persia.† While he was still in Khorasan, Yaghi Sayan the amir of Antioch had instantly sent him an envoy asking for timely help (since a very strong army of Franks held him closely besieged in Antioch) and promising to give him either the city of Antioch or very great riches if he would bring aid. Since Kerboga had with him a great army of Turks whom he had been assembling for a long time, and had been given leave by the caliph (who is the pope of the Turks)‡ to kill Christians, he set out, there and then, on the long journey to Antioch. The amir of Jerusalem came to his help with an army, and the king of Damascus brought a great number of men.§ So Kerboga collected an

* Military governor (atabeg) of Mosul (*c*.1094–1108).

† Berkyaruk, Seljuk sultan of Baghdad 1094–1105, son of Malik Shah.

‡ Abbasid caliph of Baghdad, a spiritual figurehead controlled by the Seljuk sultans. The caliph (Commander of the Faithful) was not the equivalent of the Roman pope, for whom there was no parallel in Islam.

§ Sukman ibn Ortuq ruled Jerusalem until 1098; Duqaq ruled Damascus.

immense force of pagans – Turks, Arabs, Saracens, Paulicians, Azymites, Kurds, Persians, Agulani* and many other people who could not be counted. The Agulani numbered three thousand; they fear neither spears nor arrows nor any other weapon, for they and their horses are covered all over with plates of iron. They will not use any weapons except swords when they are fighting.

All these men came to raise the siege of Antioch, so that they might scatter the company of the Franks, and when they had approached the city there met them Shams-al-Dawla, son of Yaghi Sayan the amir of Antioch, and he ran straight up to Kerboga weeping, entreating him and saying, 'Most victorious prince, I am a suppliant begging you for help, for the Franks are besieging me on all sides in the citadel of Antioch, and they have got the city in their power, and they want to drive us out of Rum and Syria and even from Khorasan. They have accomplished everything they planned, and have killed my father, and the next thing will be that they will kill me and you and all the rest of our people. I have waited a long time for assistance, so that you may help me in this peril.' Kerboga answered, 'If you want my sincere help, I will faithfully give you assistance in this peril, but you must first surrender the citadel to me, and I will put my own men in to guard it. Then you shall see how much I can help you.' Then said Shams-al-Dawla, 'If you can kill all the Franks and send me their heads, I will give you the citadel, and do homage to you, and hold it as your liege man.' 'That will not do at all,' replied Kerboga. 'You must surrender the citadel into my hands at once.' So Shams-al-Dawla gave him the citadel willy-nilly.

On the third day after we entered the city† Kerboga's vanguard came up before the walls, for his main army was encamped at the Orontes bridge, where it stormed one of the towers on the bridge and killed all the garrison in it. None of our men there survived except the leader, whom we found, bound in iron chains, when we had fought the great battle. Next day the

* See above, p. 189nn. † In fact 4–5 June 1098.

main army of the pagans moved up and approached the city, encamping between the two rivers,* where it stayed for two days. When Kerboga had received the surrender of the citadel† he called one of his amirs, whom he knew to be a truthful, kindly and peaceable man, and said to him, 'I want you to hold this citadel as my liegeman, for I have known for a very long time that you are most worthy of trust. Therefore I beg you to keep it with extreme care.' The amir replied, 'I would prefer never to do such a thing for you, but I will do it on this condition, that if the Franks drive you back and defeat you in mortal combat, I may surrender the citadel to them at once.' Then Kerboga said to him, 'I know that you are such an honourable and brave man that I will agree to anything you think fit.'

After this Kerboga went back to his army, and immediately the Turks, making mock of the Frankish troops, brought him a very poor sword all covered with rust, and a thoroughly bad wooden bow, and a spear which was quite useless, all of which they had just stolen from the poor pilgrims, and they said, 'Look at the arms which the Franks have brought to fight against us!' Then Kerboga began to chuckle, and said to all those who were present, 'Are these the warlike and splendid weapons which the Christians have brought into Asia against us, and with these do they confidently expect to drive us beyond the furthest boundaries of Khorasan, and to blot out our names beyond the rivers of the Amazons? Are these the people who drove all our forefathers out of Rum‡ and from the royal city of Antioch, which is the honoured capital of all Syria?' Then he called his scribe and said, 'Be quick and write many letters which may be read in Khorasan, in these words: "To the caliph our pope and the lord sultan our king, that most valiant warrior, and to all the most gallant knights of Khorasan, greeting and boundless honour! Enjoy yourselves, rejoicing with one accord, and fill your bellies, and let commands and injunctions

* See map p. 145.   † Still in Muslim hands; see map p. 145.
‡ A reference to Byzantine successes in northern Syria in the late tenth century under the emperors Nicephorus Phocas and John Tzimisces.

be sent throughout the whole country that all men shall give themselves up to wantonness and lust, and take their pleasure in getting many sons who shall fight bravely against the Christians and defeat them. And receive, with my good wishes, these three weapons which we have already taken from the Frankish rabble, and learn what kind of arms the Franks have brought against us. Know also that I have got all the Franks shut up in Antioch, and I hold the citadel in my power while they are down below in the city. I have them all in my hands, and I will have them either executed or led into Khorasan in most bitter captivity, because they threaten to repulse us by their weapons and to drive us out of all our lands, as they drove our forefathers out of Rum and Syria. Moreover I swear to you by Muhammad and by all the names of our gods* that I will not appear again before your face until I have conquered, by the strength of my right arm, the royal city of Antioch and all Syria, Rum, Bulgaria and even as far as Apulia, to the glory of the gods and of you and of all who are sprung from the race of the Turks." ' This was the end of the letter.†

It happened that the mother of Kerboga, who was in the city of Aleppo, came at once to him, and said to him, 'My son, are these things true, which I hear?' 'What things?' said he, and she answered, 'I have heard that you desire to join battle with the people of the Franks.' 'Know', said he, 'that this is quite true.' She cried, 'I beseech you, my son, by the names of all the gods and by your own great excellence, not to join battle with the Franks, for you are an unconquered warrior and no man has ever seen you fleeing from the battlefield before any victor. Your prowess is renowned, and brave soldiers tremble, wherever they may be, at the mere sound of your name. Surely we know well enough, my son, that you are a mighty warrior and a man of valour, so that no people, Christian or pagan, can show any

---

* A common Christian error in the early Middle Ages; in fact Islam is more rigidly monotheist than Christianity's doctrine of the Trinity.
† Clearly fictitious; all of Kerboga's utterances are designed to emphasise the alien and the exotic.

courage in your sight – men flee before you when they have but heard your name, as sheep before a raging lion. Therefore I implore you, beloved son, listen to my counsels and never let the idea of making war with the Christians occupy your mind or find a place in your counsels.' When Kerboga heard his mother's warnings he replied furiously, 'What sort of tale are you telling me, mother? I think you are mad or possessed by the furies – why, I have more amirs in my following than the whole of the Christians, both great and small.' 'O sweetest son,' replied his mother, 'the Christians alone cannot fight with you – indeed I know that they are unworthy to meet you in battle – but their god fights for them every day, and keeps them day and night under his protection, and watches over them as a shepherd watches over his flock, and suffers no people to hurt or vex them, and if anyone wishes to fight them, this same god of theirs will smite them, as he says by the mouth of David the prophet, "Scatter the people that delight in war" and again, "Pour out thine anger upon the people that have not known thee, and upon the kingdoms that have not called upon thy name." Before they are even ready to join battle, their god, mighty and powerful in battle, together with his saints, has already conquered all their enemies, and how much more will he do to you who are his own enemy, and have prepared with all your might to resist? Beloved, know also the truth of this, that those Christians are called "sons of Christ" and, by the mouth of the prophets, "sons of adoption and promise" and the apostle says that they are "heirs of Christ", to whom Christ has even now given the promised inheritance, saying by the prophets, "From the rising of the sun to the going down thereof shall be your bounds, and no man shall stand against you."* Who can contradict these words or resist them? I tell you truly that if you join battle with these men you will suffer very great loss and dishonour, and lose many of your faithful soldiers, and you will leave behind all the plunder which you have taken, and escape as a panic-stricken fugitive. You will not die now in this

* A series of misquotations; see above, p. 63n.

battle, but yet in this very year,* for this same god, when his wrath is roused, does not punish the offender at once, but when he wills he punishes him with manifest vengeance, and therefore I fear that he will condemn you to a heavy sentence. You will not, as I say, die at once, but nevertheless you will lose all that you now have.'

Then Kerboga, when he had heard his mother's words, was bitterly grieved to the depths of his heart, and he replied, 'Mother dearest, I desire to know who told you these things about the Christian people, how their god loves them so dearly, and how he has in himself such great might in battle, and how these Christians shall conquer in the battle of Antioch and take our spoils and pursue us, gaining a great victory, and how I am doomed to sudden death this very year.' His mother answered sorrowfully, 'Beloved son, more than a hundred years ago it was discovered in our Koran, as well as in the books of the infidel, that the Christian people was destined to come upon us and to defeat us in every place, and that it should rule over the pagans, and that our people should be subject to these men wherever they are; but I do not know whether these things will come to pass now or in the future. Therefore I, wretched woman that I am, have followed you from Aleppo the fairest of cities, where by my observations and careful calculations I have looked into the stars of the sky, and studied the planets and the twelve signs of the zodiac and all kinds of omens. In all of them I found prognostications that the Christian people is fated to defeat us utterly, and therefore I fear terribly for you, with bitter grief, for I may live to be bereft of you.'

Kerboga said to her, 'Mother dearest, tell me the truth about certain things which my heart will not let me believe.' 'Willingly, beloved,' said she, 'if you will tell me what you do not understand.' He answered, 'Are not Bohemund and Tancred the gods of the Franks, and do they not deliver them from their enemies? And do they not eat two thousand cows and four thousand pigs

* As Kerboga lived longer than this, it has been suggested this indicates this passage was written in 1098; this is an attractive but unnecessary inference.

at a single meal?' 'Beloved son,' said his mother, 'Bohemund and Tancred are mortal, like all other men, but their god loves them exceedingly beyond all others, and therefore he grants them excelling courage in battle. For their god – almighty is his name – is he who made the heaven and earth, the sea and all that in them is; whose throne in heaven is prepared from all eternity, whose power is everywhere to be feared.' 'Be it so,' said her son, 'yet will I not turn aside from battle with them.' So when his mother heard that he would pay no heed to her counsels, she was exceedingly sad; but she went back to Aleppo taking with her everything on which she could lay her hands.

On the third day after his arrival at Antioch Kerboga prepared for battle, and a great force of Turks came with him and approached the city from the side on which the citadel stood. We, thinking that we could resist them, prepared to fight, but their power was such that we could not withstand them, so we were forced back into the city. The gate was so terribly strait and narrow that many of the people were trampled to death in the crowd. All through that day (which was Thursday),* until the evening, some of our men were fighting outside the walls and others within. While this was going on, William of Grandmesnil, Aubrey his brother, Guy Trousseau and Lambert the Poor, who were all scared by the battle of the previous day, which had lasted until evening, let themselves down from the wall secretly during the night and fled on foot to the sea, so that both their hands and their feet were worn away to the bone.† Many others, whose names I do not know, fled with them. When they reached the ships which were in St Simeon's Port they said to the sailors, 'You poor devils, why are you staying here? All our men are dead, and we have barely escaped death ourselves, for the Turkish army is besieging the others in the city.' When the sailors heard this they were horrified, and rushed in terror to their ships and put to sea. At that moment the Turks arrived and killed everyone whom

* 10 June 1098.
† In consequence, these deserters became known derisively in the west as 'rope-danglers'.

they could catch. They burned those ships which were still in the mouth of the river and took their cargoes.

As for us who stayed in Antioch, we could not defend ourselves against the attacks from the citadel, so we built a wall between us and it, and patrolled it day and night. Meanwhile we were so short of food that we were eating our horses and asses.

In this heightened state of tension, and amid an atmosphere of religious agitation carefully orchestrated by the legate Adhemar to encourage cohesion, the spiritual came to the assistance of the temporal. Dramatic stories of divine visions experienced by two Provençal crusaders, Stephen of Valence and Peter Bartholomew, came to light the day after the mass desertion (11 June). Three days later Peter Bartholomew, as he had predicted, after digging beneath the floor of the cathedral of St Peter, discovered what observers, who included the chronicler Raymond of Aguilers, took to be the Holy Lance that had pierced the side of Christ on the Cross. Although sceptics, especially among the Norman contingent, later cast doubt on the authenticity of the relic, at the time its discovery played a central role in raising morale through emphasis on the holiness of the crusaders' mission, generating enough self-confidence (or controlled instead of panicked desperation) in the troops to make a confrontation with Kerboga's force possible. On 28 June, the newly emboldened Christian army, carrying the relic of the Holy Lance with them, sallied forth to inflict an astonishing defeat on the numerically superior Muslims. Thereafter the latent religiosity of the whole enterprise increasingly asserted itself in crusaders' own perceptions of their actions and fate, a feeling most vividly captured by Raymond of Aguilers, whose account of these events reads more like a collection of inspiring miracle stories than the narrative of a military campaign.

On the third day thereafter, being the fifth day of the same June, the crusaders were besieged by the pagans;* and thus it happened that they, who had laid siege to Turkish Antioch through

* Kerboga's army arrived 4–5 June 1098.

God's compassion, now found themselves hemmed in by the Turks through his will. To add to our fears the higher fortification, to all intents and purposes a citadel, was in their possession. Therefore, united by fear we laid siege to the fortress. But Kerboga, lord of the Turks, shortly after his arrival, in the belief that the battle would be fought outside the city, made camp approximately two miles from Antioch and in orderly ranks advanced to the town's bridge. On the first day our men bolstered the defence of the count's fort, fearful that the occupants of the citadel might seize Antioch if the Christians marched out to fight. On the other hand they felt that, if they abandoned the fortress by the bridge, the enemy would capture it and block egress for fighting because it controlled exit from the city.

Roger of Barneville, a most illustrious and beloved knight, was following the retreating Turks one day when he was seized and beheaded. Thereupon, sorrow and fear gripped our people, driving many to the desperation of flight.* Then in the ensuing encounters our foes suffered two setbacks, but on the third day they stormed the fort so forcefully that it seemed that only God's power protected it and halted the enemy, because for some unknown reason the Turks became panic-stricken while in the act of crossing the moat and overthrowing the wall, and for that reason hurriedly ran away. Following a short withdrawal they saw no cause for flight other than their fright and therefore renewed the assault. They pressed forward furiously as if to wipe out their shameful rout, but once again were intimidated by God's power and consequently Kerboga's men returned to their camp on the same day.

The crusaders burned the fort and withdrew into Antioch after their opponents returned the following day with heavy equipment. The anxiety of the Franks mounted while the enemy's confidence soared, because we had no hope outside the city and our foes held the key citadel within Antioch. These encouraging facts led the Turks to advance against us by way of the citadel; but the Christians, confident in their strategic positions and

* The night of 10–11 June 1098.

high ground, marched against the enemy and beat them in the first attack.* Then, oblivious to a counter-attack and preoccupied with spoils of battle, they suffered a disgraceful rout. At an entrance to Antioch more than one hundred Christians and a larger number of horses lost their lives; and as a result the Turks, upon entering the fortification, dreamed of attacking the city below.

A small valley, marked by a plain and water-hole, lay between our mountain and their fort. Thereupon, the Turks strained with might and main to overrun and expel us from their route because descent into Antioch was possible only through our mountain. From morning until evening the fight raged with ferocity the like of which has never been reported. In the very middle of the hail of arrows and rocks, the uninterrupted clash of weapons, and numerous deaths, our troops fell into a deep sleep, certainly a most horrible and unusual experience for us. If you wish to know, the combat came to an end at night.

Now at vigils, the time of trust in God's compassion, many gave up hope and hurriedly lowered themselves with ropes from the wall-tops; and in the city soldiers, returning from the encounter, circulated widely a rumour that mass decapitation of the defenders was in store. To add weight to the terror, they too fled even as some urged the undecided to stand steadfast.† Nevertheless, as we have said, God's pity was present even when Christians were troubled and sunk in despair, and in turn that which chastened his lascivious children likewise comforted them in adversity.

Following the capture of Antioch, the Lord, unfolding his might and goodness, selected a Provençal peasant to console us and to deliver the following message to Raymond and Adhemar.‡

'Andrew, the apostle of God and Our Lord, Jesus Christ,

* The citadel, still in Muslim hands, passed from the control of Yaghi Sayan's son, Shams al-Dawla to one of Kerboga's lieutenants, Ahmad ibn Marwan.
† The deserters of 10–11 June 1098.
‡ Peter Bartholomew reported his visions on 11 June 1098. He was hardly an average peasant, being involved in numerous expeditions in search of supplies as far as Cilicia and even planning to go to Cyprus; he was also able to recite part of the liturgy and claimed to have forgotten more of it.

warned me some time ago on four different occasions and ordered me to report to you and, upon the fall of Antioch, return to you the lance which pierced the side of our Saviour. Even today when I left with some others for the fight outside the walls of the city, I was trapped by two horsemen and almost crushed in the retreat. Dejected and listless I sank down upon a rock, whereupon St Andrew and a comrade appeared to me, a wretched sinner still staggering from affliction and fears, and warned me of added burdens if I did not hasten to deliver the lance to you.'

When the count and the bishop sought in detail the nature of the disclosures and the directives of St Andrew, the Provençal responded:

'During the Frankish investment of Antioch at the time of the first tremor of the earth,* I was terror-stricken and speechless except for "God save me." I was alone abed in my hut without the reassurance of friends; it was dark, and as I have said the shocks continued at length, thereby adding to my anxiety. At this moment two men clad in brilliant garments appeared to me. The older one had red hair sprinkled with white, a broad and bushy white beard, black eyes and an agreeable countenance, and was of medium height; his younger companion was taller, and "fair in form beyond the sons of men".

'The older man enquired, "What are you doing?"

'I, all alone, was terrified and blurted out, "Who are you?"

'Then he said, "Stand up, do not be frightened, and listen to me. I am Andrew, the apostle. Arrange a meeting of the bishop of Le Puy, the count of St Gilles and Peter Raymond of Hautpoul† and ask them: Why doesn't Adhemar preach the word, exhort, and bless the people with the Cross which he carries daily? Certainly, it would be a great blessing to them."

'And he further commanded: "Follow me and I shall reveal to you the lance of our Father, which you must give to the count because God set it aside for him at birth."

'Dressed in only a night-shirt I got out of bed and followed

* 30 December 1097.
† Peter Raymond of Hautpoul, Provençal vassal of Count Raymond.

him into Antioch to the church of the blessed apostle Peter by way of the north gate, in front of which the Saracens had constructed a mosque. Two lamps in the church brightened the interior as if it were midday. Then St Andrew told me, "Remain here," and further ordered me to stand by the column which was adjacent to the south steps leading up to the altar. While his companion remained some distance from the altar steps, St Andrew reached under ground, drew out the lance, and placed it in my hands.

'St Andrew then spoke to me: "Look upon the lance which pierced Christ's side from which the world's deliverance arose."

'As tears of joy streaked my cheeks, I grasped the lance and sobbed to St Andrew, "Lord, if you so wish I shall take it from the church and put it into the hands of the count."

'And St Andrew replied: "Wait until after the capture of Antioch, and then return with twelve men and search for the lance in the same place where I revealed it and shall now conceal it." And he buried it in the same spot. Following these revelations he conducted me over the city's walls to my hut and then vanished.

'Shortly, after reflecting upon my squalor and your eminence, I dared not come to you. Thereafter, following my departure to a fort near Edessa in search of food, on the first day of Lent* at the cock's crow St Andrew in the same habit along with his former comrade came to me, and as a great light filled the house queried: "Are you asleep?"

'Awakened by his words, I answered: "No, Lord, my sire, I am awake."

'And he asked me: "Have you delivered my recent message?"

'Then I replied: "Sire, have I not besought you to send a more worthy one to them because, frightened by my wretched state, I have not dared to go before them?"

'Again he queried: "Do you not know God's reason in leading you here, the greatness of his love for you, and his especial care in the choice of you? He ordered you here to vindicate scorn of him

* 10 February 1098.

as well as his chosen ones. His love for you is so great that the saints now resting in peace, aware of the favour of divine will, desired to return in the flesh and fight by your side. God has selected you from all mankind as grains of wheat are gathered from oats, because you stand out above all who have come before or shall come after you in merit and grace as the price of gold exceeds that of silver."

'Following their departure I fell victim to a disease which so threatened my eyesight that I started ridding myself of my limited means, when I suddenly concluded that these ills beset me because of my disobedience of the apostle's orders, and thus reassured I went back to the siege. Reflecting again upon my wretched state, I said nothing because I feared that if I reported that to you, you would cry out that I was a famished man who carried such a tale to secure food. Sometime later I was resting with my Lord William Peter* in a tent at the port of St Simeon on the eve of Palm Sunday when the blessed Andrew in the same garb of his past appearance and along with his companion revealed himself to me and said: "Why have you not delivered my message to Raymond and Adhemar?"

'And I replied: "Lord! Have I not begged you to send a more intelligent replacement, one whom they would heed; and besides you must know that the Turks kill anyone *en route* to Antioch."

'Then St Andrew countered: "Don't be afraid; the Turks will not hurt you. But tell the count not to be dipped in the River Jordan upon his arrival, but first row across in a boat; and once on the other side be sprinkled while clad in a shirt and linen breeches and thereafter keep his dried garments along with the Holy Lance." And my Lord William Peter can vouch for the conversation although he did not see St Andrew.

'Reassured I came back to the besiegers of Antioch, but I could not assemble you as I wished, and so went to the port of Mamistra. There while I waited impatiently to set sail for supplies in Cyprus, St Andrew confronted me with grave threats if I did not turn back to Antioch and repeat his instructions to you. Then as

* A fellow Provençal pilgrim.

I figured on ways that I could make the three days' journey from Mamistra to the crusading camp, I began to cry hysterically because I realised that it was impossible. So finally at the insistence of my lord and comrades, we embarked and for a whole day were pushed by oars and a favourable wind until sunset, when a sudden storm broke and drove us back to Mamistra within an hour or two. Thus blocked three times from passage to Cyprus, we went back to the port of St Simeon where I became very sick; but with the capture of Antioch I came to you and now offer my testimony for your approval.'

The bishop considered the story fraudulent, but the count immediately believed it and placed Peter Bartholomew in the custody of his chaplain, Raymond.*

On the following night Our Lord Jesus Christ revealed himself to a priest, Stephen by name, who was crying as he awaited death for himself and his friends.† Stragglers from the fight at the citadel had terrified him by reporting a Turkish descent from the mountain and the flight and disorderly retreat of the crusaders. Before his approaching death Stephen, desirous of having God as a witness, entered the church of the blessed Mary, confessed, received absolution for his sins, and began to chant hymns with his friends. He kept vigils while the others slept, repeating, 'Lord who shall live in thy dwelling? Who shall find rest on thy holy mountain?'

At this moment, a man, handsome beyond human form, appeared and asked Stephen, 'Who has entered Antioch?'

Stephen replied, 'Christians.'

Then the man queried: 'What do these Christians believe?'

The priest answered: 'They believe Christ was born of the Virgin Mary and endured agony on the Cross, died, was buried, and rose from the grave on the third day and ascended to heaven.'

Then the man enquired, 'If they are Christians, why do they dread pagan hordes?' He continued, 'Don't you recognise me?'

* i.e. Raymond of Aguilers himself; note Bishop Adhemar's initial scepticism.
† Stephen of Valence.

The priest, Stephen, answered, 'I only know that you are most majestic.'

Thereupon the man demanded, 'Pay close attention to me.'

As Stephen observed him closely, he saw appear gradually from above his head the form of a Cross more dazzling than the sun. Then the priest replied to his interrogator, 'Lord, we call images similar in appearance to you, those of Jesus Christ.'

The Lord continued, 'You have spoken correctly because I am Jesus Christ. Is it not recorded that I am the Lord, mighty and powerful in battle? And who, may I ask, is your commander?'

Stephen replied, 'Lord, we have no unified command, but we trust Adhemar more than others.'

Then Christ commanded: 'Tell the bishop that these people by their evil deeds have alienated me, and because of this he should command, "Turn from sin and I shall return to you." Later when they go to fight they shall say, "Our enemies are gathered together and boast of their might; crush their might, O Lord! and rout them so that they shall know thou, our God, alone battlest with us." And add these instructions, "My compassion shall be with you if you follow my commands for five days."'

While he spoke thus a woman, Mary, mother of Jesus Christ, whose countenance was haloed brilliantly, came near, looked towards the Lord and enquired, 'What are you telling this man?'

And Christ answered Mary, 'I asked who were the people within Antioch.'

The Lady declared, 'O my master! They are Christians who are so often in my prayers to you.'

When the priest aroused his nearby sleeping companion to witness the vision, Christ and Mary rose out of sight. The next morning,* Stephen mounted the hill, *vis-à-vis* the Turkish fort, where our princes tarried with the exception of Godfrey, who guarded the mountain bastion to the north. In a called assembly Stephen reported the above vision, swore upon the Cross to verify it, and finally signified his willingness to cross through fire or throw himself from the heights

* Probably 11 June 1098.

of a tower if necessary to convince the unbelievers.

In view of the fact that the masses believed that the princes now wished to escape to the port and only a few of them, stead-fast in the faith, did not contemplate flight during the night past, the princes swore that they would neither flee nor abandon Antioch except by common council, and thus many were reassured.* Even then only the closing of the gates of Antioch by orders of Bohemund and Adhemar prevented wholesale evacuation; and despite all precautions William of Grandmesnil† along with his brother and many clerks and laymen deserted. Yet it happened to many who fled the city in the greatest peril to encounter a more perilous brush with death from Kerboga's men.

Now reported revelations of our comrades became rife; and we too saw a wonder in the sky, namely a great star hanging over Antioch for a short time, then splitting three ways and falling into the Turkish camp. Somewhat strengthened, the crusaders eagerly anticipated the fifth day proclaimed by the priest; and on that day twelve men and Peter Bartholomew collected the proper tools and began to dig in the church of the blessed Peter, following the expulsion of all other Christians. The bishop of Orange, Raymond d'Aguilers, author of this work, Raymond of St Gilles, Pons of Balazun and Farald of Thouars‡ were among the twelve.

We had been digging until evening when some gave up hope of unearthing the lance. In the mean time after the count had gone to guard the citadel, we persuaded fresh workers to replace the weary diggers and for a time they dug furiously. But the youthful Peter Bartholomew, seeing the exhaustion of our workers, stripped his outer garments and, clad only in a shirt and barefooted, dropped into the hole. He then begged us to pray to God to return his lance to the crusaders so as to bring strength and victory to his people. Finally, prompted by his gracious com-

* 11 June 1098; a moment when the whole army almost disintegrated.

† William of Grandmesnil, of a Norman family, was Bohemund's brother-in-law.

‡ Farald of Thouars came from Poitou, outside the close-knit group of Provençals.

passion, the Lord showed us his lance and I, Raymond, author of this book, kissed the point of the lance as it barely protruded from the ground. I cannot relate the happiness and rejoicing which filled Antioch, but I can state that the lance was uncovered on the eighteenth day before the calends of July [14 June].

On the following night the blessed Andrew stood before the young revealer of the lance and told him, 'Behold, God gave the lance to the count, in fact had reserved it for him alone throughout the ages, and also made him leader of the crusaders on the condition of his devotion to God.'

When Peter Bartholomew sought mercy for the Christians, the blessed Andrew answered, 'Indeed the Lord will have pity on his people.'

And again Peter sought from the nocturnal visitor the name of his companion: 'Who was he whom he had seen so frequently accompanying him?'

The blessed Andrew said, 'Come close; kiss his foot.'

Then the Provençal approached and saw what appeared to be a fresh and bloody wound on his foot, and as he held back because of the bloody sight, the blessed Andrew commanded:

'Look upon the Father who was pierced for us on the Cross and has borne from that time forth this wound. In addition, the Lord orders you to celebrate the date of the discovery of his lance on the octave of the following week, because the uncovering of the lance at vespers prevents the celebration on that day; and thereafter on every anniversary of the day of the discovery of the lance, you shall celebrate.

'Further, tell the Christians to restrain themselves as today's reading of the epistle of my brother, Peter, teaches. (This epistle taught, "Humble yourselves under the mighty hand of God.") Also the clerks shall chant daily the following hymn, *Lustra sex qui jam peracta tempus implens corporis.** When they have chanted, *Agnus in cruce levatus immolandus stipite,*† they shall genuflect and conclude the hymn.'

* 'Now six lustra [thirty years] old, his bodily life fulfilled.'
† 'The Lamb raised for sacrifice on the post of the Cross.' Raymond's text

Later when the bishop of Orange and I enquired whether he knew the liturgy, Peter Bartholomew, under the impression that an affirmative 'I know' would have brought disbelief, answered, 'I do not know.' Although he knew some ritual, he was so bewildered at the time that he neither recalled the liturgy nor had any recollection of what he had learned from it except the *Pater Noster, Credo in Deum, Magnificat* and *Gloria in excelsis Deo*, and *Benedictus Dominus Deus Israel*. The others he had completely forgotten and only later could recall a few with difficulty.

The Gesta Francorum *confirms Raymond's general impressions.*

One day,* when our leaders were standing in the upper city before the citadel, grieving and troubled, there came to them a certain priest,† and he said, 'Gentlemen, may it please you to listen to the account of a certain vision which I have seen. One night, as I lay prostrate in the church of St Mary the mother of our Lord Jesus Christ, the Saviour of the world appeared to me with his mother and St Peter, prince of the apostles, and he stood before me and said, "Knowest thou me?" "No," said I. When I had said this, behold, an unbroken Cross appeared behind his head, and the Lord asked me a second time, saying, "Knowest thou me?" I answered, "I should not know you, except that I see about your head a Cross like that of our Saviour." He answered, "I am he." So I fell down at his feet, humbly beseeching him to help us in the trouble which had come upon us. The Lord replied, "I have given you great help, and I will help you hereafter. I granted you the city of Nicaea, and victory in all your battles, and I have led you hither and suffered with you in all the troubles which you have endured in the siege of Antioch. Behold, I gave you timely help and put you safe and sound into the city of Antioch, but you are satisfying your filthy lusts both with Christians and with loose pagan women, so that a great stench goes up to heaven." Then the gracious Virgin and blessed Peter fell at his feet, praying and beseeching him to

reads *cruce* rather than the more strictly correct *crucis*.
* 11 June 1098.   † Stephen of Valence, attached to the Provençal army.

help his people in this trouble, and blessed Peter said, "Lord, the pagans have held my house* for so long, and have done many unspeakable evil deeds therein. Now, O Lord, if thine enemies be driven out, there will be rejoicing among the angels in heaven." And the Lord said to me, "Go and say to my people that they shall return unto me, and I will return unto them, and within five days I will send them a mighty help. Let them sing each day the response 'For lo, the kings were assembled', together with the doxology." Gentlemen, if you do not believe this to be true, let me climb up this tower and throw myself down from it; if I am unhurt, believe that I speak the truth, but if I suffer any injury, then behead me or throw me into the fire.'

Then the bishop of Le Puy gave orders that the Gospels and a crucifix were to be brought, on which the man could swear to the truth of his story; and all our leaders took counsel together at that hour that they should all swear an oath that none of them, while he lived, would flee, either from fear of death or from hope of life. It is said that Bohemund took the oath first, and after him the count of St Gilles, Robert the Norman, Duke Godfrey and the count of Flanders. But Tancred swore and vowed that so long as he had forty knights to follow him, he would not turn aside either from this battle or from the march to Jerusalem. When the Christians heard of this oath they were greatly encouraged.

There was in our army there a certain pilgrim whose name was Peter.† Before we took the city of Antioch, St Andrew the apostle appeared to him, saying, 'Friend, what doest thou?' He answered 'Who are you?' The apostle answered him, 'I am Andrew the apostle. Know, my son, that if thou goest to the church of blessed Peter, when thou enterest the city, thou wilt find there the lance with which our Saviour Jesus Christ was pierced when he was hanging on the Cross.' Saying this, the apostle disappeared.

Peter was afraid to reveal the words of the apostle, so he would

---

* Antioch cathedral was dedicated to St Peter, who was regarded as the founder of the Christian Church in Antioch.

† Peter Bartholomew, a layman in the Provençal army.

not tell our pilgrims, for he thought that he had seen an apparition, and he said to the saint, 'Lord, who will believe this?' In that same hour St Andrew took him and carried him to the place where the lance was hidden in the ground.

Later on, when we were in the straits which I have just described, St Andrew appeared again, saying to Peter, 'Why hast thou not taken the lance from the earth, as I bade thee? Know of a truth that he who carries this lance in battle shall never be overcome by the enemy.' Then at once Peter revealed to our men the mystery told to him by the apostle, but they did not believe him, and turned him away, saying, 'How can we believe a thing like this?' for they were all terrified, thinking that they were at death's door. So Peter came* and swore that the whole story was quite true, since St Andrew had twice appeared to him in a vision, and had said to him, 'Arise, go and tell the people of God to have no fear, but to trust surely with their whole hearts in the One True God, and they shall be victorious everywhere, and within five days God will send them such a sign as shall fill them with joy and confidence, so that if they will fight, their enemies shall all be overcome as soon as they go out together to battle, and no one shall stand against them.' When our men heard that their enemies were destined to be altogether defeated, their spirits revived at once, and they began to encourage one another, saying, 'Let us arise, and be strong and brave, for God will soon come to our help, and he will be a mighty refuge for his people, on whom he has looked in the time of their affliction.'

Meanwhile the Turks who were up in the citadel attacked us so fiercely at all points that on one day they trapped three of our knights in a tower which stood in front of the fortress, for the pagans had sallied out and made such a sharp attack that our forces could not bear the brunt of it. Two of the knights were wounded and came out from the tower, but the third defended himself manfully all day from the Turkish attack, and fought so bravely that he overthrew two Turks at the approach to the wall,

* Probably on the same day as Stephen of Valence, 11 June, the day after the mass desertions.

breaking his own spears. On that day three spears were broken in his hands, but both the Turks were killed. He was called Hugh the Mad, and he belonged to the band of Godfrey* of Monte Scaglioso.

When the honoured Bohemund saw that he could by no means induce his followers to come up to the citadel to fight (for they stayed in the houses cowering, some for hunger and some for fear of the Turks) he was very angry, and gave immediate orders that the part of the city containing Yaghi Sayan's palace should be set on fire. When the men in the city saw this they left the houses and all their possessions and fled, some towards the citadel, some towards the gate held by the count of St Gilles, others to that held by Duke Godfrey – every man to his own people. At this moment a great storm of wind arose suddenly, so that no one could direct his course aright. The valiant Bohemund was very anxious, fearing for the safety of St Peter's and St Mary's and the other churches. The danger lasted from the third hour until midnight, and nearly two thousand churches and houses were burnt, but at midnight all the violence of the fire suddenly died down.

In this way the Turks who held the citadel fought within the city against our men day and night, and it was only our arms which kept them off us. When our men saw that they could bear this no longer (for a man with food had no time to eat, and a man with water no time to drink) they built a wall of stones and mortar between the Turks and us, and set up a tower and catapults, so that they might be safe. One band of the Turks was holding the citadel, attacking us, and another was encamped in a valley near the citadel.

That very night there appeared a fire in the sky, coming from the west, and it approached and fell upon the Turkish army, to the great astonishment of our men and of the Turks also. In the morning the Turks, who were all scared by the fire, took to flight in a panic and went to my lord Bohemund's gate, where they

* Godfrey had been killed at Dorylaeum, but his contingent apparently retained some coherence; see above, p. 73n.

encamped; but those who were in the citadel fought with our men day and night, shooting arrows and wounding or killing them. The rest of the Turks besieged the city on all sides, so that none of our men dared to go out or come in except by night and secretly. Thus we were besieged and afflicted by those pagans, whose number was beyond counting. These blasphemous enemies of God kept us so closely shut up in the city of Antioch that many of us died of hunger, for a small loaf cost a bezant, and I cannot tell you the price of wine. Our men ate the flesh of horses and asses, and sold it to one another; a hen cost 15 shillings, an egg two, and a walnut a penny. All things were very dear. So terrible was the famine that men boiled and ate the leaves of figs, vines, thistles and all kinds of trees. Others stewed the dried skins of horses, camels, asses, oxen or buffaloes, which they ate. These and many other troubles and anxieties, which I cannot describe, we suffered for the name of Christ and to set free the road to the Holy Sepulchre; and we endured this misery, hunger and fear for six-and-twenty days.*

Now it happened that, before Antioch was captured, that coward Stephen, count of Chartres, whom all our leaders had elected commander-in-chief, pretended to be very ill, and he went away shamefully to another castle which is called Alexandretta.† When we were shut up in the city, lacking help to save us, we waited each day for him to bring us aid. But he, having heard that the Turks had surrounded and besieged us, went secretly up a neighbouring mountain which stood near Antioch, and when he saw more tents than he could count he returned in terror, and hastily retreated in flight with his army. When he reached his camp he took all his goods and retraced his steps as fast as he could. Afterwards, when he met the emperor at Philomelium,‡ he asked for a private interview and said, 'I tell you truly that

* 3–28 June 1098.
† Alexandretta was a port north of Antioch; Stephen had been chosen *ductor*, whatever that implied, in March 1098, perhaps to have a supervisory or arbitration role in the fissiparous leadership (see Stephen's letter above, pp. 183–5); he fled 2 June 1098.   ‡ Near Iconium; see map p. xliv.

Antioch has been taken, but that the citadel has not fallen, and our men are all closely besieged, and I expect that by this time they have been killed by the Turks. Go back, therefore, as fast as you can, in case they find you and the men who are following you.' Then the emperor was much afraid, and he called to a secret council Guy, Bohemund's brother,* and certain other men, and said to them, 'Gentlemen, what shall we do? All our allies are closely besieged, and perhaps at this very moment they have died or been led into captivity at the hands of the Turks, according to the tale of this wretched count who has fled in such a shameful way. If you agree, let us retire quickly, lest we also suffer sudden death, even as they have died.'

When Guy, who was a very honourable knight, had heard these lies, he and all the others began to weep and to make loud lamentation, and all of them said, 'O true God, Three in One, why hast thou allowed this to be? Why hast thou permitted the people who followed thee to fall into the hands of thine enemies, and forsaken so soon those who wished to free the road to thy Holy Sepulchre? By our faith, if the word which we have heard from these scoundrels is true, we and the other Christians will forsake thee and remember thee no more, nor will one of us henceforward be so bold as to call upon thy name.' This rumour seemed so grievous to the whole army that none of them, bishop, abbot, clerk or layman, dared to call upon the name of Christ for many days. Moreover no one could comfort Guy, who wept and beat his breast and wrung his hands, crying, 'Woe's me, my lord Bohemund, honour and glory of the whole world, whom all the world feared and loved! Woe's me, sorrowful as I am! I have not even been found worthy, to my grief, to see your most excellent countenance, although there is nothing that I desire more. Who will give me a chance to die for you, my sweetest friend and lord? Why did I not die at once when I came out of my mother's womb? Why have I lived to see this accursed day? Why did I not drown in the sea, or fall off my horse and

* Guy was Bohemund's half-brother and had served in Constantinople for some years.

break my neck so that I might have died at once? Oh, that I had been so lucky as to suffer martyrdom with you, that I might behold your glorious death!' And when everyone ran to comfort him, so that he might cease from his lamentation, he controlled himself and said, 'Perhaps you believe this cowardly old fool of a knight? I tell you that I have never heard of any knightly deed which he has done. He has retreated shamefully and indecently, like a scoundrel and a wretch, and whatever the knave says, you may be sure that it is a lie.'

Meanwhile the emperor issued orders to his army, saying, 'Go and escort all the people of this country into Bulgaria.* Seek out and destroy everything in the land, so that when the Turks come they may find here nothing at all.' So, willy-nilly, our friends retreated, grieving very bitterly even to death, and many of the sick pilgrims died because they had not the strength to follow the army, so they lay down to die by the wayside. All the others went back to Constantinople.

Now we, who heard the words of the man who brought us the message of Christ through the words of his apostle, hurried at once to the place in St Peter's church which he had described, and thirteen men dug there from morning until evening. And so that man found the lance,† as he had foretold, and they all took it up with great joy and dread, and throughout all the city there was boundless rejoicing. From that hour we decided on a plan of attack, and all our leaders forthwith held a council and arranged to send a messenger to Christ's enemies the Turks, so that he might question them through an interpreter, asking confidently why they had been so vainglorious as to enter into the Christians' land and encamp there, and why they were killing and bullying the servants of Christ. When they had ended their council they found certain men, Peter the Hermit and Herluin, and said to them, 'Go to the accursed army of the Turks and give them this whole message in full, asking them why they have been

---

* The Balkans; i.e. the European provinces of the Byzantine empire.
† Peter Bartholomew, 14 June 1098; cf. Raymond of Aguilers, who was present; see above, pp. 206–14.

so rash and vainglorious as to enter the land which belongs to the Christians and to us.' When they had received this message, our envoys went off and came to that blasphemous company, where they delivered all their message to Kerboga and the others in these words: 'Our leaders and commanders are shocked to see that you have been so bold and vainglorious as to enter this land, which belongs to the Christians and to them. Perhaps (as we think and believe) you have come hither with the full intention of being christened? Or have you come to make yourselves a nuisance to the Christians in any way you can? In any case our leaders, as one man, require you to take yourselves off quickly from the land which belongs to God and the Christians, for the blessed Peter converted it long ago to the faith of Christ by his preaching. But they give you permission to take away all your goods, horses and mules, asses and camels, and to take with you all your sheep and oxen and other possessions whithersoever you may choose.'

Then Kerboga, commander-in-chief of the army of the sultan of Persia, with all his counsellors, was filled with pride, and he answered fiercely, 'We neither want nor like your god and your Christendom, and we spit upon you and upon them. We have come here because we are scandalised to think that those leaders and commanders whom you name should lay claim to the land which we have conquered from an effeminate people. Do you want to know our answer? Then go back as fast as you can, and tell your leaders that if they will all become Turks,* and renounce the god whom you worship on bended knee, and cast o your laws, we will give them this land and more besides, witff cities and castles, so that none of you shall remain a foot-soldier, but you shall all be knights as we are: and tell them that we will count them always among our dearest friends. Otherwise, let them know that they shall all be slain or led in chains to Khorasan, where they shall serve us and our children for all time, in everlasting captivity.'

Our messengers came back quickly and reported all the things

* i.e. Muslims.

which this most cruel people had said to them. (It is reported that Herluin knew both languages, and that he acted as interpreter for Peter the Hermit.*) While all this was happening our men did not know what to do, for they were afraid, being caught between two perils, the torments of hunger and the fear of the Turks.

At last, after three days spent in fasting and in processions from one church to another, our men confessed their sins and received absolution, and by faith they received the body and blood of Christ in communion, and they gave alms and arranged for masses to be celebrated. Then six lines of battle were drawn up from those who were in the city. In the first line (the vanguard) were Hugh the Great, with the French troops, and the count of Flanders; in the second Duke Godfrey and his men; in the third Robert the Norman with his knights; in the fourth the bishop of Le Puy, bearing the lance of our Saviour, and he had with him both his own men and those of Raymond, count of St Gilles, who stayed behind on the hill to guard the citadel, for fear lest the Turks should come down into the city; in the fifth Tancred with his men; in the sixth Bohemund with his army. Our bishops and priests and clerks and monks put on their holy vestments and came out with us, carrying crosses, praying and beseeching God to save us and keep us and rescue us from all evil, while others stood above the gate with holy crosses in their hands, making the sign of the Cross and blessing us. So we closed our ranks, and protected by the sign of the Cross we went out by the gate which is over against the mosque.

When Kerboga saw the Frankish squadrons, so well drawn up, coming out one after the other, he said, 'Let them come, so that we may have them the more surely in our power.' But after they were all outside the city, and he saw how great was the force of the Franks, he was much afraid,† so he told the amir who had

* Does this imply that Herluin knew Turkish, which would be notable, or Arabic, which, if he came from southern Italy or Sicily, would not be surprising?
† Kerboga's coalition was fragile, as he knew; on 28 June he was apparently caught by surprise; for a masterly reconstruction, see J. France, *Victory in the East* (Cambridge University Press, 1994), pp. 278–96.

charge of the host that if he saw a fire lighted in the vanguard he should immediately cause the whole army to be summoned to retreat, for he would know that the Turks had lost the battle.

Without delay Kerboga began to withdraw a little way towards the mountain,* and our men followed him. Then the Turkish army divided into two; one wing moved towards the sea and the other stayed in position, for they hoped to surround our men. When our leaders saw this they did likewise, and improvised a seventh line from the forces of Duke Godfrey and the count of Normandy. Count Rainald† was put in command of this squadron, which they sent to face the Turks who were coming up from the direction of the sea. The Turks joined battle with them and killed many of our men with their arrows. Meanwhile other Turkish forces were drawn up between the river and the mountain, which is two miles away, and troops began to come out on each wing, surrounding our men, throwing darts, shooting arrows, and wounding them.

Then also appeared from the mountains a countless host of men on white horses, whose banners were all white. When our men saw this, they did not understand what was happening or who these men might be, until they realised that this was the succour sent by Christ, and that the leaders were St George, St Mercurius and St Demetrius.‡ (This is quite true, for many of our men saw it.)

Meanwhile the Turks who were on the wing stretching towards the sea, realising that they could no longer withstand us, set fire to the grass, so that their fellows who were in the camp might see it and flee. They recognised the signal, seized all their valuables, and took to flight. Our men were gradually fighting their way forward towards the main Turkish army at the camp. Duke Godfrey, the count of Flanders and Hugh the Great rode along the river bank, where the strongest Turkish

* North of the city; see map p. 145.

† Possibly from Beauvais or possibly Toul.

‡ Compare the letter of Patriarch Symeon, above, pp. 165–6. Note the church dedicated to St George to the south of the city occupied by the crusaders.

force was stationed, and, defended by the sign of the Cross, were the first to make a concerted attack upon the enemy. When our other troops saw this, they attacked likewise, and the Persians and Turks began to cry out. Then we called upon the true and living God and rode against them, joining battle in the name of Jesus Christ and of the Holy Sepulchre, and by God's help we defeated them.

The Turks fled in terror and we pursued them right up to their camp, for the knights of Christ were more eager to chase them than to look for any plunder, and the pursuit continued as far as the Orontes bridge, and in the other direction as far as Tancred's castle. The enemy left his pavilions, with gold and silver and many furnishings, as well as sheep, oxen, horses, mules, camels and asses, corn, wine, flour and many other things of which we were badly in need.

The Armenians and Syrians who lived in those lands, hearing that we had overcome the Turks, rushed towards the mountain to cut off their retreat, and killed any of them whom they caught. We returned to the city with great rejoicing, praising and blessing God who had given victory to his people.

When the amir who was in charge of the citadel saw Kerboga and all the others fleeing from the battlefield before the Frankish army, he was much afraid, and he came in a great hurry to ask for a Frankish banner.* The count of St Gilles, who was there keeping watch outside the citadel, ordered his own banner to be delivered to the amir, who took it and was careful to display it upon his tower. Some men from southern Italy, who were standing by, said at once, 'This is not Bohemund's banner.' The amir questioned them, saying, 'Whose is it?' and they replied, 'It belongs to the count of St Gilles.' The amir came and took the banner and gave it back to the count, and just then the noble Bohemund came up and gave him his own banner, which he accepted with great joy. He made an agreement with my lord Bohemund that those pagans who wished to be christened might

* A sign of surrender and hence protection from indiscriminate plunder and massacre.

join his band, and that he would allow those who wished to depart to go away safe and uninjured. Bohemund agreed to the amir's terms and put his followers into the citadel at once. Not many days afterwards the amir was christened, with those who preferred to accept Christ, and my lord Bohemund caused those who wished to adhere to their own laws to be escorted into the land of the Saracens.

This battle was fought on 28 June, the vigil of the apostles Peter and Paul, in the reign of our Lord Jesus Christ, to whom be honour and glory for ever and ever. Amen.

Raymond of Aguilers took a slightly different perspective on the battle.

During this time food became so scarce that a tongueless head of a horse sold for 2 or 3 *solidi*, a goat's intestines for 5 *solidi*, and a hen for 8 or 9 *solidi*. What can I report on bread prices when hunger remained after eating 5 *solidi*'s worth? To those rich in gold, silver and clothes it was neither unusual nor burdensome to pay exorbitant costs. So prices were high because the sinful consciences of the knights lacked Christian courage. They gathered, cooked and sold green figs, and also slowly boiled hides of cattle and horses as well as neglected edibles and sold them at such a high price that anyone could eat an amount costing 2 *solidi*. The majority of the knights, expecting God's compassion, refused to slaughter their horses, but did sustain themselves with their blood.

While these and other misfortunes too unpleasant to report beset the Christians, some of our men turned traitor and informed the Turks of the wretched state of Antioch and thereby added to our burdens. These reports stirred the Turks to bold and threatening acts, one of which occurred at noon one day. Around thirty of them mounted one of our towers, and for a time created panic; but our imperilled forces, fighting with God's aid, killed some of our foes and pushed others from the battlement. At this time all of the crusaders promised to follow the commands of Bohemund for a period of fifteen days after the fight so that he could arrange for the protection of Antioch and make battle plans. This decision was made because of the Turkish threat, the illness of Count Raymond and Adhemar, and the flight of Stephen of Blois.* I call to your attention that Stephen, despite the fact that he had been chosen crusading leader before the fall of Antioch, fled following rumours of the impending battle.

As we have reported, heavenly assistance came to our defeated, burdened and distressed Christians through Peter Bartholomew, the finder of the lance, who advised us as to our actions before and during battle. He told us that the blessed Andrew commanded:

'All have displeased the Lord greatly and so have been afflicted; and you have prayed to the Lord and the Lord has hearkened to you. Now let everyone turn from sin to God and offer five alms because of the five wounds of the Lord; and if he is unable to do so let him repeat five times, *Pater Noster*. Following the completion of these commands, open the battle in the name of the Lord and let it be opened by day or night according to the princes' battle plans, because the Lord's hand will be with you. However, if anyone is doubtful of the outcome, open the gates and let him run to the Turks where he shall witness how Allah protects him. And further may any slacker who won't fight be with Judas, betrayer of Jesus Christ, who abandoned the apostles and sold the Lord to the Jews.

'In truth, let them go forth to battle with the faith of the blessed Peter, holding fast to Christ's promise to him on his resurrection and appearance on the third day; and let them go forth to battle, because this land is not pagan but is under the jurisdiction of St Peter. Your rallying cry shall be, "God aid us," and, indeed, God shall aid you. All of your deceased comrades of the journey shall fight with you with the strength and leadership of God against nine-tenths of the enemy, while you fight one-tenth. Hurry into battle lest the Lord lead an equal number of Turks

* Fled 2 June 1098.

against you and blockade Antioch so long that you will eat one another. But rest assured that the days have come which Christ foretold to the blessed Mary and to his apostles, the days in which he will hurl down and grind under foot the kingdom of the pagans, and in which he will lift up the Christian principality. But do not turn aside to the enemy tents for gold or silver.'

Then the mighty hand of God so revealed itself that he, who ordered the above commands announced to us by St Andrew, strengthened all hearts with hope and faith so that each Christian felt that he had won a victory. Their zest for combat returned as they encouraged and exhorted one another, and the crowd, paralysed by fear and poverty only a few days before, now questioned delay of battle and abused the princes.

Consequently, the chieftains set the battle date and then sent Peter the Hermit to Kerboga, atabeg of Mosul, with orders that he abandon the siege of Antioch because it was under the jurisdiction of St Peter and the Christians. But the haughty Kerboga answered that right or wrong he wished to become master of the city and the Franks, and he made the reluctant Peter the Hermit bow down before him.

At this time there arose the question of selecting some troops to guard Antioch from attacks from the citadel while others marched out to battle. So they made a stone wall and rampart on top of a hill facing the enemy, and fortified it with rocks, and garrisoned it with Raymond of Toulouse, who was seriously ill, and two hundred men. The day set for battle came, and that morning all took the sacrament, surrendered to God's will, even to death if he so wished, and to the honour of the Roman Church and the Frankish race.

The battle order provided two double lines of Provençals from the troops of Raymond and Adhemar, with footmen in the van attacking or halting on command from their leaders, and the knights following as a rearguard. The same order of battle prevailed for the troops of Bohemund, Tancred, the count of Normandy and the Franks, the duke and the Burgundians. Heralds scurried through Antioch urging each man to fight with his leader. The order of the march was set as follows: Hugh the Great, the count of Flanders, and the count of Normandy first; then the duke, the bishop, and finally Bohemund. In this manner they fell into their proper ranks below the city and before the Bridge Gate.

Oh! How blessed is the nation whose Lord is God and the people whom he has chosen for his own inheritance! Oh! How changing was the appearance of this army from sloth to activity! Only a few days before the leaders and nobles walked the streets of Antioch imploring God's help; and the commoners, crying and beating on their chests, went barefoot through the city. So dejected were the Christians that father and son, brother and brother, exchanged neither salutation nor glances as they passed on the streets. With the sudden change in spirit one could see the Christians go out as spirited horses, rattle their arms, wave their spears, and boisterously celebrate with acts and speeches. But why delay this story? The will to fight was now granted and the plans of the chieftains were executed.

In the mean time as Kerboga played chess in his tent, he learned that the Franks were marching out to fight. Troubled in his soul at this unexpected move, he summoned Mirdalin,* a Turkish refugee from Antioch and well-known courageous nobleman, and enquired, 'What goes on? Because the Franks were small in numbers did you not report the outnumbered Christians would never fight me?'

To this query Mirdalin answered, 'No, sire, I made no such report, but follow me and I shall observe them and advise you if you can overwhelm them easily.'

As our third rank of crusaders advanced, Mirdalin scouted our ranks and told Kerboga, 'The Christians will die before they flee.'

Kerboga in turn enquired, 'Can't some of the Christians be pushed back a little?'

Then Mirdalin answered, 'If all the pagan world rushed against them, they would not budge a foot.'

* Unidentified, possibly a corruption of 'amir'.

Despite his apprehension, Kerboga formed his great army into battle order and permitted the crusaders to march out of Antioch unmolested, although he could have blocked them. Fearing encircling tactics from the rear, our forces turned their battle lines towards the mountains which were two full miles from the bridge. In typical clerical procession we advanced, and, may I add, it was a procession. Priests and many monks wearing white stoles walked before the ranks of our knights, chanting and praying for God's help and the protection of the saints. Nevertheless, the Turks attacked and shot arrows; but Kerboga, no longer deaf to Christian proposals, suggested to our leaders that five or ten Turks should fight the same number of Franks, and following the outcome the army represented by the conquered knights should leave the battle in peace.

Our men responded, 'You refused when we wished this, but now that we are ready for battle let every man fight for his rights.'

As stated, we were arrayed on the plain when a detachment of Turks to the rear of us attacked a contingent of footmen, who wheeled and met the attack courageously. The enemy troops, unable to budge the footmen, kindled a fire around them so that those undaunted by swords would be swept away by fire. Because of the extremely dry grass, there was a forced withdrawal.

Now with our army outside Antioch, barefooted priests clad in priestly vestments stood upon the walls invoking God to protect his people, and by a Frankish victory bear witness to the covenant which he made holy with his blood. But in the advance from the bridge to the mountain we struggled mightily because of the encircling Turks, and in the course of this the enemy rushed upon those of us who were in Adhemar's ranks. Superior in numbers, they neither wounded anyone nor shot arrows against us, no doubt because of the protection of the Holy Lance. I was both a witness to these events and bearer of the Holy Lance. Furthermore, if the rumour is spread that Heraclius, standard-bearer of the bishop, was wounded in this mêlée, let it be known that he gave his standard to another and was far from our ranks.*

* Heraclius, viscount of Polignac.

With all of our soldiers outside Antioch our princes, as already stated, had formed eight lines; but five more appeared in our lines, thereby giving us thirteen ranks. Likewise, we shall not pass by this memorable event, one in which the Lord loosed a small but welcome shower as the Christians advanced into battle. Its drops brought to those touched by it such grace and strength that they disdained the enemy and charged forth as though nurtured in regal style. The shower affected our horses no less miraculously. In proof may I ask whose horse broke down before the fight's end although it had eaten nothing but bark and leaves of trees for eight days? Because God added soldiers to our army, we outnumbered the Turks in battle although previously we appeared outmanned.

Upon completion of our advance and battle formation, the enemy fled without giving us an opportunity to fight, and our troops then chased them until sundown. The Lord laboured surprisingly well with men and horses, for the men were not deterred by avarice, and those famished horses, scarcely led from their scanty provender into battle by their masters, now pursued without difficulty the best and fleetest Turkish steeds. The Lord reserved this further pleasure for us; namely, the defenders of the citadel, upon viewing the flight of Kerboga's men, despaired and some surrendered with the guarantee of their lives while others hastily took to flight. Despite this horrible and terrifying battle, few Turkish knights perished; on the other hand hardly a footman survived. In addition the booty included all of the Turkish tents, much gold and silver, many spoils, immeasurable amounts of grain, innumerable cattle and camels. It brought to mind the flight of the Syrians at Samaria when a measure of flour and barley was bought for a shekel. These events happened on the vigils of St Peter and St Paul, and appropriately so because through these saintly intercessors the Lord Jesus Christ brought this triumph to the pilgrim Church of the Franks; indeed it was our merciful Lord who lives and dwells with his servants through all eternity. Amen.

Anna Comnena's account of the events at Antioch and of Alexius'
refusal to risk coming to the crusaders' aid occupies a pivotal posi-
tion in her narrative: on her interpretation depends much of her
argument exonerating Alexius from accusations of treachery and of
having forfeited his rights to Antioch by abandoning the western
army to its fate. It represents special pleading at its most elaborate.
The rest of the crusade held little interest for Anna, who treated it in
a most perfunctory (and inaccurate) manner.

After his departure Bohemund, who was still keeping secret
the Armenian's promise,* battened on fine hopes, reserving to
himself the future governorship of Antioch. He addressed the
counts: 'You see how long a time already we have spent here in
misery. So far we have made no good progress. Worse still, we may
soon become the victims of famine, unless we make some better
provision for our safety.' When they asked him what he suggested,
he went on: 'Not all victories are granted by God through the
sword, nor are such results invariably achieved through battle.
What the moil of war has not produced is often gladly given after
negotiation, and friendly diplomatic manoeuvres many a time
have set up finer trophies. In my opinion it's wrong to waste our
time to no purpose; we should hurry to invent some sensible
and bold scheme to save ourselves before Kourpagan [Kerboga]
arrives. I suggest that each of us should try hard to win over the
barbarian watching his particular section. And if you approve, let
a prize be awarded to the first man who succeeds in this – the governorship of the city, say, until the arrival of the emperor's nomi-
nee, who will take over from us. Of course, even in this we may not
make any good progress.' The cunning Bohemund, who loved
power, loved it not for the sake of the Latins or their common interests, but to glorify himself. His plans and intrigues and deceptions
did not fail – the story as it unfolds will make that plain. The
counts unanimously approved of his scheme and set to work. As
day broke Bohemund immediately went off to the tower; the Armenian, according to his agreement, opened the gates. Bohemund

* The promise of Firuz to hand Antioch over to Bohemund.

leaped at once with his followers to the top of the tower as fast as he could. Besiegers and besieged alike saw him standing there on the battlements and ordering the trumpeter to sound the call to battle. An extraordinary sight could then be seen: the Turks, panic-stricken, without more ado fled through the gate at the other side of the city; a mere handful, brave warriors, were left behind to guard the citadel; the Celts outside followed in the steps of Bohemund as they climbed the ladders to the top and straightway occupied the city. Tancred, with a strong force of Celts, lost no time in pursuing the runaways, killing and wounding many of them. When Kourpagan arrived with his countless thousands to help, he found the place already in the hands of the enemy. He dug a trench, deposited in it his baggage, pitched camp and prepared to invest the city, but before he could begin the Celts made a sortie and attacked. There was a tremendous struggle, in which the Turks were victorious; the Latins were penned up inside the gates, exposed to danger from two sides – from the defenders of the citadel (the barbarians still controlled that) and from the Turks encamped beyond the walls. Bohemund, being a clever man and wishing to secure for himself the first place in the government of Antioch, again addressed the counts: 'It's not right', he said, 'that the same men should have to fight on two fronts – with enemies outside and in the city at the same time. We ought to divide up our forces in two unequal groups, proportionate to the enemies opposed to us, and then take up the challenge against them. My task will be to fight the defenders of the citadel, if, that is, you agree. The others will be concerned with the enemy outside. They will launch a violent attack on them.' Everyone agreed with this idea of Bohemund. He immediately built a small counter-wall facing the citadel and cutting it off from the rest of Antioch, a very sturdy line of defence if the war went on. After it was completed he established himself as its guardian, ever watchful, never relaxing the pressure on the defenders at every available opportunity. He fought most bravely. The other counts devoted careful attention to their own sectors, protecting the city at all points, examining the parapets and the battlements that crown the walls, making sure that no

barbarians from outside should climb up by ladders and so capture the city, that no one from inside should furtively make his
way on to the walls and then, after parley with the enemy, arrange
to betray it.

While these events were taking place at Antioch, the emperor
was much concerned to bring help personally to the Celts, but
the despoiling and utter destruction of cities and districts by
the sea held him back, however impatient. For Tzachas* held
Smyrna as though it were his own private property, and Tangripermes retained a city of the Ephesians near the sea, in which
a church had once been built in honour of the apostle St John the
Divine. One after the other the satraps occupied fortified posts,
treating the Christians like slaves and ravaging everything. They
had even taken the islands of Chios and Rhodes (in fact, all
the rest) and there they built their pirate vessels. As a result of
these activities the emperor thought it best to attend first to the
seaboard and Tzachas. He decided to leave sufficient forces on
the mainland, with a strong fleet; they would serve to throw off
and contain barbarian incursions. With the remainder of the
army he would take the road to Antioch and fight the Turks on
the way as chance offered. John Ducas, his brother-in-law,† was
summoned and to him were entrusted troops drawn from different countries and enough ships to lay siege to the coastal towns;
he also took charge of Tzachas' daughter, held prisoner along
with the others who happened at that time to be in Nicaea. John's
instructions were to make a general proclamation of the capture
of Nicaea; if it was not believed, he was then to exhibit the lady
herself to the Turkish satraps and the barbarians living in the
coastal areas. He hoped that the satraps, then in control of the
places I have mentioned, seeing her and being convinced that
the city had really fallen would surrender without a struggle in
sheer despair. So John was sent, well equipped with supplies of
all kinds. How many triumphs he achieved in the fight against
Tzachas and how he drove him out of Smyrna will be described
hereafter. He took his leave of the emperor, left the capital and

* A Greek general.   † Anna's maternal uncle.

crossed at Abydos. Caspax became admiral, with total responsibility for the naval expedition. John promised him that if he fought well he would be appointed governor of Smyrna itself (when that city was taken) and of all the neighbouring districts. While Caspax sailed as commander of the naval forces, John remained on land as tagmatarch [general]. The inhabitants of Smyrna saw Caspax and John approaching simultaneously; Ducas pitched camp a short distance from the walls, while Caspax ran his ships aground in the harbour. The men in Smyrna already knew that Nicaea had fallen and they were in no mood for fighting: they preferred to start negotiations for peace, promising to give up their city to John without a struggle and with no bloodshed, if he would swear on oath to let them go home unharmed. Ducas agreed, giving his word that Tzachas' proposal would be carried out to the letter. Thus the enemy was peacefully ejected and Caspax became supreme governor of Smyrna. At this point an incident took place which I will outline now. When Caspax had left John Ducas, a certain Smyrnaean came to him with a complaint. He said that 500 golden staters had been stolen from him by a Saracen. Caspax ordered the two parties to appear before him for judgement. The Syrian was forcibly dragged in and thought he was being hauled off to execution. In desperation for his life he drew his dagger and plunged it into Caspax's stomach; then, wheeling round, he struck at the governor's brother and wounded him in the thigh. In the great confusion that followed the Saracen ran off, but all the sailors of the fleet (including the rowers) entered the city in a disorganised mob and massacred everyone without mercy. It was a pitiable sight – some ten thousand slain in the twinkling of an eye. John Ducas, deeply moved by the murder of Caspax, once again, and for some time, devoted his whole attention to the affairs of Smyrna. He came to the city, made a thorough inspection of its defences and received accurate information from experts about the feelings of its people. The situation called for a man of courage and John appointed as the new governor a brave soldier, Hyaleas, in his opinion the outstanding candidate for the post. All the fleet was left behind to protect Smyrna, but John himself drove on to Ephesus with the army. Ephesus was then held by the satraps Tangripermes and Marakes. The enemy knew of his approach and arranged their forces, fully armed and in battle formation, on the plain outside the place. Losing not a minute the duke bore down on them with his men in disciplined ranks. The battle that ensued lasted for most of the day. Both sides were locked in combat and the issue was still undecided, when the Turks turned away and fled at speed. Many of them were killed there and prisoners were taken, not only from among the ordinary soldiers, but from the satraps, most of whom were captured. The total number reached as many as two thousand. When the emperor heard of this victory, he gave orders that they were to be scattered among the islands. The Turkish survivors went off across the River Maeander towards Polybotus and adopted a contemptuous attitude, thinking they had seen the last of Ducas. But it did not turn out like that. John left Petzeas to govern the city and taking with him all the infantry at once set out in pursuit. His troops marched in good order; there was no confusion. In fact, John followed the emperor's precepts well and controlled the advance in a manner worthy of a highly experienced general. The Turks, as I have said, had made their way across the Maeander and through the towns in that vicinity; they reached Polybotus. The duke, however, did not take the same route: he followed a shorter track, seizing Sardis and Philadelphia by surprise. Michael Cecaumenus was detailed to guard them afterwards. When John arrived at Laodicea the whole population immediately came to meet him. He treated them as deserters from the enemy, encouraged them and allowed them to dwell on their own land without interference. He did not even appoint a governor. From there he went through Choma and took Lampe, where Eustathius Camytzes was made military commander. When he finally came to Polybotus he found a strong body of Turks. An attack was launched on them just after they had deposited their baggage and in a clash a quick and decisive victory was won. Many Turks were killed and much booty, proportionate to their numbers, was recovered.

John had not yet returned and was still struggling against the Turks when the emperor was ready to march to the aid of the Celts in the Antioch region.* After wiping out many barbarians *en route*, he arrived at Philomelium with his whole army. Many towns formerly held by the Turks had been sacked. It was here that he was joined by William of Grandmesnil, Etienne, count of France, and Pierre d'Aups from Antioch.† They had been let down by ropes from the battlements of the city and had come by way of Tarsus. By them he was assured that the Celts had been reduced to a state of extreme peril; in fact, they affirmed on oath that the collapse was complete. The emperor was all the more anxious to hurry to their aid, despite the general opposition to the enterprise. But there was a widespread rumour of an imminent attack from countless hordes of barbarians: the sultan of Khorasan, learning that Alexius had set out to help the Celts, had sent his son Ishmael‡ with very strong forces from Khorasan and even more distant parts, all well armed, to stop him. Ishmael was ordered to overtake the emperor before he could reach Antioch. The news brought by the Franks from Antioch and information received about Ishmael's approach checked the plans for rescuing the Celts, however much Alexius longed to crush the furious Turkish onslaught and of course to put an end to their leader Kourpagan. As to the future, he drew the conclusion one would expect: to save a city recently captured by the Celts, but still unsettled and immediately besieged by the Agarenes, would be impossible; the Celts moreover had given up hopes of saving themselves and were planning to desert the fortifications and hand them over to the enemy, intent only on the preservation of their own lives by running away. The truth is that the Celtic race, among other characteristics, combines an independent spirit and imprudence, not to mention an absolute refusal to cultivate

* This digression is designed to excuse Alexius' slow progress towards Antioch in the wake of the crusaders.
† William of Grandmesnil, who had served Alexius in the past; Stephen of Blois; and Peter Aliphas, a veteran Norman in Alexius' service.
‡ Probably a convenient fiction.

a disciplined art of war; when fighting and warfare are imminent, inspired by passion they are irresistible (and this is evident
not only in the rank and file, but in their leaders too), charging
into the midst of the enemy's line with overwhelming abandon –
provided that the opposition everywhere gives ground; but if
their foes chance to lay ambushes with soldier-like skill and if
they meet them in a systematic manner, all their boldness van-
ishes. Generally speaking, Celts are indomitable in the opening
cavalry charge, but afterwards, because of the weight of their
armour and their own passionate nature and recklessness, it is
actually very easy to beat them. The emperor, having neither
sufficient forces to resist their great numbers, nor the power to
change the Celtic character, nor the possibility of diverting them
to some expedient policy by more reasonable advice, thought it
wise to go no further. He might lose Constantinople as well as
Antioch in his eagerness to succour them. He was afraid that if
the enormous hosts of Turks came upon him now, the people
living in the area of Philomelium might fall victims to the barbarian sword. Under the circumstances he decided to make a
general proclamation about the Agarene advance. It was immediately announced that every man and woman should leave the
place before their arrival, thus saving their own lives and as much
of their possessions as they could carry. Without delay the whole
population, men and women alike, chose to follow the emperor
. . . Such were the measures taken by Alexius with regard to the
prisoners. One part of the army was detached and then sub-
divided into many companies; they were sent out in several
directions to fight the Agarenes, wherever they were discovered
making forays; they were to hold up the Turkish advance by
force. Alexius himself, with all the barbarian prisoners and the
Christians who had come over to him, prepared to return to
Constantinople. The archsatrap Ishmael had been informed of
the emperor's departure from the capital; he had heard of the
great slaughter that followed it and of the utter destruction of
many townships on his march; he also knew that Alexius was
about to return with much booty and many captives. Ishmael

was in a difficult position: there was nothing left for him to do –
he had lost the quarry, as it were. He changed his line of march
and decided to besiege Paipert,* which had been taken and occupied shortly before by the famous Theodore Gabras. The whole
Turkish force halted by the river which flows near this place, but
the move was not unknown to Gabras, who planned a surprise
attack in the dark. The end of the Gabras affair, his origin and
character are subjects reserved for the appropriate point in the
history; we must now resume the narrative.†

The Latins, being dreadfully harassed by the famine and the
unrelenting siege, approached Peter, their bishop, who had been
defeated formerly at Helenopolis‡ (as I have already made clear)
and asked for his advice. 'You promised', he replied, 'to keep
yourselves pure until you arrived at Jerusalem. But you have
broken that promise, I think, and for that reason God no longer
helps us as he did before. You must turn again to the Lord and
weep for your sins in sackcloth and ashes, with hot tears and
nights passed in intercession, proving your repentance. Then,
and only then, will I join in seeking divine forgiveness on your
behalf.' They listened to the high priest's counsel. Some days
later, moved by some divine oracle, he called to him the leading
counts and recommended them to dig to the right of the altar§
and there, he said, they would find the Holy Nail.¶ They did as he
said, but found nothing, and returning to him in dismay told
him of their failure. He prayed even more earnestly and commanded them to make a close examination with greater care.
Again they carried out his orders exactly. This time they found
what they were looking for and running brought it to Peter, overcome with joy and religious awe. After that the revered and Holy
Nail was entrusted by them in their battles to St Gilles, for he was

* In Armenia, far to the north-west of Asia Minor; an error or a smokescreen?
† The previous passage is crucial in Anna's attempt to exonerate Alexius
from blame over Antioch; it may be thought an elaborate exercise in special
pleading.   ‡ A very confused account.
§ In the cathedral of St Peter, Antioch.
¶ Rather than the lance; a deliberate error, seeing that one relic of the Holy
Lance resided in Constantinople?

purer than the rest. On the next day they made a sortie from a
secret gate against the Turks. This was the occasion when the
count of Flanders* asked the others to grant him one request –
to be allowed to ride out at the head of their force against the
enemy, with only three companions. The request was granted,
and when the rival armies were drawn up in ranks ready for
battle, he dismounted, knelt down on the ground, and three
times in prayer implored God for help. And when all cried aloud,
'God with us!' he charged at full gallop at Kourpagan, who was
standing on a hilltop. Those who opposed them were straightway speared and hurled down. This struck terror into the hearts
of the Turks and before battle was even begun they fled. A divine
power was manifestly aiding the Christians.† What is more, in
the confusion of their flight most of the barbarians were caught
up in the currents of the river and drowned; their bodies served
as a bridge for those who came after them. When the pursuit
had gone on for a fair distance the Celts returned to the Turkish
entrenchment. The baggage was found there and all the booty
they had brought with them. Although the Celts would have
liked to take it up at once, so enormous was the plunder that they
barely had the strength to bring it into Antioch in thirty days. For
a short while they remained there, recovering from the tribulations of war. At the same time they were concerned for Antioch –
a new governor had to be appointed. Their choice fell on Bohemund, who had asked for the post before the fall of the city. He
was given overriding authority, after which the others set out on
the road to Jerusalem. Many coastal strong points were captured
along the route, but the most powerful places (which would
require a longer siege) were for the time being ignored. They
were in a hurry to reach Jerusalem. The walls were encircled and
repeatedly attacked, and after a siege of one lunar month it fell.‡
Many Saracens and Hebrews in the city were massacred. When
submission was complete, when all opposition ended, Godfrey
was invested with supreme power and nominated king.§

* Wrong date; incident an invention.   † 28 June 1098.   ‡ 15 July 1099.
§ After this, Anna proceeds to mangle the events of 1099 to 1102 together in a

News of the events at Antioch reached the west from a number of witnesses in 1098, including the crusade leadership itself and, at second hand, the people of the Italian city of Lucca. These letters testify to the continued contact of the Christian army with the west. The crusaders rightly felt the eyes as well as hopes of Christendom rested on them.

Bohemund and the Leaders of the Crusade to Pope Urban II, Antioch, 11 September 1098

To the venerable lord Pope Urban, from Bohemund, Count Raymond of St Gilles, Duke Godfrey of Lorraine, Count Robert of Normandy, Count Robert of Flanders and Count Eustace of Boulogne, greetings! and as from sons to a spiritual father: faithful service and true subjection in Christ.

We wish and desire that notice be made to you that through the great mercy of God as well as through his most manifest assistance Antioch has been taken by us; that the Turks, who had brought much shame to our Lord Jesus Christ, have been captured and slain; that we, pilgrims of Jesus Christ going to Jerusalem, have avenged the injury to God Almighty; that we who first besieged the Turks were afterwards besieged by other Turks coming from Khorasan, Jerusalem, Damascus and many other places; and how we were delivered by the mercy of Jesus Christ.

After the capture of Nicaea, we overcame as you have heard the great multitude of Turks which met us on the calends of July* in the valley of Dorylaeum and routed the mighty Suleiman and stripped him of all his lands and possessions. Having acquired and subdued all of Romania, we advanced to the siege of Antioch. In its siege we endured many hardships, especially from attacks of the neighbouring Turks and pagans rushing in upon us so frequently and in such numbers that we might truly be said to have been besieged by those whom we were besieging in Antioch.

complete mess; see *The Alexiad of Anna Comnena*, trans. E. R. A. Sewter (Penguin, 1969), pp. 308–52.   * 1 July 1098.

Finally all the battles were won and the Christian faith was exalted by their successful issue in this way: I, Bohemund, made an agreement with a certain Turk who delivered the city to me. A little before dawn on the third day before the nones of June [3 June] I placed ladders upon the wall, and thus we took the city which had been resisting Christ. We slew Cassianus, the tyrant of the city,* and many of his soldiers, and kept their wives, children and families, together with their gold and silver and all their possessions.

However, we were not able to capture the citadel of Antioch, which had been previously fortified by the Turks. But when we were ready to assail it the next day, we saw an infinite multitude of Turks moving about throughout the entire countryside. For many days we had been expecting that they would arrive to fight us while we were [still] outside the city. On the third day [after we had captured the city] they laid siege to us; and more than one hundred thousand of them entered the aforesaid citadel, hoping to rush through its gate into the section of the city below it, which was held partly by us and partly by them.

But we, stationed on another height opposite the citadel, guarded the path which was between both armies and which descended to the city so that the Turks in their great numbers could not break through. We fought inside and outside the walls night and day and finally compelled our enemies to return to their camp, through the citadel gate which led down into the city.

When they saw that they could not harm us on that side they surrounded us on all sides so that none could leave or enter the city. On that account we were all so discouraged and desolate that many of us, dying of famine and other afflictions, slaughtered and devoured our horses and asses, which were also starving.

Meanwhile with the kindest mercy of Almighty God watching over us and assisting us we found the Lord's lance with which the side of our Saviour was pierced by Longinus. It was

* Not literally true; Yaghi Sayan was murdered making his escape, possibly by local Armenians.

revealed three times to a certain servant of God by St Andrew the apostle who showed him the place where the lance lay in the church of the blessed Peter, prince of the apostles. Comforted by this discovery and by many other divine revelations, we were so strengthened that we who had previously been dejected and timid now most bravely and promptly urged each other to battle.

Thereafter having been besieged three weeks and four days, we, having confessed all our sins and entrusted ourselves to God, issued forth from the gates of the city in battle array on the eve of the feast of the apostles Peter and Paul.* We were so few that the enemy thought that we would not fight them, but would flee.

However, when we were all prepared and our foot and horse were drawn up in regular order, we boldly advanced with the Lord's lance towards the centre of the greatest strength and power of the Turks and forced them to flee from their advanced position. They, however, as was their wont, began to scatter in all directions. By occupying hills and roads wherever possible they thought to hem us in. Thus they hoped to slay us all. But we had been trained against their wiles and trickery in many a battle. The grace and mercy of God assisted us so that we who were so few in comparison with them forced them into a mass. With the right hand of God fighting on our side we compelled the Turks, thus herded together, to flee and to abandon their camps with all that they contained.

After we had overcome the Turks and pursued them for a whole day and killed many thousands of them, we returned to the city joyous and happy. Then a certain amir surrendered the citadel, previously mentioned, to Bohemund together with a thousand men in it. Through Bohemund he gladly yielded them with one accord to the Christian faith. Thus our Lord Jesus Christ delivered all of Antioch to the Roman religion and faith.

And since something sad always happens in the midst of joys, the bishop of Le Puy, whom you had sent us as your vicar, died

* 28 June 1098.

on the calends of August.* This was after the battle, in which he had taken a noble part, and after the city had been pacified.

Now therefore we your children, bereft of the father assigned to us, ask this of you, our spiritual father. Since you initiated this pilgrimage and by your sermons have caused us all to leave our lands and whatever was in them, since you have admonished us to follow Christ by carrying the Cross, and since you have urged us to exalt the name of Christ by fulfilling what you have preached, we beg you to come to us and to urge whomsoever you can to come with you. For it was here that the name of Christian originated. After the blessed Peter was enthroned in the church which we see daily, they who were formerly called Galileans† were here first and principally called Christians. Therefore what in this world would seem more proper than that you, who are the father and head of the Christian religion, should come to the principal city and capital of the Christian name and finish the war, which is your project, in person?

We have subdued the Turks and the pagans; but the heretics, Greeks and Armenians, Syrians and Jacobites, we have not been able to overcome. Therefore we ask and ask again that you, our most dear father, come as father and head to the place of your predecessor; that you who are the vicar of the blessed Peter seat yourself on his throne and use us as your obedient sons in carrying out all things properly; and that you eradicate and destroy by your authority and our strength all heresies of whatever kind. And thus you will finish with us the pilgrimage of Jesus Christ undertaken by us and proclaimed by you; and you will open to us the gates of the one and the other Jerusalem and will liberate the sepulchre of Our Lord and exalt the Christian name above all. For if you come to us and finish with us the pilgrimage that was inaugurated by you the whole world will be obedient to you. May God who liveth and reigneth for ever and ever suffer you to do this. Amen.

---

* 1 August 1098.   † The references are to Acts 1:11, 2:7 and 11:26.

The People of Lucca on Crusade to All Faithful Christians, Antioch, October 1098

To the primates, archbishops, bishops and other rectors, and to all the faithful of the lands of Christ anywhere; the clergy and people of Lucca [send] greeting full of peace and gladness in the Lord.

To the praise and glory of the Redeemer, Our Lord Jesus Christ, we are truly and faithfully making known to all [the news] which we received truly and faithfully from participants in the affairs themselves – at what time, with what great triumph, the most mighty right hand of Christ gave complete victory over the pagans to our brethren, his champions, after trial and perils. A certain citizen of ours, Bruno by name, known and very dear to all of us, in the year preceding this [1097], went with the ships of the Angles even to Antioch itself. There, as a partner in work and danger, sharer of triumph and joy, he fought along with the fighters, starved with the starving and conquered, also, with the conquering; and when the complete victory had already been achieved, and he had rejoiced three weeks there with all, he returned to us, after a happy voyage. Placing him in our midst, we received from him the pure and simple truth of the matter – lo! in his own account, as follows:

'When we who were voyaging by sea had come to Antioch, the army, which had gathered together from everywhere by land, had already surrounded the city in siege, though not very well. On the following day, our princes proceeded to the sea, for the sake of visiting us. They urged us to get together an abundant supply of wood for the construction of war engines, which we did at great expense. On the third day, moreover, before the nones of March,* that is the first Friday, our princes decided to erect a fortress at the western gate of the city. This fortress, a very short *ballista*-shot away [from the city], is now called by the name of the blessed Mary. There, on that same day, in an attack of the Turks, in which they killed 2,055 of our men, we killed eight hun-

* i.e. 5 March 1098.

dred of the enemy. From the third day, moreover, when the
fortress had been erected, until the third day before the nones of
June [3 June], our men endured many hardships, and, weakened
by hunger and the sword, they toiled there at great cost. However, on this day the city was captured in the following manner:
four brothers, noble men of Antioch, on the second day of June
promise to surrender the city to Bohemund, Robert Curtose, and
Robert, count of Flanders. These, however, with the common
assent of all our princes, at nightfall conduct the whole army to
the wall of the city, without the knowledge of the Turks. And in
the morning, when the citizens of Antioch open the gates to
receive the three named princes alone, according to promise, all
of our men suddenly rush in together. There is the greatest clamour: our men obtain all the fortified places, except the very high
citadel; the Turks – these they kill, those they hurl to destruction
over the precipice.'

VII

Divided Leadership

June 1098–January 1099

After the capture of Antioch, the crusaders spent six months re-
cuperating in northern Syria, a number of the leaders eagerly
establishing themselves in control of certain regions to the extent
that the object of Jerusalem seemed to fade as a priority, to the dis-
quiet of the mass of the remaining troops. The death of Adhemar of
Le Puy at Antioch on 1 August removed a conciliatory influence that
had reinforced unity and restrained rivalries. Now, squabbles over
ownership of Antioch, in particular between Raymond of Toulouse
and Bohemund, threatened to break up the expedition. Only after
Bohemund prevailed was Raymond persuaded to lead his army
south towards Palestine and the Holy City, and only then after his
followers had destroyed the walls of recently captured Ma'arrat,
making it impossible for the count to remain where he was and
forcing him to embark for Jerusalem, which he did, theatrically
dressed as a barefoot penitent, on 13 January 1099.

The Gesta Francorum *describes the aftermath of victory at*
Antioch.

When all our enemies had been resoundingly defeated (high
praise be to God Almighty, the Three in One) they fled hither
and thither, some of them half-dead, others wounded, and they
fell down and died in the valleys and woods and fields and by the
roadside. Christ's people, the conquering pilgrims, went back
into the city after their enemies had been defeated, exulting
in their joyful triumph. Without delay all our leaders, Duke
Godfrey, Raymond, count of St Gilles, Bohemund, the count of
Normandy and the count of Flanders, and all the others, sent the

high-born knight Hugh the Great to the emperor at Constantinople, asking him to come and take over the city and fulfil the obligations which he had undertaken towards them. Hugh went, but he never came back.*

After all these things were done, all our leaders assembled and held a council to decide how best to guide and lead the people until they should complete their journey to the Holy Sepulchre, for which they had already suffered so many perils. In this council they decided that they dared not yet enter into the land of the pagans, because in summer it is very dry and waterless, and that they would therefore wait until the beginning of November. So our leaders separated and each went off into his own territory until it should be time to resume the march. They had it announced throughout the city that if there were any poor man, lacking gold and silver, who wished to take service with them and stay on, they would gladly enrol him.

There was in the army of the count of St Gilles a certain knight whose name was Raymond Pilet.† He took into his service many knights and foot-soldiers, and set out boldly, with the army which he had collected, into the land of the Saracens. He passed by two cities and came to a castle named Tell-Mannas. The occupants of this castle, who were Syrians, surrendered it to him at once, and when his men had all been there for eight days messengers came to him, saying, 'There is a castle full of Saracens near at hand.' The knights and pilgrims of Christ went straight to that castle and besieged it on all sides, and by Christ's help they took it at once. They captured all the peasants of the district and killed those who would not be christened, but those who preferred to acknowledge Christ they spared. When this was done, our Franks came back with great joy to the first castle. On the third day they set out and came to a city named Marra‡ which was not far off, in which were assembled many Turks and

* He did, but only in 1101 to meet his death.
† Lord of Alais in the Limousin.
‡ Ma'arrat al-Numan on the road from Hamah to Aleppo; Raymond Pilet's raid took place July–August 1098.

Saracens from the city of Aleppo and from all the cities and castles round about. The barbarians came out to fight with our men who, resolving to do battle with them, put them to flight; yet the enemy rallied and went on attacking our men all through the day, and their onslaught lasted until the evening. The heat was unspeakable, and our men could not endure such fearful thirst, for they could find no water to drink, so they wanted to get back safely to their castle. The Syrians and poor pilgrims, for their sins, got into a blind panic and began to retreat in a hurry. When the Turks saw them drawing back, they began to pursue them, and victory increased their strength, so that many of our people gave up their souls to God, for love of whom they had come thither. This massacre took place on 5 July. The surviving Franks withdrew into the castle, and Raymond with his men stayed there for several days.

The other crusaders, who remained in Antioch, stayed there with joy and great gladness, having the bishop of Le Puy as their ruler and shepherd. But, as God would have it, he fell very sick, and by God's will he departed from this world, and resting in peace he fell asleep in the Lord on the feast of St Peter's Chains.* Therefore there was grief and sorrow and great mourning throughout the whole army of Christ, for the bishop was a helper of the poor and a counsellor of the rich, and he used to keep the clergy in order and preach to the knights, warning them and saying, 'None of you can be saved if he does not respect the poor and succour them; you cannot be saved without them, and they cannot survive without you. They ought every day to pray that God will show mercy towards your sins, by which you daily offend him in many ways, and therefore I beseech you, for the love of God, to be kind to them, and to help them as much as you can.'

Not long afterwards the noble Raymond, count of St Gilles, came and entered into the land of the Saracens and reached a city called al-Bara, which he attacked with his army and captured at once. He killed all the Saracens whom he found in it, both men

* 1 August 1098.

and women, great and small, and after he had established his power there he restored the town to the Christian faith, and took counsel with his most trustworthy advisers as to how he might, with due devotion, have a bishop set up in the city, to recall it to the worship of Christ, and to consecrate the house of the devil to be a temple of the true and living God, and a church dedicated to his saints. Eventually they chose an honourable and learned man* and took him to Antioch to be consecrated, and this was done. The rest of the army, which was in Antioch, stayed there with joy and gladness.

Raymond of Aguilers provides a fuller picture of the infighting.

Following the victory the Frankish leaders, Bohemund, the count, the duke, and the count of Flanders, recaptured the citadel; but Bohemund, conceiving mischief by which he brought forth sin, seized the higher towers and forcibly ousted the followers of Godfrey, the count of Flanders and the count of St Gilles from the citadel with the excuse that he had sworn to the Turk who had delivered Antioch that only he would possess it. Emboldened by this unpunished act, Bohemund came to demand the castle and gates of Antioch which Raymond, Adhemar and Godfrey had protected from the time of Kerboga's siege. With the exception of the count all yielded. Despite his enfeebled state, Raymond did not wish to let go the Bridge Gate, and prayers, promises and threats did not dissuade him.

Internal strife worried our leaders and further undermined friendly relations, so that only a few avoided disputes with their comrades or servants over theft or violence. In the absence of a judge who could or would discuss lawsuits, each person became a law unto himself. In these conditions the ailing count and bishop offered little protection to their followers. But why trifle with such petty details? Luxuriating in idleness and riches, the crusaders, contrary to God's commands, postponed the journey

* Peter of Narbonne, *c.*25 September 1098; the first Latin bishop appointed by the crusaders over a predominantly Greek Orthodox Christian community.

until the calends of November.* We believe that, if the Franks had advanced, not one city between Antioch and Jerusalem would have thrown one rock at them, so terrified and weakened at this time were the Saracen cities following the defeat of Kerboga.

In the mean time Adhemar, lord bishop of Le Puy, beloved by God and mankind, flawless in the estimation of all, departed in peace to the Lord on the calends of August.† So great was the sorrow of all Christians at the time of his passing that we, who had been eyewitnesses to it, could not describe the reactions when we turned to recording the greatness of events. The scattering of the leaders following Adhemar's death – Bohemund's return to Romania, and Godfrey's journey to Edessa – gave proof to his past usefulness to the *Militia Christi* and to its leaders.‡

On the second night following the bishop's burial in the church of the blessed Peter of Antioch, Lord Jesus, the blessed Andrew and Adhemar appeared in Raymond's chapel to Peter Bartholomew, the one who had related the location of the lance in Antioch. Then Adhemar said to Peter:

'Thanks be to God, Bohemund and all my brothers who freed me from hell. Following the uncovering of the lance, I sinned deeply and so was drawn down to hell, whipped most severely, and as you can see my head and face were burned. My soul remained in hell from the hour it passed out of my body until my miserable corpse was returned to dust. This vestment you now see is one which the Lord returned to me in the burning flames, because at the time of my ordination as bishop I had given it to a pauper for God's work. Although Gehenna boiled up and the minions of Tartarus raved against me, they injured nothing beneath the garment. Of all things brought from my native land none brought as much benefit as a candle which my friends gave as an offering for me and the 3 *denarii* which I presented to the lance. These benevolences revived me when, burning even unto

---

* 1 November 1098.   † 1 August 1098.

‡ Bohemund went to Cilicia to secure for himself the conquests of Baldwin and Tancred the previous autumn.

death, I went forth from hell. My lord, Bohemund, said that he would carry my body to Jerusalem. For his sake he shall not move my corpse from its resting place because some of the blood of the Lord with whom I am now associated remains there.

'But if he doubts my statements, let him open my tomb and he shall see my burnt head and face. I entrust my followers to my lord, the count; let Raymond deal kindly with them so that God will be compassionate and carry out his promises. Moreover, my brothers should not sorrow because of my death, because I shall be far more useful in death than in life if they are willing to keep the laws of God. I and all my departed brothers shall live with them, and I shall appear and offer better counsel than I did in life. You, my brothers, heed the burdensome and frightful pains of hell and serve God, the emancipator of man from these and other ills. Indeed, how fortunate is he who escapes the penalties of hell. The Saviour shall be able to bestow this pardon upon those who shall have kept his commandments. Also save the drippings of this candle left at dawn. Since I am dead let the count and his chosen ones select a bishop in my place, since it is improper that the see of the blessed Mary be without a bishop; and further give one of my cloaks to the church of St Andrew.'

Then the blessed Andrew paid his respects, came nearer and commanded:

'Heed God's words which I speak. Raymond,* remember the gift the Lord handed over to you, and that which you do, do in his name so that the Lord may guide your words and acts and grant your prayers. Nicaea, first city granted to you by the Lord, has been turned from him. God gave his city to you, wrested it from your enemies, only to be denied in that place later because the works of the Lord were unknown there; and if one asked the Lord's help he was scourged. However, in his goodness the Lord does not wish to abandon you; and he shall grant that which you seek, and even more than you have dared to seek, because he delivered to you the lance, which pierced his body from which ran the blood of our redemption. Remember the Lord did not

* i.e. Raymond of Toulouse.

give you this city to desecrate as you did the other, and you can certainly see that the Lord did not give it to you because of your merits.

'The Lord orders you, O Raymond, that you learn who aspires most to rule Antioch and make enquiries concerning the Lord's role in his rule. Therefore, if you and your brothers, God's custodians of Antioch, find a faithful maintainer of God's justice, give him the city. But if he schemes to hold Antioch by force, thus scorning justice and judgement, then you and your brothers seek counsel from God, and he shall give it to you. Righteous men and the true worshippers of God will not fail you; but the unrighteous, may they return to him who is the enemy of justice, and it shall be seen in what manner God will save them. Truly, upon them shall be the same curse of God and his mother as that which was placed on the falling Lucifer. If you are in accord, seek counsel in prayer, and God will give it to you.

'Further, if you are harmonious, hold counsel concerning a patriarch of your law. Do not absolve captives wishing to keep your commandments, and do not admit those who have followed the Koran in order to worship Allah of the Turks. Regard them as Turks and send two or three to prison, and they will identify others for you. Following completion of the above, ask the Lord's advice on the crusading journey and he will counsel you well. However, if you do not follow the above command, although Jerusalem is only ten days' distance, you will not reach it in ten years; and I shall lead the infidels back into their lands and one hundred of them will triumph over you. Besides, you, servants of God, entreat the Lord as did the apostles; and as he answered their prayers so shall he answer yours.

'You, Raymond and Bohemund, go to the church of the blessed Andrew, and he will give you God's best advice; and that which God places in your heart, follow it. After this visitation of the blessed Andrew, not only humble yourself before him but have your brothers do likewise. By all means let peace and love of God abide with you, Raymond and Bohemund, because if you are in accord nothing can destroy you. It behoves you first to make known the justice which you must render. Let as many men as there are from each of their bishops declare publicly their wealth and assist their poor according to their ability and to the need. Further, act according to general agreement, and if they do not wish to observe this and other just rules, restrain them. If anyone desires to possess any city given to him by God for the Christians, may he conduct himself according to the above commands. But if he shall not do so, let the count and the children of God scourge him.'

At first credited, the admonitions of St Andrew were soon ignored, for some of the crusaders said, 'Let us return Antioch to Alexius,' but others objected.

Later at the siege of Arqah as Peter Bartholomew lay dying, he summoned the count and instructed him: 'Upon your arrival at Jerusalem command the army to pray God to lengthen and continue your life and God will double your life. Moreover, upon your return put the lance within five leagues of the church of St Trophimus and have a church erected there; and upon oath make sound money there and do not permit any false acts in that place. This spot shall be called Mount of Joy, and may these things be carried out in Provence because the blessed Peter promised his disciple, Trophimus, to deliver the Holy Lance to him.'*

The interests of the poor were set aside because of strife and dissension, and nothing happened concerning the counsel which the chieftains received from St Andrew. At this time the Turks from Aleppo invested a fortress which is called Azaz.† Troubled thus, the besieged Turks asked Godfrey, who was in the vicinity, to accept their castle because henceforth they preferred only a Frankish lord. Consequently, the duke upon his return to Antioch called together Raymond, who had recovered from his illness, and all his knights and footmen whom the count had led into Hispania [Ruj] to pillage the countryside for the poor.

---

* Peter Bartholomew died 20 April 1099 at the siege of Arqah after the ordeal by fire of 8 April; Montjoie refers to the hill on the Jaffa–Jerusalem road which afforded travellers their first view of the Holy City. This anecdote breathes hindsight.   † North-east of Antioch, c.14–17 September 1098.

Godfrey also pleaded earnestly that Raymond, for God's sake as well as the honour of the Frankish race, hasten to help the apostate Turks, who now cried out to God; and he further stated that the besieged Turks made the sign of the Cross against the machines of the besiegers. Following these and other entreaties, the count marched with Godfrey; however, the Turks abandoned the siege upon receipt of this news. Consequently, upon our army's arrival at Azaz, the duke took hostages from the castle as guarantors of future loyalty, and Raymond returned to Antioch with considerable expense to his army. Here he called together his knights so that he could lead the poor people, now demoralised by hunger and weariness, into Hispania.

At the same time St Andrew appeared to Peter Bartholomew in a tent at Chastel Rouge which was occupied by the bishop of Apt, Raymond d'Aguilers, chaplain of the count, and a chaplain named Simon. Simon, upon hearing the conversation of St Andrew and Peter, covered up his head, and as he reported, heard much, but recalled only, 'Lord, I say.'*

However, the bishop of Apt added, 'I am not sure that I have dreamed or not, but an old man wearing a white stole and holding the Holy Lance of the Lord in his hands asked me, "Do you believe this is the lance of Jesus Christ?"

'Whereupon I responded, "I believe, lord!"

'When he put the question a second and third time, I answered, "Truly, I believe, lord, that this is the lance which drained the blood from the side of Jesus Christ by which all have been redeemed."'

Then the bishop of Apt shook me, Raymond d'Aguilers, as I lay sleeping close by. Upon awakening I noticed the extra light, and as if holy grace had entered my soul I enquired from my friends present whether they had felt as if they were in a group moved by great emotion, and all replied, 'No, indeed.'

While we repeated the above, Peter, the recipient of the heavenly revelation, answered, 'Indeed you did see a pleasing

* The bishop of Apt and the otherwise unknown Simon were in the Provençal force; Chastel Rouge was a fort in the Ruj valley.

light because the Father, author of all grace, stood in this spot for a long time.'

When we requested him to relate the words of his heavenly visitors, Peter reported to us and the count as follows:

'Tonight the Lord and the blessed Andrew in their accustomed form came here accompanied by a small companion, wearing a long beard and clad in linen. Then the blessed Andrew, displeased because I had abandoned the relics of his body, found in the church at Antioch, threatened me severely and continued: "After being cast head first from a mountain by the unbelievers, I broke two fingers, and following my death this man preserved them and then translated them to Antioch. But you cared little for my relics after you found them; one you allowed to be stolen, the other you shamefully discarded." Then he showed his hand which lacked two fingers.'

Peter continued: 'O count, St Andrew criticised you harshly because you are not afraid to sin grievously and evilly although you received the inexpressible gift reserved for you alone by the Lord. This is the reason the Lord gave you this sign: specifically, five days ago you gave as an offering a candle large enough to burn three days and as many nights. Yet immediately melting, it sank to the ground. This night on the contrary you offered a small candle, one scarce large enough to burn until the cock's crow, and it sheds its light with only a third of the candle melted although it is now day.

'Therefore, the Lord demands these things from you: "Undertake nothing unless you have done penance, for if you fail to do so you and your undertakings will be as a melted candle which trickles to the earth. But God will make perfect and complete all your undertakings in the name of the Lord if you do penance, and the Lord will magnify even your small efforts as he has made the little candle, which you see, last a long time." '

Raymond, although he denied the gravity of his sins, confessed and did penance after Peter Bartholomew confronted him with his sin.

Peter continued to address the count: 'O count, the blessed

Andrew objects to your advisers because they gave evil counsel for a purpose, and on account of this you are commanded to ignore their advice unless they swear not to give bad counsel knowingly to you.

'Listen well, Raymond. The Lord orders you not to dilly-dally, because he will aid you only after the capture of Jerusalem; and let no crusader ride closer than two leagues when you approach Jerusalem. If you follow instructions God will deliver the city to you.

'Following these commands St Andrew thanked me profusely because I had brought about the consecration of the church which had been constructed in his name at Antioch; and he spoke not only of these things but of other matters not pertinent at this time. After this he and his comrades ascended into space.'

The Gesta Francorum *describes the worsening relations after the Antioch conference of 1 November.*

When the appointed day (the feast of All Saints)* approached, all our leaders returned together to Antioch and began to discuss how they should continue their journey to the Holy Sepulchre, for, said they, 'The appointed day is at hand, and it is no time for any further quarrels,' for Bohemund had been asking every day for the recognition of the agreement by which all the leaders had formerly promised to give him the city, but the count of St Gilles would make no agreement and did not want to give way to Bohemund, because he was afraid of breaking his oath to the emperor. Many meetings were held in the church of St Peter in order to come to a just conclusion. Bohemund recited his agreement and showed a list of his expenses, and likewise the count of St Gilles repeated the words and the oath which he had sworn to the emperor on Bohemund's advice. The bishops, with Duke Godfrey, the counts of Flanders and Normandy and the other leaders, went apart from the rest, and entered that part of the church

* 1 November 1098.

where stands St Peter's chair, so that they might give judgement between the two parties; but afterwards, fearing lest the journey to the Holy Sepulchre might be interrupted, they would not give a clear judgement. Then said the count of St Gilles, 'Rather than abandon the journey to the Holy Sepulchre, and provided that Bohemund will come with us, I will faithfully promise to do whatever is approved by our peers, Duke Godfrey and the count of Flanders and Robert the Norman and the other leaders, saving the faith which I owe to the emperor.' Bohemund agreed to all this, and the two of them promised, putting their hands into those of the bishops, that the journey to the Holy Sepulchre should in no wise be interrupted by them. Then Bohemund took counsel with his men as to how he could garrison and victual the citadel on top of the mountain. Likewise the count of St Gilles took counsel with his men as to how he could garrison and victual the palace of Yaghi Sayan the amir, and the tower which is over the Bridge Gate (which lies on the side of the city nearest to St Simeon's Port), so that it could hold out for a long time.

The city of Antioch is a very fine and distinguished place. Within its walls are four great mountains which are exceedingly high. The citadel, a wonderful building which is exceedingly strong, stands on the highest of them. Down below lies the city, which is impressive and well planned, adorned with all kinds of splendid buildings, for there are many churches, and 360 monasteries. Its patriarch is metropolitan over 153 bishops.

This city is surrounded by two walls, the greater of which is very high and amazingly broad, built of great stones, and there are set upon it 450 towers. Everything about this city is beautiful. On the east it is shut in by four great mountains, on the west, beside the city walls, runs a river called the Orontes. This city is the centre of great authority, for it was formerly established by seventy-five kings, of whom the chief was King Antiochus, from whom it gets its name of Antioch. The Franks besieged this city for eight months and a day, and thereafter they themselves were besieged for three weeks by the Turks and other pagans, in greater number than have ever before been gathered together, whether of Christian men or pagans. Finally, by the help of God and the Holy Sepulchre, they were defeated by the Christians, and we rested in Antioch, with joy and gladness, for five months and eight days.

When this time came to an end, Raymond, count of St Gilles, set out from Antioch with his army in the month of November, and came to a city called Riha and thence to one called al-Bara. On 28 November he reached the city of Marra [Ma'arrat al-Numan], in which was assembled a great number of Saracens, Turks, Arabs and other pagans, and the count attacked it next day. Bohemund and his army followed the other counts soon afterwards, and joined forces with them on a Sunday. On the Monday they attacked the town very bravely from all sides, and pressed on with such eagerness and courage that scaling-ladders were set up against the wall, but such was the power of the pagans that on that day it was not possible to come to grips with them or to do them any harm. When our leaders saw that they could do nothing, and that they were labouring in vain, Raymond, count of St Gilles, caused a wooden siege tower to be built, and it was strong and lofty, so engineered and constructed that it ran upon four wheels. On the top storey stood many knights and Everard the Huntsman, who blew loud blasts on his horn, and underneath were armed knights who pushed the tower up to the city wall, over against one of its towers. When the pagans saw this they immediately made an engine by which they threw great stones upon our siege tower, so that they nearly killed our knights. Moreover they threw Greek fire upon the siege tower, hoping to burn and destroy it, but this time Almighty God would not let the siege tower burn, and it was higher than all the walls of the city. Our knights who were on its upper storey (William of Montpellier and many others) threw great stones down upon those who stood on the city wall, and struck them upon their shields; so that shield and man fell backwards into the city, and the man was killed. While they were doing this others held in their hands spears adorned with pennants, and tried to pull the enemy towards them with lances and hooks of iron. Thus they fought until the evening. Behind the siege tower stood the priests and clerks, clad in their holy vestments, praying and beseeching God to defend his people, and to exalt Christendom and cast down idolatry.

On the other side of the city our knights were fighting every day with the enemy, putting up scaling-ladders against the city wall, but the might of the pagans was such that they could gain no advantage. At last Gouffier of Lastours* was the first to get up the ladder on to the wall; the ladder broke at once under the weight of the crowd who followed him, but nevertheless he and some others succeeded in reaching the top of the wall. Those who had gone up cleared a space around them on the wall. Others found a fresh ladder and put it up quickly, and many knights and foot-soldiers went up it at once, but the Saracens attacked them so fiercely, from the wall and from the ground, shooting arrows and fighting hand-to-hand with spears, that many of our men were terrified and jumped off the wall. While those very gallant men who stayed on the wall were resisting the enemy attack, others, protected by the siege tower, were under-mining the defences of the city. When the Saracens saw that our men had undermined the wall they were panic-stricken and fled into the city. (This all happened on a Saturday, at the hour of vespers, when the sun was setting. It was 11 December.)

Then Bohemund sent an interpreter to the Saracen leaders to tell them that if they, with their wives and children and goods, would take refuge in a palace which lies above the gate he would save them from death. Our men all entered the city, and each seized his own share of whatever goods he found in houses or cellars, and when it was dawn they killed everyone, man or woman, whom they met in any place whatsoever. No corner of the city was clear of Saracen corpses, and one could scarcely go about the city streets except by treading on the dead bodies of the Saracens. Then Bohemund took those whom he had ordered to enter the palace, and stripped them of all their belongings, gold,

---

* Lord of Lastours; he was later said to have brought a pet lion home with him as a souvenir.

silver and other valuables, and some of them he caused to be killed, others to be taken to Antioch and sold as slaves.

The Franks stayed in that city for one month and four days, during which time the bishop of Orange died.* While we were there some of our men could not satisfy their needs, either because of the long stay or because they were so hungry, for there was no plunder to be had outside the walls. So they ripped up the bodies of the dead, because they used to find bezants hidden in their entrails, and others cut the dead flesh into slices and cooked it to eat.

Bohemund could not reach an agreement about his claims with the count of St Gilles, so he was angry and went back to Antioch. Count Raymond, without much delay, sent messengers to Antioch, asking Duke Godfrey and the count of Flanders and Robert the Norman and Bohemund to come and hold a conference with him at Riha.† All the leaders came thither, and took counsel as to how they should continue on their way to the Holy Sepulchre, for which they had set out and towards which they had marched until this time, but they could not reconcile Bohemund with Raymond, unless Count Raymond would surrender Antioch to Bohemund, and this the count was unwilling to do because of the oath which he had sworn to the emperor. Then the other counts and the duke returned to Antioch with Bohemund, but Count Raymond returned to Marra, where the poor pilgrims were, and he ordered his knights to fortify the palace, and the castle which was above the gate by the city bridge.‡

Raymond of Aguilers's account appears closer to the currents of popular feeling, at least in the Provençal army.

Soon thereafter Raymond, accompanied by the poor pilgrims and a few knights, marched into Syria where he courageously

* William; after Adhemar of Le Puy's death he tried to fill his spiritual role.
† Conference held *c.*4 January at Ruj.
‡ In fact Raymond's followers had demolished the walls (*c.*5 January) to force him to lead them south.

captured al-Bara, the first Saracen town on his route.* Here he
slaughtered thousands, returned thousands more to be sold into
slavery at Antioch, and freed those cowardly ones who surrendered before the fall of al-Bara. Thereafter, following the views
of his chaplains and princes, the count very commendably and
properly selected a priest as bishop in this manner. One of the
count's chaplains, after a general convocation, climbed on the
walls and made known to all the people Raymond's wishes.
Because the people demanded an election, the above chaplain
enquired whether there was a cleric who could receive the loyalty
of the faithful, and by opposing the pagans as much as possible
aid God and his brethren.

In the ensuing silence we called Peter, a native of Narbonne,
and publicly made plain the burden of the bishopric, and urged
that he take the post if he was determined to hold al-Bara even
unto death. When he promised the above in his administration,
the people unanimously approved him and thanked God very
much in view of the fact that they wanted a Roman bishop in the
eastern Church.† Raymond gave Peter of Narbonne one-half of
al-Bara and its environs.

The calends of November,‡ the time for the reassembling of
the crusaders and the renewal of the march, now drew near and
al-Bara was two days' journey from Antioch. As a result, Raymond left his army in al-Bara and journeyed to Antioch with
Peter, his new bishop, many captives and great booty. Here, all of
the princes with the exception of Baldwin, brother of Godfrey,
reassembled. This Baldwin,§ after digressing from the main crusading army, turned towards the Euphrates before the capture of
Antioch, seized the rich and celebrated city Edessa, and waged
many successful battles against the Turks.

Before going to other events I must tell you this tale. When
Godfrey was on his way to Antioch with twelve knights, he
encountered 150 Turks, and, not the least hesitant, prepared his

---

* *c.*25 September 1098.
† This may be wishful thinking on the author's part.   ‡ 1 November 1098.
§ Baldwin of Boulogne's Edessa detour, October 1097–February/March 1098.

arms, exhorted his knights, and courageously charged the enemy. But the Muslims, impressed by the daredevil choice of death rather than safety in flight, chose to have some of their men dismount so that the mounted Turks would be assured that their dismounted friends would not desert them. As a result during the long and violent mêlée, Godfrey's knights, equal in number to the twelve apostles and secure in their belief the duke was God's vicar, bravely charged the enemy. God gave the duke such a great victory that he killed some thirty pagans, captured a like number, and pursuing the fugitives killed or caused to be drowned many others in the adjacent swamp and river. In a joyful triumph with the captive foes carrying the heads of their slain comrades, Godfrey returned victoriously to Antioch.

Thereafter in a princely assembly in the church of the blessed Peter, the princes began to plan the resumption of the march to Jerusalem. Then some of the holders of castles and rents in the environs of Antioch asked: 'What shall be done about Antioch? Who will guard it? Alexius will not come; remember he fled when he heard Kerboga besieged us, because he had no confidence in his strength or his huge army. Shall we await him longer? Certainly, he, who forced our brothers and those coming to God's aid to retreat, will not come to support us. On the other hand if we abandon Antioch and the Turks recover it, the result will be more disastrous than the last occupation. So let us give it to Bohemund, a wise man, respected by the pagans, a man who will protect it well.'

But the count and others spoke in opposition: 'We swore upon the Cross of the Lord, the crown of thorns, and many holy relics that we would not hold without the consent of the emperor any city or castle in his dominion.'

Thus divided by contradictions, the princes became so violent that they almost took up arms. Actually, Godfrey and Robert of Flanders took the Antioch quarrel lightly and secretly favoured Bohemund's possession, but fearful of the disgrace of perjury dared not commend it to him. As a result the journey and all matters pertaining to it and the care of the poor were postponed.*

The people, upon observing this princely fiasco, began to suggest first privately and later publicly: 'It is obvious that our leaders because of cowardice or because of the oath to Alexius do not wish to lead us to Jerusalem; therefore, why can't we select a brave knight in whose loyal service we can be secure, and God willing we shall reach the Holy Sepulchre with him as our leader. My goodness! A year in the land of the pagans and the loss of two hundred thousand soldiers; isn't this enough? Let those who covet the emperor's gold or the Antiochian revenues possess them; but for us who left our homes for Christ, let us renew our march with him as leader. May the coveters of Antioch die wickedly even as its inhabitants did recently. If the Antiochian quarrel continues, let us tear down the walls; then the era of princely good will existing prior to the city's capture will return with its destruction. Otherwise, we should turn back to our lands before hunger and fatigue exhaust us.'

Swayed by these and other views, Raymond and Bohemund made a peace of discord; and on a set date orders went out to the people to prepare for resumption of the crusade. Upon completion of all the details for this march, the counts of St Gilles and Flanders along with the people on the set day marched into Syria where they besieged the wealthy and heavily populated city of Ma'arrat al-Numan, which was situated eight miles from al-Bara.† Because of a former skirmish with us in which we suffered heavy losses, the haughty citizens of the city railed at our leaders, cursed our army, and desecrated crosses fixed to their walls to anger us. On the day following our arrival, we were so angered by the natives that we openly stormed the walls and would, no doubt, have seized Ma'arrat al-Numan if we had possessed four more ladders. However, our two ladders, short and

---

* Raymond of Aguilers here refuses to shy away from the fierce divisions and rivalries within the leadership.

† Ma'arrat al-Numan was besieged from 27 November to 11–12 December 1098.

fragile, were mounted fearfully; and it was the council's decision to build machines, hurdles and mounds by which the wall could be reached, sapped and tumbled to the ground. While this went on Bohemund and his army came and laid siege to another sector of Ma'arrat al-Numan. As we stated above, we were inadequately prepared, but urged on by the newcomers' appearance we hoped to launch a new attack by filling the moat. But our new attack, more miserable than the first, was useless.

It grieves me to report that in the ensuing famine one could see more than ten thousand men scattered like cattle in the field scratching and looking, trying to find grains of wheat, barley, beans or any legume. Despite the continuing work on assault machines, some of our people, impressed by the misery around them and the audacity of the Saracens, lost hope of God's mercy and turned tail.

But God, the protector of his servants, now had mercy on his people when he saw them in the slough of despond. As a result he employed the blessed apostles Peter and Andrew to inform us of his will and of ways to appease his harsh command. In the middle of the night they entered the count's chapel and awakened Peter Bartholomew, the one to whom they had shown the lance. But Peter Bartholomew, suddenly aroused, upon seeing two ugly and filthily clad characters standing by the reliquary, naturally believed them to be thieving paupers. St Andrew was clad in an old tunic, torn at the shoulders, the left one patched with cloth, the right one bare, and he wore cheap shoes. Peter was dressed in an ankle-length, coarse linen shirt.

Then Peter Bartholomew enquired, 'Who are you, my lords, and what do you seek?'

The blessed Peter answered: 'We are God's messengers; I am Peter and this is Andrew. But we chose this habit for our appearance so that you may observe the great profits for him who serves God devotedly. In this state and garb, just as you see us, we came to God, and behold us now.'

After these remarks Peter and Andrew became brighter and more beautiful than words can express; and Peter Bartholomew, terror-stricken by the unexpected flash of light, tumbled to the ground as if dead, and in his anxiety broke into a sweat which dampened the mat upon which he had fallen. Thereupon St Peter helped him to his feet and said, 'You fell easily.'

Peter Bartholomew replied, 'Yes, my lord.'

St Peter then explained, 'So shall all disbelievers and transgressors of the Lord's command fall, but the Lord raises them as I did you after your fall if they repent their evil deeds and cry out to God. Furthermore, as your sweat remains on the mat, so surely God will lift up and remove the sins of those crying out to him. But tell me, how does the army conduct itself?'

Peter Bartholomew answered, 'Certainly, they are greatly worried by famine, and they are very miserable.'

Whereupon St Peter stormed: 'Deserters of Almighty God may well be fearful for having so forgotten the perils from which he delivered them that they failed to offer thanks. But you cried out to God when you were down and out at Antioch so that we in heaven might hear. The Lord heard you, offered you his lance as a pledge of victory to you, and gave you a marvellous and glorious triumph over the besiegers and Kerboga. You have deeply offended God; and now in what lord do you believe yourselves to be safe? Can towering mountains or hidden caves protect you? You could not be safe even on some impregnable height stocked with all necessities, because one hundred thousand foes would menace each of you. In your ranks there is murder, pillage and theft, as well as an absence of justice. There is also adultery, although it would be pleasing to God if you would marry. In the matters of justice the Lord orders that all goods in the dwelling of the violent oppressor of the poor shall be public property. If you pay your tithes the Lord is prepared to give you that which you need; but he will give Ma'arrat al-Numan to you on account of his mercy and not because of your deeds; and whenever you wish besiege it, do so because, without doubt, it will be seized.'

Following Peter's account of these events next morning to the count, Raymond along with the bishops of Orange and al-Bara called together the people; and, enticed by high hopes of capturing the city, the faithful gave generously and offered prayers to Almighty God to liberate his poor people for his name's sake only. Upon completion of these spiritual preparations, ladders were hastily made, a wooden tower erected, hurdles put together, and at the end of the day the assault was started. The besieged of Ma'arrat al-Numan hurled stones from catapults, darts, fire, hives of bees and lime upon our men who had sapped their walls; but scarcely any suffered injury because of the power and mercy of God. On the other hand, the crusaders daringly attacked the walls with rocks and ladders in an assault lasting from sunrise until sunset; indeed it was a remarkable fight in that no one rested and no one doubted the victorious outcome. Finally all called out to God to be merciful to his people and to execute the promises of his disciples.

The ever-present Lord delivered the city to us as his apostles had prophesied. Gouffier of Lastours, first to mount the walls, was followed by other Christians, who attacked the ramparts and towers; but night ended the fight and left some towers and parts of the town in Saracen hands.* The knights, anticipating a last-ditch stand of the enemy the following morning, guarded the outer walls to cut off any escapees. But some crusaders, careless of their lives because starvation had made them contemptuous of life, carried the fight to the besieged in the shades of night. Thereby the poor gained the lion's share of booty and houses in Ma'arrat al-Numan while the knights, who awaited morning to enter, found poor pickings. In the mean time the pagans hid in subterranean caves, and practically none appeared on the streets. The Christians filched all the goods above the ground, and, driven by hopes of Saracen wealth underground, smoked the enemy out of their caves with fire and sulphur fumes. When the plunder in the caves proved disappointing, they tortured to death the hapless Muslims in their reach. Some of our men had the experience of leading the Saracens through the streets, hoping to locate spoils of war, only to find their captives would

* See above, p. 259n.

lead them to wells and then suddenly jump headlong to their deaths in preference to revealing goods owned by them or others. Because of their intransigence all submitted to death. Their corpses were thrown into swamps and areas beyond the walls, and so Ma'arrat al-Numan yielded little plunder.

The knights of Bohemund, although only half-hearted in pressing the siege, acquired the greater number of towers, horses and captives, and thereby led to hard feelings between the Normans and the Provençals. Now the Lord had brought to pass a miraculous event; and, as I reported above, even though we explained to the people before the capture of Ma'arrat al-Numan the apostolic commands of Peter and Andrew, Bohemund and his comrades ridiculed us. Actually Bohemund and his Normans were more of a hindrance than a help, and naturally the entourage of Raymond was indignant because the Normans held the major share of the spoils. Finally, the lords disagreed; Raymond wanted to give the city to the bishop of al-Bara, and Bohemund held to some of his captured towers and warned, 'I shall agree to nothing with Raymond unless he cedes the Antiochian towers to me.'*

In this turmoil knights and the people asked when it would please the princes to begin the journey, for although the march had started long ago, yet each day seemed to be the start of a new crusade, for the goal had not been reached. Bohemund answered that he would not go before Easter, and it was now the time of the Nativity of our Lord. Many gave up hope and turned back on account of the scarcity of horses, the absence of Godfrey, and the exodus of many knights to Baldwin of Edessa.

At last, the bishop of al-Bara and some nobles met with the poor people and called upon Raymond for help. When the bishop ended his sermon, the knights and all the people knelt before the count, the recipient of the Holy Lance, and tearfully beseeched him to make himself leader and lord of the army. They further stated that in view of the merits of his possession of the Holy Lance and the fact that he was beholden for the Lord's

* i.e. the towers Raymond held and garrisoned.

benefaction, he would not fear to continue the journey in safety with the people. Failing to do so Raymond should hand over the lance to the masses, and they would continue the march to the Holy City under the Lord's leadership. The count temporised, fearing that the absentee princes, already envious of him, would not follow him if he set the day of departure.

Why not end this dreary story? The tears of the poor prevailed, and Raymond set the departure date on the fifteenth day while the infuriated Bohemund proclaimed throughout the town the date of departure as the fifth or sixth day, and soon thereafter returned to Antioch. Raymond and the bishop of al-Bara turned to providing a garrison, determining both the number and choice of personnel. At the same time the count requested Godfrey and the absentees from Ma'arrat al-Numan to come together in one place and make the necessary preparation for resumption of the journey. The princes met and held a conference at Chastel Rouge, which is almost half-way between Antioch and Ma'arrat al-Numan; but the meeting came to naught because the leaders and many who followed their example offered reasons for not continuing the journey. As a result Raymond offered Godfrey and Robert of Normandy 10,000 *solidi* apiece, 6,000 to Robert of Flanders, 5,000 to Tancred, and proportionately to others.*

Meantime upon reception of the news that Raymond planned to garrison Ma'arrat al-Numan with knights and footmen from the army, the poor gossiped: 'So that's it! Strife in Antioch, strife in Ma'arrat al-Numan; will there be bickering of princes and sapping of God's army in every spot which God gives to us? Let us put an end to further strife here, and for the sake of tranquillity among the leaders and peace of mind for Raymond, who worries over its loss, come and let us tear down its walls.'

Thereupon, even the sick and weak, arising from their beds

---

* The Ruj meeting was held *c.*4 January 1099 and provides a good example of how leaders expected to raise troops, i.e. by payment; the sums involved may indicate the relative size of each contingent as well as Count Raymond's disposable wealth.

and hobbling along on sticks, came all the way to the walls. An emaciated person could roll back and forth and push from the wall stones of such size that three or four yoke of oxen could scarcely budge. The bishop of al-Bara and Raymond's friends, exhorting and pleading against such vandalism, went around about the city; but those who had scrambled from the walls and hidden at their approach were quick to resume their work as soon as the guards passed by them. The more cowardly and pre-occupied ones worked at night so that almost no one was too weak or sick to help in tumbling the walls.*

Now the food shortage became so acute that the Christians ate with gusto many rotten Saracen bodies which they had pitched into the swamps two or three weeks before. This spec-tacle disgusted as many crusaders as it did strangers, and as a result of it many gave up without hope of Frankish reinforcements and turned back. The Saracens and Turks reacted thus: 'This stub-born and merciless race, unmoved by hunger, sword or other perils for one year at Antioch, now feasts on human flesh; there-fore, we ask, "Who can resist them?" ' The infidels spread stories of these and other inhuman acts of the crusaders, but we were unaware that God had made us an object of terror.†

At this time Raymond, upon his return from Ma'arrat al-Numan, was highly incensed with his followers; however, he recognised God's fine hand and ordered the foundations of the walls to be undermined when he learned that neither threats nor force on the part of the bishop of al-Bara and other leaders could dissuade the mob from its purpose. But the food shortage grew daily, and we ordered almsgiving and prayers for the journey as the appointed day approached. Meanwhile, moved by the absence of the great leaders and the weakening effect of the famine, the count of Toulouse ordered the Christians to forage for food in Hispania, and he promised that he and his knights would be in the vanguard. But some of his disgruntled followers

* This effectively forced Count Raymond to move on.
† A measured judgement; for cannibalism, L. A. M. Sumberg, 'The "Tafurs" and the First Crusade', *Medieval Studies*, xxi (1959), pp. 224–46.

complained: 'With less than three hundred knights and only a small number of footmen, shall we split our forces with some going into Hispania while others remain in the defenceless ruins of Ma'arrat al-Numan?' And they enlarged on Raymond's great instability.

Nevertheless, at last on behalf of the poor the count marched into Hispania and captured many castles, prisoners and much plunder. Upon his joyous and victorious return, following the killing of many Saracens, the infidels seized and killed six or seven of our indigent. Oddly enough, all these corpses had crosses on their right shoulder. The observers, along with Raymond, greatly comforted by the sight, offered prayers to the omnipotent God who remembered his paupers. To convince the sceptics, who remained with the baggage train near Ma'arrat al-Numan, they carried back one of the mortally wounded who was still breathing. We saw a miracle in this poor man, one so mutilated that his battered body scarcely had a spot to conceal his soul. Yet he lived seven or eight days without nourishment, all the time testifying that Jesus, to whose judgement he would surely go, was God, the creator of the Cross which he bore on his shoulder.

Ibn al-Qalanisi viewed events such as the capture of Ma'arrat al-Numan from the victims' perspective. He also chronicled the highly significant capture by the Egyptians of Jerusalem in the summer of 1098 from the Ortuqids.

For three centuries after its capture by Caliph Umar in AD 638, Jerusalem had been ruled on behalf of the caliphs of Damascus and then, from the eighth century, the caliphs of Baghdad. In the tenth century, the grip of the Abbasid caliphs weakened, Jerusalem and southern Palestine becoming a battleground between rulers of northern Syria and Egypt. With the establishment of the Shia Fatimid caliphate of Egypt in the 970s, Jerusalem fell under Egyptian political control that was only challenged by the invasion of Syria by the Seljuks after their victory over the Greeks at Manzikert in 1071. The Holy City fell to the Seljuks without a struggle in 1073 and, after a brief Egyptian restoration in 1076, remained part of the

Seljuk empire until its disintegration following the death of Sultan
Malik Shah of Baghdad in 1092.* It was to this period that some
in the west attributed a worsening of conditions for pilgrims, later
promoted, without much tangible justification, as one of the causes
of the First Crusade.

Malik Shah's brother Tutush (d. 1095) had established Ortuq, a
Turkish amir and general, as governor of Jerusalem where, follow-
ing his death in 1091, his sons, the Ortuqids Sukman and Il-Ghazi
ruled, from 1095 as vassals of Tutush's son, Duqaq of Damascus.
The invasion of northern Syria by the First Crusade in 1097–8 and
the defeats of Duqaq, Ridwan of Aleppo and Kerboga of Mosul.
gave the newly aggressive Egyptian vizier al-Afdal the chance to
recover territory lost twenty years earlier. In July 1098 he managed
to seize Jerusalem at a time when he was also entertaining ambas-
sadors from the western army.

Although, in their close diplomatic exchanges with the crusaders,
the Egyptians had previously made common cause with the in-
vaders, with control of Jerusalem and southern Palestine, they now
regarded the westerners with suspicion and increasing hostility
leading to a collapse in relations in the spring of 1099. The Fatimid
conquest of Jerusalem therefore made the crusaders' task more
difficult still.

In July 1098 news was received that al-Afdal, the commander-in-
chief, had come up from Egypt to Syria at the head of a strong
askar. He encamped before Jerusalem, where at that time were
the two amirs Sukman and Il-Ghazi, sons of Ortuq, together
with a number of their kinsmen and followers and a large body
of Turks, and sent letters to them, demanding that they should
surrender Jerusalem to him without warfare or shedding of
blood. When they refused his demand, he opened an attack on
the town, and having set up mangonels against it, which effected
a breach in the wall, he captured it and received the surrender of
the sanctuary of David† from Sukman. On his entry into it, he
shewed kindness and generosity to the two amirs, and set both

* See above, pp. xvi–xvii.   † Tower of David; see map p. 313.

them and their supporters free. They arrived in Damascus during the first ten days of September, and al-Afdal returned with his askar to Egypt.

In this year also the Franks set out with all their forces to Ma'arrat al-Numan, and having encamped over against it on 27 November, they opened an attack on the town and brought up a tower and scaling-ladders against it.

Now after the Franks had captured the city of Antioch through the devices of the armourer, who was an Armenian named Firuz, on the eve of Friday [night of Thursday, 3 June], and a series of reports were received confirming this news, the armies of Syria assembled in uncountable force and proceeded to the province of Antioch, in order to inflict a crushing blow upon the armies of the Franks. They besieged the Franks until their supplies of food were exhausted and they were reduced to eating carrion; but thereafter the Franks, though they were in the extremity of weakness, advanced in battle order against the armies of Islam, which were at the height of strength and numbers, and they broke the ranks of the Muslims and scattered their multitudes. The lords of the pedigree steeds were put to flight, and the sword was unsheathed upon the foot-soldiers who had volunteered for the cause of God, who had girt themselves for the Holy War, and were vehement in their desire to strike a blow for the faith and for the protection of the Muslims. This befell on Tuesday, 29 June 1098.*

In December 1098, the Franks made an assault on the wall of Ma'arrat al-Numan from the east and north. They pushed up the tower until it rested against the wall, and as it was higher, they deprived the Muslims of the shelter of the wall. The fighting raged round this point until sunset on 11 December, when the Franks scaled the wall, and the townsfolk were driven off it and took to flight. Prior to this, messengers had repeatedly come to them from the Franks with proposals for a settlement by negotiation and the surrender of the city, promising in return security for their lives and property, and the establishment of a [Frank-

* Actually 28 June 1098.

ish] governor amongst them, but dissension among the citizens and the foreordained decree of God prevented acceptance of these terms. So they captured the city after the hour of the sunset prayer, and a great number from both sides were killed in it. The townsfolk fled to the houses of al-Ma'arrat, to defend themselves in them, and the Franks, after promising them safety, dealt treacherously with them. They erected crosses over the town, exacted indemnities from the townsfolk and did not carry out any of the terms upon which they had agreed, but plundered everything that they found, and demanded of the people sums which they could not pay. On Thursday, 13 January 1099 they set out for Kafartab.

VIII

Miracles on the Road

January–June 1099

The march from Ma'arrat al-Numan to Jerusalem took Raymond and his Provençals the best part of five months, being punctuated by a long, fruitless siege of Arqah (February–May 1099). Gradually all the other leaders except Bohemund joined Raymond: Robert of Normandy almost immediately in January; Godfrey of Bouillon and Robert of Flanders only in mid-March. At Arqah, the final diplomatic breach with the Egyptians occurred. The crusaders now realised that speed was essential if they were to reach Jerusalem before a relief army arrived from Egypt and so avoid a rerun of the trials at Antioch. So each of the main coastal ports was avoided or deals were struck with their rulers. Only when Ramleh was reached in early June did the westerners establish their own garrisons, partly to secure the link with the coast that was to prove vital in the ensuing siege of the Holy City.

Throughout the march, which ended with their arrival before the walls of Jerusalem on 7 June, the crusaders were accompanied by visions and miracles. At Arqah, to face down his critics, Peter Bartholomew underwent an ordeal by fire (8 April) in which, depending on the witness, he suffered mortal burns or survived only to be severely mauled by a hysterical mob of supporters: either way, he died on 20 April, casting further doubt on the authenticity of the Holy Lance. However, other visions and other visionaries stepped into Peter's place to reassure the Christian host of their providential uniqueness and the close watch kept over them by the saints and by their own deceased comrades now elevated as martyrs to eternal bliss. By the time the siege of Jerusalem began, the crusaders displayed characteristics of a revivalist rally as well as an army on the march. This was no accident. Rather, it formed a vital ingredient in maintaining unity, direction and optimism.

The story is taken up by the Gesta Francorum.

When Raymond saw that he was the cause why none of the other leaders would set out on the way to the Holy Sepulchre, he went out barefoot from Marra on 13 January and reached Kafartab, where he stayed for three days and the count of Normandy joined him. The king of Shayzar [Ali ibn Munqidh] had sent many messengers to Count Raymond while he was at Marra and Kafartab,* because he wanted a treaty of peace, and he swore to pay an indemnity, and to be kind to the Christian pilgrims, so that while they were within his territory they should not suffer the least offence, and he said that he would be glad to sell them horses and food. So our men went out and came to encamp near Shayzar, on the river Orontes. When the king of Shayzar saw the Frankish camp so near to the city he was anxious, and ordered merchandise to be withheld from them unless they moved further off from the city boundary. Next day he sent two Turks, his messengers, to go with them and show them the ford over the river, and to lead them where they could find booty; so they came into a valley guarded by a castle, and seized there more than five thousand animals and plenty of corn and other goods, which were a great refreshment to the whole army of Christ. The garrison of the castle surrendered to the count, and gave him horses and refined gold, and swore on the Koran that they would do no harm to the pilgrims. We stayed there for five days, and when we set out we came rejoicing and took up our quarters in a castle belonging to Arabs, for its lord came out and made an agreement with the count. After leaving this place we reached a city which was very beautiful and full of all kinds of good things; it was called Cepkalia† and stood in a valley. Its inhabitants, on hearing of the approach of the Franks, left the city, and their gardens full of vegetables and houses full of food, and took to flight. On the third day we left this city and crossed a mountain‡ which

* See map p. xliv.   † Formerly Raphania.   ‡ The Ansariyah range.

was very high and broad, and entered the valley of Sem [the al-Buqaiah valley], which was extremely fertile, and there we stayed for nearly fifteen days. Not far off there was a castle, in which a great multitude of pagans had assembled. Our men attacked it, and would have taken it by force if the Saracens had not turned out of the gates an immense number of beasts, so that our men returned to the camp with all the good things which they had captured. At dawn our men struck their tents and came to besiege that castle, proposing to encamp there, but the pagans had fled and left the castle empty. Our men entered and found plenty of corn, wine, oil, flour and whatever they needed, so we celebrated the feast of Candlemas there with great devotion. While we were there messengers came from the city of La Chamelle,* the king of which sent to the count horses and gold, and made an agreement with him that he would not do the Christians the least harm, but that he would be kind to them and respect them. Also the king of Tripoli [Fakhr al-Malik ibn Ammar] sent to the count, proposing to make a faithful treaty of friendship with him, if he agreed, and he sent ten horses and four mules and some gold; but the count said that he would make no treaty at all with him, unless he would be christened.

When we left that valley (which was a very good place) we came on Monday in the second week in February to a castle which is called Arqah and pitched our tents around it.† This castle was full of an immense horde of pagans, Turks, Saracens, Arabs and Paulicians, who had made its fortifications exceedingly strong and defended themselves bravely. While we were there fourteen of our knights rode over to the city of Tripoli, which was quite near, and found about sixty Turks and others who had rounded up men and beasts to the number of more than fifteen hundred. Our men made the sign of the Cross and attacked them, killing six men and capturing six horses, and by God's help they won a marvellous victory.

* Literally 'she-camel'; Hims.
† The siege of Arqah lasted from mid-February to 13 May 1099.

Raymond Pilet and Raymond, viscount of Turenne,* left the main army of Count Raymond and came to the city of Tortosa,† which they attacked bravely, for it was garrisoned by many of the pagans. When night fell they withdrew into a corner where they encamped and lit many fires, so that it might appear that the whole host was there. The pagans were terrified and fled secretly in the night, leaving the city full of provisions. (It has also an excellent harbour.) Next morning our men came and attacked it from all sides, but they found it empty, so they entered it and stayed there until the siege of Arqah began. There is another city, called Maraclea, not far from this one; the amir who governed it made a treaty with our men, admitted them to the city, and put up our banner.‡

Meanwhile Duke Godfrey, Bohemund and the count of Flanders came to the city of Laodicea,§ where Bohemund broke away and went back to Antioch. The others came and laid siege to a city called Jabala.¶ But when Raymond, count of St Gilles, heard that an immense force of pagans was speeding towards us, determined to fight, he took counsel with his followers and decided to summon those of our leaders who were besieging Jabala to come to his aid. When they heard this news they made a treaty with the amir at once, and agreed with him on terms of peace, receiving a tribute of horses and gold, and so they left the city and came to our help; but the threatened attack did not come, so the said counts encamped on the other side of the river and took part in the siege of Arqah.

Not long afterwards our men rode against Tripoli, and came upon Turks, Arabs and Saracens outside the city. Our men scared them off and put them to flight, killing many of the leading men of the city. So great were the slaughter of pagans and the bloodshed that even the stream which flowed into the city ran red and stained the water in the citizens' tanks, for which reason they were full of grief and lamentation, and so frightened that none of them dared to go outside the city gate.

* Turenne in the Limousin.   † North of Tripoli; see map p. xliv.
‡ Tortosa and Maraclea fell on 17 February 1099.
§ Latakiah; Bohemund left on 1 March.   ¶ The siege lasted 2–11 March 1099.

Another day our men rode over beyond Sem and found oxen, sheep, asses and many other beasts, and they also carried off nearly three thousand camels. We went on besieging Arqah for three months, all but one day, and celebrated Easter there on 10 April. While the siege was going on our ships* put into a port near at hand, and they were laden with plenty of provisions, corn, wine, meat, cheese, barley and oil, so that the whole army was very well supplied. Many of our men, including Anselm of Ribemont,† William the Picard and many others whose names I do not know, suffered blessed martyrdom in the course of this siege. The king of Tripoli sent frequent messengers to our leaders, asking them to raise the siege and make a treaty with him. When Duke Godfrey and Raymond, count of St Gilles, and Robert the Norman and the count of Flanders heard this, and saw that the season of harvest was come, for we were eating spring beans in the middle of March and corn in the middle of April, they took counsel together and decided that it would be a very good thing to finish the journey to Jerusalem while the harvest was being gathered in.

Therefore we left the castle and came to Tripoli on Friday, 13 May, and there we stayed for three days. The king of Tripoli finally made an agreement to set free at once more than three hundred pilgrims who had been captured there, and to give us 15,000 bezants and fifteen horses of great value. He also sold us plenty of horses, asses and provisions, so that the whole army of Christ was well supplied. The treaty also stated that if we could defeat the army which the amir of Cairo‡ was preparing against our men, and could take Jerusalem, then the king of Tripoli would be christened and hold his land from our leaders. This was the lawful agreement.

We departed from the city one Monday in the month of May

* Genoese fleet moving south from St Simeon.

† Lord of Ribemont near St Quentin; author of the letters on pp. 167–70, 193–6; see below, pp. 285–5.

‡ Al-Afdal; he had taken advantage of the crusaders' arrival to capture Jerusalem in July 1098; his negotiations with the crusaders collapsed at Arqah; see above, p. 179n.

and travelled all that day and night, by a narrow and steep path, until we came to a castle called Batrun, and thence to a city on the coast called Jubayl, where we suffered badly from thirst, so that we were exhausted by the time that we reached the river called Braym [the Nahr Ibrahim]. After this we spent the night and the following day (which was Ascension Day) in crossing a cliff where the path is very narrow, and we expected to find our enemies lying in ambush, but by God's grace none of them dared to come near us.* Then our knights went on ahead of us, clearing the way, and we reached a city called Beirut which lies on the coast. From thence we came to another city called Sidon and so to another called Tyre, and from Tyre to Acre. From Acre we came to a castle named Haifa, and afterwards we encamped near Caesarea, where we celebrated Whit Sunday on 30 May. Thence we came to the city of Ramleh,† which the Saracens had evacuated for fear of the Franks. Near Ramleh is a church worthy of great reverence, for in it rests the most precious body of St George, who there suffered blessed martyrdom at the hands of the treacherous pagans for the name of Christ. While we were there our leaders took counsel together to choose a bishop‡ who might protect and build up this church, and they paid him tithes and endowed him with gold and silver, horses and other animals, so that he and his household might live in a proper and religious manner.

Raymond of Aguilers's account contains his usual differing emphases.

Encouraged by their good fortune and the propitious omens of the crosses, the foragers left their booty at Kafartab, four leagues' journey from Ma'arrat al-Numan, and those who had friends at Ma'arrat al-Numan returned with Raymond. On the appointed day the count, his clerks and the bishop of al-Bara departed and trudged along barefoot, calling out for God's mercy and the saints' protection as flames set by the departing

* The narrow pass across the Dog river; see map p. xlv.
† 3 June 1099.   ‡ Robert of Rouen.

Christians mounted the ruins of Ma'arrat al-Numan. In the rear marched Tancred with forty knights and many footmen. News of the resumption of the crusade caused nearby rulers to send Arab nobles to Raymond with prayers and many offerings and promises of future submission as well as free and saleable goods.*

We continued our march in security following their oaths and their surrender of hostages as security. But we think our guides, sent to us by the ruler of Shayzar,† led us poorly on the first day, because we lacked everything but water at the camping site; but on the next day the same guides inadvertently led us into a valley where the cattle of the ruler and of all of the vicinity had been herded on account of the fear which we had inspired. Long aware of our proposed march, the ruler of Shayzar had ordered the Saracens to flee; however, if he had commanded the entire region to block our march, it would not have been done, because we too were informed. Raymond of the Isle‡ and a comrade on this day captured the king's courier with letters urging all the natives to flee. Upon news of the capture of his messenger, the king said, 'My men, in place of hastily fleeing before the faces of the Franks as I ordered, come to them; and since God chose this race, I shall not stand in the way of their wishes.' Then the ruler blessed God, the provider of life's necessities for those who fear him.

The sight and capture of this unexpected large herd of cattle caused our knights and more affluent people to go to Shayzar and Camela [Hims] with their money to buy Arabian horses with the excuse, 'Since God took care of our nourishment, let us take care of the poor and the army'; and so we had almost one thousand of the best war horses. Day by day the poor regained health, the knights became stronger, the army seemed to multiply; and the further we marched the greater were God's benefits. Although adequately provisioned, certain men tried to persuade Raymond to turn from the route for a short time to take Jabala, a

* 13 January 1099.   † See map p. xliv.
‡ Possibly Raymond-Bertrand of l'Isle Jourdain, vassal of Raymond of Toulouse.

sea-coast town. But Tancred and other brave and good men blocked the move, arguing: 'God visited the poor and us; therefore must we turn from the journey? Are not the past hardships of battle at Antioch, cold, starvation and all human wretchedness sufficient? Why should we alone fight the whole world? Shall we kill all mankind? Think a bit; of one hundred thousand knights hardly less than one thousand remain, and of two hundred thousand armed footmen less than five thousand are left to fight. Shall we dilly-dally until all of us are liquidated? Will Christians from the west come if they hear of the fall of Antioch, Gibellum [Jabala] and other Islamic towns? No, but let us march to Jerusalem, the city of our quest, and surely God will deliver it to us; and only then will cities on our route, Gibellum, Tripoli, Tyre and Acre be evacuated by their inhabitants out of fear of the new wave of crusaders from Christendom.'

In the mean time along our march Turks and Arabs lurked in the rear, killing and robbing the infirm and straggling poor; and following two such incidents the count lay in ambush as the crusaders marched by. On the other hand the infidels with impunity and hopeful of booty pushed behind our army as in the past; but now as they rode past the ambush, Raymond and his knights rushed upon them, threw them into disorder, confused and killed them, and happily returned to the main body with their horses. Following this experience, Raymond and a large number of armed horsemen rode in the rearguard, and as a result the enemy ceased to prey upon the poor. Added to this precaution other armed knights along with the count of Normandy, Tancred and the bishop of al-Bara rode in the vanguard so that the enemy could not rout us from the front or the rear.

It is to be noted that the bishop of al-Bara left a garrison of seven knights and thirty footmen commanded by William, son of Peter of Cuniliacum, at al-Bara and on the advice of the count, who wished to increase the number of knights who marched from Ma'arrat al-Numan to Jerusalem, joined the crusading army. William, a devout and faithful man, in a short time with

God's help caused the bishop's interest to grow tenfold; and in place of thirty footmen he had seventy and also sixty or more knights.

We agreed in council to abandon the route to Damascus and to march to the sea coast because we could trade with Cyprus and other islands if our ships from Antioch rejoined us. When we followed this course, we found that the natives abandoned their cities, fortifications and well-stocked farms. Then we arrived in a very fertile valley after circling great mountains only to find some peasants haughty because of their number and an impregnable castle.* So they showed neither peaceful intentions nor indications of abandoning their fort. On the contrary, from their hilltop they rushed down upon armed squires and footmen who were foraging helter-skelter in fields, killed a few and carried the spoils to their fort. Our enraged men moved to the foot of the mountain upon which the castle was built, but the natives would not come down to meet us. As a result of a council of war, our knights and footmen formed ranks, climbed the mountain on three sides and routed the peasants. Thirty thousand Saracens occupied the fort, a fact which with its location gave them a chance to run into the fortification or on up the higher slopes. As a result they held us back for a time.

But when we yelled our battle-cry, 'God help us! God help us!' almost one hundred of the terror-stricken infidels fell dead either from fright or the press of their comrades at the castle gates; and, of course, outside the wall where we fought there was great plunder in cattle, horses and sheep. While the count and his knights pressed the fight, our low-born ones became satiated with the booty; and first our poor, one by one, then our poor footmen and finally our poor knights left the scene to return to their tents some ten miles away.

At the same time Raymond commanded his knights and people to take quarters; but the Saracens, who descended from the mountain-top along with those in the castle, saw the depleted ranks of the crusaders and began to organise their broken ranks

* Krak des Chevaliers, 28–9 January 1099.

for consolidation. Raymond, neglectful of this new strategy, almost lost contact with his knights on a very steep and rocky path on which horses went single file. Confronted by this danger, he faked an advance with his men as if to attack those descending from the mountain-top. In the split second of the Saracens' hesitation, the crusaders wheeled and turned to the apparent security of the valley. Foiled by this trick, the two contingents of the enemy, those on the mountain and those in the castle, upon seeing our descent joined forces and rushed the count's men. In the press of the attack some of the crusaders dismounted while others rode headlong over steep places and thus perilously missed death, but some died heroically.

Certainly, Raymond never had been in such danger of loss of his life. As a result he was so provoked with himself and his troops that upon his return to the army he accused his knights in council of unauthorised abandonment of the battle and imperilment of his life. Then all vowed to continue the siege until by God's grace the castle was razed. But God, the guide and protector of Christians from all disasters, so terrorised the defenders that in their precipitate haste they left their dead unburied. In the morning only spoils of war and a ghost castle awaited us.

The legates of the amir of Camela [Hims] and the king of Tripoli, in camp at this time, were so impressed by the sight of our courage and strength that they begged Raymond to permit them to leave upon a promise of speedy return. Shortly after their departure along with our envoys, they returned with rich gifts and many horses. This resulted from fear which seized the whole area after our capture of the hitherto impregnable castle. In addition, inhabitants of the region sent word to Raymond along with gifts and supplications, and prayed to him to send his standards and seals until he could receive their cities and castles. I mention that it was a custom in our army to respect the standard of any Frank and to refrain from an attack thereafter. Consequently, the king of Tripoli placed the count's standard on his castles.

As a result of this turn of fortune, the fame of the count of Toulouse seemed to be excelled by no leader of the past. On their journey to Tripoli as envoys, our knights were impressed by the royal wealth, the rich dominion and the populous city. Therefore, they persuaded Raymond that the king of Tripoli would in four or five days give him gold and silver to his heart's content if he laid siege to Arqah, a strongly defended place, one unconquerable by human force. On account of their wishes we invested Arqah and thereby caused courageous men to suffer unknown troubles. Sad to say, we bore heavy losses, including many illustrious knights. One of these, Pons of Balazun, lost his life from a rock hurled by a petrary, and it was because of his prayers that I have carried on this work which I have taken the trouble to write for all of the Orthodox, especially those across the Alps and for you, revered head of Viviers.*

I shall take care with the inspiration of God, the real author of these events, to complete the remainder of my report with the same love with which I began, and pray and beseech that all who shall hear these things shall believe in their truth. May God burden me with the horrors of hell and blot me from the book of life if I, out of zeal or hatred of anyone, add anything to this book except that which I believed or saw. Although ignorant of many things, I know that since my advancement to the priesthood on God's crusade, it is my duty to obey God and so relate the truth rather than fabricate lies. I wish to carry on with the same charity in my history as is exhorted by the apostle when he observed, 'Charity never fails.' May God aid me.

During the protracted siege our ships from Antioch and Latakiah, along with Venetian and Greek vessels, anchored with grain, wine, barley, pork and other marketable goods. However, the sailors soon sailed back to the ports of Latakiah and Tortosa in view of the fact that Arqah lay a mile from the sea, and the ships had no place to dock.† The Saracens had abandoned before the siege of Arqah Tortosa, a city well fortified by inner and outer walls and well provisioned. They left it on account of the fear

* Testimony to initial joint authorship to support the introductory dedication. The 'revered head of Viviers' is Leodegar, bishop of Viviers, to whom the *Historia* was dedicated.　　† More like fifteen miles.

which God had instilled in the Saracens and Arabs of the area, a fear which caused them to believe that we were all-powerful and bent on ruthless devastation of their lands.

Yet God, unwilling to forward a siege which we undertook more for unjust interests than for him, showered us with all kinds of misfortune. Strangely enough, the Christians, who had been eager and prepared for former battles, now were indisposed or ineffectual, and the inspired soldiers of Christ who did attempt anything were either wounded or found their efforts fruitless.

At the siege of Arqah Anselm of Ribemont died gloriously.* Arising one morning, he summoned priests to him, confessed his omissions and sins, invoked God's mercy and told them of the imminence of his death. While they stood shocked by the news since they saw Anselm hale and hearty, he explained: 'Don't be astonished; listen to me. Last night I saw Lord Engelrand of St Paul, who lost his life at Ma'arrat al-Numan, and I, fully conscious enquired, "What goes here? You were dead, and behold now you are alive."†

'Lord Engelrand replied, "Those who die in Christ's service never die."

'Again I interrogated him, this time concerning the source of his exceptional beauty, and he answered, "It is not astonishing since I live in a beautiful home."

'Immediately, he showed me a home in heaven so beautiful that I could conceive of nothing to equal it. While I stood shocked at the sight, Lord Engelrand said, "A much more beautiful one is in preparation for you tomorrow," and thereupon he ascended.'

Following this widely publicised narration, Anselm on this same day advanced to combat some Saracens who had stealthily sneaked out of their fort, hoping to steal something or inflict injury upon someone. In the ensuing mêlée Anselm fought courageously, but was hit on the head by a rock from a catapult.

* *c*.25 February 1099.

† Raymond adds verisimilitude by extending the dramatis personae, important in proving that the dead were martyrs and continued to help the living.

So he left this world to dwell in his heavenly home prepared for him by God.

After this a legate of the king of Babylon [Egypt], along with our released envoys who had been captives for one year, came to Arqah.* This king was still undecided on his choice of us or the Turks, and so we offered his legate these terms. If he would aid us in Jerusalem or return Jerusalem and its belongings to us, we would turn over, as we seized them, all his former cities wrested from him by the Turks. Moreover, we would divide with him all other Turkish cities not in his domain but captured with his aid. Rumour had it that the Turks promised that, if the king of Babylon would ally with them against us, they would worship Ali, kinsman of Muhammad whom he worshipped,† would accept his money, pay some tribute, and agree to other concessions unknown to us.

The king of Babylon, because of letters from Alexius with information concerning us which we found in his tents after the battle of Ascalon,‡ knew that our army was small and that the emperor plotted our destruction. He had as a result of these and other things held our envoys for a year in Babylon. But now when reports came of our entry into his lands and its attendant destruction of villages and fields and all else, he informed us that two or three hundred of us at a time and unarmed could go to Jerusalem, and return after worshipping the Lord. Confident of God's mercy, we scoffed at the offer and let him know that if he did not return Jerusalem unreservedly we would move against Babylon.§

I remind you that the amir occupied Jerusalem at this time, because upon receipt of the news of the Turkish disaster at Antioch he laid siege to Jerusalem in the knowledge that the often defeated and routed Turks would not battle against him. He received Jerusalem following the handing over of great gifts to the defenders, and then made offerings of candles and incense at the Sepulchre of the Lord on Mount Calvary.

---

* For the Egyptian negotiations, see above, p. 179n.
† A surprisingly well-informed reference to Shiite belief.
‡ Al-Afdal abandoned his camp 12 August 1099.   § i.e. Cairo and Egypt.

But let us turn back to the siege of Arqah, for as we have reported, in the midst of our army's toil there, news came that the pope of the Turks and great hordes, who followed him since he was of Muhammad's stock, were on their way to fight us. The army was alerted for battle-readiness and the bishop of al-Bara was despatched to Godfrey and the count of Flanders at Jabala,* a fortification overlooking the sea, midway between Arqah and Antioch and about two days' journey from each. Following reception of our distress call, the duke and the count of Flanders abandoned the siege and rushed to our aid; but in the interim we learned that it was a false rumour circulated by the Saracens to frighten us and thereby gain respite from the siege. After the union of the armies, the count's entourage boasted of their Arabian horses and riches, bestowed upon them by God in Saracen lands because they faced death for his sake. However, there were some who claimed that they were poverty-stricken.

So because of the great number of poor and infirm, the public was urged to give a tenth of all spoils of war. The authorised division went as follows: one-fourth to the priests who administered their masses, one-fourth to the bishop, and one-half to Peter the Hermit, the authorised custodian of the poor, the clergy and the people. In turn, of this sum Peter gave equally to the clergy and the people. Consequently, God so multiplied the number of horses and camels, as well as other necessities for the army, that wonder and astonishment grew among the crusaders. This sudden prosperity brought such contention and haughtiness to the leaders that God's most devout Christians longed for poverty and dreadful conflict to threaten us.

The king of Tripoli offered us 15,000 gold pieces of Saracen money plus horses, she-mules, many garments, and even more of such rewards in succeeding years. To give this offer meaning, one gold piece was equivalent to 8 or 9 *solidi*. Our money in circulation included *Pictavani* [Poitou], *Cartensis* [Chartres], *Manses* [Mans], *Luccenses* [Lucca], *Valanzani* [Valence], *Melgorienses* [Melgueil], and *Pogesi* [Puy], the last named being two for

* *c.*11 March 1099.

one of the others. In addition, the lord of Gibellum [Jabala], fearful of another siege, sent our leaders tribute of 5,000 gold pieces, horses, she-mules and an abundant supply of wine.

Now we were well provisioned because many gifts from castles and cities other than Gibellum were sent to us. Moreover, some of the Saracens, prompted by fear or because of zeal for our way of life, anathematised Muhammad and all of his progeny and were baptised. Because of this new-found wealth each of our princes despatched messengers with letters to Saracen cities stating that he was the lord of the crusaders. Such was the ill conduct of our princes at this time, and Tancred was the greatest of the agitators. You will recall that Tancred had accepted 5,000 *solidi* and two thoroughbred Arabian horses from Raymond for his services on the journey to Jerusalem; but now he wished to join the forces of Godfrey. So he and Raymond quarrelled, and finally Tancred wickedly deserted the count.

Many visions, sent to us by God, were announced now; and I, author of this book, relate the following revelation under the name of the one who witnessed it.

'In the year of the Incarnation of our Lord, 1099, in the seventh indiction, twenty-sixth epact, in the fifth concurrence, on the fifth of April, at night when I, Peter Bartholomew, rested in the count's chapel during the siege of Arqah, I thought of the priest to whom the Lord revealed himself with the Cross at the time of Kerboga's siege; and as I wondered why he had never revealed himself to me on the Cross, lo and behold, I saw the Lord, the apostles Peter and Andrew, and a large, heavy, dark-complexioned, big-eyed and almost bald stranger coming into the chapel.

'The Lord then asked, "What are you doing?"

'I replied, "I am standing here."

'The Lord continued, "You were almost overwhelmed by sin like the others, but what are your thoughts now?"

'I answered, "Lord, Father, I was reflecting upon the priest and your apparition on the Cross to him."

'The Lord said, "I am aware of it"; and he went on to say,

"Believe I am the Lord for whom you have gone crusading and that I underwent the Passion on the Cross at Jerusalem for your sins, and if you so believe you shall see."

'Then I saw a Cross made of two pieces of black, round, unpolished, rough, ill-fitted wood with the exception of notched and supporting middle joints.

'The Lord commanded, "Look upon the Cross which you are seeking," and there upon the Cross the Lord was stretched and crucified just as in the Passion. Peter, on the right, supported him with his head, Andrew on the left held his shoulders, and the stranger to the rear sustained him with his hands.

'The Lord continued his instructions: "Report to my people this vision. Do you see my five wounds? Like these the crusaders stand in five ranks. Those of the first rank fear not spears, swords or any kind of torment, and they resemble me who went to Jerusalem, fearing not swords, lances, clubs, sticks and last, even the Cross. They die for me as I died for them, and together we reside spiritually, one in the other. Upon their death they are seated on God's right, the place where I sat after my Resurrection and Ascension. Those of the second rank are auxiliaries of the first, a rearguard as well as a shelter in case of flight. This rank, I may say, resembles the apostles, who followed and partook of food with me. Those of the third rank act as a service of supplies, furnishing such things as stones and spears to those who fight, and they remind me of those who smote their breasts and cried out against the injustice as I was hanging on the Cross and suffering my Passion. Those of the fourth rank shut themselves up in their houses and tend to their own business when war arises, because they believe that victory lies not in my strength but in human wisdom. They are like my crucifiers who said, he deserves death; to the Cross with him because he claims to be a king, the Son of God. Those of the fifth rank, hearing the noise of battle, view it at a distance, seek its cause, display cowardice rather than bravery, and take no risks for me or their brothers. In fact, under the guise of caution they invite those wishing to join the fray or at least to furnish arms to sit on the sidelines;

and so they are similar to the betrayers, Judas and the judge, Pontius Pilate."

'The Lord was hanging naked on the Cross with the exception of a linen loincloth of a neutral shade of black and red, bordered by white, red and green bands; and the cloth hung from his loins to his knees. After this the Cross disappeared, and the Lord remained in his former garb. Then I said to him, "Lord, God, if I report this, they will not believe me."

'The Lord replied, "Would you like to know the doubters?"

'I added, "Indeed, I would."

'Then Christ commanded: "Have the count call the leaders and the people together, and have them line up as if for battle or a siege, and at the proper time let the best-known herald give the battle-cry, God help us, three times, and have him try to complete the military array. Then, as I said to you, you shall see the ranks, and along with the other believers recognise the unbelievers."

'Then I asked, "What shall we do with the doubters?"

'The Lord answered: "Show them no mercy, kill them; they are my betrayers, brothers of Judas Iscariot. Give their worldly goods to the first rank proportionate to their need; and by this act you will find the right way which you so far have circumvented. Just as other revelations came to pass as predicted, so shall these. By the way, do you know what race I especially esteem?"

'I replied, "The Jewish race."

'The Lord said: "I entertain hatred against them as unbelievers and rank them the lowest of all races.* Therefore, be sure you are not unbelievers, or else you will be with the Jews, and I shall choose other people and carry to fulfilment for them my promises which I made to you."

'The Lord further commanded that I relate the following to the crusaders. "Why do you fear to bring to pass justice? Let me ask you, what excels justice? I wish them to follow this procedure – appoint judges by families and relatives. If one commits an offence against another, let the plaintiff ask, Brother, would you

* A standard expression of eleventh- and twelfth-century anti-Semitism.

like to be treated this way? If the aggressor continues, let the plaintiff charge him in accordance with his legal right. Thereupon, let the judge feel free to take all of the possessions of the defendant, giving one-half to the plaintiff and one-half to the authorities. If for any cause the judge equivocates, go to him and tell him that if he doesn't set this right, he shall not be absolved even to the end of the world unless you free him. Do you know how burdensome an interdict can be? I commanded Adam not to touch the tree of knowledge, namely good and evil. He broke my command, so he and his descendants were in miserable bondage until I came as a mortal and redeemed them by my crucifixion. Of tithes, I shall say, some are to be commended because they gave as commanded, and I shall reward them and make them outstanding."

'Following the Lord's statement, I requested him out of the goodness of his heart that he return to me the knowledge of the services recently taken from me at Antioch. The Lord then asked me, "Is your knowledge not sufficient for relating what you know? Yet you wish to know much more."

'Suddenly, I grew confident of my wisdom, and I sought nothing more. Then, the Lord enquired, "Is your present knowledge sufficient?"

'I replied, "It is enough!"

'Then the Lord continued, "What did I tell you? Respond."

'Now I was blank, and when he pressed me for repetition of his words, I confessed, "Lord, I know nothing."

'The Lord replied, "Go and relate what you know, and that will be adequate." '

When we related these things to the brethren, some said they would never believe that God carried on a conversation with such a man, overlooking princes and bishops in showing himself to an illiterate yokel; and they went so far as to cast doubts on the Holy Lance. Consequently, we called together those to whom the lance had formerly been revealed; and then we summoned Arnulf, chaplain of the count of Normandy, and chief, as it were, of the unbelievers although a highly respected man because of his erudition.* We then questioned him concerning his doubts.

He replied that he was sceptical because Bishop Adhemar had questioned the authenticity of the lance. Thereupon, a priest, Peter Desiderius, responded; 'After the death of Adhemar, I saw him and the blessed Nicholas and finally he told me: "I now reside in the heavenly hosts of St Nicholas,† but because I hesitated to believe in the Lord's lance, when I, of all people, should have accepted it, I was led into hell. The hairs on the right side of my head and one-half of my beard were singed; and although I am not now chastised, I cannot see the Lord clearly until the full growth of my hair and beard returns." ' Peter Desiderius told this and many other revelations which came to pass later, but we shall relate these in due course.

Ebrard, a priest, came forward and reported: 'I went to Tripoli shortly before Antioch's capture, and was there keeping body and soul together when I heard of Kerboga's siege of the crusaders.‡ Upon receipt of this news, I learned that entrance and exit to Antioch was openly impossible, and I also heard of many real misfortunes as well as imaginary ones spread by Saracen lies. So in the fear of death I took refuge in a church and fell down before the statue of the Virgin Mary. For several days, tearfully and prayerfully, I implored through her intercession God's mercy, all the time fasting and beseeching her: "O most kind Lady these are pilgrims, who abandoned their children, wives and worldly goods in the name of Christ, and for you, and now they have journeyed here from faraway places, and now battle for your son. Have compassion on them and think, O Lady, of the opinion of your Son and you, also, in their lands if you deliver them to the Turks."

'Muttering and groaning I went over and over these and like things when a Christian Syrian came and said to me, "Be of good

* Meeting c.6–7 April 1099. Arnulf of Chocques, elected patriarch of Jerusalem 1 August 1099, deposed in favour of Daimbert of Pisa, elected again in 1112, briefly suspended 1115, died 1118. Controversy clung to him.

† St Nicholas of Lyra, specially venerated at Bari in Italy; Peter Desiderius was a Provençal priest.

‡ Unlikely that a priest travelled so far through hostile territory.

cheer and stop crying"; and he continued: "A little while ago I stood before the portals of the church of the blessed Mary, Christ's mother, and a clerk in white vestments appeared. When I asked his name and home he answered, I am Mark, the evangelist, recently of Alexandria, and I detoured here because of the church of the blessed Mary."

'I further enquired concerning his destination, and Mark answered: "Christ now resides in Antioch and commands his disciples to join him and aid in the battle which the Franks must wage with the Turks," and then he departed.

'When I was still doubtful, sad and tearful, the same Syrian reassured me: "You must understand that it is recorded in the Gospel of the blessed Peter that the Christian people who are destined to capture Jerusalem shall first be besieged in Antioch and cannot break out until they find the Holy Lance." '

Ebrard then testified: 'If anyone is sceptical, light an ordeal fire, and in God's name and in testimony to this I shall cross it.'

Another priest, Stephen of Valence, a respectable and good person, approached and added to this testimony. 'In the most trying ordeals at Antioch, the Lord Jesus talked to me, and in the presence of his most blessed mother, the Virgin Mary, promised that on the following fifth day he would be compassionate and end the Christians' toil if they returned to him whole-heartedly. I believe the Lord was true to his word, because the lance was uncovered on the fifth day. Now, if you don't believe me, I say that immediately after this vision, I offered Adhemar as testimony to undergo the ordeal by fire in the presence of the crowd or at his request to jump from the highest tower, and I now offer the same to you.'

The bishop of Apt, adding to our growing list of witnesses, came forward and testified: 'Only God knows whether I saw this in a dream or not, because certainly I do not.* Anyhow, a man in white clothes stood in front of me, held in his hands the Lord's lance, this lance, I say, and asked me, "Do you believe this is the lance of the Lord?"

* The bishop of Apt had doubted the lance.

'I responded, "Surely, O Lord." But because I sounded uncon-vinced, he harshly demanded two more responses from me and I repeated, "I believe this is the lance of my Lord, Jesus Christ," and immediately he disappeared.'

Then I, author of this book, before the brotherhood and the bishop, added to the evidence. 'I was there in the church of St Peter when the lance was unearthed, and I kissed its point before it was completely uncovered, and there are in the army many other witnesses along with me.' I continued: 'There is a priest, Bertrand of Le Puy, a member of Adhemar's household during his lifetime, who was deathly ill at Antioch. At this time Adhe-mar and his standard-bearer, Heraclius, who had been hit in the face with an arrow and killed when he had courageously at-tacked the Turks in the most furious battle at Antioch, appeared to Bertrand.

'Adhemar then asked, "What are you doing, Bertrand?"

'Heraclius answered, "Lord, he is sick."

'The bishop responded, "He is sick because he is a doubter."

'Bertrand then whispered, "Lord, do I not believe in the lance of the Lord as I do in the Lord's Passion?"

'Adhemar admonished him, "This is not enough; you should believe in more." '

Although extraneous, because it is notable, I shall jot down the ensuing for the benefit of the worthy. 'When the ill and wobbly Bertrand had to sit down before Adhemar and his lord, Heraclius, he saw, as he sat there, the jagged arrow wound which ended the worldly cares of Heraclius. Bertrand then questioned, "Lord, we thought that your wound had healed, but what is this?"

'Heraclius replied: "That is a good question. Upon coming to the Lord, Jesus Christ, I prayed him to leave my wound unclosed, because it brought my life to an end and so, by the Lord's will, it remains unhealed." Adhemar and Heraclius not only reported this to Bertrand, but they added other things not pertinent to this account.'

Arnulf credited the lance and confessed after hearing these

and other revelations. He further promised the bishop of al-Bara to do public penance because of his scepticism; but when he came on an appointed day to a council, he stated that he fully believed in the lance; yet he equivocated by saying that he would do penance only after consultation with his lord.

The news of Arnulf's stand caused Peter Bartholomew to become righteously indignant like a guileless but truthful man, and he blurted out: 'I not only wish, but I beg that you set ablaze a fire, and I shall take the ordeal of fire with the Holy Lance in my hands; and if it is really the Lord's lance, I shall emerge unsinged. But if it is a false lance, I shall be consumed by fire. I offer to do this because I see that no one believes in revelations or witnesses.'

This satisfied the crowd, and we set the occasion for the ordeal by fire on the day of the Lord's Passion on the Cross for our salvation; and we ordered Peter Bartholomew to fast. Four days later on Good Friday as day broke, the pile of wood was started and was completed after midday.* Some sixty thousand noblemen and people crowded there along with barefooted churchmen in sacerdotal garments. Dry olive branches were stacked in two piles, four feet in height, about one foot apart, and thirteen feet in length.

As the fire was started and flames shot into the air, I, Raymond, in the presence of the crowd declared: 'If Omnipotent God talked to this man in person, and St Andrew revealed the Holy Lance to him at vigils, let him walk through the fire unharmed; but if this is a lie, let Peter Bartholomew and the lance he carries be consumed by fire.' As they knelt the crowd responded, 'Amen.' The searing heat rose 30 cubits into the air and no one could come close to it.

Then Peter Bartholomew, clad in a simple tunic, on bended knees before the bishop of al-Bara took God as a witness that he had once seen Christ in person on the Cross, had received from him the above revelations as well as those from St Peter and St Andrew, and that reports in the name of St Peter, St Andrew or

* 8 April 1099.

Christ were not his fabrications. He further added that, if he had lied, he would never make it through the burning pile. He prayed that God would forgive him for his transgressions against God and his neighbours, and likewise the same to the bishop, the priests and the viewers of this ordeal. Forthwith the bishop handed him the lance, and Peter genuflected, made the sign of the Cross, walked into the flaming pile bravely and undaunted, briefly lingered in its midst, and finally by God's grace emerged from the flames.

To this day some of the observers there claim that they saw this sign; namely, a bird, flying over Peter's head before he emerged from the fiery grave, circled and plunged into the fire. Both Ebrard, formerly mentioned and later a resident in Jerusalem for God's sake, and William Bonofilius, a respectable and excellent knight of Arles, testified to the above. William Malus Puer, a respected knight from Béziers, reported that a man, dressed in priestly garments with a chasuble drawn over his head, entered the flames before Peter did so.* William stated that he began to cry when he failed to see the man walk out of the fire, because he had mistaken him for Peter Bartholomew and believed that Peter had been consumed by the flames.

In the huge crowd many things were not seen, but many revelations and acts we certainly know but shall not report for fear of boring the reader; and besides, three capable witnesses are sufficient for all judgements. But this we cannot omit. After Peter crossed through the fire, the frenzied crowd grabbed burning sticks and glowing coals so that shortly after only the blackened ground remained. Later through these relics, in which the people had faith, the Lord performed many worthy acts.

Peter walked through the fire, and his tunic and the Holy Lance which was wrapped in the most exquisite cloth, were left unsinged. As he emerged Peter waved to the crowd, raised the lance, and screamed out, 'God help us.' Whereupon the crowd seized him, seized him, I say, and pulled him along the ground.

* The priest Ebrard and the two lay Provençal witnesses are introduced to lend weight to Raymond of Aguilers's conviction.

Almost everyone from the mob pushed and shoved, thinking Peter was near by and hoping to touch him or snatch a piece of his clothing. The mob made three or four gashes on his legs in the tussle, and cracked his backbone. We think that Peter would have died there if Raymond Pilet, a renowned and courageous knight, had not with the aid of numerous comrades charged the milling mob, and at the risk of death snatched him from them. But we cannot write more because of our anxiety and distress.*

After Peter's wounds were bound up, he rested where Raymond Pilet had carried him. We enquired what caused him to pause in the fire. He answered: 'The Lord met me in the flames, held my hand, and said: "Because of your doubts of the uncovering of the Holy Lance at the time of St Andrew's revelation, you shall not cross without wounds; but you shall not see hell." Following these words the Lord disappeared.' Peter continued, 'Do you wish to see my burns?' His wounds were severe, but the burns on his legs were trivial.

Then we assembled the sceptics so that they could examine his face, head, hair and other parts of his body and so ascertain the truth of Peter's revelations for which he had undergone the ordeal of fire. Many, upon examining his face and body, praised God with these words: 'God, who freed this man from such searing flames, flames so hot we believed not an arrow could cross unscorched, most certainly can be our protector in the midst of pagan swords.'

Peter afterwards called Raymond of Aguilers, the count's chaplain, and demanded: 'Why did you want me to submit to the ordeal of fire in proof of my revelations of the Holy Lance and God's instructions? Certainly, I know your wishy-washy thoughts,' and he revealed Raymond's thoughts.

When Raymond denied these thoughts, Peter pinned him down: 'This absolute proof you cannot deny because I found out the other night from the Virgin Mary and Adhemar the truth.

---

* The ambiguity of the outcome of the ordeal is not at all uncommon in contemporary judicial ordeals when the verdict owes as much to the observers' motives as to any physical results.

I was very astonished to learn that although you entertained no doubts concerning the words of the Lord and his apostles, you wished me at my peril to hold this proof of these same revelations.'

Upon Peter's detection of his lies and his guilt before God, Raymond of Aguilers cried in anguish; and thereupon Peter consoled him: 'I do not wish you to be despondent because the most blessed Virgin Mary and the blessed Andrew will gain pardon for you before God if you pray earnestly to them.'

In the mean time quarrels split the army, but God, our guide and Lord, patched up these differences so that his benefactions would not be lost. The ruler of Tripoli, a city close to our camp, upon learning of the quarrels scoffed at the demands for tribute made by our envoys: 'Who are the Franks? What about their knights? How powerful are they? Think about it; the Frankish army has laid siege to Arqah for three months, and although only four leagues away I have neither experienced an attack nor seen a single armed man. Franks, come to Tripoli, be seen, and let us test your knights. Why should I pay tribute to unseen faces and unknown might?'*

This report caused public questioning: 'Behold, how have we profited from disputes and hard feelings? God is reviled and we are held in contempt.'

These sentiments unified the princes, who ordered the bishop of al-Bara and some of the army to protect the camp while they, along with footmen and knights in customary formation, would attack the ramparts of Tripoli. On the date set when our army marched in such order, the Tripolitans, confident in their tumultuous crowds, came against us in battle array. A very solid and high wall of an aqueduct leading to Tripoli formed a narrow trail between the city and the sea, which surrounds Tripoli on three sides.

As a result the Saracens fortified the above-mentioned wall of the aqueduct so that in case of reverses they could pass back

---

* The amir tended to be friendlier than this implies; perhaps the author was influenced by Count Raymond's later interest in capturing the city.

and forth as if from fort to fort. Upon the sight of the Tripolitans, confident in their battle site and arms, the crusaders, footmen and knights, prayed to God, brandished their spears and
crowded together. Their advance upon the ranks of the enemy
was more of a procession, in that if you watched the march you
would have thought and reported that they went forth as friends
rather than foes. The Lord paralysed the Tripolitans with fear,
and hardly anyone fled after the first clash of arms. Now the land
stank with Moorish blood, and the aqueduct was choked with
their corpses. It was a delightful sight as the swirling waters of the
aqueduct tumbled the headless bodies of nobles and rabble into
Tripoli. We lost one or two men, but the Turks are reported to
have had seven hundred killed.

After the victory our leaders returned to Arqah with the booty
and announced: 'Today the king of Tripoli saw us, and we in turn
saw approaches to Tripoli, and we studied means of assault. If
you now agree we will let the king of Tripoli test the mettle of
our knights tomorrow.' Thereupon on our return the following
day not a soul ventured outside Tripoli. Thereafter the king of
Tripoli proposed to our commanders that he would give them
15,000 gold pieces, horses, mules, clothing, provisions and an
open public market. He would, in addition, turn over all Christian captives if we would abandon the siege of Arqah.

Emissaries from the emperor Alexius arrived in camp at this
time protesting at Bohemund's possession of Antioch in contradiction of oaths made to the *basileus*. I break my narrative
by stating that Bohemund now held Antioch, for he violently
chased out Raymond's men from the towers they guarded when
he heard that the count had set out from Ma'arrat al-Numan
into Syria. The Byzantine envoy further stated that Alexius
would give large sums of gold and silver, and that crusaders
should await him until the feast of St John so that he could journey with them to Jerusalem. It is well to mention that it was now
near Easter.*

* 10 April 1099. Raymond of Aguilers was remarkably candid about the
leaders' rows and ambitions.

Many, among whom was the count of St Gilles, argued: 'Let us delay our march for the arrival of Alexius. We shall have his gifts. His presence will assure trade by land and sea, and we shall be united under his leadership. All cities will lay down their arms, and Alexius may possess or destroy them as he wishes. There is a chance also that crusaders, broken by long and constant adversities, would, if they reached Jerusalem, prefer to return to their homes as soon as they had seen its walls. Weigh carefully the number and extent of perils confronting those who are anxious to complete their vows. Let us step up the siege of Arqah so that in a month the garrison will capitulate or be forcibly seized. On the other hand if we decide the siege is hopeless, and news of our abandonment of it spreads afar, we, an army known for successful termination of its projects, will be mocked.'

In contradiction others argued, 'The emperor has always harmed, deceived and connived against us. Now that he realises he is weak and we are strong through God's grace, he seeks to turn us from the Holy Sepulchre in fear that word of our success will cause others to follow in our footsteps. Let those he has often offended by words and acts beware of vain trust in him. Let us renew our march to Jerusalem, place our trust in Christ our leader, who has freed us from hopeless peril as well as shielded us from the deeds and deceits of Alexius, and then we shall, by God's promise, easily gain our dreams. Upon news of the capture of Jerusalem and open commerce, he shall respond with works as well as gifts rather than deceitful words.'

The majority of the people agreed with the latter view, but their wishes and the counsel of the princes encountered difficulties. These difficulties arose because of the large entourage of Count Raymond and because he had without the other leaders braved death with the people and had made numerous large private gifts.

In this impasse we proclaimed fasting, prayers and alms to the people with the hope that Omnipotent God, who had guided us across so many lands, would condescend to communicate his will. So the prayers of the faithful prevailed with God. Bishop Adhemar appeared to Stephen of Valence, of whom we have already written concerning his vision of the Lord on the Cross, and struck him with a rod as he was walking home one night, calling out: 'Stephen.'

Stephen responded, 'Lord,' and upon turning around recognised Adhemar.

Adhemar then demanded: 'Why have you ignored so many times my commands concerning the Cross of the Lord, as well as those of our mother, the Virgin Mary? I speak of the Cross which was in my front ranks; let it be carried in the army. Tell me, what relic is better than the Cross? Has this Cross not been stoned enough for you? Or has it not guided you to the Holy Lance? Now our Lady, the blessed Virgin Mary, says that without this Cross you will have no wisdom.'

Thereupon Stephen cried, 'O dearest Lord, where is the blessed Mary?'

Immediately Adhemar revealed Mary, wondrous in form and attire, standing nine or ten cubits from him along with the blessed Agatha and a virgin holding two candles.* Stephen then spoke to Adhemar, who was standing beside Mary: 'Lord, many are the rumours in the army, among them that your hair and beard were burned in hell and many like uncredited stories. So I earnestly request you to give me one of the candles to carry to the count in testimony of your commands.'

Then Adhemar replied, 'Look at my face; do you not see it burned?' Then the bishop walked to the Virgin Mary, learned her will, returned to Stephen, and reported: 'You cannot get your wish, but the ring on your finger is useless to you, and you should not wear it. Therefore go and present it to Raymond and tell him: "The Virgin, very sainted mother, sends this ring to you; and with each failure call to mind the Lady, donor of this ring, and implore her, and God will help you." '

Again Stephen enquired concerning instructions for his brother, and Adhemar answered: 'Have him persuade the bishop-elect to perform three masses to the Lord for the souls of our

* The traditional iconography shows St Agatha holding pincers and instruments of torture.

relatives. Our mother Mary orders that henceforth the Holy Lance shall not be shown unless carried by a priest clad in sacred vestments and that the Cross precede it in this manner.' Then Adhemar held the Cross suspended from a spear and a man clad in sacerdotal garments with the Holy Lance in his hands followed as the Bishop gave this response: *Gaude Maria Virgo, cunctas hereses sola interemisti.** Hundreds of thousands of countless voices joined in the heavenly choir and the company of saints vanished.

The next morning Stephen first asked whether we had the lance, and upon seeing it broke into tears as he began to relate the above visitation, things heard and seen. Touched by this, the count sent William Hugh of Monteil, brother of the bishop of Le Puy, to Latakiah, where Adhemar's cross and hood had been left.

In the mean time, Peter Bartholomew, debilitated by illness resulting from his crushing blows and wounds, called the count and other leaders to him and told them: 'Death comes near, and I am well aware that in the presence of God I shall be judged for all my evil deeds, words or thoughts. In God's sight and your presence I bear witness to him now that I fabricated nothing concerning all the things I reported to you as coming from God and the apostles. Without doubt, you will see the fulfilment of my words if you faithfully serve God.' After this Peter, on the hour set by God, died peacefully and was buried on the spot where he crossed through the fire with the Holy Lance.†

At this time Raymond and other crusading chieftains asked natives of the region which was the best and least difficult route to Jerusalem. Consequently, some Syrians came to us, and I shall use their coming to digress a bit. Some sixty thousand Christian inhabitants have been in possession of the Lebanon mountains and its environs for many years. These Christians are addressed as Surians since they are close to Tyre, now commonly called

* 'Rejoice, O Virgin Mary, that alone hast destroyed all heresies.'
† Awkwardly for Raymond of Aguilers, despite his laying of the blame for his injuries on the overenthusiastic mobbing Peter Bartholomew received after the ordeal.

Sur. When the Saracens and the Turks rose to power through God's will, many of the Surians under their bondage for four hundred years or more were compelled to forsake their country and Christian law.

But if some because of God's grace defied the pagans, they were forced to hand over their beautiful children to be circumcised and trained in the Koran. Furthermore, fathers were murdered, while mothers were abused and their children snatched from their arms. The flaming evil passions of this race of men incited them to tear down churches of God and the saints, break to pieces images, gouge out the eyes of the more indestructible and use the statues as targets for their arrows. They tumbled altars and made mosques of the great churches. But if some poor tormented Christian soul wanted an image of God or a saint in his home, he had to pay for it month after month, year after year, or else see it trampled and crushed in filth. What I am about to relate is really too disagreeable. They placed youths in brothels and exchanged their sisters for wine for more lewdness.

Mothers were afraid to cry in public over these and other afflictions. But why should I waste so much time on the Syrians? Surely this race plotted against the Holy of Holies and his inheritance. Had not God by his order and initiative armed brutish animals against similar evils as he did once in our presence, the Franks could have met misfortunes like those of the Surians. But this covers the subject sufficiently.

The Surians, whom I have discussed above, in a meeting with Raymond of St Gilles, were questioned upon the route and answered: 'The Damascus route is flat, well stocked with food, but waterless for two days. The road through the Lebanon mountains is safe, bountiful in necessities, but very tough for camels and pack animals. Still another way, skirting the sea, has many passes so narrow that fifty or a hundred Saracens could hold back all of the human race. Yet it is recorded in our Gospel of the blessed Peter that if you are the destined captors of Jerusalem, you will journey by the sea coast, although its hazards make it appear impossible to us. This Gospel, written among us, contains not only your choice of routes, but many of your past acts and the course of future actions.'*

In the back-and-forth clash of opinions, William Hugh of Monteil returned with the above-mentioned Cross.† The sight of the Cross so agitated the entourage of the count concerning the journey that contrary to the advice of Raymond and other princes they burned their shelters and were the first to leave Arqah.

Raymond broke into tears and began to despise himself and others, but God ignored his feeling in deference to the people's will. On the other hand Godfrey, very anxious to renew the march, incited the masses. So upon leaving that hateful and abominable siege of Arqah, we arrived at Tripoli where Raymond, against the unanimous opposition of the leaders, tried to persuade them with entreaties and rewards to invest Tripoli.

St Andrew now revealed himself to Peter Desiderius, a person referred to before, and commanded: 'Go and inform the count: "Stop pestering yourself and others, because you can expect no aid until Jerusalem is first captured. Do not be disturbed over the uncompleted siege of Arqah; and further do not burden yourself if it and other cities on the way do not fall now. Actually, a battle, in which these as well as many other cities will be conquered, is imminent. So stop worrying yourself and your followers, and in his name give generously God's gifts to you; and further be a comrade and faithful friend to your men. God will give you Jerusalem, Alexandria and Babylon [Cairo] if you do so; but if you do not, you shall neither obtain God's promised rewards nor shall you henceforth have a legacy until you are in inescapable want." '

The count only gave lip-service to these words of the priest, because he ignored them by his acts and denied them by being stingy with the great riches acquired from the king of Tripoli. Moreover, he irritated his followers with chidings and invective. Peter Desiderius related this and many other matters, part of which we report in this book.

* An apocryphal work of Christian devotion.
† William Hugh of Monteil, Adhemar's brother; his Cross is used to maintain Provençal spiritual credentials.

Peter Desiderius had come to me, Raymond of Aguilers, long before when we thought of leaving Antioch and told me that he had a vision in which a person came to him and commanded: 'Go to the church of the blessed Leontius,* where you will find the relics of four saints; pick them up and carry them to Jerusalem.' The person went on to show Peter the relics and the reliquary, and told him the names of the saints. Yet Peter was sceptical of the vision after waking, and prayed and besought God to assure him a second time that this was his revelation. So in a few days the same saint reappeared to Peter, and threatened him because of neglect of God's orders. He specified that if the relics were not moved by the fifth day of the week, great harm would come to him and his lord Isoard, count of Die,† a man faithful to God according to his light, and by his judgement and goodness useful to us.

I repeated this story to the bishop of Orange, Raymond of St Gilles and others after Peter told it to me. Soon after we came to the church of St Leontius bearing candles which we offered along with vows to God and to the saints of the same church. We asked God, who made these relics holy, to assign them as our comrades and aids, and these saints, rather than scorning the fellowship of pilgrims and God's exiles, out of Christian love would be bound to us and in turn would bind us to God.

On the next morning accompanied by Peter Desiderius, we came to the place of the reliquaries of saints, and just as he had related found relics of St Cyprian, St Omechius, St Leontius and St John Chrysostom. Here we also found a chest with relics which the priest could not identify. Upon questioning, the natives were at odds on identification. Some replied that they belonged to St Mercurius, while others gave the names of various saints. Regardless of their obscurity, Peter Desiderius wished to pick them up and place them with the others.

Then I, Raymond, in the presence of all the group strongly urged: 'If this saint wishes to journey with us to Jerusalem, let him announce his name and wish, or else let him remain in this

* A saint of Tripoli.   † Isoard of Die travelled with Count Raymond.

casket. Shall we add to our burden by carrying these unknown bones?' As a result of my words the unidentified bones were abandoned at that time.

On the night following the priest's collection and wrapping of the other relics in cloths and a coverlet, a handsome youth of about fifteen stood before this priest at vigils and asked, 'Why didn't you carry my relics today with the others?'

The priest then enquired, 'Who are you?'

The young man continued his questioning, 'Don't you know the name of the standard-bearer of this army?'

Peter admitted, 'No, sir.'

Upon the priest's same answer a second time, the young man stormed, 'You tell me the truth.'

Then Peter replied, 'Lord, it is said that St George is the standard-bearer of this army.'

The youth then said, 'Correct you are. I am St George, and I command you to pick up my relics and place them with the others.'*

However, as days passed without the priest's execution of the command, St George returned and harshly demanded: 'Don't let morning pass without picking up my relics. Take also a vial of the blood of the Virgin Mary and the martyr Thecla which you will find close by, and then sing mass.' This time Peter Desiderius found all of these things and carried out the orders of St George.

Before we continue our story, we must mention those men who dared to sail through the strange and vast surface of the Mediterranean and the ocean out of love of crusading. These English, upon receipt of news of the crusades launched in the name of God's vengeance against those who desecrated the land of Christ's nativity and his apostles, set sail on the Anglican sea, and thus rounding the coast of Spain, bearing across the ocean and ploughing through the waves of the Mediterranean, after great trials arrived at Antioch and Latakiah in advance of our army. The English as well as the Genoese assured us commerce from Cyprus and other islands and so proved helpful. Daily these

* George was a local saint; his shrine was at Lydda.

ships sailed to and fro over the sea thereby frightening the Saracens and thus making Greek shipping safe. However, when the English saw us leave for Jerusalem and observed the oak wood of their ships rotting with age to the point that of the thirty original vessels only nine or ten remained, some of them abandoned ship and disembarked while others burned their boats and hastened to join the march to Jerusalem.

Our princes loitered before Tripoli until God instilled such a desire to continue the journey that all restraints were removed. So contrary to our custom and to the orders of the princes, we left at evening, rambled along all night, and arrived at Beirut the next day. Then after sudden capture of a pass, Bucca Torta, by our vanguard, we arrived in Acre unhindered and within a few days.* The king of Acre, fearful of a siege and anxious for us to leave, swore to Raymond as follows: he would yield himself and Acre to the crusaders if we seized Jerusalem or if we remained in the region of Judaea for twenty days without the king of Babylon [Cairo] engaging us in battle, or if we defeated the above king. In the mean time the king of Acre promised friendship. After this we departed from Acre one day at evening time and encamped by nearby swamps.

As is customary at such time, while some ran back and forth below the camp in search of necessities, and others sought the location of their friends' tents from acquaintances, a hawk soaring over the army dropped a mortally wounded pigeon into the bustling camp. The bishop of Apt upon picking up the bird found a letter which it carried.

The letter ran as follows: 'Greetings from the king of Acre to the duke of Caesarea. A generation of dogs, a foolish, headstrong, disorderly race has gone through my land. If you value your way of life, you and others of the faith should bring harm to them since you can easily do what you wish. Transmit this message to other cities and strongholds.' In the morning when the army was ordered at ease, the contents of the letter were made public. Thus God's kindness was revealed to us, a kindness which

* The host left Tripoli 16 May; Acre 24–5 May 1099.

prevented birds in flight from harming us and one which caused our enemies' secrets to be revealed.*

So we extolled and gave thanks to Omnipotent God and then departed fearlessly and briskly, frequently walking back and forth in the ranks. Upon news of our crossing of a nearby river, the Saracen inhabitants of Ramleh abandoned their forts and arms as well as much grain in the field and harvested crops. So when we arrived on the next day, we were certain that God fought for us. Here we made pledges to St George, our avowed leader, and our chieftains and the public decided to select a bishop, because here we found the first church of Israel. We also felt that St George would be our intercessor with God and would be our faithful leader through his dwelling place.†

Since Ramleh is fifteen miles from Jerusalem, we had a conference there. Some argued: 'Delay the journey now and turn to Egypt and Babylon; if through God's grace we could conquer the kingdom of Egypt, we would not only acquire Jerusalem, but also Alexandria, Babylon and many kingdoms. On the other hand, if we march to Jerusalem and abandon the siege because of a water shortage, we shall never succeed.'

The other group argued: 'Despite a force of hardly fifteen hundred knights and a small number of armed footmen, some favour an expedition to strange and remote lands cut off from aid of our people. Consequently, we would have little chance of holding a captured city or possessing a route of escape if necessary. This is no good. Let's stick to our course, and let God take care of the siege, the thirst, the famine and other things for his servants.'

---

* The letter is fiction.
† The adoption of local saints is intriguing, implying the crusaders' catholic embrace of a full religious landscape. Ramleh was reached 3 June 1099.

IX

Jerusalem

June–August 1099

Nearly three years after leaving their homes in the west, on 7 June 1099 the crusader forces finally reached their objective, Jerusalem. Fulcher of Chartres, who would live there for more than a quarter of a century after 1100, describes the Holy City as he knew it.

The city of Jerusalem is located in a mountainous region which is devoid of trees, streams, and springs excepting only the Pool of Siloam, which is a bowshot from the city. Sometimes it has enough water, and sometimes a deficiency due to a slight drainage. This little spring is in the valley at the foot of Mount Sion in the course of the Brook Kedron which, in wintertime, is accustomed to flow through the centre of the valley of Josaphat.*

The many cisterns inside the city, reserved for winter rains, have a sufficiency of water. More, at which men and beasts are refreshed, are also found outside the city.

It is generally conceded that the city is laid out in such proper proportion that it seems neither too small nor too large. Its width from wall to wall is that of four bowshots. To the west is the Tower of David with the city wall on each flank; to the south is Mount Sion a little closer than a bowshot; and to the east, the Mount of Olives a thousand paces outside the city.

The aforesaid Tower of David is of solid masonry half-way up, of large squared blocks sealed with molten lead. Fifteen or twenty men, if well supplied with food, could defend it from all assaults of an enemy.

In the same city is the Temple of the Lord, round in shape,

* Eyewitness account as Fulcher lived in Jerusalem 1100–28. See map p. 313.

built where Solomon in ancient times erected the earlier magnificent Temple. Although it can in no way be compared in appearance to the former building, still this one· is of marvellous workmanship and most splendid appearance.*

The Church of the Lord's Sepulchre is likewise circular in form. It was never closed in at the top but always admits the light through a permanent aperture ingeniously fashioned under the direction of a skilful architect.†

I cannot, I dare not, I know not how to enumerate the many objects which it now contains or contained in the past lest in some way I deceive those reading or hearing about the matter. In the middle of the Temple, when we first entered it and for fifteen years thereafter,‡ was a certain native rock. It was said that the Ark of the Lord's Covenant along with the urn and tables of Moses was sealed inside it, that Josiah, king of Judah, ordered it to be placed there, saying, 'You shall never carry it from this place.' For he foresaw the future Captivity.

But this contradicts what we read in the descriptions of Jeremiah, in the second Book of the Maccabees, that he himself hid it in Arabia, saying that it would not be found until many peoples should be gathered together. Jeremiah was a contemporary of King Josiah; however, the king died before Jeremiah.

They said that the angel of the Lord had stood upon the aforesaid rock and destroyed the people because of the enumeration of the people foolishly made by David and displeasing to the Lord. Moreover this rock, because it disfigured the Temple of the Lord, was afterwards covered over and paved with marble. Now an altar is placed above it, and there the clergy have fitted up a choir. All the Saracens held the Temple of the Lord in great veneration. Here rather than elsewhere they preferred to say the prayers of their faith although such prayers were wasted because offered to an idol set up in the name of

* Dome of the Rock.
† For the building history of the Holy Sepulchre, see M. Biddle, *The Tomb of Christ* (Sutton, 1999).
‡ This description of the Dome of the Rock was clearly written in 1115.

Muhammad. They allowed no Christian to enter the Temple.

Another temple, called the Temple of Solomon, is large and wonderful, but it is not the one that Solomon built. This one, because of our poverty, could not be maintained in the condition in which we found it. Wherefore it is already in large part destroyed.*

There were gutters in the streets of the city through which in time of rain all filth was washed away.

The emperor Aelius Hadrian† decorated this city magnificently and fittingly adorned the streets and squares with pavements. In his honour Jerusalem was called Aelia. For these and many other reasons Jerusalem is a most renowned and glorious city.

The siege of Jerusalem lasted from 7 June until the city was taken by storm on 15 July. The crusader army divided into two main groups: Raymond and the Provençals camped before the Sion Gate to the south of the city while the rest, under Godfrey of Bouillon and Robert of Normandy, laid siege first to the north-western corner of the city before transferring to positions opposite the Damascus Gate in the northern walls. The two eyewitness accounts – the Gesta Francorum *and Raymond of Aguilers – reflect this division, even though both seem to have most information from the Provençal army.*

Early assaults failed to make an impression on the city walls. Only after timber and engineers arrived from a Christian fleet that had put in at Jaffa could effective siege engines be constructed. After a religious procession around the walls on 8 July, preparations for a major attack began, fuelled by rumours of an Egyptian relief army. The final assault was launched on two sides of the city at once, the crusaders keeping in touch by means of signallers on the Mount of Olives. A breach in the northern wall on 15 July soon led to the capitulation of the city and one of the most grotesque massacres in medieval warfare, 'the wine press of the Lord', as Raymond of Aguilers, quoting from the Book of Revelation, described it.

* The al-Aqsa mosque; Baldwin I stripped its roof of lead to sell.
† Emperor Hadrian, AD 117–38.

The Gesta Francorum

We, rejoicing and exulting, came to the city of Jerusalem on Tuesday 6 June* and established a very thorough siege. Robert the Norman took up his station on the north, next to the church of St Stephen the Protomartyr, who was stoned there for the name of Christ, and Robert count of Flanders was next to him. Duke Godfrey and Tancred besieged the city from the west. The count of St Gilles was on the south, that is to say on Mount Sion, near the church of St Mary the mother of the Lord, where the Lord shared the Last Supper with his disciples.

On the third day some of our men – Raymond Pilet, Raymond of Turenne and many others – went off to fight, and found two hundred Arabs. The knights of Christ fought against these misbelievers, and by God's help bravely defeated them, killing many and capturing thirty horses. On the Monday† we pressed upon the city in such a vigorous assault that if our scaling-ladders had been ready we should have taken it. We did indeed destroy the curtain wall, and against the great wall we set up one ladder, up which our knights climbed and fought hand-to-hand with the Saracens and those who were defending the city, using swords and spears. We lost many men, but the enemy lost more. During this siege we could not buy bread for nearly ten days, until a messenger arrived from our ships,‡ and we suffered so badly from thirst that we had to take our horses and other beasts six miles to water, enduring great terror and apprehension on the way. The Pool of Siloam, at the foot of Mount Sion, kept us going, but water was sold very dearly in the army.

After the messenger from our ships arrived, our leaders took counsel and decided to send knights who might provide a faithful guard for the men and ships who were in the harbour of Jaffa. At dawn a hundred knights set out from the army of Raymond, count of St Gilles. They included Raymond Pilet, Achard of

---

* Actually 7 June; for the siege see map opposite.
† 13 June; this account is mainly from the Provençal perspective at Mount Sion.　　‡ The Genoese fleet and others at Jaffa.

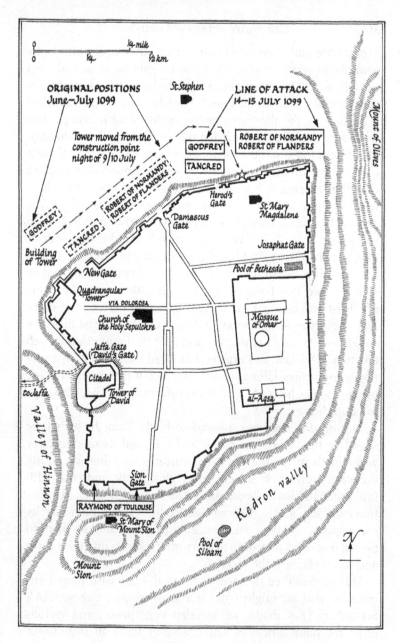

The siege of Jerusalem, June–July 1099

Montmerle and William of Sabran, and they rode confidently towards the port. Then thirty of our knights got separated from the others, and fell in with seven hundred Arabs, Turks and Saracens from the army of the amir.* The Christian knights attacked them bravely, but they were such a mighty force in comparison with ours that they surrounded our men and killed Achard of Montmerle† and some poor foot-soldiers. While our men were thus surrounded and all expecting death, a messenger reached the others, saying to Raymond Pilet, 'Why are you staying here with your knights? Look! All our men are trapped by the Arabs and Turks, and perhaps at this very moment they are all dead, so bring help, bring help!' When our men heard this they rode at once as hard as they could, and came quickly to where the others were fighting. When the pagans saw the Christian knights they split up into two bands, but our men called upon the name of Christ and charged these misbelievers so fiercely that every knight overthrew his opponent. When the enemy saw that they could not stand up to the brave attack of the Franks they turned tail, panic-stricken, and our men pursued them for the space of nearly four miles, killing many of them, but they spared the life of one so that he could give them information. They also captured 103 horses.

During this siege, we suffered so badly from thirst that we sewed up the skins of oxen and buffaloes, and we used to carry water in them for the distance of nearly six miles. We drank the water from these vessels, although it stank, and what with foul water and barley bread we suffered great distress and affliction every day, for the Saracens used to lie in wait for our men by every spring and pool, where they killed them and cut them to pieces; moreover they used to carry off the beasts into their caves and secret places in the rocks.

Our leaders then decided to attack the city with [siege] engines, so that we might enter it and worship at our Saviour's Sepulchre. They made two wooden siege towers and various other mechanical devices. Duke Godfrey filled his siege tower

* Perhaps from Egypt.   † A Burgundian castellan.

with machines, and so did Count Raymond, but they had to get the timber from far afield. When the Saracens saw our men making these machines, they built up the city wall and its towers by night, so that they were exceedingly strong. When, however, our leaders saw which was the weakest spot in the city's defences, they had a machine and a siege tower transported round to the eastern side one Saturday night.* They set up these engines at dawn, and spent Sunday, Monday and Tuesday† in preparing the siege tower and fitting it out, while the count of St Gilles was getting his engine ready on the southern side. All this time we were suffering so badly from the shortage of water that for one penny a man could not buy sufficient to quench his thirst.

On Wednesday and Thursday‡ we launched a fierce attack upon the city, both by day and by night, from all sides, but before we attacked our bishops and priests preached to us, and told us to go in procession round Jerusalem to the glory of God, and to pray and give alms and fast as faithful men should do.§ On Friday at dawn¶ we attacked the city from all sides but could achieve nothing, so that we were all astounded and very much afraid, yet, when that hour came when Our Lord Jesus Christ deigned to suffer for us upon the Cross, our knights were fighting bravely on the siege tower, led by Duke Godfrey and Count Eustace his brother. At that moment one of our knights, called Lethold [of Tournai], succeeded in getting on to the wall. As soon as he reached it, all the defenders fled along the walls and through the city, and our men went after them, killing them and cutting them down as far as Solomon's Temple,** where there was such a massacre that our men were wading up to their ankles in enemy blood.

Count Raymond was bringing up his army and a siege tower from the south to the neighbourhood of the wall, but between the wall and the tower there was a deep pit. Our leaders discussed how they should fill the pit, and they had it announced that if

---

* 9 July 1099.   † 10–12 July 1099.   ‡ 13–14 July 1099.
§ Probably on 8 July 1099.   ¶ 15 July 1099.
** The al-Aqsa mosque on the Temple Mount.

anyone would bring three stones to cast into that pit he should have a penny. It took three days and nights to fill the pit, and when it was full they took the siege tower up to the wall. The defenders fought against our men with amazing courage, casting fire and stones. But when the count heard that the Franks were in the city he said to his men, 'Why are you so slow? Look! All the other Franks are in the city already!' Then the amir who held David's Tower* surrendered to the count, and opened for him the gate where the pilgrims used to pay their taxes,† so our men entered the city, chasing the Saracens and killing them up to Solomon's Temple, where they took refuge and fought hard against our men for the whole day, so that all the temple was streaming with their blood. At last, when the pagans were defeated, our men took many prisoners, both men and women, in the temple. They killed whom they chose, and whom they chose they saved alive. On the roof of the Temple of Solomon were crowded great numbers of pagans of both sexes, to whom Tancred and Gaston of Béarn‡ gave their banners.

After this our men rushed round the whole city, seizing gold and silver, horses and mules, and houses full of all sorts of goods, and they all came rejoicing and weeping from excess of gladness to worship at the Sepulchre of our Saviour Jesus, and there they fulfilled their vows to him. Next morning they went cautiously up on to the Temple roof and attacked the Saracens, both men and women, cutting off their heads with drawn swords. Some of the Saracens threw themselves down headlong from the Temple. Tancred was extremely angry when he saw this.

Our leaders then took counsel and ordered that every man should give alms and pray that God would choose for himself whomsoever he wished, to rule over the others and to govern the city. They also commanded that all the Saracen corpses should be thrown outside the city because of the fearful stench, for almost the whole city was full of their dead bodies. So the surviving Saracens dragged the dead ones out in front of the

* See map p. 313.   † The Jaffa Gate.
‡ Gaston IV, viscount of Béarn in the foothills of the Pyrenees.

gates, and piled them up in mounds as big as houses. No one has ever seen or heard of such a slaughter of pagans, for they were burned on pyres like pyramids, and no one save God alone knows how many there were. Count Raymond, however, caused the amir and those who were with him to be taken to Ascalon, safe and sound.

Raymond of Aguilers

We packed our camels, oxen and other beasts of burden and left for Jerusalem after taking leave of the bishop and his garrison. In the mad scramble caused by our greed to seize castles and villas, we failed to remember and held valueless the command of Peter Bartholomew that we were not to approach within two leagues of Jerusalem unless barefoot. It was customary that no one seized a castle or town flying one of our standards and first touched by one of our men. So driven by ambition, many got out of bed at midnight and, unaccompanied by their comrades, captured all of the mountain forts and villas in the plains of the Jordan. But a few who held God's command dear marched along barefoot, sending up deep sighs to God because of the flouting of his will, but they recalled not one friend or comrade from the vain course. When we approached Jerusalem on this haughty march, the townspeople struck our vanguard, wounded some horses seriously as well as many men, and killed three or four from our ranks.

In turning to the siege we note that Godfrey, the count of Flanders, and the count of Normandy encamped to the north and invested Jerusalem from the centrally located church of St Stephen to the angular tower adjacent to the Tower of David.* Raymond along with his army established himself on the west and laid siege to the city from the duke's line to the foot of Mount Sion. However, a ravine between his camp and the walls prevented an even approach and caused the count to wish to change his camp and location.

* See map p. 313.

One day while Raymond was encircling Jerusalem he stopped and visited the church of Mount Sion, where he heard of God's miracles there and was so impressed that he addressed the princes and those present: 'What would happen to us if we abandon these sacred gifts of God and the Saracens should seize them, and, perhaps, defile and break them because of their hatred of the crusaders? Who knows that these gifts of God may not be tests of the intensity of our love for him? This I do know, namely, failure to guard the church of Mount Sion zealously will cause him to withhold like spots in Jerusalem.'

Thereupon in contradiction of the wishes of the princes the count of Toulouse ordered the moving of his camp to Mount Sion. This move caused him to suffer such ill will from his people that they neither wished to change camp nor to keep watch through the night, and so with the exception of a few who went to Mount Sion all the others remained in the original camp. But the count daily garrisoned his stand by paying his knights and footmen large sums of money.

I shall now digress by listing some of the sacred things there: the tombs of David, Solomon and the protomartyr, St Stephen. There the blessed Mary died; Christ ate there, and following his Resurrection appeared to his disciples and to Thomas. In that very same place the apostles were aroused by the coming of the Holy Spirit.

One day following the investment of Jerusalem a hermit on the Mount of Olives told some princes there, 'The Lord will give you Jerusalem if you will storm it tomorrow until the ninth hour.'

The Christians replied, 'We do not have any siege machinery.'

Then the hermit said, 'God is so omnipotent that if he wishes, you could scale the wall with one ladder. He is with those who work for the truth.'

So they stormed Jerusalem the next morning until the third hour with such siege weapons as they could improvise during the night. They broke the outer wall, forced the Saracens back to the inner wall, and a few crusaders climbed atop the inner fortification. At the very moment capture was imminent, the assault was broken off by sloth and fear.*

Following this reverse the Christians went foraging in the neighbourhood and ignored preparations for a new attack, each preferring to gratify his palate and belly. Even more detestable was the fact that they failed to pray to God to deliver them from the many great evils threatening their very existence. New threats came from the Saracens who had covered the mouths of wells, destroyed the cisterns and choked the flow of springs, all of which brings to mind the Lord, who 'turneth rivers into a wilderness and water springs into dry grounds . . . for the wickedness of them that dwell therein'.† So for the above reason water was very scarce.

The Pool of Siloam,‡ a great fountain at the foot of Mount Sion, flows every third day; but formerly, according to the natives, it flowed only on Saturday and was on other days marshy. Certainly, we offer no explanation of this phenomenon other than God's will. According to reports, when it gushed forth on the third day the frantic and violent push to drink the water caused men to throw themselves into the pool and many beasts of burden and cattle to perish there in the scramble. The strong in a deadly fashion pushed and shoved through the pool, choked with dead animals and filled with struggling humanity, to the rocky mouth of the flow, while the weaker had to be content with the dirtier water.

The weak sprawled on the ground by the fountain with gaping mouths made speechless by their parched tongues, and with outstretched hands begged for water from the more fortunate ones. In the fields stood horses, mules, cattle, sheep and many other animals too weak to take another step. There they shrivelled, died from thirst and rotted in their tracks, and filled the air with the stench of death.

This unfortunate turn forced the Christians to lug water from a spring some two or three leagues away and to water their cattle

* 12 June; the first attack 13 June 1099.   † Psalms 107:33–4.
‡ South-east corner of Jerusalem: see map p. 313.

there. But the Saracens learned that our unarmed men passed back and forth through rough terrain and so ambushed, killed and captured many of them and led away their cattle and flocks. Water brought in for sale in containers was sky-high, and 5 or 6 *nummi* [pennies] was an inadequate sum for a day's supply of pure water for one person.

The mention of wine was seldom if ever made. The thirst, already unbearable, was made worse by the searing heat, the choking dust and the strong winds. But why should I waste time on these mortal things? Only a few thought of God or the essentials of the siege. The crusaders did not pray for God's mercy and so we ignored God in our chastisement, and he in turn did not provide for ingrates.

At this time news of the anchoring of six of our ships at Jaffa came to us as well as demands from the sailors that we send a garrison to protect the towers of Jaffa and their ships in the port. Jaffa is almost one day's journey away and is the nearest port to Jerusalem, but little remains of the demolished place except one intact tower of a badly wrecked castle. The crusaders gladly sent Count Geldemar Carpinel with twenty knights and some fifty footmen; then in his wake Raymond Pilet with fifty knights, and last William Sabran and his entourage. Four hundred crack Arab troops and two hundred Turks stood in the way when Geldemar arrived at a plain near Ramleh.*

Geldemar drew up his knights and archers in the front ranks because of his small numbers, and confident in God's help immediately marched against the enemy. The opposition, sure that they could annihilate the Christians, rushed forward, shot arrows, and circled around. They killed four knights as well as Achard of Montmerle, a noble young man and well-known knight. They also wiped out all of our archers and wounded others from Geldemar's force, but not without heavy losses to themselves.

* 18 June 1099; Geldemar Carpinel was an ally of Godfrey of Bouillon, who gave him Haifa in 1100; William, lord of Sabran, was a Provençal follower of Count Raymond.

Despite these casualties neither did the pagan attack diminish nor did the strength of our knights, truly *Christi militia*, weaken. Rather, inspired by wounds and even death, they carried the attack more energetically as they underwent greater pressure. Finally, beset by fatigue rather than fear, the leaders of the small band noticed a cloud of dust on the horizon at a time when they were about to break away. This sight was caused by Raymond Pilet and his men who gave spurs to their horses, and in the mad charge kicked up so much dust that the enemy believed there was a large approaching force.

So by God's grace the enemy was routed and put to flight and around two hundred were killed and great booty was captured. The spoils may be accounted for by a custom among pagans; namely, if they were in flight and hotly pursued they would fling down their arms, then their garments, and finally their saddle-bags. Thus our small number of knights slew the enemy until weary and kept the spoils of those who fled.

Following the fight and the collection and division of the booty, our knights went to Jaffa where the sailors joyously received them with bread, wine and fish. Now heedless of danger they neglected their ships and posted no seaward look-outs in the crow's nest. Soon the happy and heedless sailors found themselves surrounded from the sea by their enemies, largely through their negligence in posting watchers. At daybreak they saw they had no chance to fight the superior force, so they left their ships and bore only the spoils. Thus in a fashion our force returned to Jerusalem both victorious and vanquished. One plundering ship, absent at the time, escaped capture. Laden with booty upon its return to Jaffa, it saw the Christian fleet surrounded by a superior force. Reversing its course, it returned by oar and sail to Latakiah and reported to our associates and friends the true state of affairs at Jerusalem.

We know that we got our just deserts, because we had no faith in God's messages. Consequently, the crusaders gave up hope of God's mercy and so marched down to the plain of Jordan. There they gathered palms, and were baptised in the Jordan river; and since they had viewed Jerusalem, they planned to give up the siege, go to Jaffa and, in whatsoever manner they could, return home; but the Lord took care of the ships for his unbelievers.

We now called a meeting because of the general quarrels among the leaders and specifically because Tancred had seized Bethlehem.* There he had flown his banner over the church of the Lord's Nativity as if over a temporal possession. The assembly also posed the question of the election of one of the princes as a guardian of Jerusalem in case God gave it to us. It was argued that it was common effort which would win it, but it would be common neglect that would lose it if no one protected it.

But the bishops and the clergy objected by saying: 'It is wrong to elect a king where the Lord suffered and was crowned. Suppose that in the elected one's heart he said, "I sit upon the throne of David, and I possess his dominion." Suppose he became a David, degenerate in faith and goodness, the Lord would, no doubt, overthrow him and be angry with the place and the people. Moreover, the prophet cries out, "When the Holy of Holies shall have come, unction will cease," because it was made clear to all people that he had come. But let us select an advocate to guard Jerusalem and to divide the tributes and rents among the protectors of the city.' As a result of these and other reasons, the election was not held until eight days after the fall of Jerusalem. Nothing good came from this quarrel, and only work and grief doubled each day upon the people.

Finally, a compassionate and kind Lord, both for his respect and for preventing the pagans from mocking his laws by questioning, 'Where is their God?', told us through a message from Adhemar, bishop of Le Puy, how to appease him and gain his mercy. But we spread God's commands publicly without connecting them with his name in fear that the people would disobey them and so be punished more severely because of their guilt. The gracious Lord sent numerous messengers to us but, since they were our brothers, their testimony was held worthless.

* 6 June 1099.

At this time Adhemar instructed Peter Desiderius:* 'Command the princes and the public, "Crusaders from distant lands, now here to worship God and Lord of all armies, free yourselves from the filthy world, and each one of you turn your back on sin. Then take off your shoes and in your naked feet walk around Jerusalem and don't forget to fast. If you follow these orders, at the end of nine days the city will fall after a violent assault; but if not, the Lord will increase all the misfortunes of the past." '

Following this report of Peter Desiderius to his lord, Count Isoard, to Adhemar's brother, William Hugh, and to some clerks, these confidants called a general assembly and spoke as follows:

'Men, fellows, you know the causes of the journey and our great weariness, and also that we heedlessly procrastinate in building weapons to besiege Jerusalem. Further, we not only neglect to make God friendly with us but even displease him in every way imaginable in all things; also we even drive him out and make him an outcast because of our filthy deeds. Now if you think it proper, let bygones be bygones, and let a spirit of forgiveness pervade the Christian brotherhood. Following this let us lose our pride in the sight of God, walk around the Holy City barefoot, and implore the loving kindness of God through the intercession of the saints.

'Pray, we say, that Almighty God, who abdicated his heavenly lordship and became human for us and of us, his servants, and who humbly sitting upon an ass entered Jerusalem in a procession flanked by crowds waving and paying great honours only to suffer the Passion on the Cross as a sacrifice for us; pray, we say, that he may throw open the gates of Jerusalem and yield it to us to the glory and honour of his name, while he makes judgement of his enemies, who gained it unjustly, defiled the place of his Passion and burial, and who now work hard to exclude us from the great benefits of the shrine of his divine degradation and our redemption.'

The above instruction met with general approval, and an order

* Clearly, in Raymond's narrative, he has taken the place left by Peter Bartholomew; perhaps less dangerous, being a priest.

went out that on the sixth day of the week clergymen with crosses and relics of saints should lead a procession with knights and the able-bodied men following, blowing trumpets, brandishing arms and marching barefoot. We gladly followed the orders of God and the princes, and when we marched to the Mount of Olives we preached to the people on the spot of Christ's Ascension after the Resurrection. At this time we exhorted them: 'We followed the Lord to the spot of Ascension and since we can do no more, let us forgive those who have hurt us so that Almighty God can be merciful to us.'

I need not say more on this topic. A spirit of forgiveness came over the army and along with liberal donations we implored God's mercy. We urged that he should not forsake his people at the last moment after he had brought them gloriously and marvellously thus far in their quest of the Holy Sepulchre. God now was on our side because our bad luck now turned to good and all went well.

Despite many omissions of events, I cannot overlook this one: during the noisy march around Jerusalem, the Saracens and Turks walked along the top of their walls poking fun at us, and they blasphemed with blows and vulgar acts crosses placed on yoked gibbets along the walkways. We, in turn, confident of the nearness of God's compassion, because of these very abuses pressed forward by day and night the final assault preparations.*

Godfrey and the counts of Normandy and Flanders appointed Gaston of Béarn to supervise the labourers who were building wattles, ramparts and siege instruments. The assignment fell to this nobleman because of ability and honesty. It proved to be a wise choice, because Gaston instituted a division of labour and speeded the job while the princes attended to the hauling of wooden materials. Count Raymond also put William Ricau† in charge of similar operations on Mount Sion and gave the bishop of al-Bara the job of supervising the Saracens and other work-

* The procession occurred 8 July 1099.
† William Embriaco and his brother Hugh commanded Genoese galleys; machines began to be built 15 June 1099.

men hauling timbers. Raymond's men forced the Saracens from captured castles and towns to work as serfs. You could see fifty or sixty of them carrying on their shoulders a building beam too heavy for four pairs of oxen to drag. But I shall not bother you with more details.

Collectively, we pressed the work, we laboured, built and co-operated, and neither sloth nor unwillingness retarded our work. Only the artisans, who were paid from public collections, and the men of Raymond, who got wages from his treasury, worked for money. Certainly, the hand of the Lord was in our work. Soon preparations were completed and after a council the leaders ordered: 'The fifth day will be the zero hour.* In the mean time devote yourselves to prayers, vigils and alms, and give your beasts of burden and servants to the artisans and carpenters for the work of dragging in beams, poles, stakes and branches necessary for the construction of mantelets. Knights, the construction quota of two of you shall be one crooked mantelet or one ladder. Work hard for God, because our job is almost ended.' All gladly turned their shoulders to the task, and orders went out for the attack position of princes and the disposition of siege machinery.

The besieged Saracens observed the completed siege weapons and so bolstered the weak spots that a successful attack seemed hopeless. Godfrey and the counts of Flanders and Normandy now noted the Saracen build-up, and consequently throughout the night before the set day of attack shifted their siege weapons, both wattles and towers, to a position between the church of the blessed Stephen and the valley of Josaphat. Believe me, the disjointing, transporting over a mile and erecting of these machines was no small job. The Saracens were thunderstruck next morning at the sight of the changed position of our machines and tents, and, I hasten to add, so were we, the faithful, who saw the hand of the Lord in this.

To brief you on the move to the north, I must say that two factors motivated the change of position. The flat surface offered a better approach to the walls by our instruments of war, and the

* Perhaps 9 July 1099.

very remoteness and weakness of this northern place had caused the Saracens to leave it unfortified. The count of Toulouse laboured no less at Mount Sion to the south and received aid from William Embriacus and his Genoese sailors, who, as I related earlier, lost their ships at Jaffa, but had salvaged ropes, hammers, nails, axes, mattocks and hatchets, all indispensable tools.* Now I shall leave off any more details and go on with the story of the storming of Jerusalem.

The day of the fight dawned and the assault began. But at this point we wish to add these statistics. To the best of our and other estimates there were sixty thousand combatants in Jerusalem, and women and children without number. On our side we had not more than twelve thousand able-bodied men, along with many disabled and poor people; and as I think, no more than twelve to thirteen hundred knights. We introduce these figures and contrasts to show you that all affairs, be they great or small, undertaken in the Lord's name will succeed, as the following pages of my book will prove.

First, we began to push our towers against their walls and then all the hellish din of battle broke loose; from all parts stones hurled from *tormenta* and *petrariae* flew through the air, and arrows pelted like hail.† But God's servants, resolute in their faith regardless of the outcome of death or immediate vengeance on the pagans, endured this attack patiently. The fight was indecisive at this point, and as the machines came close to the walls defenders rained down upon the Christians stones, arrows, flaming wood and straw, and threw mallets of wood wrapped with ignited pitch, wax, sulphur, tow and rags on the machines. I wish to explain that the mallets were fastened with nails so that they stuck in whatever part they hit and then burned. These projectiles of wood and straw thrown by the defenders kindled fires which held back those whom swords, high walls and deep ditches had not disconcerted.

---

* The ships had foundered or been scuttled 18–19 June 1099. The wooden equipment, not least masts for artillery-throwing missiles, proved crucial.
† The attack began 14 July 1099.

The deeds performed in the day-long battle were so marvellous that we doubt that history recorded any greater. We, assured of divine mercy, again prayed to our leader and guide, all-powerful God. With the coming of night, fear settled down on both camps. With the outer wall broken and the ditch filled, speedy access was open to the inner wall, and the Saracens feared the fall of Jerusalem that night or the following day. The crusaders, in turn, were apprehensive lest the Saracens would strengthen their cause by finding a way to burn the nearby machines. Alertness, labour and sleepless anxiety prevailed in both camps, and on our side confident hope, but on theirs gnawing dismay. The Christians besieged the city willingly for the Lord, and the pagans resisted reluctantly for Muhammad's laws.

Incredible activity in both camps went on during the night. At the break of dawn* our men eagerly rolled their siege weapons into place only to be met by the Saracens, who blocked us with their machines which outnumbered ours nine or ten to one. I shall not linger on this detail because this was the ninth day, the day which the priest had predicted would mark the fall of Jerusalem. Despite the splintering of our siege engines by the rain of stones and the lagging spirits of our bone-tired troops, the always dominant, unconquerable mercy of God was ever present in our travail. However, I cannot pass by this interesting incident. When two women tried to cast a spell over one of our *petrariae*, one of the stones from the same machine hurtled whistling through the air and smashed the lives out of the two witches as well as the lives of the three nearby small girls, and thus broke the spell.

At midday we were in a state of confusion, a phase of fatigue and hopelessness brought on by the stubborn resistance of many remaining defenders, the lofty and seemingly impregnable walls, and the overwhelming defensive skill of the Saracens. As we wavered and the pagans took new heart, the ever-present healing compassion of God came to us and changed our melancholy to gladness. At the very moment when a council debated the wisdom of withdrawing our machines since many were burned or

* 15 July 1099.

badly shattered, a knight, whose name is unknown to me, sig-
nalled with his shield from the Mount of Olives to the count and
others to move forward.* This had a psychological effect on our
spent forces, and some revitalised crusaders renewed the attacks
against the walls while others began to climb ladders and ropes.
At the same time a youth shot arrows ablaze with cotton pads
against the ramparts of the Saracens which defended against
the wooden tower of Godfrey and the two counts. Soon mounting flames drove the defenders from the ramparts. Hurriedly
Godfrey lowered the drawbridge which had defended the tower,
and as it swung from the middle of the tower it bridged the
wall, and the crusaders, unafraid and undaunted, poured into
the stricken city.

Tancred and Godfrey in the vanguard spilled an incredible
amount of blood, and their comrades, close at their heels, now
brought suffering to the Saracens. Now I must tell you of an
astonishing circumstance; namely, in one part of the city resistance had practically ceased, but in the area near Mount Sion the
Saracens fought fiercely with Raymond's forces as if they had
not been defeated. With the fall of Jerusalem and its towers one
could see marvellous works. Some of the pagans were mercifully
beheaded, others pierced by arrows plunged from towers, and yet
others, tortured for a long time, were burned to death in searing
flames. Piles of heads, hands and feet lay in the houses and
streets, and indeed there was a running to and fro of men and
knights over the corpses.

Let me tell you that so far these are few and petty details, but it
is another story when we come to the Temple of Solomon, the
accustomed place for chanting rites and services. Shall we relate
what took place there? If we told you, you would not believe us.
So it is sufficient to relate that in the Temple of Solomon and the
portico crusaders rode in blood to the knees and bridles of their
horses.† In my opinion this was poetic justice that the Temple of
Solomon should receive the blood of pagans who blasphemed

---

* See map p. 313, to show how this could have worked.
† This passage is based on Revelation 14:20.

God there for many years. Jerusalem was now littered with bodies and stained with blood, and the few survivors fled to the Tower of David and surrendered it to Raymond upon a pledge of security. With the fall of the city it was rewarding to see the worship of the pilgrims at the Holy Sepulchre, the clapping of hands, the rejoicing and singing of a new song to the Lord. Their souls offered to the victorious and triumphant God prayers of praise which they could not explain in words.

A new day, new gladness, new and everlasting happiness, and the fulfilment of our toil and love brought forth new words and songs for all. This day, which I affirm will be celebrated in the centuries to come, changed our grief and struggles into gladness and rejoicing. I further state that this day ended all paganism, confirmed Christianity and restored our faith. 'This is the day which the Lord has made; we shall rejoice and be glad in it,'* and deservedly because on this day God shone upon us and blessed us.

Many saw Lord Adhemar, bishop of Le Puy, in Jerusalem on this day, and many also asserted that he led the way over the walls urging the knights and people to follow him. It is also noteworthy that on this day the apostles were thrown out of Jerusalem and dispersed throughout all the world. On this day the children of the apostles freed the city for God and the Fathers. This day, the ides of July, shall be commemorated to the praise and glory of the name of God, who in response to the prayers of his Church returned in faith and blessing to his children Jerusalem as well as its lands which he had pledged to the Fathers. At this time we also chanted the office of the Resurrection, since on this day he, who by his might, arose from the dead, restored us through his kindness.

Fulcher of Chartres, although not an eyewitness to the siege, constructed his account from the experiences of others, basing it on the Gesta *and Raymond of Aguilers.*

* Psalms 118:24.

When the Franks beheld the city and realised that it would be difficult to take, our leaders ordered wooden ladders to be made. By carrying these to the wall and erecting them, and climbing with fierce energy to the top of the wall, they hoped with the help of God to enter the city.

These ladders were made, and on the seventh day after the arrival our leaders gave the command for the attack. At the sound of the trumpets at daybreak our men attacked the city on all sides with remarkable energy. But when they had continued the attack up to the sixth hour of the day and were not able to enter by means of the ladders which they had prepared because the ladders were too few, they reluctantly gave up the assault.

Then after consultation our leaders ordered the engineers to make machines of war. They hoped when these were moved up to the walls to attain the desired result with the help of God. Therefore this was done.

Meanwhile, however, our men did not suffer from lack of bread or meat. Yet because the area was dry, unwatered and without streams our men as well as their beasts suffered for lack of water to drink. Wherefore, because necessity demanded it, they brought water daily to the siege from four or five miles away, laboriously carrying it in the skins of animals.

When the machines were ready, namely battering rams and *scrofae*, our men again prepared to attack the city. Among those contrivances they put together a tower made of short pieces of timber because there was no large stuff in that area. When the command was given they transported the tower, in sections, by night to a corner of the city. In the morning they quickly erected it, all assembled, not far from the wall, together with *petrariae* and other auxiliary weapons which they had prepared. After they had set it up and well protected it on the outside with hides, they pushed it little by little nearer the wall.

Then some soldiers, few it is true but brave, climbed upon the tower at a signal from the trumpet. The Saracens nevertheless set up a defence against them. With *fundibula* they hurled small burning brands soaked in oil and grease against the tower and the soldiers in it. Therefore many on both sides met sudden death in this fighting.*

From the side where they were located, namely Mount Sion, Count Raymond and his men launched a heavy attack with their machines. From the other side where Duke Godfrey, Count Robert of Normandy and Robert of Flanders were stationed there was a still greater assault upon the wall. These were the events of that day.

The next day at the sound of the trumpets they undertook the same task with still more vigour. As a result they made a breach in the wall by battering it in one place with rams. The Saracens had suspended two timbers in front of the battlements and tied them there with ropes as a protection against the stones hurled at them by their assailants. But what they did for their advantage later turned to their detriment, by divine providence. For when the Franks had moved the aforesaid tower up to the wall they used falchions to cut the ropes by means of which the two beams were suspended. With these timbers they contrived a bridge and skilfully extended it from the tower to the top of the wall.

Already one stone tower on the wall, at which those working our machines had thrown flaming brands, was afire. This fire, gradually fed by the wooden material in the tower, caused so much smoke and flame that none of the city guards could remain there any longer.

Soon therefore the Franks gloriously entered the city at noon on the day known as *dies Veneris* [Friday], the day on which Christ redeemed the whole world on the Cross.† Amid the sound of trumpets and with everything in an uproar they attacked boldly, shouting 'God help us!' At once they raised a banner on the top of the wall. The pagans were completely terrified, for they all exchanged their former boldness for headlong flight through the narrow streets of the city. The more swiftly they fled the more swiftly they were pursued.

* For *scrofae* and *petrariae*, see above, p. 115n; *fundibula* were slings. Sieges often turned on the use of artillery and other engines; Antioch was an exception.   † 15 July 1099.

Count Raymond and his men, who were strongly pressing the offensive in another part of the city, did not notice this until they saw the Saracens jumping off from the top of the wall. When they noticed it they ran with the greatest exultation as fast as they could into the city and joined their companions in pursuing and slaying their wicked enemies without ceasing.

Some of the latter, Arabs as well as Ethiopians,* fled into the Tower of David, and others shut themselves up in the Temples of the Lord and of Solomon. In the courts of these buildings a fierce attack was pressed upon the Saracens. There was no place where they could escape our swordsmen.

Many of the Saracens who had climbed to the top of the Temple of Solomon in their flight were shot to death with arrows and fell headlong from the roof. Nearly ten thousand were beheaded in this Temple. If you had been there your feet would have been stained to the ankles in the blood of the slain. What shall I say? None of them were left alive. Neither women nor children were spared.

How astonishing it would have seemed to you to see our squires and footmen, after they had discovered the trickery of the Saracens, split open the bellies of those they had just slain in order to extract from the intestines the bezants which the Saracens had gulped down their loathsome throats while alive! For the same reason a few days later our men made a great heap of corpses and burned them to ashes in order to find more easily the above-mentioned gold.†

And also Tancred rushed into the Temple of the Lord and seized much gold and silver and many precious stones. But he restored these things, putting them or their equivalent back into the Holy Place. This was in spite of the fact that no divine services were conducted there at that time. The Saracens had practised their rule of idolatry there with superstitious rite and moreover had not allowed any Christian to enter.

* Black Nubians provided a significant element in the Egyptian army.
† The details are Fulcher's own.

With drawn swords our men ran through the city
Not sparing anyone, even those begging for mercy.
The crowd fell just as rotten apples fall
From shaken branches and acorns from swaying oaks.*

After this great slaughter they entered the houses of the citizens, seizing whatever they found in them. This was done in such a way that whoever first entered a house, whether he was rich or poor, was not challenged by any other Frank. He was to occupy and own the house or palace and whatever he found in it as if it were entirely his own. Thus they mutually agreed upon this right of possession. In this way many poor people became wealthy.

Then the clergy and laity, going to the Lord's Sepulchre and his most glorious Temple, singing a new canticle to the Lord in a resounding voice of exultation, and making offerings and most humble supplications, joyously visited the Holy Places as they had long desired to do.

O day so ardently desired! O time of times the most memorable! O deed before all other deeds! Desired indeed because in the inner longing of the heart it had always been hoped by all believers in the Catholic faith that the place in which the Creator of all creatures, God made man, in his manifold pity for mankind, had by his birth, death and resurrection, conferred the gift of redemption, would be restored to its pristine dignity by those believing and trusting in him. They desired that this place, so long contaminated by the superstition of the pagan inhabitants, should be cleansed from their contagion.

It was a time truly memorable and justly so because in this place everything that our Lord God Jesus Christ did or taught on earth, as man living amongst men, was recalled and renewed in the memory of true believers. And this same work which the Lord chose to accomplish through his people, his dearly beloved children and family, chosen, I believe, for this task, shall resound and continue memorable in the tongues of all nations until the end of time.

* From Ovid, *Metamorphoses*, vii. 585–6.

On 22 July the conquerors elected Godfrey of Bouillon as ruler of the captured city. More or less his first duty was to lead the western army against the expected Egyptian relief force under the vizier al-Adil which was destroyed outside the walls of Ascalon on 12 August, consolidating the newly won Christian hold over the Holy City. Following this triumph, most of the surviving crusaders, a tiny fraction of those who set off three years earlier, embarked for home, the light of their extraordinary achievements shining brightly on their helms, as it has shone for nine hundred years.

Raymond of Aguilers

With the passage of six or seven days the princes on the eighth day, according to their custom, solemnly turned to the election of a king to run the government, collect the taxes of the region, protect the countryside from further devastation, and to serve as a counsellor to the people. In the course of these discussions some of the clergy came together and gave their views to the princes. 'We applaud your move, but since spiritual matters precede temporal ones, righteous and proper procedure demands that you first elect a spiritual leader and after that elect a secular ruler; and if you do not we shall not recognise your choice.' This only angered the princes and hastened the election.*

I must add that the clergy was weakened at this time, first by the death of Lord Adhemar, bishop of Le Puy, who had restrained the army, consoling them with admirable acts and sermons, just as did Moses. Then William of Orange, a respected man and bishop dedicated to our protection, soon died in Ma'arrat al-Numan. Thus with the death of these good men only the bishop of al-Bara and a few others stood up to the princes. The bishop of Martirano,† who followed a crooked course when he fraudulently gained the church of Bethlehem, was captured in three or four days by the Saracens, and thereafter never made his appearance among us.

Disdainful of our advice and protest, the princes encouraged

* 17–18 July 1099.   † In Calabria.

Raymond of St Gilles to accept the kingship; but he confessed that he shuddered at the name of king in Jerusalem; however, he said that he would not stand in the way of its acceptance by another. So they elected Godfrey and gave him the Holy Sepulchre. Then Godfrey demanded the Tower of David from Raymond, and the count countered by saying that he planned to remain in the region until Easter, and during that time he wished himself and his men to be treated properly. The duke replied that he would abandon the Tower last of all, and so an impasse between the two developed. The counts of Flanders and Normandy favoured Godfrey as well as almost all of Raymond's entourage. Raymond's men thought that the count would return to Languedoc as soon as he lost the Tower of David. This was not the only opposition of the Provençals to Raymond, because earlier they spread malicious lies to block his election as king.

Abandoned by comrades and friends, Raymond surrendered the tower to the bishop of al-Bara for judgement, only to find that the bishop surrendered it to Godfrey without waiting for a decision. Upon being accused of breaking trust, the bishop charged that he had done so under duress and had been manhandled. I learned that many weapons were carried into the quarters of the bishop, namely the house of the patriarch which was located near the church of the Holy Sepulchre. The bishop talked about the use of physical force against him and secretly blamed Raymond's men.

Following the loss of the tower, the count, in a huff at his followers, flared out, saying that he had been dishonoured and would leave the country. So we travelled from Jerusalem to Jericho, gathered palms, and came to the Jordan. Following the instructions of Peter Bartholomew, we made a raft of small branches, placed Raymond on it, and paddled across the river. We then ordered the assembled crowd to pray for the lives of the count and the other princes. With Count Raymond clad only in shirt and new breeches, we carried out the order concerning baptism, but why God's man, Peter Bartholomew, issued such an order we have not the slightest idea until the present time.

Upon our return to Jerusalem after this task, Arnulf, chaplain of the count of Normandy, was elected by some as patriarch contrary to the wishes of the good clergymen, who objected on the grounds that he was not a subdeacon and was of priestly origin.* To cap it all he was accused of being a philanderer on the journey, even to the point that he was the object of smutty stories. Needless to say, the ambitious Arnulf ignored canonical decrees, his disgraceful birth and lack of conscience, berated the good clergy, and had himself elevated to the patriarchal seat to the accompaniment of hymns, chants and great applause of the people. Arnulf was not frightened by the divine punishment of the bishop of Martirano, the inciter and director of Arnulf's elevation, for he continued to take benefices from clergymen who had altars in the Lord's Sepulchre or from those who received fees for its care.

Once in power Arnulf sought to locate, with the help of the inhabitants, the Cross worshipped by pilgrims before the Turkish capture of Jerusalem. They knew nothing of its location, going so far as to prove their words by oath and other signs, but they were finally forced to say, 'Revelation shows that you are God's chosen people, that you have been freed from trials and given Jerusalem and many other cities not by your great strength but by a wrathful God who blinded the blasphemers. The Lord, your leader, threw open the gates of impregnable cities and won terrifying battles for you. Since God is on your side why should we obstinately hide his relics from you?' Then after leading the crusaders to a hall in the church, they uncovered and surrendered the Cross.† So we were glad and praised and thanked Almighty God who not only restored to us the city of his Passion but the symbols of his crucifixion and victory so that we might clasp him more closely in the arms of faith, surer because we now saw the relics of our salvation.

* Arnulf of Chocques's election 1 August 1099, perhaps deliberately exactly one year after the death of Adhemar of Le Puy.
† 5 August 1099; a very convenient find, especially in the light of the previous controversies over relics.

At this time, as we have previously reported, Godfrey held Jerusalem by agreement, and Raymond was exasperated by grief and injustice over the loss of the Tower of David, undoubtedly the key to the kingdom of Judaea. As a result he made plans to return with a great part of his Provençals. However, news came that the king of Babylon [al-Afdal, vizier of Egypt] had arrived in Ascalon with a large force of pagans with the purpose of storming Jerusalem, killing all of the Franks twenty years of age and above, and capturing the rest along with their women. He would, so rumour held, mate the young Frankish males with women of his race and the Frankish women with young males of his land and thereby breed a warrior race from Frankish stock.

His grandiose schemes led him to boast he would give the same treatment to Antioch and Bohemund; further, that he would wear the crown of Damascus and the remaining cities. Moreover, upon due consideration of his mighty hosts of soldiers and knights, he held the Turks were nothing and the Franks, conquerors of the Turks, were nothing. Still unsatisfied, he blasphemed God by saying that he would destroy the Lord's birthplace, the manger where the Lord had lain, the place of the Passion and Golgotha, purportedly the spot where blood gushed from the crucified Lord, the Lord's burial grave, and all other sacred spots in Jerusalem and its environs. He further boasted that he would unearth these relics, break them into small pieces, and scatter their dust over the sea so that the Franks would no longer search beyond their lands for relics of the Lord now lost in the oblivion of the sea.

Our princes and clergy assembled upon news of this and other rumours concerning the vast hordes of this tyrant gathered at Ascalon, a city removed from us by a journey of a day and one-half. The assembled crusaders marched barefoot before the Holy Sepulchre and tearfully begged mercy from the Lord, asking him to free his people whom he had made conquerors in the past. They also besought him not to permit the further profanation of the place of his sanctification, which had just been purified for his name's sake. Then we came to the Temple of the Lord [the

Dome of the Rock] barefoot, imploring his mercy with songs, hymns and saintly treasures, and there in soul and body poured forth our prayers before God. We urged that he remember the pouring forth of his blessing in the same place: 'If your people have sinned against you and changing have done penance and coming have prayed in this place, listen to them from heaven, O Lord, and free them from the hands of their enemies.'

Following the blessing of the bishop, the leaders drew up the battle plans and means of protection of Jerusalem. Then Godfrey and his knights departed to verify the rumours regarding the amir, and upon arriving at the plains of Ramleh despatched the bishop of Martirano to report to the counts in Jerusalem on the state of affairs. Now certain of a battle, the leaders issued a call to the able-bodied, prayed to God, marched out of Jerusalem in full armour carrying the Holy Lance, and on the same day came to the plains. On the following day our united armies moved forward in squadrons with guards drawn up on all sides.*

At sundown we approached a river which is on the road from Jerusalem to Ascalon, and we saw Arabs pasturing flocks of sheep and large herds of cattle and camels. So we sent two hundred knights to reconnoitre, because the large number of Arabs and livestock made us believe that a fight would ensue. In the mean time, as we have written, we marched in nine ranks, three to the rear, three to the front and three in the middle so that attack would be met in three ranks with the middle one always available to bolster the others. The Arab herdsmen fled at the sight of our knights, but had God favoured them as he did us they, no doubt, would have defended their animals. Actually they numbered three thousand while our army possibly had twelve hundred knights and no more than nine thousand footmen. Following their flight we seized unbelievable amounts of booty, and killed and captured a few Arabs. Since it was late in the day we pitched camp, and then we compelled the captives to

---

* Godfrey left to scout 9 August; the main body moved towards Ascalon on 11 August; the battle was fought on 12 August 1099; Raymond later carried the lance on the crusade of 1101.

reveal their plans, state of preparations and their numbers. The captives stated that the Arabs wished to invest Jerusalem and drive out, take captive or kill the Franks. They added that the amir, who camped five leagues away, would march against us the next day. The herders ventured no absolute estimate of the size of their army since it increased daily. Regarding their role, they said that they were herders who planned to sell their animals to the Babylonian army.

The crusaders, ready for the ensuing conflict, forgave one another sins of commission and omission, and became so stirred that they hardly credited reports of the preparedness of the enemy. In their assurance they believed the Arabs to be more timid than deer and more innocuous than sheep. This assurance was born from our belief that God was with us as in other trials and that on account of the pagans' blasphemy he would on his own initiative punish them even if our cause was weak. Thus we preferred to think of God as defender and ourselves as his helpers.

Orders then were given throughout the army that all be prepared for battle at dawn, that each one join the forces of his leader, and that no one should touch booty until after the battle, under pain of excommunication. We spent a wretched night with no tents, little bread, no wine, very little grain and salt; but at least the meat supply was plentiful as sand, and so we ate meat and used mutton for bread.

At the crack of dawn the alert army was called to battle ranks by the blare of trumpets and horns. Thus we set out at daybreak with guards arranged on all sides as previously reported and moved towards the camp of Muhammad. The Arabs remained in their camp in the belief that at news of their coming we would remain close to our walls. Reports had come to them of the slaughter and flight of the herders and brought this response: 'The Franks came for booty and will now return.' Actually they had daily reports on the desertions in Jerusalem, the small size of our army, and the enfeebled state of our people and horses. Confident in their size and strength, they were sure that they could drown us and our camp in their spit. Their stargazers and sooth-sayers, so we heard, advised against moving camp or fighting until the seventh day of the week, with the warning that an earlier date would be disadvantageous.

We moved forward in nine ranks, as stated above, and God multiplied his army to the point that we seemed to equal the Arab forces. This miracle came when the animals we had freed formed herds, and without a directing hand followed us, stood when we stood, ran when we ran, and marched forward when we marched forward. We could neither estimate the amount of costly goods nor compute the sum total of arms and tents seized. The Arabs, upon seeing the slaughter of many of their comrades, the eager and secure ransacking of their camp, gave up the fight and decided, 'Since we must flee, why delay? If today, these Christians, exhausted from the march and almost dead tired from hunger and thirst, smashed our forces with one attack, what could they do refreshed, restored and victorious against us half-alive, weakened and terrified?'

Consequently, with morale broken the Arabs with a few exceptions returned to Ascalon, which lay about a mile from our camp. Raymond decided to send Bohemund, a Turk, to the amir with a plan for peace but reminded him that he had been reluctant to free Jerusalem and had fought us. Bohemund, at the same time, was to size up the situation, and to see whether the amir planned to flee or to fight, and how he reacted to his defeat. Bohemund, although a Turk, was multilingual, clever and shrewd as well as loyal to us. He was called Bohemund because the great Bohemund received him at the baptismal font when he turned apostate and came to us with his wife and arms.

The Gesta Francorum

On the eighth day after the city was taken* they chose Duke Godfrey as its ruler, so that he might fight against the pagans and protect the Christians. Likewise a most experienced and distin-

---

* 22 July 1099.

guished man called Arnulf was chosen as patriarch, on the feast of St Peter's Chains.* (This city was captured by God's Christians on 15 July, which was a Friday.)

While all this was happening, a messenger came to Tancred and Count Eustace, asking them to make ready and go to receive the surrender of the town of Nablus; so they set out, taking with them many knights and foot-soldiers, and came to the city, the inhabitants of which surrendered at once. Then Duke Godfrey summoned them to come quickly, for the amir of Cairo was getting ready to fight with us at Ascalon, so they went quickly into the mountains, looking for Saracens to fight, and came to Caesarea, from whence they came along the coast towards Ramleh, where they found many Arabs who had been sent as scouts before the main army. Our men chased them and captured several, who gave us a full report as to where their army was, and its numbers, and where it was planning to fight with the Christians. When Tancred heard this, he sent a messenger straight off to Jerusalem to Duke Godfrey and the patriarch and all the other leaders, saying, 'There is going to be a battle at Ascalon, so come quickly with all the forces you can muster!' Then the duke had everyone summoned so that they might go faithfully prepared to fight our enemies at Ascalon. He himself, with the patriarch, Robert count of Flanders and the bishop of Martirano,† went with them on Tuesday,‡ but the count of St Gilles and Robert the Norman said that they would not go unless they knew for certain that there would be a battle, so they ordered their knights to go out and see whether the battle was really going to take place, and to come back as soon as possible, for they themselves were all ready to set out. The knights went out, saw the preparations for the battle and came straight back to report what they had seen with their own eyes. The duke at once summoned the bishop of Martirano and bade him go to Jerusalem to tell the knights there to get ready to come to the field of battle.

* 1 August 1099.   † Arnulf, bishop of Martirano in southern Italy.
‡ 9 August 1099.

On Wednesday those lords went out and rode to battle. The bishop of Martirano was returning from Jerusalem, bearing messages to the duke and the patriarch, when the Saracens met him, and they captured him and took him away with them. Peter the Hermit stayed in Jerusalem to admonish and encourage all the Greek and Latin priests and the clerks to go in procession devoutly to the honour of God, and to pray and give alms, so that God might grant his people victory. The clerks and priests put on their holy vestments and led the procession to the Temple of our Lord,* where they sang masses and orisons, praying that God would defend his people.

Meanwhile the patriarch and the bishops and the other leaders were assembled at the river which lies on this side of Ascalon. They carried off from thence many animals, oxen, camels and sheep, and other goods. About three hundred Arabs came up, and our men attacked them and captured two, driving the rest back to their own army. When evening came, the patriarch had it announced throughout all the host that every man should be ready for battle at dawn, and that anyone who turned aside for plunder before the battle was finished should be excommunicated, but that thereafter they might return with great joy to take whatever the Lord should grant.

At daybreak on Friday† our men entered a beautiful valley near the coast and drew up their lines of battle. The duke, the count of Normandy, the count of St Gilles, the count of Flanders, Count Eustace, Tancred and Gaston each drew up his own men, and foot-soldiers with archers were ordered to precede the knights. All this was thus arranged, and they joined battle at once in the name of Our Lord Jesus Christ. Duke Godfrey with his men fought on the left wing, the count of St Gilles on the right (near the sea), while the counts of Normandy and Flanders, with Tancred and all the rest, rode in the centre, and thus our men began gradually to advance. The pagans, for their part, stood ready for battle. Each of them had, hanging round his neck, a

---

* Probably the Holy Sepulchre, although the Franks usually called the Dome of the Rock the Temple of the Lord.　† 12 August 1099.

bottle from which he could drink while he was pursuing us, but by God's grace this was not to be.

The count of Normandy, seeing that the amir's standard had a golden apple on the top of the pole, which was covered with silver, rushed straight at its bearer and gave him a mortal wound. The count of Flanders made a determined attack from the other side, and Tancred charged straight into the middle of the enemy camp. When the pagans saw this, they began to flee at once. (There was an innumerable multitude of pagans, and nobody knows how many there were save God alone.) The battle was terrible, but the power of God was with us, so mighty and so strong that we gained the victory at once. The enemies of God stood about blinded and bewildered; although their eyes were open they could not see the knights of Christ and they dared not stand fast against them, for they were terror-stricken by the power of God. Some in their panic climbed up trees, hoping to hide, but our men killed them with arrows and spears and swords, and cast them down to the ground. Others threw themselves flat on the ground, not daring to stand up against us, so our men slaughtered them as one slaughters beasts in a shambles. The count of St Gilles, who was near the sea, killed any number of them. Some jumped into the sea and others fled hither and thither.

So the amir reached the city [Ascalon], grieving and lamenting, and saying as he wept, 'O spirits of the gods! Who has ever seen or heard of such things as these? Such power, such courage, such an army as has never been overcome by anyone, to be defeated by such a wretched little force of Christians! Woe's me, sad and miserable man that I am! What more can I say? I have been beaten by a force of beggars, unarmed and poverty-stricken, who have nothing but a bag and a scrip. And this is the army which is now pursuing the Egyptians, who often used to give alms to these people when they went round our country begging. I led two hundred thousand soldiers hither to battle, and now I see them all fleeing with slack reins down the road to Cairo, and they have not the courage to rally against the Franks.

I swear by Muhammad and by the glory of all the gods that I will never raise another army, because I have been defeated by a strange people. I brought all sorts of weapons and engines to besiege these men in Jerusalem, and it is they who have attacked me two days' march outside the city. Woe's me! What more can I say? I shall be held up to everlasting scorn in the land of Cairo.'

Our men captured the amir's standard, which the count of Normandy redeemed for twenty marks of silver and gave to the patriarch in honour of God and the Holy Sepulchre. The amir's sword was bought for 60 bezants. So by God's will our enemies were defeated. All the ships from the lands of the pagans were there, but when the crews saw the amir fleeing with his army they hoisted sail at once and made for the open sea. Our men went back to the enemy camp and found innumerable spoils of gold and silver, piles of riches, and all kinds of animals, weapons and tools. They took what they wanted and burned the rest.

Then our men came back to Jerusalem rejoicing, bearing with them all sorts of provisions which they needed. This battle was fought on 12 August, by the mercy of our Lord Jesus Christ, to whom be honour and glory, now and for ever, world without end. May every soul say 'Amen'!

Fulcher of Chartres

All the people of the Lord's army in the Holy City chose Godfrey prince of the realm* because of the nobility of his character, military skill, patient conduct, no less than for his elegance of manners, to protect and govern it.

Then, too, they placed canons in the church of the Lord's Sepulchre and in his Temple to serve him. Moreover they decided at that time that a patriarch should not be created as yet

---

* A slightly ambiguous phrase (*regni principem*) that matched a disagreement over authority between Godfrey and the Church led by Daimbert of Pisa as patriarch of Jerusalem in 1100.

until they had enquired from the Roman pope whom he wished to place in authority.*

Meanwhile some Turks and Arabs and about five hundred black Ethiopians who had taken refuge in the Tower of David begged of Count Raymond, who was quartered near that citadel, that on condition they leave their money there, they be allowed to depart with their lives. He conceded this, and they withdrew to Ascalon.

At that time it pleased God that a small piece of the Lord's Cross should be found in a secret place. It had been hidden in ancient times by holy men. And now by the will of God it was discovered by a certain Syrian who with the knowledge of his father had carefully concealed and preserved it. This piece, fashioned in the form of a cross, partly covered by gold and silver work, they all carried aloft to the Lord's Sepulchre and thence to the Temple, singing triumphantly and giving thanks to God, who through all this time had preserved for himself and us this, his treasure and ours.

Moreover the king of Babylon and the commander of his forces, Lavedalius [al-Afdal] by name, when they heard that the Franks had already entered their territories for the purpose of subjecting the Babylonian kingdom to themselves, gathered by edict a multitude of Turks, Arabs and Ethiopians and hastened to go to fight against them. And when they had heard through another set of messengers that Jerusalem had been captured with such fury the aforesaid commander waxed wroth and hurried to do battle with the invaders or besiege them confined within the city.

When the Franks learned this they adopted a plan of great boldness. They marched their forces towards Ascalon against those tyrants, taking with them the wood of the life-bearing Cross mentioned above.†

* Characteristically, Fulcher ignores the bitter dispute following the election of Arnulf of Chocques as patriarch and his subsequent deposition in favour of Archbishop Daimbert of Pisa.
† Raymond of Aguilers talks instead of the Holy Lance: see above, p. 338.

One day* when the Franks were scouring around Ascalon and awaiting battle they discovered considerable booty in oxen, camels, sheep and goats. When our men had gathered these beasts near their tents at the end of the day, our leaders decreed by strict proclamation that the men should not drive their quarry with them on the morrow, when battle was expected, so that they should be unencumbered and the more free to fight.

The next morning the Franks learned from the scouts that had been sent out that the pagans were advancing. When this was known the tribunes and centurions at once formed their men into wings and phalanxes, arranged them in the best way for battle and proceeded boldly against the enemy with banners aloft.

You might have seen the animals mentioned above advancing of their own will to the right and left of our formation as if by command; yet they were driven by no one. In this way many of the pagans, at a distance seeing the animals proceeding with our soldiers, concluded that the whole array was the army of the Franks.

However, the pagans, an innumerable multitude, approached our formations like a stag thrusting forward the branches of his horns. They divided their advance formation, uncovering a flying wing of Arabs and managing to encircle our rear. As a result Duke Godfrey went back with a heavy body of mailed knights and rescued the rear line. The other princes advanced, some in the first line, others in the second.

When foe had approached foe at a distance of a stone's throw or less, our footmen began to shoot arrows into their opponents, whose lines were extended. Soon the lance took the place of the arrow as our knights, as if mutually agreed under oath, made a violent onslaught. In the slaughter the slower of the horses of the enemy were thrown over on their riders. In the short space of an hour many bodies became pale and lifeless.

Many of the enemy in their flight climbed to the tops of trees. Yet here they were shot with arrows and, mortally wounded, fell

* 11 August 1099.

miserably to earth. In the sweeping attack the Saracens perished on all sides. Those who escaped fled through their camp to the walls of Ascalon. This city is 720 stades from Jerusalem.

Lavedalius, their leader, who had hitherto despised the Franks, now in the very first encounter turned his back in precipitate flight. He thus involuntarily abandoned his tent, which was pitched among the rest and was stored with much money. Thither the Franks returned, joyous in victory, and, reunited, gave thanks to God.

Then they entered the tents of the enemy and found vast princely wealth: gold, silver, long cloaks, other clothing, and precious stones. These latter were of twelve kinds, jasper, sapphire, chalcedony, emerald, sardonyx, sardius, chrysolite, beryl, topaz, chrysoprasus, jacinth and amethyst.* They also found many vessels and many kinds of things such as helmets decorated with gold, the finest rings, wonderful swords, grain, flour and much else.

Our men spent the night there and, by being very watchful, guarded themselves well. For they thought that on the following day the fighting would be renewed by the Saracens, but these latter, exceedingly terrified, all fled that same night. When in the morning this fact was ascertained by scouts, the Franks, in voices overflowing with praise, blessed and glorified God, who had permitted so many thousands of infidels to be scattered by a tiny army of Christians. 'Blessed therefore be God who hath not given us as a prey to their teeth!' 'Blessed is the nation whose God is the Lord!'†

Had not these very Babylonians threatened, saying, 'Let us go and capture Jerusalem with the Franks enclosed therein. After slaying them all let us tear down that Sepulchre so dear to them, and cast the stones of the building out of the city, and let no further mention of the Sepulchre ever be made again!' But with God's mercy this was brought to naught. Instead the Franks loaded the very horses and camels with the money of the Saracens. Not being able to carry to the Holy City the tents and all the

* Revelation 21:19–20.   † Psalms 124:6, 33:12.

spears, bows and arrows thrown on the ground, they committed them all to the flames and then returned rejoicing to Jerusalem.

After these things were accomplished, some of the people wished to return to their native lands. As soon as they had bathed in the waters of the Jordan and had collected palm branches near Jericho, in what was said to be the Garden of Abraham,* Robert, count of the Normans, and Robert, count of Flanders, set out by ship for Constantinople and from there returned to France to their possessions. Raymond, however, returned to Latakiah in Syria, left his wife† there, and went on to Constantinople, expecting to return.‡ Duke Godfrey, keeping Tancred and several others with him, ruled the government at Jerusalem which, with the consent of all, he had undertaken to maintain.

---

* Palm-leaves from Jericho, the northernmost tropical oasis, were brought home by pilgrims as evidence of the completion of their pilgrimage; hence the nickname 'palmers'.   † Elvira of León and Castile.

‡ Again Fulcher sidesteps an ugly confrontation between the leaders at Latakiah in August 1099.

X

Rejoicing and Lamentation

September 1099–1105

In the west, news of the victory at Jerusalem provoked explosive delight, although the crusade's preacher, Urban II, died on 29 July 1099, a fortnight after the Holy City fell, unaware of the crowning if bloody success of his vision. Providence appeared to have vindicated western ambition and the Christian faith. News spread; those who had failed to honour their vows were shamed or bullied into joining up for new expeditions. In Syria, the associates of Baldwin of Boulogne and Bohemund were now able to make their pilgrimage, not without danger but assured of a welcome at the end of it. The memory of these remarkable events lingered, not least in popular media such as songs. A new legend had been created.

Godfrey of Bouillon, Raymond of St Gilles and Daimbert to Pope Paschal II, Laodicea, September 1099

To lord Paschal, pope of the Roman Church, to all the bishops, and to the whole Christian people, from the archbishop of Pisa, Duke Godfrey, now, by the grace of God, defender of the church of the Holy Sepulchre, Raymond, count of St Gilles, and the whole army of God, which is in the land of Israel, greeting.

Multiply your supplications and prayers in the sight of God with joy and thanksgiving, since God has manifested his mercy in fulfilling by our hands what he had promised in ancient times. For after the capture of Nicaea, the whole army, made up of more than three hundred thousand soldiers, departed thence. And, although this army was so great that it could have in a single day covered all Romania and drunk up all the rivers and eaten up all the growing things, yet the Lord conducted them amid so great abundance that a ram was sold for a penny and an ox for twelve pennies or less. Moreover, although the princes and kings of the Saracens rose up against us, yet, by God's will, they were easily conquered and overcome. Because, indeed, some were puffed up by these successes, God opposed to us Antioch, impregnable to human strength. And there he detained us for nine months and so humbled us in the siege that there were scarcely a hundred good horses in our whole army. God opened to us the abundance of his blessing and mercy and led us into the city, and delivered the Turks and all of their possessions into our power.

Inasmuch as we thought that these had been acquired by our own strength and did not worthily magnify God who had done this, we were beset by so great a multitude of Turks that no one dared to venture forth at any point from the city. Moreover, hunger so weakened us that some could scarcely refrain from eating human flesh. It would be tedious to narrate all the miseries which we suffered in that city. But God looked down upon his people whom he had so long chastised and mercifully consoled them. Therefore, he at first revealed to us, as a recompense for our tribulation and as a pledge of victory, his lance which had lain hidden since the days of the apostles. Next, he so fortified the hearts of the men, that they who from sickness or hunger had been unable to walk now were imbued with strength to seize their weapons and manfully to fight against the enemy.

After we had triumphed over the enemy, as our army was wasting away at Antioch from sickness and weariness and was especially hindered by the dissensions among the leaders, we proceeded into Syria, stormed Barra [al-Bara] and Marra [Ma'arrat al-Numan], cities of the Saracens, and captured the fortresses in that country. And while we were delaying there, there was so great a famine in the army that the Christian people now ate the putrid bodies of the Saracens. Finally, by the divine admonition, we entered into the interior of Hispania [Ruj], and the most bountiful, merciful and victorious hand of the omnipotent Father was with us. For the cities and fortresses of the country through which we were proceeding sent ambassadors to us with many gifts and offered to aid us and to surrender their walled places. But because our army was not large and it was the unanimous wish to hasten to Jerusalem, we accepted their pledges and made them tributaries. One of the cities forsooth, which was on the sea coast, had more men than there were in our whole army. And when those at Antioch and Laodicea and Archas [Arqah] heard how the hand of the Lord was with us, many from the army who had remained in those cities followed us to Tyre. Therefore, with the Lord's companionship and aid, we proceeded thus as far as Jerusalem.

And after the army had suffered greatly in the siege, especially on account of the lack of water, a council was held and the bishops and princes ordered that all with bare feet should march around the walls of the city, in order that he who entered it humbly in our behalf might be moved by our humility to open it to us and to exercise judgement upon his enemies. God was appeased by this humility and on the eighth day after the humiliation he delivered the city and his enemies to us. It was the day indeed on which the primitive Church was driven thence, and on which the festival of the dispersion of the apostles is celebrated. And if you desire to know what was done with the enemy who were found there, know that in Solomon's Porch* and in his Temple our men rode in the blood of the Saracens up to the knees of their horses.

Then, when we were considering who ought to hold the city, and some moved by love for their country and kinsmen wished to return home, it was announced to us that the king of Babylon had come to Ascalon with an innumerable multitude of soldiers. His purpose was, as he said, to lead the Franks, who were in Jerusalem, into captivity, and to take Antioch by storm. But God had determined otherwise in regard to us.

Therefore, when we learned that the army of the Babylonians was at Ascalon, we went down to meet them, leaving our baggage and the sick in Jerusalem with a garrison. When our army was in sight of the enemy, upon our knees we invoked the aid of the

* On the Temple Mount, outside the al-Aqsa mosque.

Lord, that he who in our other adversities had strengthened the Christian faith might in the present battle break the strength of the Saracens and of the devil and extend the kingdom of the Church of Christ from sea to sea, over the whole world. There was no delay; God was present when we cried for his aid, and furnished us with so great boldness, that one who saw us rush upon the enemy would have taken us for a herd of deer hastening to quench their thirst in running water. It was wonderful, indeed, since there were in our army not more than five thousand horsemen and fifteen thousand foot-soldiers, and there were probably in the enemy's army one hundred thousand horsemen and four hundred thousand foot-soldiers.* Then God appeared wonderful to his servants. For before we engaged in fighting, by our very onset alone, he turned this multitude in flight and scattered all their weapons, so that if they wished afterwards to attack us, they did not have the weapons in which they trusted. There can be no question how great the spoils were, since the treasures of the king of Babylon were captured. More than one hundred thousand Moors perished there by the sword. Moreover, their panic was so great that about two thousand were suffocated at the gate of the city. Those who perished in the sea were innumerable. Many were entangled in the thickets. The whole world was certainly fighting for us, and if many of ours had not been detained in plundering the camp, few of the great multitude of the enemy would have been able to escape from the battle.

And although it may be tedious, the following must not be omitted: on the day preceding the battle the army captured many thousands of camels, oxen and sheep. By the command of the princes these were divided among the people. When we advanced to battle, wonderful to relate, the camels formed in many squadrons and the sheep and oxen did the same. Moreover, these animals accompanied us, halting when we halted, advancing when we advanced, and charging when we charged. The clouds [of dust] protected us from the heat of the sun and cooled us.

Accordingly, after celebrating the victory, the army returned to

* An obvious exaggeration.

Jerusalem. Duke Godfrey remained there; the count of St Gilles, Robert, count of Normandy, and Robert, count of Flanders, returned to Laodicea. There they found the fleet belonging to the Pisans and to Bohemund. After the archbishop of Pisa had established peace between Bohemund and our leaders, Raymond prepared to return to Jerusalem for the sake of God and his brethren.

Therefore, we call upon you of the Catholic Church of Christ and of the whole Latin Church to exult in the so admirable bravery and devotion of your brethren, in the so glorious and very desirable retribution of the Omnipotent God, and in the so devoutedly hoped-for remission of all our sins through the grace of God. And we pray that he may make you – namely, all bishops, clerks and monks who are leading devout lives, and all the laity – to sit down at the right hand of God, who liveth and reigneth God for ever and ever. And we ask and beseech you in the name of our Lord Jesus, who has ever been with us and aided us and freed us from all our tribulations, to be mindful of your brethren who return to you, by doing them kindnesses and by paying their debts, in order that God may recompense you and absolve you from all your sins and grant you a share in all the blessings which either we or they have deserved in the sight of the Lord. Amen.

Manasses II, Archbishop of Rheims, to Lambert, Bishop of Arras, 1099*

Manasses, by grace of God archbishop of Rheims, to Lambert, his brother, bishop of Arras; greeting in Jesus Christ.

Be it known to you, dearest brother, that a true and joyful rumour has recently come to our ears, which we believe to have come down not from human knowledge, but from the divine majesty – to wit: Jerusalem stands on high with joy and gladness which it has so gloriously received from God in our times. Jerusalem, the city of our redemption and glory, delights with

* Lambert had attended the Council of Clermont and had preserved a copy of the crusade decree: see above, p. 23.

inconceivable joy, because through the effort and incomparable might of the sons of God it has been liberated from most cruel pagan servitude. And let us also be joyful, whose Christian faith in such times as these has been placed in a mirror of eternal clarity.

We, therefore admonished, summoned and compelled, not only through the letters of the lord Pope Paschal, but, also, through the most humble prayers of Duke Godfrey, whom the army of Christ by divine direction elevated as king, as well as through the mellifluous entreaties of Lord Arnulf, whom they have unanimously chosen as patriarch of the see of Jerusalem* – we command with equal affection that you have every one of your parish churches, without fail, pray with fasts and almsgiving that the King of Kings and the Lord of Lords crown the king of the Christians with victory against the enemy, and the patriarch with religion and wisdom against the sects and deceptions of heretics. We command, likewise, and admonish, through your obedience, that you constrain by threat all who vowed to go on the expedition and took the sign of the Cross upon themselves to set out for Jerusalem, if they are vigorous of body and have the means to accomplish the journey. As for the others, however, do not cease skilfully and most devoutly to admonish them not to neglect aiding the people of God, so that not only the first, but likewise the last, may receive the shilling which is promised to those labouring in the vineyard. Farewell.

Pray for the bishop of Le Puy, for the bishop of Orange, for Anselm of Ribemont, and for all the others who lie at rest, crowned with so glorious a martyrdom.

Fulcher of Chartres, who remained with Baldwin at Edessa, notes his master's fulfilment of his vow.

Lord Bohemund, a man wise and strong, was at that time ruling in Antioch while Lord Baldwin, a brother of the aforesaid Godfrey, ruled Edessa and the neighbouring country on the other

* Arnulf of Chocques, 1 August 1099.

side of the River Euphrates.* When they heard that Jerusalem had been taken by their colleagues who had preceded them, they rejoiced and returned praise and prayers to God.

But if those who were first in speed of journey to Jerusalem had done well and advantageously, still it was not to be doubted that these latter two with their companions would be as brave although following later.

For it was necessary that the land and the cities taken from the Turks with such difficulty should be carefully guarded. These if rashly left unprotected might be conquered in a sudden attack by the Turks, now driven back as far as Persia. In this case great harm would befall all the Franks, both going to Jerusalem and returning. Perhaps it was divine providence which delayed Bohemund and Baldwin, judging that they would be more useful in what remained to be done than in what had been done.

Oh, how many times, meanwhile, was this same Baldwin wearied in the battles against the Turks in the lands of Mesopotamia! How many Turkish heads were cut off there it would be impossible to say. Often it happened that Baldwin with his few men fought a great multitude of the enemy and with the help of God rejoiced in triumph.†

Now when Bohemund through messengers suggested to Baldwin that they both with their men should finish the journey to Jerusalem, which they had not yet completed, Baldwin in good time arranged his affairs and prepared to go.

But then when Baldwin heard that the Turks had invaded one section of his country he delayed starting on the trip. Since he had not yet gathered his little army for this journey to Jerusalem, he went against the Turks with only a few men. One day the Turks, thinking that Baldwin had already begun his journey, were feeling secure in their tents when they saw the white banner which Baldwin carried. They were terrified and fled as quickly as possible. After he had pursued them a little way with his few men

* Fulcher is once again an eyewitness of Baldwin of Edessa's movements.
† Fulcher eggs the pudding of praise for Baldwin as a Christian warrior to conceal his absence from the capture of Antioch and Jerusalem.

he returned to the project which he had previously undertaken.*

Beginning the journey and passing Antioch to the right, he came to Latakiah where he bought provisions for the journey and reloaded the pack animals. Then we set out. It was in the month of November. After we had passed by Jabala we came up to Bohemund encamped in his tents before a certain town called Banyas.

With him was a certain Pisan archbishop named Daimbert, who had come by sea to the port of Latakiah with some Tuscans and Italians and there had waited to go with us. A certain bishop from Apulia was there too. A third was with Lord Baldwin.† Of those thus assembled in friendship we estimated the number to be twenty-five thousand of both sexes, mounted and on foot.

When we entered the interior lands of the Saracens, we were unable to obtain from the hostile inhabitants bread or anything else to eat. No one would give or sell, and as more and more of our provisions were being consumed it happened that many suffered grievously from hunger. The horses and beasts of burden suffered doubly from lack of food. They walked but had nothing to eat.

But in those cultivated fields through which we passed during our march there were certain ripe plants which the common folk called 'honey-cane' and which were very much like reeds.‡ The name is compounded from 'cane' and 'honey', whence the expression 'wood honey' I think, because the latter is skilfully made from these canes. In our hunger we chewed them all day because of the taste of honey. However, this helped but little.

Verily for the love of God we endured these and many other hardships such as hunger, cold and heavy rains. Many men, starving, ate horses, asses and camels. Moreover we were very often tormented by excessive cold and frequent rainstorms, for the heat of the sun was not sufficient to enable us to have our sodden clothes dried when another rain would harass us for four or five days.

* Probably in November 1099.
† The bishop from Apulia may have been from Ariano; with Baldwin may have been Benedict of Edessa.   ‡ Sugar cane.

I saw many people who had no tents die from chills from the rains. I, Fulcher of Chartres, who was with them, saw many persons of both sexes and a great many beasts die one day because of these freezing rains. It would be too long to tell and too tedious to hear since no anxiety, no misery missed the people of God.

Often many Franks were killed by Saracens lurking around the narrow paths along the way or were captured when they went in search of food. You might have seen knights of noble birth who had become foot-soldiers, having lost their horses in one way or another. You might have seen also, because of the lack of beasts of burden, goats and wethers taken from the Saracens greatly fatigued by the baggage loaded upon them and with their backs made sore by the chafing of their packs.

Twice on the way, and no oftener, we had bread and grain, purchased at a very high price, to wit, at Tripoli and at Caesarea.* From this it is evident that one cannot acquire anything great without corresponding effort. It was indeed a momentous event when we arrived at Jerusalem.

With this visit to Jerusalem our protracted task was finished. When we gazed upon the much-longed-for Holy of Holies we were filled with immense joy. Oh, how often we recalled to mind the prophecy of David which said, 'We shall worship in the place where his feet have stood.'† Truly we saw that prophecy fulfilled in us at that moment, however much it likewise pertained to others. 'Thither' indeed we went up, 'the tribes, the tribes of the Lord to confess his name'‡ in his Holy Place.

On the day of our entrance into Jerusalem the receding sun, having completed its winter descent, resumed its ascending course.§

When we had visited the Lord's Sepulchre and his most glorious Temple and the other Holy Places, we went on the fourth day to Bethlehem to celebrate the Nativity of the Lord. We wanted to assist personally that night in the prayers at the manger where the revered mother Mary gave birth to Jesus.

* Still in Muslim hands.   † Psalms 132:7.
‡ Psalms 122:4.   § 21 December 1099.

After we had finished the appropriate devotions that night and had celebrated the third mass, we returned to Jerusalem in the third hour of the day.*

Oh, what a stench there was around the walls of the city, both within and without, from the rotting bodies of the Saracens slain by our comrades at the time of the capture of the city, lying wherever they had been hunted down!

After we and our beasts had been refreshed for a while with a much-needed rest, and after the duke and the other chief men had chosen the above-mentioned Lord Daimbert to be patriarch in the church of the Holy Sepulchre,† we replenished supplies, loaded our beasts and went down to the River Jordan.

Some of the army, the last to arrive, chose to remain in Jerusalem; others that had come first preferred to go with us. Duke Godfrey continued to rule the territory of Jerusalem with a firm hand as before.

One of many songs composed in celebration of the events of 1099 is the following, commonly referred to by the title 'Nomen a Solemnibus'.

This feast is named from solemn rites   it takes the name
    Solemnicum
Therefore we all will solemnise   all except a certain monk,
Serracus, who has maimed himself   by cutting off his private
    parts;
Because he has we will accept him   just as if he were a
    demon;
Let him mourn, and mourn alone   and stand accused before
    Aeacus!‡

    Let us exalt, and let us sing a canticle of victory,
    And let us sing, as sing we must, the praises due to
        glory's king,

* 9 a.m., 25 December 1099.
† The dispute with Arnulf, already elected 1 August, is concealed.
‡ In Greek mythology, one of the three judges of the Underworld.

Who today has saved the city   David's city* from the
   pagans!

   Refrain
   The festival begins,
   We cherish now the day
   When Dagon lies in pieces smashed
   And Amalek defeated, quashed†
   The sons of Hagar driven back
   Jerusalem is snatched away
   Restored again to Christian ways,
   And so we celebrate the day!

This city, the most beautiful,   noblest of all, had first a King
In this city vast and great   that King was pleasing to the
   Lord
Here on account of humankind   that King wished to be
   crucified
Here to this city came the Spirit   who resounded to apostles.

   City wond'rous, fire descending, fire descending once a
      year,
   This it shows us, generations, how God loves it through
      the ages,
   Be it honoured, be it filled up, be it filled with kings and
      peoples!

   Refrain

This city is from heaven blessed   set in the heavens, how it
   loves
Of law the tabernacle true   Temple of Ark of Covenant
Shelter of wretched of the earth   of all the poor the sanctuary,
Never will you have to fear   as long as you reside in it.

* Jerusalem.
† Old Testament enemies of the Israelites; Dagon was a Philistine god, the
Amalekites a hostile tribe.

With the brightness of its light, the city outshines sun
    and moon
With its holiness this city conquers and absorbs all cities
Gebuseus Areuna* does not choose his place in vain.

Refrain

*The view from the Near East was very different. In the volatile
frontier region of Syria and Palestine, caught between the Seljuks of
Iraq and Anatolia, the Fatimids of Egypt, the Armenians of Cilicia
and Syria, and the Byzantines, conquest and changes in lordship
were hardly uncommon. The greatest shock to the Muslim world lay
rather in the massacres that accompanied the Frankish advance.
The Franks' assault and capture of Ma'arrat al-Numan (27 November–12 December 1098),† a desperate business for both sides,
ended in the destruction and removal of its inhabitants, leaving a
livid scar on the memory kept fresh by refugees:*

I do not know whether it is a pasturing place for wild beasts
    or my house, my native residence . . .
I turned towards it and asked, my voice choked with tears,
    my heart torn with affliction and love.
'O house, why has destiny pronounced such an unjust
    sentence on us?'‡

*Ibn al-Qalanisi provides an equally mournful account of the sack of
Jerusalem.*

Thereafter they proceeded towards Jerusalem in the middle of
June of this year, and the people fled in panic from their abodes
before them. They descended first upon Ramleh, and captured
it after the ripening of the crops. Thence they marched to
Jerusalem, the inhabitants of which they engaged and block-
aded, and having set up the tower against the city they brought

* Areuna the Jebusite; see 2 Samuel 24:16–24.   † See above, pp. 263–7.
‡ C. Hillenbrand, *The Crusades: Islamic Perspectives* (Edinburgh, 1999), p. 71.

it forward to the wall. At length news reached them that al-Afdal* was on his way from Egypt with a mighty army to engage in the Holy War against them, and to destroy them, and to succour and protect the city against them. They therefore attacked the city with increased vigour, and prolonged the battle that day until the daylight faded, then withdrew from it, after promising the inhabitants to renew the attack upon them on the morrow. The townsfolk descended from the wall at sunset, whereupon the Franks renewed their assault upon it, climbed up the tower, and gained a footing on the city wall. The defenders were driven down, and the Franks stormed the town and gained possession of it. A number of the townsfolk fled to the sanctuary [of David], and a great host were killed. The Jews assembled in the synagogue, and the Franks burned it over their heads. The sanctuary was surrendered to them on guarantee of safety on 14 July of this year, and they destroyed the shrines and the tomb of Abraham. Al-Afdal arrived with the Egyptian armies, but found himself forestalled, and having been reinforced by the troops from the Sahil,† encamped outside Ascalon on 4 August, to await the arrival of the fleet by sea and of the Arab levies. The army of the Franks advanced against him and attacked him in great force. The Egyptian army was thrown back towards Ascalon, al-Afdal himself taking refuge in the city.‡ The swords of the Franks were given mastery over the Muslims, and death was meted out to the footmen, volunteers and townsfolk, about ten thousand souls, and the camp was plundered. Al-Afdal set out for Egypt with his officers, and the Franks besieged Ascalon, until at length the townsmen agreed to pay them 20,000 dinars as protection money, and to deliver this sum to them forthwith. They therefore set about collecting this amount from the inhabitants of the town, but it befell that a quarrel broke out between the [Frankish] leaders, and they retired without having received any of the money. It is said

* Vizier of Egypt.
† The name given to the Palestinian coastal plain and maritime cities from Beirut to Ascalon.   ‡ 12 August 1099.

that the number of the people of Ascalon who were killed in this campaign – that is to say of the witnesses, men of substance, merchants and youths, exclusive of the regular levies – amounted to 2,700 souls.

The carnage meted out to the citizens of Jerusalem after its fall on 15 July 1099 lived as a burning testimony to the Franks' inhumanity not only among Muslims but also for the Jewish communities of the Near East whose brethren had been butchered, ransomed or expelled, their synagogue burnt, their holy books plundered. The Cairo Geniza (literally 'lumber room') preserved a uniquely rich collection largely of correspondence and legal and commercial documents deposited by the Jewish community of Old Cairo from the tenth to the thirteenth century. Most are written in Arabic but in Hebrew script, a significant example of cultural transmission and accommodation. A few record the immediate practical as well as psychological aftermath of the Jerusalem conquest and massacre, an example of the opposite. In the context described by Ibn al-Qalanisi, the Cairo Geniza documents provide urgent, personal details of a community, the Jews of Jerusalem, raped and destroyed by the zealots of Christianity.

The Jewish Community of Cairo to the Community of Ascalon, soon after the fall of Jerusalem

Boundless [blessings ...] from the Lord of Peace, who makes peace, [and the angels of peace, and from the Torah,] [the per]fect, all the paths of which are peace, [may come upon] the excellent [congrega]tions, the communal assembly of Ascalon [with greetings from us,] the community at Cairo, known as the residential city, your loving brothers, who enquire about your welfare and wish you all the best. May it please our God to accept from us all prayers and supplications on your behalf.

We beg to inform you – may God grant you permanent welfare and bestow upon you his mercy and grace – that we received tidings of the great disaster and all-comprising visitation, which befell our brothers, the Jews living in the Holy City, may God restore it for ever, the holy Torah scrolls, and the captives, suffering multiple vexations inflicted upon them by the enemies of God and haters of his people. We assembled at His Excellency, our lord, His Hon(our), Great(ness) and Hol(iness), our master and teacher Mevorakh, 'Leader of the Deliberations', 'Sage of the Yeshiva', 'the Great Council', etc.,* and found him, his garments rent, sitting on the floor, and shedding tears about what had happened. He addressed us, admonishing and urging us to donate sums for redeeming the Torah scrolls and the people of God held in captivity by the wicked kingdom, may God destroy and exterminate it.

We were moved by his warm and heart-winning words – may God preserve his high rank – and, responding to him, collected 123 dinars for retrieving the Torah scrolls and ransoming the remnants of Israel who had escaped from the sword.

This sum we handed over to Mr Mansur, son of Mr——, known as 'the son of the schoolmistress', to bring it to Ascalon. He will let you know what he is carrying and how he acted. We explained to him how he should proceed in this matter. We are sending you these lines in a great hurry because we are afraid lest our sins may cause failure and, God forbid, our iniquities will be visited upon us. For indeed we are unable to control and console ourselves. Our kidneys are in flames, because of the burning of the house of our God, our glorious sanctuary, may God forgive – our sun has darkened and our stature is bent . . .

The Leaders of the Community of Ascalon to the Jewish Community in Alexandria or Cairo, Summer 1100

We thank the Most High who gave us the opportunity of fulfilling this pious deed, and granted to you to take a share in it with us. We spent the money for the ransom of some of the captives, after due consideration of the instructions contained in your

* Head of the Jewish community in Egypt.

letter, that is, we send what was available to those who [had already been ransomed(?)].

We did not fail to reply to what you had written us, and indeed we answered, but we were seeking a man who would bring our reply to you. Afterwards it happened that these illnesses came upon us: plague, pestilence and leprosy, which filled our minds with anxiety, that we ourselves or some of our relatives might be stricken with disease. A man whom we trust went from here and must have explained to you the position with respect to the sums you had sent: that they reached us safely and that they were spent in the manner indicated [in your letter].

News still reaches us that among those who were redeemed from the Franks and remained in Ascalon some are in danger of dying of want. Others remained in captivity, and yet others were killed before the eyes of the rest, who themselves were killed afterwards with all manner of tortures; [for the enemy murdered them] in order to give vent to their anger on them.

We did not hear of a single man of Israel who was in such plight without exerting ourselves to do all that was in our power to save him.

The Most High has granted opportunities of relief and deliverance to individual fugitives, of which the first and most perfect instance – after the compassion of heaven – has been the presence in Ascalon of the honourable sheikh Abu 'l-Fadl Sahl son of Yusha son of Shaya (may God preserve him), an agent of the sultan (may God bestow glory upon his victories), whose influence is great in Alexandria where his word is very much heeded. He arranged matters wisely and took great pain in securing the ransom; but it would require a lengthy discourse to explain how he did it. But he could only ransom some of the people and had to leave the others. In the end, all those who could be ransomed from them [the Franks] were liberated, and only a few whom they kept remained in their hands, including a boy of about eight years of age, and a man, known as [?] the son of the Tustari's wife. It is reported that the Franks urged the latter to embrace the Christian faith of his own free will and promised to treat him well, but he told them, how could he become a Christian priest and be left in peace by them [the Jews], who had disbursed on his behalf a great sum? Until this day these captives remain in their [Franks'] hands; as well as those who were taken to Antioch, but these are few; and not counting those who abjured their faith because they lost patience as it was not possible to ransom them, and because they despaired of being permitted to go free.

We have not heard, praise be to the Most High, that the accursed ones who are called Ashkenazim [Germans] violated or raped women, as did the others.*

Now, among those who have reached safety are some who escaped on the second and third days following the battle and left with the governor who was granted safe conduct; and others who, after having being caught by the Franks, remained in their hands for some time and escaped in the end; these are but few. The majority consists of those who were ransomed. To our sorrow, some of them ended their lives under all kind of suffering and affliction. The privations which they had to endure caused some of them to leave for this country without food or protection against the cold, and they died on the way.

Others in a similar way perished at sea; and yet others, after having arrived here safely, became exposed to a 'change of air'; they came at the height of the plague, and a number of them died. We had, at the time, reported the arrival of each group.

And when the aforementioned honoured sheikh arrived, he brought a group of them, i.e., the bulk of those who had reached Ascalon; he spent the sabbath and celebrated Passover with them on the way in the manner as is required by such circumstances. He contracted a private loan for the sum that he had to pay the camel drivers and for their maintenance on the way, as well as the caravan guards and for other expenses, after having already spent other sums of money, which he did not charge to the community. All this is in addition to the money that was borrowed and spent in order to buy back 230 volumes, one

* i.e. in contrast with Muslims when they sacked cities.

hundred codices and eight Torah scrolls. All these are communal property and are now in Ascalon.

The community, after having disbursed about 500 dinars for the actual ransom of the individuals, for maintenance of some of them and for the ransom, as mentioned above, of the sacred books, remained indebted for the sum of 200 dinars. This is in addition to what has been spent on behalf of those who have been arriving from the beginning until now, on water and other drinks, medical treatment, maintenance and, in so far as possible, clothing. If it could be calculated how much this has cost over such a long period, the sum would indeed be great.

Had the accepted practice been followed, that is, of selling three Jewish captives for 100 [dinars], the whole available sum would have been spent for the ransom of only a few. However, the grace of the Lord, may his name be exalted, and his ever-ready mercy, have been bestowed upon these wretched people, the oppressed, the captives, the poor and indigent, who may, indeed, groan, lament and cry out as it is written: 'Thou hast given us like sheep appointed for meat, and hast scattered us among the heathen. Thou sellest thy people for nought and dost not increase thy wealth by their price.'* And we ourselves may say: 'Except the Lord of hosts had left unto us a very small remnant, we should have been as Sodom, and we should have been like unto Gomorrah.'† We declare that all the silver which we have weighed [i.e. the money we have spent] in this catastrophe, from the beginning until now is but light and insignificant in relation to its magnitude and the greatness of the sorrow it has entailed.

Some adduce as an excuse the impoverishment of this class of financial magnates and property holders ... and [?] the harshness of the winter season ... and ... enfeebled it.

We could not refrain ourselves from reporting what we know and the outcome of what we have done in this juncture, for we are convinced that you, just like ourselves, regret and mourn for those who have died and strive for the preservation of those

* Psalm 44:12–13.　　　† Isaiah 1:9.

who are alive; especially since your determination to distinguish yourselves was clearly shown and the loftiness of your aspiration and generosity became apparent. You were the first and the most consistent in the fulfilment of this 'good deed' which you were granted to perform, and which gained for you great superiority over the other communities as well as much honour. Thus, you may be, indeed, compared with that class of people to whom it was assigned to perform generous deeds and to strive to do praiseworthy acts, as it is written: 'And he came with the heads of the people, he executed the justice of the Lord, and his judgement with Israel.'*

   We have already indicated that we remained in debt of over 200 dinars, apart from the moneys that are required for the maintenance of the captives who remained in Ascalon – they number more than twenty persons – for their transfer and other needs until they arrive here. Among those who are in Ascalon is the honoured elder Abi al-Khayr Mubarak, the son of the teacher Hiba ibn Nasan (may God protect him for a long time). It is well known how much he is revered, wise, God-fearing and endowed with high virtues; he is bound by an old vow not to benefit in anything from charity together with the whole of the community, but only from what is explicitly destined for him by name. [He should be enabled] to come here, after [you] our lords, elders and masters – may God preserve your happiness – have graciously offered us the sum needed for cancelling the debt incurred for the ransom of our and your brethren. Gird now your loins together with us in this matter, and it will be accounted for you as a mark of merit in the future, as it has been in the past . . . the generous deed which you began, by helping us to lighten our burden and by assisting us with your generosity in order to put us back on our feet, for we have no one in this country to whom we could write as we are writing to you. It is proper that we should turn to you and cause you some disturbance. The main tenor of this letter ought to be read out to your [entire] community, after you have announced that everyone must

* Deuteronomy 33:21.

attend [the meeting]. For the benefit will [thus] be complete and general, both to those who pay and to those who receive payment. For it is unlikely that there should lack among the public those who had made a vow, or those who had undertaken an obligation to perform 'holy deeds' which have not yet been determined; such should, then, be invited to contribute as much as may be seen fitting. Or there may be those who had previously intended to make contribution to charity, or others may wish to make a specific contribution to one cause rather than to another. In this manner you will achieve your purpose, and deal with us in your accustomed generosity and excellent manner . . . and you will deserve, through this charitable act, to acquire 'both worlds'. Only rarely does such a juncture present itself, in which 'commerce' is beneficial and 'business' entirely profitable. We do not call your attention to such a matter in order to remind you of the duty of doing it, but . . . your own lofty [virtues] are the strongest urger and reminder.

We despatched a messenger to you and what he will tell you about the details of this misfortune exempts us from discoursing on it at a greater length. We beg of you, may God preserve you in long life, to deal with him kindly until he returns; and concerning that which God may cause him [to collect] amongst you – may God preserve you – if you could write out for him a bill of exchange, it would make things easier for him, since he is but a messenger, and speed up his return. If this cannot be done, arrange that an exact statement of how much has been collected be made, and have your letter sent through him [the messenger] and mention the sum in it. The God of Israel, etc. . . . .

The writer of the above, the pained, sorrowful and grieving Yeshaya ha-Kohen ibn Masliah the Enlightened sends respectful greetings to all the gentlemen, and begs them to accept his apology. They are not unaware of what he has gone through from the time he took leave of them until this day.

David ben Rabbi Shelomo ben Rabbi . . . sends his greeting to your excellencies and begs you to note . . . al-Fadl Abu . . .

Hanina ibn Mansur ibn Ubayd (peace be on him) reserves for the venerable lords and masters, may God preserve Their Excellencies, the best greeting and most excellent salutation and attention; expresses his longing for them and begs them to take note of the contents of this letter. Peace.

At some point in 1100 a Jewish pilgrim in Egypt, unable to reach Palestine because of the war, wrote home to North Africa or Spain expressing his frustration.

If I attempted to describe my longing for you, my lord, my brother and cousin – may God prolong your days and make permanent your honour, success, happiness, health and welfare; and [...] subdue your enemies – all the paper in the world would not suffice. My longing will but increase and double, just as the days will grow and double. May the Creator of the world presently make us meet together in joy when I return under his guidance to my homeland and to the inheritance of my fathers in complete happiness, so that we rejoice and be happy through his great mercy and his vast bounty; and thus may be his will!

You may remember, my lord, that many years ago I left our country to seek God's mercy and help in my poverty, to behold Jerusalem and return thereupon. However, when I was in Alexandria God brought about circumstances which caused a slight delay. Afterwards, however, 'the sea grew stormy', and many armed bands made their appearance in Palestine; 'and he who went forth and he who came had no peace', so that hardly one survivor out of a whole group came back to us from Palestine and told us that scarcely anyone could save himself from those armed bands, since they were so numerous and were gathered round . . . every town. There was further the journey through the desert, among [the bedouins] and whoever escaped from the one, fell into the hands of the other. Moreover, mutinies [spread throughout the country and reached] even Alexandria, so that we ourselves were besieged several times and the city was ruined; . . . the end however was good, for the sultan – may God bestow glory upon his victories – conquered the city and caused justice to abound in it in a manner unprecedented in the history of any king in the world; not even a dirham was looted from anyone. Thus I had come to hope that because of his justice and strength God would give the land into his hands, and I should thereupon go to Jerusalem in safety and tranquillity. For this reason I proceeded from Alexandria to Cairo, in order to start [my journey] from there.

When, however, God had given Jerusalem, the blessed, into his hands* this state of affairs continued for too short a time to allow for making a journey there. The Franks arrived and killed everybody in the city, whether of Ishmael or of Israel; and the few who survived the slaughter were made prisoners. Some of these have been ransomed since, while others are still in captivity in all parts of the world.

Now, all of us had anticipated that our sultan – may God bestow glory upon his victories† – would set out against them [the Franks] with his troops and chase them away. But time after time our hope failed. Yet, to this very present moment we do hope that God will give his [the sultan's] enemies into his hands. For it is inevitable that the armies will join in battle this year; and, if God grants us victory through him [the sultan] and he conquers Jerusalem – and so it may be, with God's will – I for one shall not be amongst those who will linger, but shall go there to behold the city; and shall afterwards return straight to you – if God wills it. My salvation is in God, for this [is unlike] the other previous occasions [of making a pilgrimage to Jerusalem]. God, indeed, will exonerate me, since at my age I cannot afford to delay and wait any longer; I want to return home under any circumstances, if I still remain alive – whether I shall have seen Jerusalem or have given up the hope of doing it – both of which are possible.

You know, of course, my lord, what has happened to us in the course of the last five years: the plague, the illnesses and ailments have continued unabated for four successive years. As a result of

* i.e. the sultan's. † A significant allegiance.

this the wealthy became impoverished and a great number of people died of the plague, so that entire families perished in it. I, too, was affected with a grave illness, from which I recovered only about a year ago; then I was taken ill the following year so that (on the margin) for four years I have remained [. . .]. He who has said: 'The evil diseases of Egypt'* . . . he who hiccups does not live . . . ailments and will die . . . otherwise . . . will remain alive.

At about the same time, a noblewoman in Tripoli, left destitute and a refugee by the fall of Jerusalem, wrote to her relatives describing her plight and begging for aid for herself and her children.

[My lord and] illustrious master, may God make your welfare and happiness permanent. [I have to convey] to you, my dear boy, something which I shall immediately describe . . . Abu 'l-Khayr [was] with al-Muntasir. Al-Muntasir died [and Abu 'l-Khayr disappeared]. Consequently we are lacking clothing and food to a degree I am unable to describe. But [our relative] Joseph was not remiss in providing us with cash, wheat and other things. Moreover, he returned to me the collaterals, which I had given him, so that I could place them with someone else. God the exalted deserves thanks and has imposed on us to thank him. You must write him a letter of thanks . . .

About the books of Abu 'l-Khayr I learned only in Tripoli. For the crate was locked and I learned about its contents only in Tripoli . . . I witnessed much bloodshed and experienced everything terrible. I was told that, as soon as al-Muntasir died, Abu 'l-Khayr disappeared. He had books and I [pawned] his books and yours for 5 dinars. Your letters concerning them have arrived. If the nagid [head of the Egyptian Jews] – may God keep him in his honoured position – manages to send 5 dinars, he will do so in the way of charity and thus ransom all the books, whereupon I shall send them to you. If he [Abu 'l-Khayr] is all right, he will ransom them and send them [to you].

* Deuteronomy 7:15.

I learned that Abu 'l-Wafa was taken by the bedouins at the time when his brother disappeared. I am a luckless young woman, suffering both by the hunger of the family, and especially the baby girl, who are with me, and by the bad news I heard about my boy. If my lord, the nagid, has sworn that he would not go to my aid and visits on me the iniquities committed by Abu 'l-Khayr, have mercy upon me, your sister and your mother, as far as you are able to do so.

As far as I am concerned, by our religion, it is better to be captured by the crusaders, for the prisoners find someone who gives them food and drink, but I, by our religion, am completely without clothing, and I and my children are starving.

Now, do not neglect me. Be mindful of the family bonds and the blood. Show your affection for me by writing to me.

The brother of this man was not remiss towards him, when he first arrived here, until he sued them for an inheritance. This led to a complete rupture between them, and no one of them talks to me ... Miserable days have come upon me. Must it be so? At the time when I was in Jerusalem, your letters and contributions came to me plentifully, as is proper between two sisters, but now you cut me.

I am writing these lines while the people are on the point of sailing. I have not described in this letter even a fraction of my real state.

Accept for yourself my greeting of peace. And may God extend his peace to my lord the nagid and my lord the Haver.* Greetings also to your mother and sister, and to his excellency, your paternal uncle. And regards to everyone under your care.

To my lord and illustrious master ... Abu 'l-Ala, may God keep him.

[From] his grate[ful] A[bu 'l-] Rida. Convey and be rewarded!

The Muslims had no less cause to lament. The contemporary Iraqi poet, Abu 'l-Muzaffar al-Abiwardi (d. 1113), looked to turn the catastrophe into a call for Islamic renewal.

* Hebrew member of the *yeshiva* or scholarly academy.

We have mingled blood with flowing tears, and there is no
    room left in us for pity.

To shed tears is a man's worst weapon when the swords stir
    up the embers of war.

Sons of Islam, behind you are battles in which heads rolled
    at your feet.

Dare you slumber in the blessed shade of safety, where life
    is as soft as an orchard flower?

How can the eye sleep between the lids at a time of disasters
    that would waken any sleeper?

While your Syrian brothers can only sleep on the backs of
    their chargers, or in vultures' bellies!

Must the foreigners feed on our ignominy, while you trail
    behind you the train of a pleasant life, like men whose
    world is at peace?

When blood has been spilt, when sweet girls must for
    shame hide their lovely faces in their hands!

When the white swords' points are red with blood, and the
    iron of the brown lances is stained with gore!

At the sound of sword hammering on lance young chil-
    dren's hair turns white.

This is war, and the man who shuns the whirlpool to save
    his life shall grind his teeth in penitence.

This is war, and the infidel's sword is naked in his hand,
    ready to be sheathed again in men's necks and skulls.

This is war, and he who lies in the tomb at Medina seems to
    raise his voice and cry: 'O sons of Hashim!*

I see my people slow to raise the lance against the enemy: I
    see the faith resting on feeble pillars.

For fear of death the Muslims are evading the fire of battle,
    refusing to believe that death will surely strike them.'

Must the Arab champions then suffer with resignation,
    while the gallant Persians shut their eyes to their dis-
    honour?

* The Prophet rebuking his successors, unworthy caliphs.

Some heeded such appeals. In 1105, Ali ibn Tahir al-Sulami (d. 1106), a Damascene religious lawyer and philology teacher at the Great Mosque, read to seminar groups from his new book the Kitab al-jihad (The Book of Jihad, *or Holy War). While the Muslim obligation to perform* jihad (*i.e. struggle) referred chiefly to internal spiritual self-improvement, the so-called lesser* jihad, *the external armed struggle against the infidel, could be revived when the faith was threatened. Al-Sulami, reminding his audience of this, explained the need for a new Holy War to restore Islam in a decidedly secular but acute historical analysis of the past that simultaneously supplied a clear blueprint for a future Muslim counter-attack.*

A number fell upon the island of Sicily at a time of difference and competition, and likewise they gained possession of town after town in Spain.* When mutually confirmatory reports reached them of the state of this country – the disagreement of its lords, the dissensions of its dignitaries, together with its disorder and disturbance – they carried out their resolution of going out to it, and Jerusalem was the summit of their wishes.

Then they looked down from Syria on disunited kingdoms, hearts in disagreement and differing opinions, linked with secret resentments. Thereby their ambitions grew in strength, and extended to what they beheld. They continued assiduously in the Holy War against the Muslims, while the Muslims did not trouble about them or join forces to fight them, leaving to each other the encounter until they [i.e. the Franks] made themselves rulers of lands beyond their utmost hopes ... Their hopes expand inasmuch as they see their enemies content to be at peace with them, so that they are convinced that all the lands will become theirs, and all the people prisoners in their hands. May God who is near and answers in his munificence humble their thoughts by uniting the community and setting it in order.

---

* Referring to the Norman conquest of Sicily after 1060 and the reinvigorated *reconquista* in Spain.

Appendix

THE COMMANDERS

ADHEMAR OF MONTEIL, bishop of Le Puy. Papal legate on crusade; close associate of Urban II 1095–6; travelled in Raymond of Toulouse's Provençal army; as adept at military command as at prayer, diplomacy and reconciling the factious crusade leaders. Died 1 August 1098 at Antioch.

AL-AFDAL, Armenian mercenary and vizier of Egypt at the time of the First Crusade; conquered Jerusalem 1098; defeated at Ascalon in his attempt to recapture it in August 1099.

ALEXIUS I COMNENUS, Byzantine emperor, usurped imperial throne 1081; invited western help against the Muslims in 1095.

BALDWIN OF BOULOGNE, younger brother of Godfrey of Bouillon and Eustace III, count of Boulogne. Initially trained for Church, his career of single-minded, acquisitive adventurism brought him the county of Edessa (1098) and the crown of Jerusalem (1100–18); thrice married, once bigamously, probably a homosexual.

BERKYARUK, son of Malik Shah, Seljuk sultan of Baghdad during the First Crusade.

BOHEMUND, prince of Taranto. Son of Robert Guiscard of Hauteville, who had made himself duke of Apulia in southern Italy. Failed in attempts to win himself a territory in the Balkans in 1080s. The crusade offered him a chance of acquiring a principality in his own right. The expedition's best field commander. Ruler of Antioch 1098; led another failed assault on Byzantine Balkans 1107–8.

DUQAQ, son of Tutush, nephew of Malik Shah, Seljuk ruler of Damascus during the First Crusade.

EUSTACE III, count of Boulogne, elder brother of Godfrey of Bouillon and Baldwin of Boulogne; travelled separately; somewhat shadowy presence in the sources for the crusade; returned to the west with seemingly few eastern ambitions, although tempted to succeed Baldwin as king of Jerusalem in 1118.

GODFREY OF BOUILLON, duke of Lower Lorraine, a supporter of Henry IV against Gregory VII; campaigned against the papacy in Italy 1084; leader of army from Lorraine and Rhineland; probably had no intention of returning; surprise choice as ruler of conquered Jerusalem 1099–1100; his memory and legend were more glamorous than his career.

HUGH THE GREAT, count of Vermandois, younger brother of King Philip I of France. Led recruits from royal lands in northern France. First of the great secular lords to reach Constantinople, he was subsequently overshadowed by the wealthier or more militarily accomplished leaders; left Antioch on a diplomatic mission to Alexius I; returned east 1101 only to meet his death.

KERBOGA, Turkish military governor (atabeg) of Mosul; led major relief expedition against the crusaders at Antioch; defeated June 1098.

KILIJ ARSLAN I, Seljuk sultan of Rum (Anatolia) defeated by crusaders at Nicaea and Dorylaeum 1097.

MALIK SHAH, great Seljuk sultan of Baghdad whose death in 1092 precipitated political faction-fighting in Iraq and Syria that presented the First Crusade with a divided enemy.

PETER THE HERMIT, holy man from northern France; conducted his own successful preaching and recruiting tour of northern France, Lorraine and western Germany 1095–6; led substantial military force to Constantinople summer 1096 which was destroyed by Turks; later joined main expedition to Jerusalem. Some regarded him as having initiated the whole enterprise.

RAYMOND IV, count of Toulouse and St Gilles; oldest of crusade leaders with close contacts 1095–6 with Urban II; led Provençal and southern French army; thwarted of ambitions at Antioch and Jerusalem, he spent his last years trying to establish his power at Tripoli.

RIDWAN, son of Tutush, nephew of Malik Shah, ruler of Aleppo at time of First Crusade.

ROBERT II CURTHOSE, duke of Normandy 1087–1106, eldest son of William the Conqueror. Mortgaged duchy to younger brother William II Rufus to pay for his crusade. Unsuccessful ruler; deprived of duchy and imprisoned for life by youngest brother Henry I in 1106.

ROBERT II, count of Flanders. One of western Europe's wealthiest rulers, his father Robert I had provided knights for Byzantium in early 1090s. Active on the crusade campaign; had no intention of staying in the east.

STEPHEN, count of Blois and Chartres, henpecked husband of the termagant Adela, daughter of William the Conqueror. Appointed *ductor* of the crusade army at Antioch March 1098; deserted June 1098; bullied by his ashamed wife to return; killed at Ramleh 1102. Father of King Stephen of England.

TANCRED, nephew of Bohemund; despite his relative youth, he quickly acquired a prominent position through his skills as a fighter and commander always eager to take responsibility, as in Cilicia in 1097 or at Bethlehem in June 1099; regent, then ruler, of Antioch after 1105.

TATICIUS, Turkish eunuch and experienced Byzantine general assigned to crusaders for the march from Nicaea to Antioch; his departure before the fall of Antioch allowed Bohemund a free hand in its capture and retention.

URBAN II, Odo of Lagery, former prior of the powerful Burgundian monastery of Cluny, pope 1088–99; inspiration and organiser of the First Crusade 1095–6.

WALTER of Poissy, lord of Boissy SansAvoir, nicknamed 'Penniless' (*sans avoir*); leader of early contingent of crusaders inspired in part by Peter the Hermit; first western commander to reach Constantinople July 1096; killed near Nicaea, October 1096.

YAGHI SAYAN, Turkish governor of Antioch in 1097, notorious for ruthless regime; murdered after fall of Antioch 1098.

Further Reading

Still the best succinct and scholarly short history of the crusades is H. E. Mayer, *The Crusades* (2nd edn, Oxford University Press, 1988). For a more expansive treatment, see C. Tyerman, *God's War: A New History of the Crusades* (Allen Lane, 2006). The most seductive if often untrustworthy modern narrative of the First Crusade remains S. Runciman, *A History of the Crusades*, vol. 1, *The First Crusade* (Cambridge University Press, 1951, and many reprints since); also, now, T. Asbridge, *The First Crusade* (Free Press, 2004). For attempts to define what contemporaries tended to assume or avoid, see J. Riley-Smith, *What Were the Crusades?* (4th edn, Palgrave Macmillan, 2009); C. Tyerman, *The Invention of the Crusades* (Macmillan, 1998); and N. Housley, *Contesting the Crusades* (Blackwell, 2006). The cultural milieu was exhaustively and magisterially exposed and explored by C. Erdmann in his classic *The Origin of the Idea of Crusade* (1935; trans. edn, Princeton University Press, 1977), although he has not lacked critics, who prefer to see the phenomenon of 1095 as less predictable, more exceptional, less political or more pious. Nonetheless, modern study of crusade origins begins with Erdmann. R. Chazan, *European Jewry and the First Crusade* (University of California Press, 1987), examines the dark aspect of the Jewish pogrom of 1096 and, by implication, much else. Discussion of the acceptability of war by the religion of the Beatitudes prompts F. H. Russell, *The Just War in the Middle Ages* (Cambridge University Press, 1975), and, more narrowly, M. Bull, *Knightly Piety and the Lay Response to the First Crusade* (Clarendon Press, 1993), and W. J. Purkis, *Crusading Spirituality in the Holy Land and Iberia c.1095–c.1187* (The Boydell Press, 2008). What drove men to join up and what they experienced on campaign concerns N. Housley, *Fighting for the Cross* (Yale University Press, 2008), and J. Riley-Smith, *The First Crusade and the Idea of Crusading* (Athlone, 1986), which also considers the role contemporary interpreters played in transmitting a coherent inspirational understanding of the events. How the crusade was presented at the time and later is discussed by C. Tyerman, *The Debate on the Crusades* (Manchester University Press, 2011). The First Crusade as warfare has encouraged the wonderful study by J. France, *Victory in the East* (Cambridge University Press, 1994). For a recent attempt at a sociological analysis, see C. Kostick, *The Social Structure of the First Crusade* (Brill, 2008). Most biographies of the western leaders in English now creak with age. For the crusade's place in ecclesiastical politics, consult C. Morris, *The Papal Monarchy* (Clarendon Press, 1989). Islamic attitudes have become increasingly clear to non-Arabists through, for example, P. Holt, *The Age of the Crusades* (Longman, 1986), and, especially, C. Hillenbrand, *The Crusades: Islamic Perspectives* (Edinburgh University Press, 1999). A. Maalouf, *The Crusade Through Arab Eyes* (Al Saqi Books, 1984), says much about modern Arab opinions but little else. Many important aspects of the First Crusade are discussed in *The First Crusade: Origins and Impact* (Manchester University Press, 1997), ed. J. Phillips. Alexius I awaits a modern English-language biography; meanwhile, for the Byzantine background, see M. Angold, *The Byzantine Empire* (Longman, 1984), and J. Harris, *Byzantium and the Crusades* (Hambledon, 2003). For a different, but no more nor less plausible contemporary narrative of the First Crusade, see S. Edgington's translation of Albert of Aachen, *Historia Ierosolimitana* (Oxford University Press, 2007).

Acknowledgements

Every effort has been made to trace the copyright-holders of the copyright material in this book and to provide correct details of copyright. Penguin regrets any oversight and, upon written notification, will rectify any omission in future reprints or editions.

ABU 'L-MUZAFFAR AL-ABIWARDI. Poem on the loss of Jerusalem, 1099, from Francesco Gabrieli, *Arab Historians of the Crusades* (Routledge, 1969). Reprinted by permission of Taylor & Francis Books Ltd.

ALBERT OF AACHEN. Extracts from *History of Jerusalem*, from *Historia Hierosolymitana*, in *Recueil des historiens des croisades: historiens occidentaux*, iv (Académie des Inscriptions et Belles Lettres, Paris, 1879), translated by Henry Maas. Copyright © The Folio Society Ltd 2004.

—— Extracts from *History of Jerusalem*, from August C. Krey, *The First Crusade: The Accounts of Eye Witnesses and Participants* (Princeton University Press, 1921).

ALI IBN TAHIR AL-SULAMI. Extract from *Kitab al-Jihad* calling for a jihad, 1105, following the fall of Jerusalem, from P. M. Holt, *The Age of the Crusades* (Longman, 1986). Reprinted by permission of Pearson Education Ltd.

ANNA COMNENA. Extracts from *The Alexiad of Anna Comnena*, translated by E. R. A. Sewter (Penguin Classics, 1969). Reprinted by permission of Penguin Books Ltd.

ANONYMOUS. Charter recording Nivello's donation to the abbey of St Peter of Chartres, 1096, from Louise Riley-Smith and Jonathan Riley-Smith, *The Crusades: Idea and Reality 1095–1274* (Edward Arnold, 1981). Reprinted by permission of the authors.

—— Extracts from *Gesta Francorum et aliorum Hierosolimitano-rum: The Deeds of the Franks and the Other Pilgrims to Jerusalem*, edited and translated by Rosalind Hill (1962), reprinted by permission of Oxford University Press.

——Letter to North Africa or Spain, 1100, from Shlomo D. Goitein, 'Contemporary Letters on the Capture of Jerusalem by the Crusaders', *Journal of Jewish Studies*, iii (1952), pp. 162–77. Reprinted by permission of the *Journal of Jewish Studies*, Oxford.

——Letter to relatives, *c.*1100, from Shlomo D. Goitein, 'Tyre–Tripoli–'Arqa: Geniza Documents from the Beginning of the Crusader Period', *Jewish Quarterly Review*, lxvi (1975), pp. 69–88. Reprinted by permission of the University of Pennsylvania Press.

——'The Narrative of the Old Persecutions' (or 'Mainz Anonym-ous'), from Shlomo Eidelberg (ed. and trans.), *The Jews and the Crusaders: The Hebrew Chronicles of the First and Second Crusades* (University of Wisconsin Press, 1977). Reprinted by permission of the estate of Shlomo Eidelberg.

——'Nomen a Solemnibus', from E. Peters (ed.), *The First Crusade* (University of Pennsylvania Press, 1998). Reprinted by permission of the University of Pennsylvania Press.

ANSELM OF RIBEMONT. Letters to Manasses II of Rheims, from Dana C. Munro (ed. and trans.), *Letters of the Crusaders* (Department of History of the University of Pennsylvania, 1894).

BOHEMUND AND THE LEADERS OF THE CRUSADE. Letter to Urban II, 11 September 1098, from Fulcher of Chartres, *A History of the Expedition to Jerusalem 1095–1127*, translated by Frances Rita Ryan and edited by Harold S. Fink (University of Tennessee Press, 1969). Copyright © 1969 by the University of Tennessee Press. Reprinted by permission of the University of Tennessee Press.

FULCHER OF CHARTRES. Extracts from Fulcher of Chartres, *A History of the Expedition to Jerusalem 1095–1127*, translated by

Frances Rita Ryan and edited by Harold S. Fink (University of Tennessee Press, 1969). Copyright © 1969 by the University of Tennessee Press. Reprinted by permission of the University of Tennessee Press.

FULK RECHIN. Account of Urban II's visit, February 1096, from E. Peters (ed.), *The First Crusade* (University of Pennsylvania Press, 1998). Reprinted by permission of the University of Pennsylvania Press.

GODFREY OF BOUILLON ET AL. Letter to Paschal II, September 1099, from Dana C. Munro (ed. and trans.), *Letters of the Crusaders* (Department of History of the University of Pennsylvania, 1894).

GUIBERT OF NOGENT. Extracts from Book II of *The Deeds of God through the Franks*, from Robert Levine (trans.), *The Deeds of God through the Franks* (Boydell Press, 1997). Reprinted by permission of Boydell & Brewer Ltd.

IBN AL-QALANASI. Extracts from *The Damascus Chronicle*, from H. A. R. Gibb (trans.), *The Damascus Chronicle of the Crusades*, University of London Historical Series, no. v (Luzac & Co, 1932).

JEWISH COMMUNITY OF CAIRO. Letter to the community of Ascalon, soon after the fall of Jerusalem, July 1099, from Shlomo D. Goitein, 'Geniza Sources for the Crusader Period', in B. Kedar, H. Mayer and R. Smail (eds), *Outremer* (Yad Izhak Ben-Zvi, Jerusalem, 1982). Reprinted by permission of Yad Izhak Ben-Zvi.

LEADERS OF THE ASCALON COMMUNITY. Letter to the Jewish community in Alexandria or Cairo, summer 1100, from Shlomo D. Goitein, 'Contemporary Letters on the Capture of Jerusalem by the Crusaders', *Journal of Jewish Studies*, iii (1952), pp. 162–77. Reprinted by permission of the *Journal of Jewish Studies*, Oxford.

MANASSES II OF RHEIMS. Letter to Lambert of Arras, 1099, from August C. Krey, *The First Crusade: The Accounts of Eye Witnesses and Participants* (Princeton University Press, 1921).

PATRIARCH OF JERUSALEM. Letter to the Church in the west, January 1098, from August C. Krey, *The First Crusade: The Accounts of Eye Witnesses and Participants* (Princeton University Press, 1921).

PEOPLE OF LUCCA ON CRUSADE. Letter to all faithful Christians, October 1098, from August C. Krey, *The First Crusade: The Accounts of Eye Witnesses and Participants* (Princeton University Press, 1921).

RAYMOND OF AGUILERS. Extracts from *The History of the Frankish Conquerors of Jerusalem*, from John Hugh Hill and Laurita L. Hill (trans.), *Historia Francorum qui Ceperunt Iherusalem* (Memoirs of the American Philosophical Society, volume 71, 1968). Reprinted by permission of the American Philosophical Society.

ROBERT OF RHEIMS. Extract from *Historia Hierosolymitana*, reporting Urban II's speech at Clermont, 27 November 1095, from Dana C. Munro (ed. and trans.), *Urban and the Crusaders* (Department of History of the University of Pennsylvania, 1894).

STEPHEN OF BLOIS. Letter to his wife Adela, 29 March 1098, from Dana C. Munro (ed.), *Letters of the Crusaders* (Department of History of the University of Pennsylvania, 1894).

URBAN II. Letters to the monks of Vallombrosa, 7 October 1096, and to the counts of Besalú et al., *c.* January 1096–July 1099, from Louise Riley-Smith and Jonathan Riley-Smith, *The Crusades: Idea and Reality 1095–1274* (Edward Arnold, 1981). Reprinted by permission of the authors.

——Letter to the faithful in Flanders, December 1095, from August C. Krey, *The First Crusade: The Accounts of Eye Witnesses and Participants* (Princeton University Press, 1921).

——Letter to his supporters in Bologna, September 1096, from E. Peters (ed.), *The First Crusade* (University of Pennsylvania Press, 1998). Reprinted by permission of the University of Pennsylvania Press.

Index

Abi al-Khayr Mubarak, 367, 371–2

Abu 'l-Rida, 372

Abu 'l-Ala, 372

Abu 'l-Fadl Sahl, sheikh, son of Yusha, 364

Abu 'l-Muzaffar al-Abiwardi, 372

Abu 'l-Wafa, 372

Abu Yala Hamza ibn Asad al-Tamimi, *see* Ibn al-Qalanisi

Achard, castellan of Montmerle: joins crusade, 71; killed at siege of Jerusalem, 312, 314, 320

Acre, 279, 307

Adana (Athena), 134, 136, 155

Adela, wife of Stephen of Blois, 182–3

Adhemar, bishop of Le Puy (papal legate): appears in visions, 300–2, 329; in battle of Antioch (June 1098), 222, 227, 229, 243; in beleaguered Antioch, 204; at capture of Antioch, 190; captured and beaten by Pechenegs, 104; death, xxi, 243, 246, 248, 250, 334, 336n; at Dorylaeum, 125–7, 131, 132n; illness, 226; leadership of crusade, 20, 25, 71, 96, 103; on march to Antioch, 168; message to crusader victors in Jerusalem, 322–3; Raymond of Aguilers accompanies, xxv–xxvi; departs for east with Raymond of Toulouse, xx; scepticism over Holy Lance and reported visions, xxvi, 206–7, 209–11, 215, 292–4; at siege of Antioch, 151–2, 154, 158, 170; at siege of Nicaea, 102, 109–10, 112; takes Cross at Clermont, 1, 11; Urban II recruits, xix

al-Adil, vizier, 334

Adrianople, 58, 61

al-Afdal (Lavedalius), vizier of Egypt: in crusaders' agreements with kings of Tripoli and Acre, 278, 307; defeated at Ascalon, 337, 339, 341, 343–5, 347, 351–2, 361; negotiations with crusaders, 179n, 286; occupies and protects Jerusalem, 271–2, 278n, 361; Raymond of Toulouse removes to Ascalon, 317

Agarenes, 66, 162

Agatha, St, 301

Ahmad ibn Marwan, 206n

Alard of Spiniaeco, 169

Albert of Aachen: condemns persecution of Jews, 31; *Historia Hierosolymitana*, xxiii, xxxii, 32; on Peter the Hermit, 32

Aleppo, crusader captives in, 65

Alexandretta, 218

Alexandria, Jewish community in, 363, 369–70

Alexius I Comnenus, Byzantine emperor: advises crusaders on methods of fighting Turks, 86, 93; in Anna Comnena's account, xv–xvi, xxix–xxxii, 65–6, 68, 70, 231, 233, 236–8; appeals to Urban II for support, vii, xv–xvi, xviii–xix, 12; attacks Godfrey's army at Constantinople, 72; Bohemund's relations with, xxix–xxx, 86–93; compensates crusader commanders for lack of booty, 108, 120–2; crusader leaders swear oath of fealty to, xx, xxviii, 79, 83–5, 89–90, 94n, 101–2, 122; crusaders request to take over Antioch, 247, 253, 299–300; crusaders seek revenge on for Larissa victory, 79; crusaders' supposed promise to deliver first captured city to, 165; envoys protest at Bohemund's possession of Antioch, 299;

Alexius I Comnenus (*continued*)
expedites crusaders' departure
from Constantinople, 64, 84; fails to
relieve crusaders at Antioch, xxi,
xxv, xxix, 231, 233, 236–8; in *Gesta
Francorum*, xxiv–xxv; learns of
destruction of crusader armies in
Asia Minor, 65; negotiates surrender of Nicaea, 108, 114, 117, 120–3,
126; and Peter the Hermit, 31, 61–2,
68–9, 70; Raymond IV of Toulouse's
relations with, xxvi, 92–4, 105–6;
resists crusaders' attacks on Constantinople, 80–3, 100; rumoured
approach to siege of Antioch, 155;
sends boats to siege of Nicaea, 111,
113; sends messages to Raymond of
Toulouse, 105; Stephen of Blois
reports situation in Antioch to,
218–19; supplies finances and provisions to crusaders, xx–xxi, 62–3, 72;
welcomes Hugh of Vermandois,
74–6; withdraws from Akshehir, 220
Ali ibn Munqidh, king of Shayzar, 275,
280
Allenby, General Edmund Henry Hyn-
man, xii
Amalfi, 72
Amircaradigum, 129
Andrew, St: appears to Peter
Bartholomew, 206–9, 213, 215–16,
227, 242, 250–1, 253–6, 264, 288;
appears to Peter Desiderius, 304
Andronopolis, valley of, 74
Anna Comnena: *Alexiad*, xv, xxiv,
xxix–xxxii; on Alexius I Comnenus' actions, 65–6, 68, 70, 231, 233,
236–8; on arrival of crusaders in
Constantinople, 74; on Bohemund,
86, 90–2; on events at Antioch and
Alexius' refusal to aid crusaders, 231;
on fighting priest, 78n; on Muslim
practices, 67; on Peter the Hermit,
31; political exile, xxix; on siege of
Nicaea, 115–16; on Taticius' departure from siege of Antioch, 161

Anseau of Caien, 169
Anselm of Ribemont: death at Arqah,
278, 285; on fall of Antioch, 193;
messages to Manasses II, 167–70, 193
anti-Semitism, *see* Jews
Anti-Taurus Mountains, 133, 161n
Antioch: Alexius I fails to relieve, xxi,
xxv, xxix, 231, 233, 236–8; Anna
Comnena on, 231–3, 238–9; Anselm
of Ribemont on, 169–70, 193–6;
battle of (28 June 1098), 222–5,
227–30, 238–40; Bohemund occupies, xxi, xxv, 186–91, 299; crusader
captives in, 65–8; crusaders confined in by Kerboga's force, 197–200,
203–5, 217–19, 272; crusaders march
on, 124, 133–4, 137–8; described, 149,
257; deserters from, 203–4, 212, 236;
disputes over ownership, 246, 249,
252, 256–7, 260, 262, 299; falls to crusaders, 186–96, 231–3, 246; famine
and starvation in, 218, 225; Fulcher
on, 144–8; *Gesta Francorum* on,
xxiv, 156–61, 177–82; Ibn al-
Qalanisi's account of siege, 162–3;
Muslim defenders make attacks on
besiegers, 150–2, 156, 158, 172; offered
to Bohemund on capture, 155; patriarch Symeon's message to Church
in west from, 165–6; provisioning
by sea, 172; Raymond of Aguilers
on, 148–55, 158n, 170–7; relief forces
repulsed, 143, 153n, 158, 170, 177, 189;
ships supply marchers to Jerusalem,
284; siege of (1097–8), xix, xxi, 143,
331n; Stephen of Bois at, 183–4;
Turks evacuate, 137; Turks hold citadel, 217–18, 227, 232, 242, 245; victory
reported to Urban II at Lucca, 240–5;
visions and miracles at, xxvi, 204–16
Antioch, Lake, battle of (1098), 143,
171n, 177n, 178–9, 185, 194n
Aoxianus, prince of Antioch, 146
Apt, bishop of, 254, 293, 307
Aregh, castle, 156, 178
Ariano, bishop of Apulia, 356

Armenian Christians, xv–xvi, 134, 137

Arnulf, bishop of Martirano, 334, 336, 338, 341–2

Arnulf of Chocques, patriarch of Jerusalem, 291, 292n, 294–5, 336, 341–2, 345n, 354, 358n

Arqah, siege of (1099), xxvi, 253, 274, 276–8, 284–7, 299, 304, 351

Artah, 164

Ascalon: al-Afdal arrives in, 337; boasts and threats, 337; Egyptian army defeated at (1099), xxi, 286, 338n, 339–47, 351, 361; Jerusalem prisoners taken to, 317; Jewish community in, 362–4, 367

Asia Minor: crusader armies destroyed in, 62, 64–5, 69–70; crusaders march across, xxi, 64

Assam, prince, 183

Aubrey, brother of William of Grandmesnil, 203

Aubrey of Cagnano, 73

Augustopolis, 125

Azaz, 253–4

'Bad-crown' (follower of Bohemund), 190

Baghras, 164

Baldric of Dol, xxiv

Baldwin, count of Mons in Hainault, 63

Baldwin Chalderuns, 169

Baldwin of Boulogne, king of Jerusalem: at Constantinople, 72, 85, 88; Fulcher of Chartres accompanies to Edessa, xxvii, 140, 354; joins crusade, xx, 63; knights desert to, 267; leaves for Jerusalem, 355–6; raids Cilicia, xxi, 134–6, 250n, 261; rule in Jerusalem, xxviii; as ruler of Edessa, xxi, 138, 140–2, 354–5; strips lead of roof of al-Aqsa mosque, 311n

Baldwin of Ghent, 169

Baltic, commercial interests in, xi

Banyas, 356

al-Bara (Barra), 158n, 164, 248, 258, 261, 281, 350

Barker, Ernest, xii

Baruch, son of Isaac, 46

Batrun, 279

Beirut, 279

Benedict, bishop of Edessa, 356n

Berkyaruk, sultan of Baghdad, 161n, 197

Bernard of Béziers, 152

Berta, queen of Philip I, 15

Bertrada, countess, wife of Fulk of Anjou, 15

Bertrand of Le Puy, 294

Besalú, count of, 27

Bethlehem, 322

Bodin, Slav leader, 103n

Boel of Chartres, 73

Bohemund, Turkish emissary, 340

Bohemund of Taranto: actions in beleaguered Antioch, 217, 219, 226; agreement with surrendering amir in Antioch citadel, 224–5, 242; Anna Comnena on, xxx–xxxi, 68, 86, 90–3, 231; Antioch offered to by brotherhood of knights, 155, 262; appearance, xxx–xxxi; in Armenia, 136–7; in battle of Antioch (June 1098), 222, 227–8; besieges Amalfi, 72; besieges Nicaea, 101, 109, 111–12, 116; and building of castle at St Simeon, 180, 193; at capture of Ma'arrat, 259–60, 264, 267; confers with Firuz, 161–2, 177, 188–9; departs from Antioch for Cilicia, 250; disputes over ownership of Antioch, 246, 249, 256–7, 260, 262–3; at Dorylaeum, 124–7, 131–3; forages in Saracen territory, 157–9; forces cross Hellespont, 108; in *Gesta Francorum*, xxiv, 62, 71, 86; as governor of Antioch, 239, 354–5; greed, 123; journey to and stay in Constantinople, 86–8; Kerboga on, 202–3; leads crusading force, xx, 62, 72–4, 96; leaves for Jerusalem, 355–6;

Bohemund of Taranto (*continued*)
leaves Ma'arrat for Antioch, 268;
not on march to Jerusalem, 274;
occupies Antioch, xxi, xxv, 4, 144,
189–91, 193–5, 231–2, 241, 245, 299; in
Peter Bartholomew's vision of
Adhemar, 250–2; pleads poverty,
154; rebukes William the Carpenter
for attempted desertion, 160; relations with Alexius I, xxix–xxx,
86, 88–93, 107; reports Antioch victory to Urban II, 240–3; requests
Raymond of Toulouse make pact
with Alexius I, 105; returns to Antioch (1099), 277; sea crossing, 76,
79; at siege of Antioch, 150–5, 157,
159, 162, 172–3, 175, 178, 181, 185,
188–9; swears oath of fealty to
Alexius I, 89, 92, 101; takes oath of
commitment, 215; and Taticius'
departure from Antioch, 162; victory at battle of Lake Antioch,
178–9; withdraws from Nicaea, 123;
Yaghi Sayan's head given to, 192
Bolianuth, 185
Bologna, Urban preaches in, 25
Braym, river (Nahr Ibrahim), 279
Bruno of Lucca, 244
Bucca Torta (pass), 307
Bulgars, 57–8, 60–1, 99, 104
Byzantine empire: crusader relations
with, xxviii, 104; dependence on
foreign mercenaries, 155n; and First
Crusade, xv–xvi; Manzikert defeat
(1071), xvi; papacy seeks alliance
with, xviii; successes in northern
Syria, 199n; *see also* Alexius I Com-
nenus, Byzantine emperor

Cabalium, 76
Caesarea, 279, 341, 357
Caesarea, Cappadocia, 137, 139n
Caesarea, duke of, 307
Calonymus, son of Meshullam, rabbi,
47–8
Camela (Hims), 280

Camela, amir of, 283
cannibalism, 260, 269
Caspax, admiral, 234
Cathar heresy, x
Cepkalia (formerly Raphania), 275
Cerdaña, count of, 27
Chanson d'Antioche, xxii, 32
Charlemagne, emperor, 3, 13, 63n
Chartres, abbey of St Peter of, 28–9
Chastel Rouge, 268
Chios, 233
Cibotus, 65, 111, 115–16
Cilicia, xxi, 134–5
Clarebold, 35–6
Clermont (Auvergne), council of
(1095), xix, xxviii, 1, 6, 14, 20, 22, 28,
95
Cologne, Jews massacred in, 30, 34
Coloman I, king of Hungary, 57, 60
Comana, 137n
Comitissa, viscountess of Châteaudun,
29
Constantine Euphorbenus Catacalon,
70
Constantinople: crusader armies
reach, xx, 55–6, 58–9, 61, 63, 72,
74, 77–9, 83–5, 87–8, 96, 100, 106–7;
crusaders attack and desecrate
(1096–7), 64, 79–84; described,
100–1; sacked (1204), ix
Coxon, 137–8
Cremona, 27
Cross, *see* True Cross
crusades and crusading, ideology of,
vi–xiv
Cumans, 104

Dacia, 67
Daimbert of Pisa, patriarch of Jeru-
salem, 292n, 344n, 345n, 349, 353,
356, 358
Danishmends, oppose Seljuk Turks, xvi
David ben Rabbi Shelomo ben Rabbi,
368
Devol, treaty of (1108), xxx
Dorylaeum, battle of (1097), xxi,

xxiv, 116, 124–32, 169n

Duqaq, Shams al-Malik, ruler of Damascus, attempts relief of Antioch, 143, 153n, 158n, 164, 185, 193, 194n, 197, 271

Dyrrhachium (Durazzo, Epidamnus), 68, 71, 75–6, 96, 99, 104; battle of (1085), 90

Ebrard, priest, 292–3, 296

Edessa, Armenia: Baldwin of Boulogne reaches and rules, xxi, 138, 140–2, 261, 354; Godfrey's journey to, 250

Egypt: army defeated at Ascalon, xxi, 338n, 339–40, 351–2; Fatimid Shiite caliphs rule in, xvii, 270; forces capture Jerusalem, 270–1, 278n, 286; Jewish community in, 363–4; negotiations at Antioch, 172n, 179, 182

Ekkehard of Aura, xxiv

Elias, 75

Elkhanes, 69

Elvira of Leon and Castile, wife of Raymond IV of Toulouse, 348

Emich, count of Flonheim: atrocities against Jews, 30, 34–5, 46–7; leads crusading force, xx, 36; turns back in Balkans, 55

Empurias, count of, 27

Engelrand of St Paul, 285

England, supports crusade, 306–7

Epirus, 67

Ethiopians (Nubians), serve in Egyptian army, 332

Eustace III, count of Boulogne: and battle of Ascalon, 342; in Fulcher of Chartres's *Historia*, xxviii; joins crusade, xx; reports Antioch victory to Urban II, 240; at siege of Jerusalem, 315; and surrender of Nablus, 341

Eustathius Camytzes, 235

Everard III of Le Puiset, viscount of Chartres, 71

Everard the Huntsman, 258

Faisal, amir, king of Iraq, xiii

Fakhr al-Malik ibn Ammar, king of Tripoli, 276, 278, 283–4, 287, 298–9, 304

Farald of Thouars, 212

Fatimids, rule in Egypt, xvii

First Crusade: campaigns, xxi; commanders disagree, xxi; constituent armies, xx; motive, 28; numbers of participants, xix; raised, xv, xviii, 1–9, 11, 13–15, 21–2; reinforced, xxi; sources and writings on, xxii–xxxii, 32

Firuz (?Armenian Christian of Antioch), 161n, 162, 177, 186, 188–90, 231n, 272

Flanders (and Low Countries): crusader army from, xx; Urban II preaches in, 24

Folkmar, leads crusading force, xx, 38, 55

France: anti-Jewish acts in, 37; and crusading ideology, xii ; famine, 20–1

Francis of Assisi, St, prefers conversion over combat, x

Frederick I (Barbarossa), Holy Roman emperor, viii

Fulcher, brother of Budellus of Chartres, 186

Fulcher of Chartres: accompanies Baldwin to Edessa, xxvii, 140, 142, 354; accompanies Stephen of Blois, 95; on Baldwin of Boulogne's rise to power, 138; on battle of Ascalon, 344–5; in Constantinople, 61; describes Jerusalem, 309; on Dorylaeum, 125, 129, 133n; *Historia Hierosolymitana*, xxii–xxiii, xxvi–xxviii, 95; ignores disputes between leaders, 345n, 348n; on siege and fall of Jerusalem, 329–33, 344, 354–5; on siege of Antioch, 144; on siege of Nicaea, 114; on Urban II's Clermont address, 5

Fulk Rechin ('the Sour'), count of Anjou, 15, 23

Gaston IV, viscount of Béarn, 316, 324, 342

Geldemar Carpinel, count, 320

Genoa, fleet and seamen support crusade, 278n, 306, 312n, 324n, 326

Geoffrey, count of Ruscinolo, 73, 87

George, St, 306, 308

George Palaeologus, xxxi, 123

Germany: disputes with papacy, 13; *see also* Rhineland

Gesta Francorum: on advance towards Antioch, 134; on aftermath of Antioch, 246, 256; on capture of Antioch, 187–8; on crossing Hellespont and siege of Nicaea, 108–11; on discovery of Holy Lance, 214; on Dorylaeum, 125–6, 133n; and fate of People's Crusade, 62; on march to Jerusalem, 275; narrative, xxiv–xxv; on occupation of Antioch, 197; on progress of second army, 71; secular nature, xxvi; on siege of Antioch, 156–61, 177–82; on siege and capture of Jerusalem, 311, 312–13, 340; as source, xxii–xxiv

Ghazi Gumushtigin, Malik (?Tanisman), Danishmend sultan, 124

Gibbon, Edward, xii

Godfrey Burel, 59–60

Godfrey of Bouillon, duke of Lower Lorraine, ruler of Jerusalem: in Armenia, 136; in attack on Turks at Antioch, 222–3; attacks Constantinople, 82–3; at battle of Ascalon, 342, 346; in beleaguered Antioch, 217; at capture of Antioch, 190; as crusader leader, viii, xx, 63, 68, 96; death, xxviii; departs for east, 71; departs for Edessa, 250; departs from Jerusalem to Ramleh, 338; and disputes over ownership of Antioch, 249, 256–7, 262; at Dorylaeum, 125–7, 130, 132n; elected ruler of Jerusalem, 334–5, 337, 340, 344; fighting on march to Antioch, 158; foray against Turks on return to

Antioch, 261–2; in Fulcher of Chartres's *Historia*, xxviii; illness at Antioch, 151; letter to Pope Paschal II, 349; on march to Jerusalem, 274, 277–8, 304; meets Alexius I in Constantinople, 88; Peter of Narbonne's mission to, 287; Raymond calls to conference at Ruj, 260, 268; reaches Constantinople, 72, 78–9; remains in Jerusalem as ruler, 348, 353, 358; reports Antioch victory to Urban II, 240; restrains Raymond of Toulouse in Constantinople, 90, 107; sends messenger to Alexius I to take over Antioch, 246; at siege of Antioch, 174, 186; at siege of Jerusalem, 311, 312, 314–15, 317, 324–5, 328, 331; at siege of Nicaea, 101, 109, 111–12, 116; swears oath of fealty to Alexius I, 83–5, 101; takes oath of commitment, 215; Tancred joins, 288; Turks request to accept Azaz castle, 253–4

Godfrey of Monte Scaglioso, 73n, 217

Gottschalk, leads crusading force, xx, 34, 55

Gouffier, lord of Lastours, 259, 266

Gregory VII, pope, xviii, 12, 13n

Guibert of Nogent: on crusading armies reaching Constantinople, 55; *Gesta Dei per Francos*, 11–12; as source, xxiv, xxxii; on Urban II's call for crusade, 11, 22n

Guibert of Ravenna, anti-pope, 25n, 97

Guy de Hauteville, Bohemund's half-brother, 219

Guy of Vitreio, 169

Guy Trousseau, 203

Hadrian, Roman emperor, 311

Haifa, 279

al-Hakim, caliph of Egypt, destroys church of Holy Sepulchre, xvii

Hamelin, brother of Nivello, 29

Hamelnuth, 185

Hanina ibn Mansur ibn Ubayd, 369

Harim, near Antioch, 171n

Helenopolis, 69–70, 238

Henry IV, German western emperor: excommunicated by Urban II, xviii; in Investiture Wars, xvii, 5, 13n, 25n; protects Jews, 30, 39

Heraclea, 124n, 134–5, 139

Heraclius, viscount of Polignac, 229, 294

heresy (Christian), x

Herluin, 220, 222

Hermann of Cannes, 73

Hilduin of Mazingarbe, 169

Hispania (valley of Ruj), 151–3, 254, 269–70, 350; *see also* Ruj

Historia Belli Sacri, xxiii

Holy Lance: Anna Comnena on, 238; authenticity questioned, xxvi, 206–7, 209–11, 215, 274, 291, 292–4; carried at battle of Ascalon, 345n; carried into battle at Antioch, 222, 229, 238, 242; discovered at Antioch, xxvi, 204, 207–8, 212–13, 215–16, 220, 242, 251, 253–4; Raymond of Toulouse carries, 238, 267–8, 339n; in visions, 302

Holy Land, lacks strategic and commercial interest to crusaders, xi

Holy Roman empire, Investiture Wars with papacy, xvii

Hospitallers of St John, historical influence, xiii

Hugh ('the Great'), count of Vermandois: advises Godfrey to yield to Alexius I, 82; in battle of Antioch (June 1098), 222–3, 228; at Dorylaeum, 125–7, 130; fighting on march to Antioch, 168; leads crusading army, xx, 71, 95–6; mission to Alexius I to take over Antioch, 247; reception by Alexius I, 74–6

Hugh, viscount of Châteaudun, 29

Hugh Embriaco, 324n

Hugh of Calniaco, 169

Hugh of Rheims, 169

Hugh the Mad, 217

Hugo, abbot of Cluny, 12

Hume, David, vii

Humphrey Fitz-Ralph, 73

Humphrey (?Geoffrey) of Monte Scaglioso, 73, 128

Hungary: crusading forces in, 55–7, 59, 63, 68; Emich marches to, 35–6; Peter the Hermit in, 55–6, 59–60, 63

Huy (monastery), 32

Hyaleas, 234

Iberia, commercial interests in, xi

Ibn al-Qalanisi (Abu Yala Hamza ibn Asad al-Tamimi): on capture of Ma'arrat al-Numan, 270–3; on fall of Antioch, 192; on fall of Jerusalem and battle of Ascalon, 360–2; on siege of Antioch, 162–3

Iconium, 135, 138, 168

Il-Ghazi, Ortuqid ruler of Jerusalem, 164n, 271

Investiture Wars (11th century), xvii, 13

Isaac, son of Daniel, 42

Isaac, son of Moses, rabbi, 48

Ishmael, son of sultan of Khorasan, 236–7

Isoard, count of Die, 305, 323

Isoard of Ganges, 173

Isoard of Mouzon, 71

Israel, state created, xiii

Jabala (Gibellum), 277, 287, 288

Jaffa, 320–2, 326

Janah al-Dawla, 164

Jerusalem: Baldwin of Boulogne rules, xxviii; capture reported to west, 349–54; captured (1099), xxi, 311, 316–17, 328–9, 332–3, 341, 349; captured by Allenby (1917), xii; as crusaders' aim, vii, ix, xv, xviii–xix, xxviii, 16–19, 23, 246–7, 262–3, 268; crusaders in, 337–8; crusaders reach, 309; Dome of the Rock, 310; Egyptians capture (1098), 270–1, 278n, 286; Fulcher of Chartres describes, 309–11; Fulcher of Chartres reaches with Baldwin

Jerusalem (*continued*)
and Bohemund, 357–8; Godfrey elected ruler, 334–5, 337, 340, 344; Godfrey remains to govern after departure of crusaders, 348, 353, 358; history of conflicts over, 270–1; Holy Sepulchre church destroyed, xvii; Jews in, ix, 362–3, 370; massacre and sack of, ix, xxvii, 311, 316–17, 328–9, 332–3, 360, 362–3; negotiations with al-Afdal over, 286; Peter the Hermit's pilgrimage to, 32–3; Raymond of Toulouse leads march towards, 246, 263, 268, 274–81, 302–3, 307–8; siege of, 274, 311, 312–17, 317–29, 330–1; visions and miracles on march to, 274–5; water shortage, 319–20

Jesus Christ, appears in visions, 33, 206, 210–11, 213–14, 250, 255, 288–91

Jews: Jesus's reported contempt for, 290; libels against, 40n; massacred and persecuted in Jerusalem and Middle East, ix, 362–72; massacred in Rhineland, ix, xv, xx, xxxii, 30, 34–5, 37–54; pogroms against, xiv, 30

jihad (Holy War), call for, 374

John, bishop of Speyer, 39–40

John, duke of Dyrrhachium, 74–5

John II Comnenus, Byzantine emperor: Anna Comnena's disapproval of, xxix; violates truce with crusaders, 104

John Ducas, Alexius I Comnenus' brother-in-law, 233–6

John Tzimisces, Byzantine emperor, 199n

Jubayl, 279

Judah, son of Isaac, rabbi, 46

Kafartab, 273, 275, 279

al-Kamil, al-Malik, sultan of Egypt, Francis of Assisi visits, x

Kerboga (Kourpagan), atabeg of Mosul: defeat and withdrawal at Antioch (June 1098), 204, 222–4, 228–30, 239, 265, 271; mother advises, 200–3; Peter the Hermit's embassy to, 220–2, 227; relief force at Antioch, xxiv, 143–4, 161n, 162, 164, 189n, 196, 197–205, 231–2, 236, 249, 292

Khorasan, 65

Kilij Arslan, father of Kilij Arslan I, 134

Kilij Arslan I, Seljuk sultan of Rum: Bohemund attacks at Dorylaeum, 124–5, 129, 132–3; raises forces against crusaders, 163; and siege of Nicaea, 108, 116, 119, 167; withdraws from Nicaea, 134

Krak des Chevaliers, 282n, 283

La Chamelle, 276

Lake Antioch, *see* Antioch, Lake

Lambert, bishop of Arras, 23, 353

Lambert the Poor, 203

Languedoc, suppression of heresies in, x

Larissa, battle of (1083), 79, 90

Latakiah, 143, 169, 277, 284, 302, 321, 348, 351, 356

Lefke, 124, 130n, 132n

Leodegar, bishop of Viviers, 284n

Lethold of Tournai, 315

Lisiard of Flanders, 169

Lombardy, forces from, xix, 62

Longinus, 241

Lorraine: and crusade, 31–2; Jews massacred in, 34

Louis I (the Pious), king of France, 3

Louis IX, St, king of France, viii

Lucca, 240, 244

Ma'arrat al-Numan (Marra): besieged and captured, 246–7, 258–60, 263–70, 272–3, 279–80, 299, 350, 360; cannibalism in, 260, 269

Macedonia, 74

Mahomerie, La, 172n, 175n, 180n, 185n, 195n, 244–5

Mainz, 37–8

Malik Shah, sultan of Baghdad, xvi, 271

Malregard, Mount, near Antioch, 157
Mamistra (Manustra), 134, 136, 155, 209–10
Manasses II, archbishop of Rheims: letter to Lambert, bishop of Arras, 353; messages from Anselm of Ribemont, 167, 193
Manasses of Clermont, 169
Manuel Butumites, Greek admiral, 75, 94–5, 117, 119–20, 122–4
Manuel I Comnenus, Byzantine emperor, Anna Comnena's disapproval of, xxix
Manzikert, battle of (1071), xvi, xviii, 6n
Maraclea, 277
Marakes, satrap, 235
Marash, 138, 140
Marianus Mavrocatacalon, 77–8
Mark, St, evangelist, 293
Mary, Virgin, appears in visions, 211, 301–2
Menahem, son of David, rabbi, 48
Meshullam, son of Isaac, 42
Michael Cecaumenus, 235
Mina (Jewish woman), 43–4
Mirdalin, 228
Miriathos, 130
Monastras, Greek general, 121–2
Montjoie (Mount of Joy), 253
Moshe bar Yekuthiel, rabbi, 39–40
al-Muntasir, 371

Nablus, 341
Narrative of the Old Persecutions, The (or *Mainz Anonymous*), 37
Nicaea: as capital of Rum, xvi; captured (1097), xxi, 115, 117–18, 120–2, 165, 168, 183, 193, 349; crusaders guard, 124; crusaders reach, xix, 69, 94–6, 102, 109; siege of, xxx, 95, 101, 108–19, 167
Nicephorus Bryennius ('Caesar'), xxix, xxxi, 80–2
Nicephorus Phocas, Byzantine emperor, 199n
Nicholas Mavrocatacalon, 74, 76–7

Nicholas of Lyre, St, 292
Nicomedia, 64
Nish, Bulgaria, 58, 61
Nivello of Chartres, 28
'Nomen a Solemnibus' (song), 358–60
Normans, in south Italy, xvii

Odo, bishop of Ostia (Urban II's nephew), 12n
Odo of Vernolio, 169
Opus, Greek general, 83
Ortuq, amir, 271
Ortuqids, 270, 271
Ottoman empire, xi–xii

Paipert, Armenia, 238
papacy: advocates Church reform, xviii; Investiture Wars with Holy Roman empire, xvii; seeks alliance with Byzantines, xvii–xviii, 10n; *see also* Gregory VII; Paschal II; Urban II
Paschal II, pope, 13; letter for crusader leaders on capture of Jerusalem, 349
Paul of Samosata, 128n
Peace of God decree, 8n, 9
Peasants' (or People's) Crusade, 54, 62
Pechenegs (Patzinaks), 60–1, 72, 87, 104
Pegasius, Greek naval commander, 84
Pelecanum, 94, 118, 122–3
People's Crusade, *see* Peasants' Crusade
Pepin the Short, Carolingian king, 13
Peter, St, appears in visions, 214–15, 253, 264–5, 288
Peter, seneschal of Castillon, 137
Peter Bartholomew: advises on actions at battle of Antioch, 226; death after ordeal by fire, 253n, 274, 295–8, 302; discovers Holy Lance, xxvi, 204, 207–8, 212–13, 216, 220; instructions on transporting Raymond of Toulouse, 335; knowledge of part of liturgy, 206n, 214; mission to Jabala, 287; visions, 206–9, 213, 215–16, 250, 253–6, 264–5, 288
Peter d'Aupis (or Aliphas), 137, 236
Peter Desiderius, 292, 304–6, 323

Peter of Narbonne, bishop of al-Bara: and Arnulf's scepticism over Holy Lance, 295; and attack on Tripoli, 298; established as bishop, 249, 261; influence on crusader leaders, 334; on march to Jerusalem, 279, 281–2, 287; and power disputes in Jerusalem, 335; at siege and capture of Ma'arrat, 265, 267, 269; at siege of Jerusalem, 324

Peter of Roaix, 137

Peter Rainaud, 104

Peter Raymond of Hautpoul, 137, 207

Peter the Hermit: Albert of Aachen's account of, xxxii, 57; allocation of goods to, 287; Anna Comnena on, 66, 68, 79, 238; army destroyed in Asia Minor, 62, 65, 69–70, 101n, 113; attempts to desert from siege of Antioch, 143, 159; betrayed by Alexius, 113; career and influence on crusade, 31–4, 55; embassy to Kerboga, 220, 222, 227; in Jerusalem, 342; leads crusading force, xx, 55–6, 59–61, 63, 66, 68, 96; persecution of Jews in Rhineland, 30–1; pilgrimage to Jerusalem, 32–3; reaches Constantinople, 55–6, 59, 61–2, 63; retires to Huy monastery, 32; visions, 33

Peter Tudebode, *Historia*, xxii–xxiv

Petzeas, 235

Philip I ('the Fat'), king of France: excommunicated, xviii, 15; Fulcher of Chartres on, 5

Philippopolis, 58, 61, 75

Philomelium, 218, 236, 237

Piacenza, council of (1095), xviii

Polybotus, 235

Pons of Balazun, xxvi, 212, 284

Pontius Rainaud, 104

Protestants and Protestantism, xi

Rachel, Mistress, daughter of Isaac, 50–1

Rainald, count (?of Beauvais or Toul), 223

Rainald, Italian lord, 64

Ralph, count, 83–4

Ralph of Caen, *Gesta Tancredi*, xxiii

Ramleh, battle of (1102), 183; crusaders reach on march to Jerusalem, 274, 279, 308; Godfrey leaves Jerusalem for, 338, 341

Ranulf of the principality of Salerno, 73

Raymond, viscount of Turenne, 277, 312

Raymond 'de Castello', 170

Raymond of Aguilers: on battle of Antioch (June 1098), 225; on carrying Holy Lance to battle of Ascalon, 345n; on discovery of Holy Lance, 204, 213, 220n; and disputes over ownership of Antioch, 249, 260, 263n, 299n; on Dorylaeum, 126, 132, 133n; on election of Godfrey as ruler of Jerusalem, 334–5; *Historia Francorum* (or *Liber*), as source, xxii–xxvii; on Kerboga's beleaguering of Antioch, 205; on march to Jerusalem, 279; on money values, 287; on Peter Bartholomew's ordeal by fire, 296n, 297–8, 302n; on Provençal army's journey to east, 102; on siege and capture of Jerusalem, 311, 317–29; on siege of Antioch, 148–55, 158n, 170–7; on siege of Nicaea, 111; takes custody of Peter Bartholomew, 210, 212

Raymond of the Isle (?Raymond-Bertrand of l'Isle Jourdain), 280

Raymond IV of Toulouse (count of St Gilles): Acre promised to, 307; advocates waiting for arrival of Alexius I, 300; aids apostate Turks, 254; in Armenia, 136; arrives at Constantinople, 88–90, 106, 108; and attack on Tripoli, 298n, 304; attacks and captures al-Bara, 248, 258–61; at battle of Ascalon, 340–3; bears papal banner, 75n; in beleaguered Antioch, 217; besieges Ma'arrat, 263, 267;

builds and fortifies La Mahomerie, 180; calls conference at Ruj, 260, 268; on capture of Antioch, 186; carries Holy Lance, 238, 267–8, 338n; declines kingship of Jerusalem, 335; dispute with Godfrey in Jerusalem, 335; at Dorylaeum, 12, 125, 127, 130n, 132n; fighting on march to Antioch, 168; and food shortages in Ma'arrat, 269–70; in *Gesta Francorum*, xxv, 71; guards citadel at Antioch, 222, 224, 227; illness, 133, 175, 226–7; leads crusader force, xx, 71, 96, 103–5; leaves Jerusalem for Constantinople, 348, 353; letter to Pope Paschal II, 349; and loss of Tower of David, 337, 345; orders destruction of Ma'arrat, 269; and ownership of Antioch, 246, 249, 256–7, 260; payments to fellow leaders, 268; Peter Bartholomew delivers visionary messages to, 206–7, 210, 212, 251–2, 254–6; on Peter Desiderius' vision, 305; raids in Hispania, 270, 302; Raymond of Aguilers accompanies as chaplain, xxv; reaches Nicaea, 94n; relations with Alexius I, xxvi, 93–4, 106–7; reports Antioch victory to Urban II, 240; rewards Tancred, 177; at siege and capture of Jerusalem, 311, 312, 315, 317–18, 324–6, 328–9, 331–2; at siege of Antioch, 148, 151–2, 172–3, 175, 180, 185, 194–5; at siege of Nicaea, 101–2, 110–12, 116–18, 148, 167; swears oath to Alexius I, 90, 94n, 101, 256, 260; takes army towards Jerusalem, 246, 263, 268, 274–6, 278, 279–84, 302–4; takes oath of commitment, 215

Raymond Pilet, lord of Alais, xxv, 247–8, 277, 297, 312, 314, 320

Reformation, effect of, xi

Reinald of Broyes, 60

Rhineland, Jews massacred in, ix, xv, xx, xxxii, 30–1, 34, 37–54

Rhodes, 233

Richard I, king of England, viii, xiii

Richard, son of Count Ranulf of Caiazzo, 73

Richard, son of Count William of the principality of Salerno, 71, 73, 76, 78, 108; at Dorylaeum, 127

Ridwan, ruler of Aleppo, Antioch relief force repulsed, 143, 170n, 177n, 185, 193–4, 271

Robert, abbot (Anselm of Ribemont's chaplain), 169

Robert I, count of Flanders, xvi

Robert II, count of Flanders: in battle of Antioch (June 1098), 222–3, 228, 239; at battle of Ascalon, 341, 343; and battle of Dorylaeum, 126, 131; besieges Ma'arrat, 263; at capture of Antioch, 190, 194, 245; at Constantinople, 90, 95, 107; favours Godfrey as ruler of Jerusalem, 335; forages in Saracen territory, 157–8; Guibert of Nogent copies, 12; joins crusade, xx, 71, 96; on march to Jerusalem, 274, 277–8, 281; and ownership of Antioch, 246, 249, 256–7, 262; Peter of Narbonne's mission to, 287; Raymond calls to conference at Ruj, 260, 268; reports Antioch victory to Urban II, 240; returns to France, 348, 353; at siege of Antioch, 150–3, 186; at siege of Jerusalem, 312, 317, 324–5, 331; at siege of Nicaea, 101–2; takes oath of commitment, 215; travels to east, 98

Robert, duke of Normandy: in battle of Antioch (June 1098), 227–8; at battle of Ascalon, 342–4; and battle of Dorylaeum, 125–6, 131, 132n; and capture of Antioch, 245; at Constantinople, 95; favours Godfrey as ruler of Jerusalem, 335; Fulcher of Chartres serves, xxvii–xxviii; leads crusading force, xx, 71, 96; on march to Jerusalem, 274, 278; meets Urban II, 97; and ownership of

Robert, duke of Normandy (*continued*)
Antioch, 246, 256–7; Raymond calls
to conference at Ruj, 260, 268; reports
Antioch victory to Urban II, 240;
returns to France, 348, 353; at siege of
Antioch, 150–1; at siege of Jerusalem,
311, 312, 317, 324–5, 331; at siege of
Nicaea, 110, 112–13; takes oath
of commitment, 215; winters in
Calabria, 98

Robert Fitz-Gerard, 178

Robert Fitz-Toustan, 73

Robert Guiscard, xvii, 92n

Robert of Ansa, 73, 127

Robert of Paris, 169

Robert of Rheims, xxii, xxiv, xxxii, 1

Robert of Rouen, bishop of Ramleh,
279n

Robert of Sourdeval, 73

Rodomer the Bulgarian, 121–2

Rodosto (Tekirdagh), 105

Roger Borsa, duke of Apulia, 73n

Roger of Barneville, 110, 205

Roger the Great, brother of Robert
Guiscard, 73

Roussillon, count of, 27

Ruj (Riha), 164; conference (1099), 260,
268

Rum, sultanate established, xvi

Runciman, Sir Steven, viii

Rusa, 88, 105, 138

Ruthard, bishop of Mainz, 35, 45, 48

St Gilles, count of, *see* Raymond IV of
Toulouse

St Reparata, abbot of, 26

St Simeon: castle (La Mahomerie)
built at, 180, 182; Turkish reinforcements arrive at, 143

Saladin (Salah ed Din Yusuf), sultan,
viii, xiii

Samosata, 141

Sanxado, son of Aoxianus of Antioch,
146

Second Crusade, and persecution of
Jews, 31

Seljuk Turks: rule in Asia Minor, xvi,
6n, 9, 101n; rule in Jerusalem, 270–1

Sem, 278

Serres, 88

Shams al-Dawla, son of Yaghi Sayan,
185, 198, 206n

Shayzar, 275, 280

Shiites, xvi

Sicily, Normans conquer, xvii

Sidon, 279

Simeon of Armenia, 136

Simha ha-Cohen, 43

Simon, chaplain, 254

Slavonia, 102–4

Slavs, attack crusader army, 103

Smyrna, 233–5

Sofia, 58, 61

Song of Roland, ix

Spain, Christian expansion in, xviii

Stephen, count of Blois and Chartres:
Anna Comnena on, 236; and battle
of Dorylaeum, 125, 131; command
at siege of Antioch, 143; in Constantinople, 95; fighting on march
to Antioch, 168; flees from Antioch,
144, 182, 186, 218, 226; Fulcher of
Chartres serves, xxvii–xxviii; killed
at Ramleh, 183; leads crusading
force, xx, 96, 98; letter to wife
Adela, 183–5; meets Urban II, 97;
at Nicaea, 102, 110, 114; qualities,
182

Stephen II, pope, 13

Stephen of Valence, 204, 210–11, 214,
216n, 293, 300–2

Strait (or Arm) of St George (Bosporus and Sea of Marmara), 9,
59

Sukman ibn Ortuq, amir of Jerusalem,
164, 193n, 197, 271

al-Sulami, Ali ibn Tahir, *Kitab al-jihad*,
374

Suleiman ibn Qutulmish, Seljuk
sultan, 240

Sur, 279

Symeon, Greek patriarch of Jerusalem:

message to Church in west, from Antioch 165–6, 223n; Peter the Hermit visits, 32–3; relations with Alexius, xvii; role in crusade, 31–2

Syria: crusaders march to, xxi; under Saracen rule, 302–3

Tancred, prince of Galilee, regent of Antioch: Baldwin takes Tarsus from, 140; in battle of Antioch (June 1098), 222, 227; at battle of Ascalon, 342–3; and battle of Dorylaeum, 125–6; at capture of Antioch, 188, 232; captures Bethlehem, 322; crosses Hellespont, 108; deserts Raymond and joins Godfrey, 288; fortifies hill at Antioch, 159, 177; joins crusade, xx, 73; on journey to Constantinople, 87–8; Kerboga on, 202–3; on march to Jerusalem, 280–1; oath of allegiance to Alexius I, 123; pursues and brings back Peter the Hermit and William the Carpenter to Antioch, 159; raids Cilicia, xxi, 134–6, 250n; Raymond makes payment to, 268, 288; remains in Jerusalem with Godfrey, 348; at siege and capture of Jerusalem, 312, 316, 328, 332; at siege of Antioch, 160; at siege of Nicaea, 109; and surrender of Nablus, 341; swears oath of commitment, 215

Tangripermes, satrap, 233, 235

Tarragona, 27

Tarsus, 134, 136, 140, 169

Tasso, Torquato, *Gerusalemme Liberata*, xxii

Taticius, Greek general: and Anna Comnena's history, xxxi; and battle of Dorylaeum, 132n; departs from siege of Antioch, 143, 154–5, 160–2; escorts and protects crusaders, 123–4; leads Byzantine force, xxi; at siege of Nicaea, 119

Tell Bashir (Turbezel), 140

Tell-Mannas, 247

Templars, historical influence, xiii

Theodore Gabras, 238

Thomas (of Emich's company), 35–6

Thorus, governor of Edessa, 140n, 141n

Tortosa, 277, 284

Tripoli, 276–7, 284, 298–9, 304, 307, 357

Truce of God, 9

True Cross, fragment recovered in Jerusalem, 336, 345

Tudela, siege of (1087), 160n

Turcopoles, 72, 87, 111, 115

Tursol, 155

Tutush, Seljuk prince, 271

Tyre, 279

Tzachas, Greek general, 233–4

Tzitas, 119

Umar, caliph of Damascus, 270

Urban II, pope: advocates good relations with eastern Church, 10n; Alexius I Comnenus appeals to for support, vii, xv, xviii; background, 12; Bohemund and leaders report Antioch victory to, 240–3; Clermont address calling crusade, xviii–xx, xxviii, 1–9, 11, 13–20, 22, 95; death, 349; disputes with Holy Roman emperor, xviii; letters, xxxii; meets crusaders near Lucca, 97; opposed by anti-pope Guibert, 97–8; and Peter the Hermit, 31; promotes crusade on European tours, 23–7, 62–3

Urso, son of Nivello, 29

Uzes, 104

Vallombrosa, Urban preaches crusade in, 26

Varangian Guard (Byzantium), xvi

Walo, constable, 195

Walter II of Poissy, lord of Boissy SansAvoir: army destroyed in Asia Minor, 62, 65; killed, 96; leads crusading force, xx, 57–8, 96; reaches Constantinople, 55, 58

Wieselburg, 35
William, archbishop of Tyre, *Historia*, 32
William, bishop of Orange, 133, 212, 214, 260, 265, 305, 334
William I (the Conqueror), king of England, xix, 75n
William, lord of Sabran, 314, 320
William, son of Emma, 71, 128
William, son of Peter of Cuniliacum, 281
William, viscount of Melun ('the Carpenter'), 75, 159–60
William Bonofilius, 296
William Embriaco, 324, 326
William Hugh of Monteil, Adhemar's brother, 302, 304, 323
William Malus Puer, 296
William of Grandmesnil, 203, 212, 236
William of Montpellier, 137, 258

William Peter, lord, 209
William the Picard, 278
women: accompany crusaders, 127, 131; besieged in Antioch, 181; expelled from army, 147

Xerigordus, castle, 64, 69

Yaghi Sayan (Cassianus), governor of Antioch: in defence of Antioch, 164, 173–4; palace burnt, 217; seized in flight and beheaded by Armenians, 187, 191–2, 241; sends for help, 185, 194, 197
Yeshaya ha-Kohen ibn Masliah the Enlightened, 368

Zacharias, pope, 13
Zionism, xiii
Zipporah, wife of Meshullam, 42

THE STORY OF PENGUIN CLASSICS

Before 1946 ... 'Classics' are mainly the domain of academics and students; readable editions for everyone else are almost unheard of. This all changes when a little-known classicist, E. V. Rieu, presents Penguin founder Allen Lane with the translation of Homer's *Odyssey* that he has been working on in his spare time.

1946 Penguin Classics debuts with *The Odyssey*, which promptly sells three million copies. Suddenly, classics are no longer for the privileged few.

1950s Rieu, now series editor, turns to professional writers for the best modern, readable translations, including Dorothy L. Sayers's *Inferno* and Robert Graves's unexpurgated *Twelve Caesars*.

1960s The Classics are given the distinctive black covers that have remained a constant throughout the life of the series. Rieu retires in 1964, hailing the Penguin Classics list as 'the greatest educative force of the twentieth century.'

1970s A new generation of translators swells the Penguin Classics ranks, introducing readers of English to classics of world literature from more than twenty languages. The list grows to encompass more history, philosophy, science, religion and politics.

1980s The Penguin American Library launches with titles such as *Uncle Tom's Cabin*, and joins forces with Penguin Classics to provide the most comprehensive library of world literature available from any paperback publisher.

1990s The launch of Penguin Audiobooks brings the classics to a listening audience for the first time, and in 1999 the worldwide launch of the Penguin Classics website extends their reach to the global online community.

The 21st Century Penguin Classics are completely redesigned for the first time in nearly twenty years. This world-famous series now consists of more than 1300 titles, making the widest range of the best books ever written available to millions – and constantly redefining what makes a 'classic'.

The Odyssey continues ...

The best books ever written

PENGUIN 🐧 CLASSICS

SINCE 1946

Find out more at www.penguinclassics.com